Internet of Things and Cyber Physical Systems

The quantity, diversity, and sophistication of Internet of Things (IoT) items are rapidly increasing, posing significant issues but also innovative solutions for forensic science. Such systems are becoming increasingly common in public locations, businesses, universities, residences, and other shared offices, producing enormous amounts of data at rapid speeds in a variety of forms. IoT devices can be used as suspects, digital witnesses, or instruments of crime and cyberattacks, posing new investigation problems, forensic issues, security threats, legal concerns, privacy concerns, and ethical dilemmas. A cyberattack on IoT devices might target the device itself or associated systems, particularly vital infrastructure.

This book discusses the advancements in IoT and Cyber Physical Systems (CPS) forensics. The first objective is to learn and understand the fundamentals of IoT forensics. This objective will answer the question of why and how IoT has evolved as one of the most promising and widely accepted technologies across the globe and has many widely accepted applications.

The second objective is to learn how to use CPS to address many computational problems. CPS forensics is a promising domain, and there are various advancements in this field. This book is structured so that the topics of discussion are relevant to each reader's major or interests. The book's goal is to help each reader to see the relevance of IoT and CPS forensics to his or her career or interests.

This book not only presents numerous case studies from a global perspective, but it also compiles a large amount of literature and research from a database. As a result, this book effectively demonstrates the concerns, difficulties, and trends surrounding the topic while also encouraging readers to think globally. The main goal of this project is to encourage both researchers and practitioners to share and exchange their experiences and recent studies between academia and industry.

Advances in Cybersecurity Management

Series Editors: Yassine Maleh and Ahmed A. Abd El-Latif

The *Advances in Cybersecurity Management* series is a knowledge resource for practitioners, scientists, and researchers working in the various fields of cybersecurity, hacking, digital forensics, cyber warfare, viruses, or critical infrastructure. It explores the complexity of the business environment and the rapidly changing risk landscape in which it must operate.

IT Governance and Information Security: Guides, Standards, and Frameworks
Yassine Maleh, Abdelkebir Sahid, Mamoun Alazab, Mustapha Belaissaoui

Security Engineering for Embedded and Cyber-Physical Systems
Saad Motahhir, Yassine Maleh

Internet of Things and Cyber Physical Systems: Security and Forensics
Keshav Kaushik, Susheela Dahiya, Akashdeep Bhardwaj, Yassine Maleh

For more information about this series, please visit: https://www.routledge.com/Advances-in-Cybersecurity-Management/book-series/AICM

Internet of Things and Cyber Physical Systems
Security and Forensics

Edited by
Keshav Kaushik, Susheela Dahiya,
Akashdeep Bhardwaj, and Yassine Maleh

CRC Press
Taylor & Francis Group
Boca Raton London New York

CRC Press is an imprint of the
Taylor & Francis Group, an **informa** business

First edition published 2023
by CRC Press
6000 Broken Sound Parkway NW, Suite 300, Boca Raton, FL 33487-2742

and by CRC Press
4 Park Square, Milton Park, Abingdon, Oxon, OX14 4RN

CRC Press is an imprint of Taylor & Francis Group, LLC

Library of Congress Cataloging-in-Publication Data
Names: Kaushik, Keshav, editor. | Dahiya, Susheela, editor. | Bhardwaj, Akashdeep, 1971- editor. |
Maleh, Yassine, 1987- editor.
Title: Internet of things and cyber physical systems : security and forensics / edited by Keshav Kaushik,
Susheela Dahiya, Akashdeep Bhardwaj, and Yassine Maleh.
Description: First edition. | Boca Raton : CRC Press, 2023. | Includes bibliographical references and index.
Identifiers: LCCN 2022033187 (print) | LCCN 2022033188 (ebook) | ISBN 9781032254067 (hbk) |
ISBN 9781032254081 (pbk) | ISBN 9781003283003 (ebk)
Subjects: LCSH: Internet of things--Security measures. | Cooperating objects (Computer systems)--Security
measures. | Digital forensic science.
Classification: LCC TK5105.8857 .I5788 2023 (print) | LCC TK5105.8857 (ebook) |
DDC 004.67/8--dc23/eng/20221017
LC record available at https://lccn.loc.gov/2022033187
LC ebook record available at https://lccn.loc.gov/2022033188

ISBN: 978-1-032-25406-7 (hbk)
ISBN: 978-1-032-25408-1 (pbk)
ISBN: 978-1-003-28300-3 (ebk)

DOI: 10.1201/9781003283003

Typeset in Times
by MPS Limited, Dehradun

Contents

About the Editors

Keshav Kaushik is an experienced educator with over eight years of teaching and research experience in Cybersecurity, Digital Forensics, and the Internet of Things. He is working as an Assistant Professor (Senior Scale) in the systemic cluster under the School of Computer Science at the University of Petroleum and Energy Studies, Dehradun, India. He has published 60+ research papers in International Journals and has presented at reputed International Conferences. He is a Certified Ethical Hacker (CEH) v11, CQI and IRCA Certified ISO/IEC 27001:2013 Lead Auditor, Quick Heal Academy Certified Cyber Security Professional (QCSP), and IBM Cybersecurity Analyst. He has acted as a keynote speaker and delivered 50+ professional talks on various national and international platforms. He has edited over ten books with reputed international publishers like Springer, Taylor and Francis, IGI Global, Bentham Science, etc. He has also chaired various special sessions at international conferences and has served as a reviewer in peer-reviewed journals and conference.

Dr. Susheela Dahiya is currently working as an Associate Professor in the Department of Computer Science and Engineering at Graphic Era Hill University, Dehradun, Uttarakhand, India. She has received her M. Tech. (Computer Science & Engineering) in 2008 and Ph.D. degree in 2015 from the Indian Institute of Technology Roorkee. She had also qualified in the Graduate Aptitude Test in Engineering and National Eligibility Test in Computer Science. She has more than 9 years of academic/research/industry experience. Her research interests include Image & Video Processing, IoT, Cyber Security, Cloud Computing, and Deep Learning. She has authored several research papers in renowned conferences, Scopus & SCI journals and edited books.

Dr. Akashdeep Bhardwaj is working as professor (cyber security & digital forensics) at the University of Petroleum & Energy Studies (UPES), Dehradun, India. An eminent IT industry expert with over 25 years of experience in areas such as cybersecurity, digital forensics, and IT management operations, Dr. Akashdeep leads projects and mentors graduate, masters, and doctoral students. Dr. Bhardwaj holds a Ph.D. in computer science, post-graduate diploma in management (equivalent to an MBA), and an engineering degree in computer science. Dr. Akashdeep has published several books and research papers in highly referred journals. He has worked as an IT technology and cybersecurity leader for various multinational organizations. He is certified in several cybersecurity technologies, compliance audits, and information security and holds vendor certifications from Microsoft, Cisco, and VMware.

Dr. Yassine Maleh is an associate professor of cybersecurity and IT governance at Sultan Moulay Slimane University, Morocco. He is the founding chair of IEEE Consultant Network Morocco and founding president of the African Research Center of Information Technology & Cybersecurity. He is a senior member of IEEE and a member of the International Association of Engineers (IAENG) and the

Machine Intelligence Research Labs. Dr. Maleh has made contributions in the fields of information security and privacy, Internet of Things security, and wireless and constrained networks security. His research interests include information security and privacy, Internet of Things, network security, information systems, and IT governance. He has published over 50 papers (book chapters, international journals, and conferences/workshops), eight edited books, and three authored books. He is the editor-in-chief of the *International Journal of Information Security and Privacy* and the *International Journal of Smart Security Technologies* (IJSST). He serves as an associate editor for *IEEE Access* (2019 Impact Factor 4.098), the *International Journal of Digital Crime and Forensics* (IJDCF), and the *International Journal of Information Security and Privacy* (IJISP). He is a series editor of Advances in Cybersecurity Management by CRC Press/Taylor & Francis. He was also a guest editor of a special issue on Recent Advances on Cyber Security and Privacy for Cloud-of-Things in the *International Journal of Digital Crime and Forensics* (IJDCF), Volume 10, Issue 3, July–September 2019. He has served and continues to serve on executive and technical program committees and as a reviewer of numerous international conferences and journals such as *Elsevier Ad Hoc Networks, IEEE Network Magazine, IEEE Sensor Journal, ICT Express*, and *Springer Cluster Computing*. He was the publicity chair of BCCA 2019 and the general chair of the MLBDACP 19 symposium and ICI2C'21 Conference. He also received the Publon Top 1% Reviewer Award for the years 2018 and 2019.

Contributors

A. A. Awoseyi
First Technical University
Nigeria

A. A. Yusuf
Federal University of Petroleum
    Resources
Nigeria

Abhilasha Chauhan
Department of Computer Science and
    Engineering
School of Computing
DIT University
Dehardun, Uttarakhand, India

Akshat Agarwal
Department of Computer Science
Amity School of Engineering and
    Technology
Amity University
Haryana, India

Ankit Garg
School of Computing (SOC)
University of Engineering & Technology
Roorkee, India

Ankit Kumar Singh
NIT Jamshedpur
India

Anuj Kumar Singh
School of Computing (SOC)
University of Engineering & Technology
Roorkee, India

A. O. Eyitayo
First Technical University
Nigeria

Arun Velu
Equifax
Atlanta, USA

F. O. Onipede
First Technical University
Nigeria

Gesu Thakur
School of Computing
University of Engineering and
    Technology Roorkee
Roorkee, Uttarakhand, India

H. A. Badmus
First Technical University
Nigeria

J. E. T. Akinsola
First Technical University
Nigeria

Kritika Puruhit
JIET
Jodhpur, Rajasthan, India

Luxmi Sapra
Graphic Era Hill University
Dehardun, Uttarakhand, India

M. A. Adeagbo
First Technical University
Nigeria

Meenu Vijarania
Centre of Excellence, Department of
    Computer Science
School of Engineering and Technology
K.R. Mangalam University
Gurugram, Haryana, India

Naved Alam
Jamia Hamdard
New Delhi, India

Pawan Whig
Vivekananda Institute of Professional
    Studies
New Delhi, India

Priyank Parmar
Rashtriya Raksha University
Gujarat, India

Rajesh Kumar
Department of Computer Engineering
J.C Bose University of Science
    and Technology
YMCA
Faridabad, Haryana, India

Ravi Sheth
Rashtriya Raksha University
Gujarat, India

Rewa Sharma
Department of Computer Engineering
J.C Bose University of Science and
    Technology
YMCA
Faridabad, Haryana, India

R. O. Abimbola
First Technical University
Nigeria

R. O. Olopade
First Technical University
Nigeria

Sameeka Saini
Indian Institute of Technology
Roorkee, Uttarakhand, India

Shama Kouser
Jazan University
Saudi Arabia

S. O. Abdul-Yakeen
First Technical University
Nigeria

S. O. Osonuga
First Technical University
Nigeria

Swati Gupta
Centre of Excellence, Department of
    Computer Science
School of Engineering and Technology
K.R. Mangalam University
Gurugram, Haryana, India

Vinita Sharma
Amity University
Noida, India

1 Emerging Trends in Security, Cybercrime, and Digital Forensics in the Context of the Internet of Things

Sameeka Saini
Indian Institute of Technology, Roorkee, Uttarakhand, India

Abhilasha Chauhan
Department of Computer Science and Engineering, School of Computing, DIT University, Dehardun, Uttarakhand, India

Luxmi Sapra
Graphic Era Hill University, Dehardun, Uttarakhand, India

Gesu Thakur
Professor, School of Computing, University of Engineering and Technology Roorkee, Roorkee, Uttarakhand, India

CONTENTS

1.1 INTRODUCTION

A term coined by Kevin Ashton, "IoT" (i.e. Internet of Things) is the trending buzzword in the industry these days. The IoT has become an attractive, interesting, and most demanding area for all researchers and experts. It is gaining popularity because it can connect devices with each other without human intervention and therefore make technology and devices smart. The inspiration behind the IoT is to enhance the quality of services provided to people, to enhance the use of resources, and to improve people's quality of life. The tremendous increase in the use of IoT devices also has reduced the gap between the physical and digital world. IoT technology comprises sensors or smart devices, connectivity, data processing, and user interface. The smart IoT nodes or sensors are capable of providing lightweight data, retrieving and approving cloud-based resources for gathering and extracting information, and then using that information to make effective decisions [1].

The IoT has wide applications in agriculture as smart devices are used to monitor soil, temperature, moisture, etc. to help harvest crops better. In healthcare, smart devices are used to gather and communicate data about patients to doctors for early diagnosis of diseases. In the home, smart devices provide ease and comfort to people. In education, the smart classroom helps students learn and understand better. In a smart city, the smart components of the city make it a smarter and safer place to live, provide entertainment, etc. Figure 1.1 highlights some major application areas of the IoT.

IoT-enabled devices are large-scale devices that allow many people to communicate, and they generate massive amounts of data. IoT devices are also called smart devices because they use sophisticated algorithms with powerful hardware to make decisions based on sensed, gathered data. The sensors or smart devices are those that sense and perceive the surrounding environment. IoT systems consist of billions of heterogeneous objects that work together to make devices smart. Some IoT devices are lightweight and small in size, so they can utilize less energy, for example, smart watches and smart lenses. The IoT requires constant connectivity for sensing, storing, and analyzing the data [2]. The IoT is trending in e-business also, where it is helpful in payment, logistics, and inventory regions [3]. Advancement in the healthcare sector is

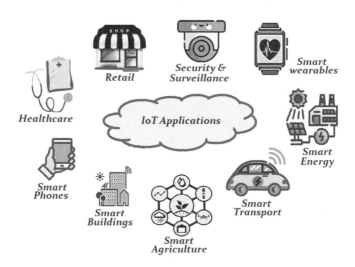

FIGURE 1.1   Internet of Things applications.

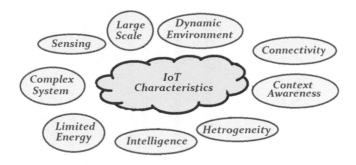

FIGURE 1.2 Characteristics of the Internet of Things.

also gaining popularity these days as, with the help of the IoT, diseases are detected and cured earlier and efficiently [4,5].

Figure 1.2 shows some of the characteristics of IoT technologies.

IoT technologies are used to transfer sensed data to the cloud or any central storage through technologies such as RFID, ZigBee, Bluetooth, WiFi, and Near-field Communication, NFC. The IoT has many benefits, including making better use of technology, minimizing human effort, being cost effective, and saving time and resources. The IoT's weaknesses are security and privacy. Other weaknesses include complexity, flexibility, and compliance. With the frequent use of IoT technologies, new horizons for attackers have also been opened. Sensitive data are always at risk for cyberattack.

1.2 NECESSARY TERMINOLOGY

Forensics describes the evidence that is collected for solving a crime, for example, fingerprints, DNA, footprints, etc. The forensic scientist inspects and examines evidence from crime scenes. Consider a crime where a guilty criminal ran away. Now, the work of the forensic team comes into play. The forensic team collects the evidence, such as blood spots, fingerprints, hair, or other trace evidence that will help to prove the criminal guilty in court. There are certain terms that are used frequently. Table 1.1 lists the basic terminology, definitions, and examples.

1.3 DIGITAL AND IoT FORENSICS

Security of data from cyberattackers or opponents is both important and crucial at the same time. In the past few years, there has been a tremendous increase in the rate of cybercrimes worldwide. The rate of cybercrime (incidents per lakh population) has increased from 3.3% in 2019 to 3.7% in 2020 in India, as per the NCRB (National Crime Records Bureau) [9]. The following Table 1.2 shows the crimes under IPC and SLL from 2018 to 2020 in India [9].

Crimes that involve computers, smartphones, networks, or the Internet to steal information or commit fraud to gain fame or financial pleasure are generally termed cybercrime. There are various crimes that are listed under cybercrime, such as

TABLE 1.1
Basic Terminology With Examples

	Terms	Definition	Example
1	Authentication	The term used to define one's identity or prove one's identity [6].	For example, opening an email by entering an email ID and password; if the information is correct, one can access all the services of the email.
2	Authorization	Authorization is giving approval to someone to perform something or to access some data. It is basically used to express an access policy [6].	For example, a house owner has all rights and authorization to access their property and to do anything with it.
3	Security	The state where one feels safe, secure, and free from threats.	For example, using an antivirus gives security from malicious attacks and viruses.
4	Confidentiality	The information is shared only between the sender and receiver, and it is kept secret and secure from a third person.	For example, a customer's personal information is kept confidential between merchant and customer.
5	Privacy	Rights one has to control their private information and how it's used. On the other hand, security refers to how personal information is protected from threats [7].	For example, when we download some software and install it, we have to accept and agree on specific terms and privacy policies.
6	IoT	The Internet of Things defines the integration of smart devices that are interconnected for sharing or exchanging information over the Internet.	For example, a smart home consists of automatic doors; smoke detectors; gas leak sensors; smart windows; and smart appliances such as a refrigerator, air conditioners, TV, microwave, etc.
7	Cybercrime	These criminal activities that involve computers or the Internet are done for financial purposes or to gain fame or publicity.	For example, credit card fraud, spoofing, sending fake emails, and online stalking and harassing are all cybercrimes.
8	Digital Forensics	Digital forensics is the process of collecting, analyzing, and preserving evidence that can be used in court to convict a person of a crime [8].	For example, we can examine a smartphone or laptop to find evidence of a cybercrime that occurred in a bank.

9	IoT Forensics	This is the branch of digital forensics that examines sensors or smart (IoT) devices to collect proof of a crime. IoT forensics can be divided into three types: IoT device level, network forensics, and cloud forensics [8].	For example, the photographs a person has viewed or any video a person has recorded can be used as evidence of a crime in court trials.
10	Computer Forensics	In this method, evidence against crime is collected in a lab with the help of hard disks, USB drives, memory devices, cloud space, phone data, or any digital device.	For example, from the location of a person's mobile phone we can prove the person's presence at the time of a crime.
11	Network Forensics	This is the branch of forensics that compares or analyzes the network traffic versus a crime's proof [7].	For example, if data are stolen by attackers who ask for a ransom, we can examine the network to determine the location or IP address of the attackers.
12	Mobile Device Forensics	The mobile device is used to collect data against a crime by using mobile texts/emails, the phone's pictures/videos, contact details, or taped phone conversations.	For example, in a kidnapping, police can tap the mobile phone to determine the location of the caller.
13	Database Forensics	This is the branch of digital forensics that examines the database and metadata and uses them as a tool for solving crime and proving crime in court.	For example, we can check the database of the victim in a bank fraud case.

TABLE 1.2

Crimes Under IPC and SLL for Duration 2018 to 2020 in India

	Years	Projected Population (in Lakhs)	Percentage of IPC Crimes to Total Cognizable Crimes
1	2018	13233.8	61.7
2	2019	13376.1	62.6
3	2020	13533.9	64.4

identity theft, copyright fraud, child pornography, digital piracy, money extortion for data, money laundering, spam, cyberbullying and stalking, online job fraud, phishing, IoT hacking, hacking, logical bombs, and a lot more. The cases registered against cybercrime are alarming, and attackers are constantly inventing new ways to harm their victims. Figure 1.3 shows the cybercrime cases in the various states of India in 2020.

To investigate cybercrime, we need the help of forensics. The evidence can be extracted from the IoT or smart devices such as mobile phones, laptops, databases, networks, etc. Forensics is the simple process consisting of the following stages, as shown in Figure 1.4.

The investigation process is started as soon as any crime is detected or reported. The goal of computer forensics is to gather and analyze the digital evidence collected from the computer to prove the cybercrime in court. First of all, we identify where the evidence is located and in which form. Next, we preserve that evidence so that no one can tamper with it. Next, tools and techniques are examined, and evidence is assessed for its accuracy. In the end, a detailed report is generated regarding the above steps. Other computer forensics branches include email forensics, database forensics, memory forensics, network forensics, mobile forensics, Web forensics, and multimedia forensics.

Digital forensics and IoT forensics are two different terms where IoT forensics can be considered a subdivision of digital forensics. Both aim to recognize and extract digital information in a legal way from an IoT or smart device, sensors, an internal network, or the cloud [10]. IoT forensics can be divided into three main parts: cloud forensics, network forensics, and IoT device level forensics. Figure 1.5 depicts these three levels in detail [11].

As stated, forensics is the technique used to investigate a crime or to collect evidence that can prove a crime. The same forensics investigation tools are used in IoT forensics. The benefit of using the investigation tools includes the ability to search quickly through a huge amount of data, the ability to choose one's own language and perform the investigation oneself, and the ability to recover data that have been deleted intentionally or accidentally. It is always preferred if we consider more than one tool for the investigation process. The reports generated by the forensics tools contain every big and small detail of evidence; hence, they can be used to prove a crime. Some forensics tools are freely available, and some come with a cost. Some tools are used only for Windows OS, some are for mobile OS,

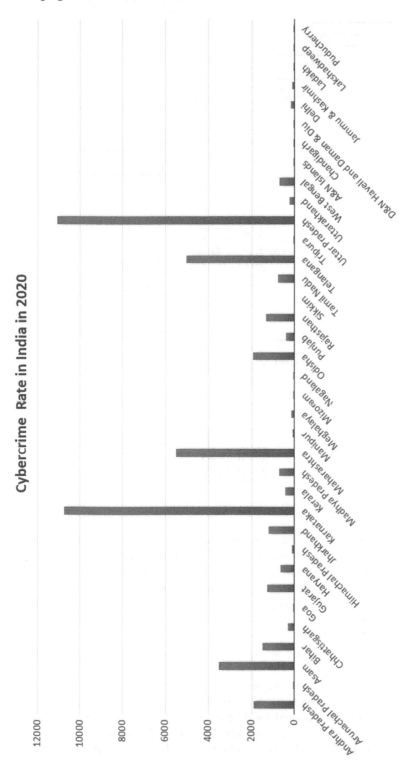

FIGURE 1.3 Cybercrime rate in the various states of India in 2020 (Data from NCRB).

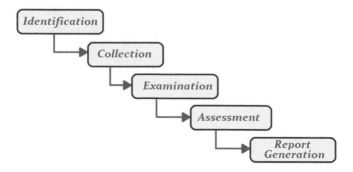

FIGURE 1.4   Steps of forensics.

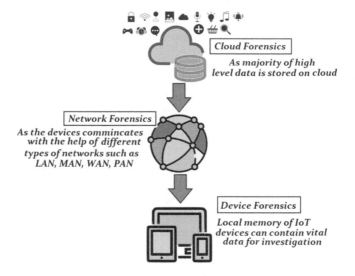

FIGURE 1.5   The IoT forensics. (Data from Atlam, 2020).

and some are so flexible that they can be used on any platform. Table 1.3 shows some of the important recent tools that are used in forensics [12].

A variety of free and paid forensics tools are available, and it is important to document the tools and methods used. Also, the information on version and model used in forensics investigation should be clear. The main drawbacks to using these tools are as follows [13,14]:

1. Because the source code is kept secret by the manufacturer, it lacks transparency.
2. These tools sometimes modify existing data.
3. The forensics specialist needs to maintain all the records.
4. There is no precise standard for determining and verifying the outcomes.
5. Some software may take a lot of time to execute the results.
6. Understanding them and gaining command of them is a hard task.

TABLE 1.3
Computer Forensics Tools

	Tools Name	Platform	Description
1	Autopsy	Windows/mac OS/Linux	The software uses the sleuth kit to collect evidence from computer devices. This tool is maintained by Basis Technology Corp. The GUI demonstrates results from a forensics search.
2	Sleuth Kit	Windows/Unix	It is the toolkit and library that provides Graphical User Interface (GUI) and Command Line Interface (CLI) for digital forensics examination for Windows and Unix. It is used to extract data from storage devices.
3	FTK (Forensic toolkit)	Windows	Developed by Access Data, this toolkit scans hard disks for different information. It has detail potential to scan and recover deleted data also.
4	SPEKTOR Forensic Intelligence	Unix	Designed by the English company Evidence Talks, this tool is used to conduct digital investigation on location or in a forensics lab.
5	COFEE	Windows	Computer Onlire Forensic Evidence Extractor (COFEE) is a toolkit developed by Microsoft. It performs live analysis and uses a USB drive.
6	Elcomsoft	Windows, mac OS	This is privately owned, free software that unlocks data, recovers passwords, and decrypts files in digital forensics investigation.
7	EnCase	Windows	Developed by Guidance Software, it allows one to recover evidence from seized storage devices. It uses pictures, documents, browsing history, registration information, etc.
8	PTK Forensics	LAMP	It is a paid commercial GUI tool used as a sleuth kit. It uses hash signature (basically SHA-1 and MD5) for media confirmation and consistency purposes.
9	The Coroner's Toolkit	Unix	It is a free CLI security tool developed by Dan Farmer that is basically used to gather evidence from UNIX systems.
10	CMAT (Compile Memory Analysis tool)	Windows	It is used to extract information from memory dump and uncover malware.

Sometimes IoT security and IoT forensics are considered to be the same, but there is a difference between them. IoT security means securing the IoT smart device so that no opponent or attacker can steal the data or can get access to confidential data. But IoT forensics doesn't claim that. Its work comes into the picture when the crime has already been done. IoT forensics gathers the evidence that can be used to prove the crime against the culprit in court.

Digital forensics is helpful because it is used to identify what was stolen, how it was stolen, and how data were replicated or disseminated. Apart from this, sometimes it can be used to identify the duration of unauthorized access on any network. In recent years, as cybercrime has increased, so has the requirement and need for digital forensics. Also, digital forensics gathers evidence from a variety of areas, such as mobile phones, computers, laptops, handprints or footprints, etc. so it is easy to prove the crime against the culprit.

Similarly, IoT forensics is required because of the weakness of the IoT (i.e. security). IoT devices are considered to be vulnerable devices. IoT devices with public interfaces are unprotected and are at more risk because they can let malware in easily in any public or private network [15]. Some of the examples include phishing, SQL injection attacks, commandeering cloud-based CCTVs, node/device tempering, data leakage, identity theft, cyberbullying, ransomware, etc., targeting various smart devices and Voice over Internet Protocol (VoIP) devices. The attacks that can be performed on IoT devices can be categorized as attacks on IoT hardware, IoT data, and IoT software. Following are some reasons, application-wise, why IoT forensics is required.

1. IoT forensics in healthcare: One of the major applications of the IoT is in the healthcare sector, where one can find smart equipment and wearable devices that help patients to keep track of their health, and doctors can monitor patients remotely. For a fitness tracker, a malicious person can accumulate the data and sell it to an insurance company or can threaten the victim with the compromised device. In the case of medical data, identity theft is increasing alarmingly [15]. Smart wearable devices are also a good source of data, generated from built-in sensors. Smart wearables are used in the healthcare sector to gather sensitive data on patients that can be analyzed to check the progress of patients' health. This data can be used as forensics to disprove the incorrect testimony of a suspect or to trace the actions of a victim. Other types of attacks may include disrupting emergency services, disrupting monitoring services, or sending fake or wrong information. For this reason, the study of wearables has become more attractive to forensics.

2. IoT forensics in smart buildings: Smart homes are located in residential areas, and office buildings can be made smart with the help of sensors and technology to save energy and resources and to make life comfortable and easy. For example, automated lighting systems, air conditioners, refrigerators, washing machines, smoke detectors, etc. are controlled through the Internet. But this easy technology can be attacked by criminals who access and break down the system. Criminals can manipulate the system and break smart locks to intrude into smart houses when the owners are away. Also, hackers can break into the smoke detector system, which will

open the emergency exit of the home; thus, they gain access to the house for robbery. Other types of attacks include tampering with smart meters or disabling water, gas, or electricity supplies. IoT forensics can help by detecting these moments by camera and then recording them and sending that video to a connected or registered mobile phone.

3. IoT forensics in smart parking: Vehicles that use green energy to keep the environment healthy and save energy are called smart IoT vehicles. Smart parking ensures parking of vehicles in proper places and spaces. Through sensors and connected devices, users can find empty parking for their vehicles. Because the locking system of the vehicles is through the Internet and sensors, hackers can break into the system and steal the vehicle. Other attacks include controlling the car from the attacker's phone, stopping the car's engine, and altering the car's GPS signal. So, forensics are required in this field.

4. IoT forensics in smartphones: Smartphones contain lots of data: phone call recordings, messages, photos, videos, etc. Mobile phones are devices that can send or receive data from WiFi access points, Bluetooth, etc. Hackers can delete the data or alter the data after a crime, so forensics is important.

5. IoT forensics in the smart grid: Old meters are replaced by new and innovative smart meters that use IoT technology to generate bills per consumer use on their smartphones. But hackers can spoof usernames and addresses, can perform denial of service attacks, or can gain unauthorized access by breaching the network. So, forensics can play a crucial role here also.

In the IoT environment, various applications help to collect evidence. As the first phase of the evidence life cycle, it is important and necessary to check on every detail to collect strong evidence against any crime. The IoT network contains a rich set of data and evidence that can be collected via smart devices. The following Table 1.4 shows some of the sources of evidence from IoT-based applications [16].

TABLE 1.4
Sources of Evidence

	IoT Application Area	Sources of Evidence
1	Smart Buildings	Data from applications on connected smartphones, CCTVs, local networks, and smart appliances such as TV, fridge, AC, etc.
2	Smart Vehicles	Data from GPS system, sensor network, automotive applications on smartphones, etc.
3	Smartphones	Data from memory cards, contact lists, text messages, call details, files, etc.
4	Smart Wearables	Data from applications on wearable devices, cloud data, biometric information, etc.
5	IoT Industry	Data from cloud storage and applications such as details of import/export, profit/loss, employee information, other important records, etc.
6	Smart Hospitals	Data from the cloud and applications such as patients' personal records, medical history, hospital staff information, medicine information, billing information, etc.

1.4 CHALLENGES AND ISSUES IN IoT FORENSICS

The IoT – being the most used, demanding, and recent technology – is also considered the most challenging one. As the IoT is dynamic in nature, all the devices are connected with each other with the help of the Internet for communication. The ease of connection and access of IoT devices opens a new horizon for hackers and attackers to gain access to the network and plant viruses or malware on the devices. The major problem that arises in this technology is security. It's difficult to ensure security in IoT devices. A lot of research is being carried out to enhance the security of IoT devices. Figures 1.6 depicts some of the major challenges faced by IoT devices or networks.

Major challenges for the IoT environment are security concerns such as confidentiality, access control, protected communication, and protected storage of data [17]. Let's discuss the above stated issues in detail with proper examples.

1. Security: This term is used to specify the techniques of protection used to secure the IoT network. IoT security is the combination of techniques, tools, and approaches toward he prevention from malicious attackers. It is the practice that keeps devices safe. This factor basically considers two cases: (1) to make sure that all sensed, collected, and stored data are kept safe or transferred securely; (2) to detect and remove the vulnerabilities in IoT components. The solution to this problem is to encrypt the data with strong encryption algorithms. For example, in any bank the CCTV captures all the details, and these data are stored centrally on cloud storage. If robbers get access to that, they can delete the recording of that day and can remove the evidence of robbery.
2. Authentication: In the IoT, authentication is used to prove the identity of authorized persons. Key generation and deployment is a major challenge in the IoT environment [18]. In the IoT, to prevent any data leak, only authorized persons should access, alter, or insert data. Devices should have a strong authentication mechanism. For example, a username and strong password are used to authenticate IoT devices in the network.
3. Privacy: Privacy is the concern where private and sensitive information is leaked to unauthorized people. For example, all the devices connected in

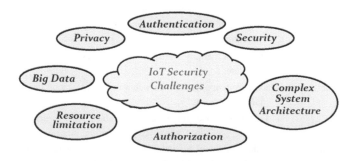

FIGURE 1.6 The challenges faced by IoT technologies.

the IoT are constantly transmitting delicate personal information, such as name, contact details, residential details, credit/debit card information, health-card information, etc. For example, if we are purchasing any product online and paying online, we need to insert our private information, Then, we need to protect this information.

4. Authorization: For securing IoT networks, providing authorization and access control mechanisms plays an important role. Access to information should be provided only after successful authentication of authentic users. This can be achieved by using two-factor authentication and keeping strong passwords. For example, in any IoT network if the username and password are weak, any attacker can guess the password and can hack the network.

5. Big Data: As the IoT is a network of various connected devices, data are constantly being created and shared between them with the help of cloud storage, so we have a large amount of sensitive data. It is the key foundation of "big data." So, we have to keep these crucial data safe and secure, and most importantly, integrity must be maintained. So, the main problem arises in maintaining integrity of the message. For example, if any patient's data are recorded and stored on the cloud, the hacker can change the patient's medical history and health statistics if proper measures are not taken.

6. Resource Limitation: The IoT network contains devices that are small and lightweight, mostly battery operated. So, high-security algorithms that take up a lot of space and time complexity make them operate slower. Moreover, we cannot execute intricate processing on them. They need lightweight, small, but strong encryption algorithms. For example, a small network that controls traffic for a small area can sense data and store data on the cloud by using small amounts of energy, but in the case of marine cargo or monitoring airport traffic, a big infrastructure and a big, strong cryptographic algorithm with large storage space is needed.

7. System Resilience: Another challenge is system resilience; that is, when the system is hacked and data are breached, how does the system react to protect itself from further damage? For example, in a network, if one node is attacked and the system realizes it, then how does it protect the other nodes from getting infected?

8. Complex System Architecture: The IoT involves large, heterogeneous nodes and devices that include sensors, storage, and computing devices, making it more complex to manage and keep safe and secure from hackers. The extra people, nodes, interaction, and boundaries increase the risk of safety breaches.

The challenges faced by investigators in IoT forensics consider the size of objects; the location, such as local or remote; the ease of access; the significance of recognized collected devices; legal issues; wireless networks; the availability of tools, etc. The objective remains the same as in physical crime – to collect the correct evidence in the given time. Digital crime also involves the steps of determining the crime, analyzing the crime, identifying the culprit, and then proving it by collecting various valid evidence [19]. Also, it includes cloud forensics as cloud storage is important in the IoT context as it contains large, sensitive data. The IoT soon is going to expand its boundaries from smart homes to smart thinking to smart cars, and we won't be amazed by seeing it being abused by attackers. We can categorize the major challenges faced by an investigator during the forensics process as follows [4]:

1. Identification of evidence
2. Acquisition of evidence
3. Preserving and protecting evidence
4. Analysis and correlation of evidence
5. Attack and deficit attribution
6. Presentation of evidence.

According to forensic researchers, legal aspects play an important role in creating problems. Figure 1.7 shows the major challenges faced by investigators during the forensics process.

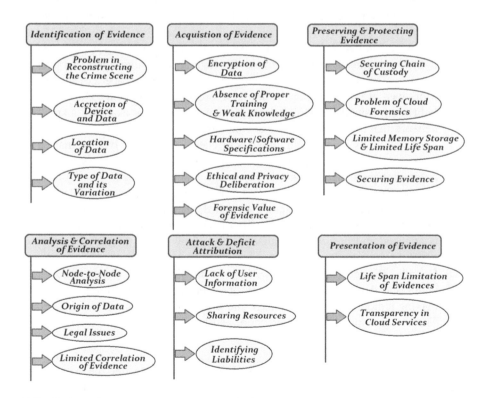

FIGURE 1.7 The major challenges faced by investigators during forensics.

1. Identification of Evidence: The first and foremost examination in forensics is to search and examine for evidence. It seems to be difficult as the investigator may not know where the data are stored physically. The problem faced during this phase is that sometimes it's difficult to reconstruct the crime scene to collect proof. In digital forensics this problem is not possible, but because the IoT considers real-time, independent interaction between various devices or nodes, it's difficult to examine the scope of the damage. Another difficulty is to select which data to select and which to discard as the IoT deals with a huge amount of data. While communicating, IoT devices can migrate between different locations physically and can be confined with single or many hosts, so locating evidence faces challenges. In digital forensics, the objects are limited to the computer, laptop, or mobile phone, but in the case of the IoT, the device types are various and heterogeneous. Some devices are so small that they are unnoticeable, such as medical equipment sensors that collect data from the patient's body for diagnosing a disease. Also, due to short battery life, some devices are hard to detect.

2. Acquisition of Evidence: After identifying the device, the next step is to collect evidence. This step is crucial as an error in this phase can result in making the whole investigation process invalid [13]. The problem faced in this phase is lack of training and knowledge of investigators. As the saying goes, incomplete information is always dangerous. The investigator should be trained regarding the whole process, its importance, and the tools available and how to use them. Another issue is data encryption. Data are stored on the cloud after performing an end-to-end strong encryption algorithm. But due to this, the user can hide or manipulate the data, so the cloud provider should have the decryption key. Also, another problem faced is extraction of evidence from IoT nodes because they can have different hardware and operating systems. Privacy and ethical issues are also concerns while collecting and accessing personal data of various people [4].

3. Preserving and Protecting Evidence: After identifying and collecting evidence, the next crucial thing is to preserve and maintain its integrity. Chain of custody is a logical series that registers and maintains sequence of custody, transfer, temperament, scrutiny, and control of all types of evidence, both electronic and physical. It documents the particulars of investigators who handled evidence, along with the date, time, and purpose. Securing the chain of custody is a challenge as it contains all the necessary and sensitive information about all evidence [20]. Figure 1.8 shows the detailed process of chain of custody and its stages.

   Another challenge in this stage is limited memory storage space in IoT devices. The size of IoT devices is already small, and they are battery operated, so the data that they store have less space. As IoT

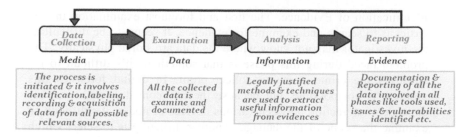

FIGURE 1.8 Process of chain of custody.

devices are performing continuously, they can override the data or even discard some data, which can result in losing important evidence. The Cloud Security Alliance (CSA) conducted a survey and gave the top 12 threats to cloud computing, which include insecure Application Programming Interface (APIs), account hacking, system vulnerabilities, data breaches, data loss, malicious insider attacks, Denial of Service attack (DoS), etc. [21]. The chain of custody and IoT data are stored and rely on the cloud completely, so any intruder who gains access can modify or delete the data [22]. Also, some vendors of cloud storage do not provide all the information and do not maintain transparency regarding the internal structure of their cloud storage [23]. The duration of stored data on the cloud is not specified.

4. Analysis and Correlation of Evidence: In the analysis phase, the investigator may not get the chance to examine all data as the data generated are numerous and their source of origin is not known to the investigator because the IoT network contains heterogeneous nodes. Another issue is that the majority of IoT nodes do not maintain metadata (e.g. time, geographical location info, copyright info), which makes correlation and logical consistency of evidence impossible. In some crimes, if the data are broken and stored at various nodes that are geographical places apart and are in different countries or states, then it is difficult to regulate them as they fall in different jurisdictions.

5. Attack and Deficit Attribution: The investigation process always tries to find out the criminal, but if the evidence is found at one node of the IoT network, it does not guarantee that after identifying that device it will lead to the criminal. Some cloud vendors ask for minimal user information while signing up and accessing the services, and this leads to problems in the investigation process [24]. In digital forensics, only a single device is tampered with, but in the IoT, where multiple users are connected, this leads to problems identifying the correct owner and lists of illegal and legal activities. Most of the recent and modern companies provide private devices for work, which makes identifying liabilities tough [25,26].

6. Presentation of Evidence: The last but most challenging phase is to present the collected and analyzed evidence in front of courtrooms with juries. It

may be possible that the juries have a basic understanding of cloud technology and forensics, but they may not be experts in everything. So, it will be challenging to explain to them everything in technical terms in a short span of time [13].

1.5   IoT FORENSICS APPROACHES AND TECHNIQUES

The IoT makes impactful applications in healthcare, entertainment, education, and various sectors but lacks in security and privacy [27,28]. It is the most popular and vulnerable area that attracts hackers and attackers to breach security and commit a crime. After the crime, attackers try to remove or alter the evidence. In both concept and practice, researchers over the last few years have been continuously working on making the IoT secure and getting accurate evidence from IoT forensics. A lot of models and frameworks were proposed from 1995 until now. There are various frameworks adopting the same main stages to choose from for any investigation. In the end, the choice depends on the assessment method and strategies of the investigator. The early models that were suggested by researchers included the Scientific Crime Scene Investigation (SCSI) model [29], Digital Forensic Investigation model (DFIM) [30], Enhanced Digital Investigation Process (EDIP) model [31], General Digital Forensic Framework model [32], Extended Model of Cyber Crime Investigation(EMCI) [33], and Computer Forensics – Secure, Analyse, Present(CFSAP) model [34]. These models were just theoretical frameworks that were presented before the IoT became popular technology. They were not supposed to resolve the issues mentioned in this chapter; however, they formed a basis for the recent digital forensics discipline.

From 2005 to 2015, researchers worked and adapted various challenges that are faced in the IoT and cloud computing. Some of the famous models include the Computer Forensic Field Triage Process (CFFTPM) model [35], the Common Process Model for IR and the forensics model [36], and the Digital Forensic Investigation Framework Mapping Process [37]; for Malaysian investigation, the process digital forensic model [38], digital forensic multi-component view model [39], Systematic Digital Forensic (SDFIM) model [40]; for cloud conceptual, integrated digital forensic framework model [41]; for cloud forensics, workflow management & processing model [42], DFS digital forensic as service model [43], FAIoT model [44], and many more. From 2016 to 2021, advancement was made on recent theoretical frameworks, and they became more advanced against attacks and crimes: MSM mobility forensic model [45], LoS (Last on Scene) model [46], IoT dots [47], Blockchain-based forensics model [48] as Blockchain is used to provide security to IoT applications [49], Trust-IoV model [50], etc.

Table 1.5 shows the brief summary of work done in this aspect by various researchers.

TABLE 1.5

Previous Research on Digital and IoT Forensics

Paper Details	Proposed Methodology	Details and Benefits
[51]	GrAALF Log Forensics	The author proposed an effectual loading, storing, dispensation, interrogating, and demonstration of logs for computer forensics. The methodology provides real-time forensic analysis of event logs. The source code of GrAALF was also released as open source software.
[52]	Data Recovery & Computer Forensics	The authors analyzed computer forensics and data recovery relationships. They also referred to anti-forensics and its applications, computer forensics technology, and its process.
[53]	Computer Forensics and Cybercrime	They focused on improving search and seizure and discovery information. The method was established with managing the evidence, change of custody, and evidence rule.
[54]	Wearables	Data from applications on wearable devices, cloud data, biometric information, etc.
[55]	IoT Industry	Data from cloud storage and applications such as details of import/export, profit/loss, details of employees, other important records, etc.
[56]	Smart Hospitals	Data from the cloud and applications such as the patient's personal record, medical history, hospital staff information, medicine information, billing information, etc.
[57]	IoT Forensics	By examining the good and bad impact of IoT forensics, the author categorized the literature work and investigated recent work. They discussed the forensic process, processing of data, layers of process, models, tools, and phases of IoT forensics.
[58]	IoT Forensics based Digital Witness Technique.	They applied the PRoFIT technique for IoT forensics, and the digital witness technique was proposed for privacy and securing data sharing.
[59]	Computer Forensics for Cloud	The author proposed recommendations against privacy in cloud computing.
[60]	Memory Forensics	The author focuses on major limitations such as issues in data exchange, incompleteness of data, exe file, inconsistencies, and incompleteness of data in the context of memory forensics.
[61]	Computer Memory Forensics	The author suggested a survey on computer memory forensics, including technological changes, a current scenario, critical analysis of techniques, future research directions, etc.

1.6 CONCLUSION

The IoT's characteristics have brought change and have impacted our lives in both positive and harmful ways. IoT smart devices have wide application areas that are gaining popularity, are expanding their roots in every possible area, and are perfectly merging with recent technologies. This exponential growth has also offered new openings for cyber criminals and attackers. By considering the complex nature and fast growth of IoT networks, security has become an important issue that needs to be analyzed. The IoT also contributes to collecting and preserving lots of data that can help in gathering forensics evidence. To fully function, IoT devices are dependent on cloud services, which creates lots of challenges for investigators when collecting evidence. The challenges are faced in each state, starting from finding evidence on the device to the last stage of presenting the evidence to prove the culprit guilty against that crime. In this chapter, we have discussed IoT and its applications, some important terminology, digital forensics, IoT forensics, challenges faced by investigators, and the recent work done in securing IoT platforms and also getting proper evidence from them. The various tools used in IoT forensics, along with their advantages and disadvantages, were also discussed in this work. Many researchers are working in this area to protect the IoT network against cyber criminals, but still there are many open issues that need to be focused on more, and there is a need to work more to make it stronger and improved against vulnerabilities.

REFERENCES

[1] Conti, M., et al. "Internet of Things security and forensics: Challenges and opportunities." Future Generation Computer Systems 78 (2018): 544–546.

[2] Atlam, H. F., and G. B. Wills. "IoT security, privacy, safety and ethics." Digital Twin Technologies and Smart Cities. Springer, Cham, 2020. 123–149.

[3] Kaushik, K., and S. Dahiya. "Security and privacy in IoT based e-business and retail," in 2018 International Conference on System Modeling & Advancement in Research Trends (SMART). IEEE, 2018.

[4] Kaushik, K., S. Dahiya, and R. Sharma. "Internet of Things advancements in healthcare." Internet of Things. CRC Press, 2021: 19–32.

[5] [online] https://auth0.com/docs/get-started/identity-fundamentals/authentication-and-authorization

[6] Kelly, G., and B. McKenzie. "Security, privacy, and confidentiality issues on the Internet." Journal of Medical Internet Research 4.2 (2002): e12.

[7] Guan, Y. "Network forensics." Managing Information Security. Syngress, 2014. 313–334. https://www.sciencedirect.com/book/9780124166882/managing-information-security#book-descriptio

[8] Stoyanova, M., et al. "A survey on the internet of things (IoT) forensics: Challenges, approaches, and open issues." IEEE Communications Surveys & Tutorials 22.2 (2020): 1191–1221.

[9] [Online] ncrb.gov.in

[10] Alabdulsalam, S., et al. "Internet of Things forensics–challenges and a case study." IFIP International Conference on Digital Forensics. Springer, Cham, 2018.

[11] Atlam, H. F., et al. "Security, cybercrime and digital forensics for IoT." Principles of Internet of Things (IoT) Ecosystem: Insight Paradigm. Springer, Cham, 2020. 551–577.

[12] [Online] https://en.wikipedia.org/wiki/List_of_digital_forensics_tools.

[13] Zawoad, S., and R. Hasan. "Digital forensics in the age of big data: Challenges, approaches, and opportunities," in 2015 IEEE 17th International Conference on High Performance Computing and Communications, 2015 IEEE 7th International Symposium on Cyberspace Safety and Security, and 2015 IEEE 12th International Conference on Embedded Software and Systems. IEEE, 2015.

[14] Arshad, H., A. B. Jantan, and O. I. Abiodun. "Digital forensics: Review of issues in scientific validation of digital evidence." Journal of Information Processing Systems 14, no. 2 (2018): 346–376.

[15] Akatyev, N., and J. I. James. "Evidence identification in IoT networks based on threat assessment." Future Generation Computer Systems 93 (2019): 814–821.

[16] Hou, J., et al. "A survey on digital forensics in Internet of Things." IEEE Internet of Things Journal 7.1 (2019): 1–15.

[17] Zarpelão, B. B., et al. "A survey of intrusion detection in Internet of Things." Journal of Network and Computer Applications 84 (2017): 25–37.

[18] Yang, Y., et al. "Towards lightweight anonymous entity authentication for IoT applications." Australasian Conference on Information Security and Privacy. Springer, Cham, 2016.

[19] MacDermott, A., T. Baker, and Q. Shi. "IoT forensics: Challenges for the IoA era," in 2018 9th IFIP International Conference on New Technologies, Mobility and Security (NTMS). IEEE, 2018.

[20] Alex, M. E., and R. Kishore. "Forensics framework for cloud computing." Computers and Electrical Engineering 60 (May 2017): 193–205.

[21] Cloud Computing Top Threats in 2016, Cloud Security Alliance, Singapore, 2016.

[22] Duncan, B., A. Happe, and A. Bratterud. "Using unikernels to address the cloud forensic problem and help achieve EU GDPR compliance," in Proc. 9th Int. Conf. Cloud Computing GRIDs Virtual. Cloud Computing, Feb. 2018: 71–76.

[23] O'Shaughnessy, S. and A. Keane. "Impact of cloud computing on digital forensic investigations," in Proc. IFIP Adv. Inf. Commun. Technol., vol. 410, 2013: 291–303.

[24] Lillis, D., B. Becker, T. O'Sullivan, and M. Scanlon. "Current challenges and future research areas for digital forensic investigation," in Proc. 11th ADFSL Conf. Digit. Forensics Security Law (CDFSL), Daytona Beach, FL, USA, May 2016.

[25] Rana, N., G. Sansanwal, K. Khatter, and S. Singh. "Taxonomy of digital forensics: Investigation tools and challenges." arXiv: 1709.06529, Aug. 2017.

[26] Das, D., U. Shaw, and S. P. Medhi. "Realizing digital forensics as a big data challenge," in 4th International Conference on Computing for Sustainable Global Development, 2017.

[27] Singh, K., K. Kaushik, Ahatsham, and V. Shahare. Role and impact of wearables in iot healthcare. In: Raju, K., Govardhan, A., Rani, B., Sridevi, R., Murty, M. (eds) Proceedings of the Third International Conference on Computational Intelligence and Informatics. Advances in Intelligent Systems and Computing, vol 1090. Springer, Singapore, 2020. 10.1007/978-981-15-1480-7_67.

[28] Kaushik, K., and K. Singh. "Security and trust in IoT communications: Role and impact." Intelligent Communication, Control and Devices. Springer, Singapore, 2020 :791–798.

[29] Du, X., N.-A. Le-Khac, and M. Scanlon. "Evaluation of digital forensic process models with respect to digital forensics as a service." arXiv preprint arXiv:1708.01730, 2017.

[30] Kruse II, W. G., and J. G. Heiser. "Computer forensics: Incident response essentials." Pearson Education, 2001.

[31] Baryamureeba, V., and F. Tushabe. "The enhanced digital investigation process model." Digital Investigation, 2004.

[32] Casey, E. Digital Evidence and Computer Crime, 2nd Edition, Elsevier Academic Press, 2004.

[33] Ciardhuain, S. "An extended model of cybercrime investigation." International Journal of Digital Evidence 3, no. 1 (2004): 1–22.

[34] Mohay, G. M. "Computer and intrusion forensics." Artech House, 2003.

[35] Rogers, M. K., et al. "Computer forensics field triage process model." Journal of Digital Forensics, Security and Law 1.2 (2006): 2.

[36] Freiling, F. C., and B. Schwittay. "A common process model for incident response and computer forensics." IMF 2007: IT-Incident Management & IT-Forensics7 (2007):19–40.

[37] Selamat, S. R., R. Yusof, and S. Sahib. "Mapping process of digital forensic investigation framework." International Journal of Computer Science and Network Security 8.10 (2008): 163–169.

[38] Perumal, S. "Digital forensic model based on Malaysian investigation process." International Journal of Computer Science and Network Security 9.8 (2009): 38–44.

[39] Grobler, C. P., C. P. Louwrens, and S. H. von Solms. "A multi-component view of digital forensics," in 2010 International Conference on Availability, Reliability and Security. IEEE, 2010.

[40] Agarwal, A., et al. "Systematic digital forensic investigation model." International Journal of Computer Science and Security (IJCSS) 5.1 (2011): 118–131.

[41] Martini, B., and K.-K. R. Choo. "An integrated conceptual digital forensic framework for cloud computing." Digital investigation 9.2 (2012): 71–80.

[42] Wen, Y., et al. "Forensics-as-a-service (faas): Computer forensic workflow management and processing using cloud," in The Fifth International Conferences on Pervasive Patterns and Applications, 2013.

[43] Van Baar, R. B., H. M. A. van Beek, and E. J. Van Eijk. "Digital Forensics as a Service: A game changer." Digital Investigation 11 (2014): S54–S62.

[44] Zawoad, S., and R. Hasan. "Faiot: Towards building a forensics aware eco system for the internet of things," in 2015 IEEE International Conference on Services Computing. IEEE, 2015.

[45] Rahman, K. M. S., M. Bishop, and A. Holt. "Internet of Things mobility forensics," in de Proceedings of the 2016 Information Security Research and Education (INSuRE), 2016.

[46] Harbawi, M., and A. Varol. "An improved digital evidence acquisition model for the Internet of Things forensic I: A theoretical framework," in 2017 5th International Symposium on Digital Forensic and Security (ISDFS). IEEE, 2017.

[47] Babun, L., et al. "Iotdots: A digital forensics framework for smart environments." arXiv preprint arXiv:1809.00745, 2018.

[48] Ryu, J. H., et al. "A blockchain-based decentralized efficient investigation framework for IoT digital forensics." The Journal of Supercomputing 75.8 (2019): 4372–4387.

[49] Saini, S., et al. "Blockchain technology: A smart and efficient way for securing IoT communication," in 2021 2nd International Conference on Intelligent Engineering and Management (ICIEM). IEEE, 2021.

[50] Hossain, Md M., R. Hasan, and S. Zawoad. "Trust-IoV: A trustworthy forensic investigation framework for the internet of vehicles (IoV)." ICIOT, 2017.

[51] Setayeshfar, O., et al. "GrAALF: Supporting graphical analysis of audit logs for forensics." Software Impacts 8 (2021): 100068.

[52] Duan, R., and X. Zhang. "Research on computer forensics technology based on data recovery." Journal of Physics: Conference Series 1648, no. 3 (2020). IOP Publishing.

[53] Akay, Y. V. "Computer forensics and cyber crime handling." Jurnal Teknik Informatika 15.4 (2020): 291–296.

[54] Shalaginov, A., A. Iqbal, and J. Olegård. "IoT digital forensics readiness in the edge: A roadmap for acquiring digital evidences from intelligent smart applications." International Conference on Edge Computing. Springer, Cham, 2020.

[55] Amato, F., et al. "A semantic-based methodology for digital forensics analysis." Journal of Parallel and Distributed Computing 138 (2020): 172–177.

[56] Otieno, G. R., and L. Dinga. "Legal Issues in Computer Forensics and Digital Evidence Admissibility." 2020.

[57] Yaqoob, I., et al. "Internet of things forensics: Recent advances, taxonomy, requirements, and open challenges." Future Generation Computer Systems 92 (2019): 265–275.

[58] Nieto, A., R. Rios, and J. Lopez. "IoT-forensics meets privacy: Towards cooperative digital investigations." Sensors 18.2 (2018): 492.

[59] Kumar, R. A., M. V. Kumar, and R. Sreejith. "Privacy issues in cloud computing for computer forensics: An analysis." Networking and Communication Engineering 10.8 (2018): 152–154.

[60] Uroz, D., and R. J. Rodríguez. "On challenges in verifying trusted executable files in memory forensics." Forensic Science International: Digital Investigation 32 (2020): 300917.

[61] Case, A., and G. G. Richard III. "Memory forensics: The path forward." Digital Investigation 20 (2017): 23–33.

2 Internet of Things (IoT): Security, Cybercrimes, and Digital Forensics

Ankit Garg and Anuj Kumar Singh
School of Computing (SOC), University of Engineering &
Technology, Roorkee, India

CONTENTS

DOI: 10.1201/9781003283003-2

2.1 INTRODUCTION

Internet of Things (IoT) technology is one of the most appealing study areas. It influences a variety of researchers and government sectors due to the emergence of its new technologies and their limitless powers. The IoT simply refers to the expansion of computing and network capabilities to include not only computers and mobile phones, but also a wide range of other devices and sensors throughout the globe [1]. The IoT has the ability to connect and share useful and sensitive data among physical and virtual items that are physically connected to the Internet. To connect the IoT devices throughout the network, either wired or wireless communication technologies are used. The potential connection of various IoT devices and exchange of information among heterogeneous integrated IoT-enabled devices can improve our standard of living [2]. The exponential growth in network technologies, communication systems, and advanced security mechanisms allow the IoT to establish secure connections among billions of things. Statista [3] estimates that the number of IoT objects will reach 75 billion by 2025. Security is one of the primary concerns that threatens the adoption of various IoT devices. Because of the IoT's varied and dynamic nature, protecting data from IoT devices is a complex task. Building an efficient and dependable security approach is now one of the most important things to think about.

Despite the fact that various researchers have proposed multiple security solutions to the IoT security challenge, a solid security approach to ensure data confidentiality, privacy, integrity, and trust have yet to be discovered [4]. Digital forensics has grown in importance, and more research needs to be carried out to develop new investigative techniques. Various techniques under digital forensics are being utilized to drastically minimize the number of cybercrime incidents. As the Internet and communication technology have improved, the number of security risks and cybercrimes has increased substantially [5]. The number of data records compromised worldwide in the first six months of 2018 topped 4.5 billion [3]. This number grows every day as a result of an inability to detect attackers and successfully repel attacks. The acquisition of legal evidence contained in digital media is aided by digital forensics. It also saves time throughout the investigation process by detecting contaminated or stolen data, which may otherwise take hours to identify. The IoT has become a big target for violence and criminals because of billions of heterogeneous devices storing sensitive and valuable data. Despite the tremendous advantages that the IoT provides in various applications, it creates a host of forensics challenges. The IoT system has billions of devices with insufficient security, making it an easy target for a variety of cyberattacks. Furthermore, due to the wide range of IoT devices, typical investigative frameworks are ineffective. As a result, developing an IoT-based investigative framework that can adapt to various devices and situations in the IoT system should be one of the top priorities for security experts.

This chapter provides knowledge on IoT security, cybercrime, and digital forensics. Section 2.2 introduces IoT technology. Section 2.3 presents various layers that are key components of IoT architecture. Section 2.4 explains IoT mechanisms and their building blocks in terms of IoT fundamental components and devices.

Section 2.5 explores various significant features of the IoT. Section 2.6 showcases various communication technologies are being used to exchange information from one IoT system to another. Further, in the subsections, various wireless communication technologies are explained. Section 2.7 elaborates on various challenges that are being faced in IoT systems. Section 2.8 provides a detailed discussion on various security threats and their consequences in IoT systems. The section explains how the security threats affect the performance of each layer of the IoT architecture. Section 2.9 provides various security solutions that are related to each layer of the IoT architecture. Section 2.10 introduces digital forensics, and its subsection discusses different phases that are involved in the process of digital investigation. Section 2.11 presents a total of three digital forensics schemes such as network forensics, device-level forensics, and cloud forensics that are widely used in IoT forensics. Further, the subsections of this section explore various types of solutions that have been suggested by the researchers to improve all the stages of the investigation process. In addition to this, this section presents various issues in digital forensics. To improve the investigation process, the section suggests different components that can be included in the real-time investigation process. In the end, Section 2.12, the chapter concludes by providing future directions that give deep insight to researchers to develop new schemes in the field of digital forensics.

2.2 IOT TECHNOLOGY

The IoT is a new technology that has emerged as a result of recent breakthroughs in the area of information technology (IT). The IoT refers to the capacity of many devices across the globe to be connected and interact with one another via the Internet. Currently, billions of IoT users are connected to one another over the TCP/IP protocol suite and communicate various forms of data throughout the day [6].

With the exponential growth of the available resources and advanced technologies over the Internet, opinions are shared and data are exchanged in over 100 countries. According to researchers and practitioners, the IoT is "An open and complete network of intelligent things with the potential to auto-organize, exchange information, data, as well as resources, reacting effectively to the face of problems and holds the opportunities in the network environment" [7]. The IoT is one of the emerging IT technologies that has attracted the interest of IT specialists all around the world. It has the capability of linking useful resources over the Internet at any time to establish a networked architecture for all IoT-enabled devices. The IoT has given each of its users a distinct identity; it may be thought of as a worldwide network that connects things and provides its unbreakable digital services to its users. The IoT system includes a number of applications that have a significant effect on practically every aspect of our everyday lives, including smart homes, smart cities, smart transport, linked cars, interconnected healthcare systems, and many more [6]. In 5G-enabled services, sometimes a high-speed data transfer is required. Therefore, to improve the rate of data transfer, IoT architectures are introducing artificial intelligence technologies. The inclusion of blockchain technology ensures a secure and trusted environment for all the IoT-enabled devices that are being connected with the IoT network [8,9]. Figure 2.1 shows some useful

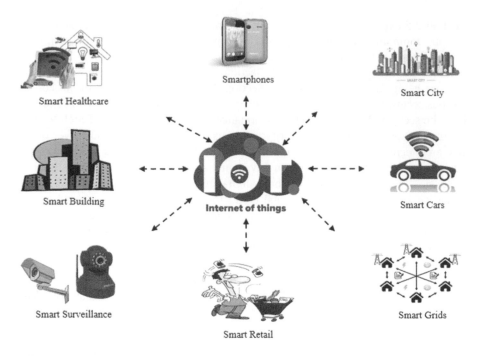

FIGURE 2.1   Applications of the Internet of Things (IoT).

applications of the IoT that improve our standard of living and are included in various activities of our daily life.

2.3   LAYERED ARCHITECTURE OF IOT

In the IoT, there are a variety of data-gathering technologies. The wireless sensor network (WSN) is the most extensively utilized technology, and it combines multi-hopping and self-organization to keep control of the communication nodes. The interconnections of all the scattered nodes are controlled by the central unit in the WSN [10]. Each node is equipped with sensors that can sense pressure, light, and heat. This system functions as an integrated model in which IoT nodes accomplish various significant activities such as sensing, data collection, and transformation of raw data into meaningful information. The WSN system is capable of analyzing data, measuring them, and transmitting them to various IoT-based applications [11]. In literature [12], it has been stressed that an open architecture for IoT-enabled devices is very useful to interlink a diverse range of network applications. In addition to this, IoT design should be adaptive to allow the integration of data and worlds with the Internet. Researchers in their studies have suggested different architecture levels in IoT architecture. Different layers in the architecture perform their assigned tasks and provide insights to the researchers to carry out more theoretical investigation. In Figure 2.2, different IoT layers such as the perception layer, network layer, support layer, and application layer are shown.

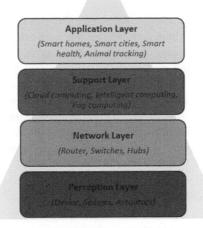

FIGURE 2.2   Different layers in IoT architecture.

Descriptions of the layers that are the key components of any IoT architecture are given below.

1. *Perception Layer:* In this layer, some recent technologies such as nano-technology, tagging technology, sensors, and intelligence technology are being used to recognize IoT-enabled physical objects. The integration of advanced technologies helps to gather useful data and information via interconnected sensors over the IoT network [13].
2. *Network Layer:* Communication systems, broadcast networks, WSNs, optical transmission networks, and closed IP carriers all fall under this tier. This layer is responsible for sending obtained information to the central controller so that the information can be read [14].
3. *Support Layer:* The IoT's core processing unit is found in the support layer, which converts the signal into another form. It also transfers the processed data to storage and makes it accessible whenever it is needed. The application layer and the support layer have a strong relationship, allowing IoT devices to execute all of their duties efficiently [15].
4. *Application Layer:* This layer comprises unique applications that have been specifically built to meet the requirements of the industry or users such as smart transportation systems, smart houses, and smart mining process monitoring systems [16].

2.4   IOT MECHANISMS AND THEIR BUILDING BLOCKS

The IoT can interconnect everything at any moment by utilizing network channels. The precise configuration of IoT-enabled devices, their identification, and exploitation of sensing devices are required to integrate heterogeneous components of the IoT system. Chandrakanth et al. [17] have suggested various fundamental components of the IoT system, which are given below.

1. *Hardware:* This component comprises all the IoT sensors, hardware devices to initiate communication over the network, and central units to process and transform the data into a meaningful form. The central processing unit of the IoT system also performs data management tasks and the exchange of sensitive information among the users.
2. *Middleware:* This component is mainly used for data analysis and management. In an IoT system, cloud computing is a middleware component that integrates various conventional technologies such as service-oriented architecture, distributed computing, hardware visualization, and grid computing [18].
3. *Presentation:* This component is widely used by consumers to visualize and interpret the data.

In efficient IoT systems, the seamless communication and exchange of sensitive information among heterogeneous networks can only be possible by the unification of IoT building blocks [19]. With the proper incorporation of building blocks into the networks, all the subtle issues related to compatibility and interoperability can be resolved. The most critical devices of an IoT network are listed below.

1. *Sensors:* Sensors are used to identify the physical attributes of interconnected IoT-enabled objects. These attributes can be temperature, weight, acceleration, and sound.
2. *Aggregator:* This component executes mathematical operations and transforms raw data into a more usable format.
3. *E-utility:* An e-utility is a piece of software or hardware that analyzes all the data it receives.
4. *Communication Channel:* A communication channel is a conduit for transferring stored data. The flow of information can be wired or wireless depending upon the requirement of the user.
5. *Decision Triggers:* These are utilized to offer outcomes to meet the primary goal of IoT devices.

2.5   CRUCIAL FEATURES OF IOT

The IoT arose from the combination of electromechanical systems and wireless communication technologies that provides several benefits [20]. IoT systems consist of several traits that are listed below.

1. *Interconnectivity:* The IoT is a fast-evolving technology that provides an integrated global information system. It facilitates the connectivity of all communication devices, which speeds up global communication [21].
2. *Things-Related Services:* The IoT provides a wide range of services to the users of IoT networks. These services utilize the physical IoT-enabled

devices in the IoT-based environment. Therefore, the IoT has established itself as a recent technology.

3. *Heterogeneity:* In the IoT network, the interconnection among the IoT-enabled devices depends upon the type of hardware and network platforms. Heterogeneity among hardware and network platforms deals with different types of challenges and provides concrete solutions to a variety of network activities [22].

4. *Dynamic Changes:* IoT devices can alter their functioning modes based on the requirements. The IoT-enabled devices interconnected within the smart home or building have the potential of wakefulness and sleep, as well as mechanically connecting and disconnecting with other integrated IoT-enabled devices.

5. *Large Scale:* The IoT network interconnects a wide variety of sensors and other useful devices. Researchers and practitioners have predicted that by the end of the year 2025 the number of interconnected IoT objects will reach up to 75 billion [3]. Therefore, the exponential growth of network devices establishes a large-scale network system that facilitates effective communication among IoT users.

2.6 DIFFERENT COMMUNICATION TECHNOLOGIES OF IOT

The IoT consists of a variety of items and gadgets. For proper functioning of all the interconnected devices, various communication protocols are being used over the IoT network. The interconnected devices generate a massive amount of data that is required to be managed through data processing services. The data can be in the form of images, text, video, audio, and other multimedia elements. To store and send high-resolution images over the network necessitates high storage requirements and efficient communication channels. Researchers have suggested various image retargeting techniques that can be used to minimize the aspect ration of the images [23–26]. To provide the new services to the users, billions of heterogeneous devices are interlinked together, which is not an easy task. Therefore, communication protocols are regarded as a critical component that enables all of the interconnected components to exchange useful and sensitive information [1]. The primary communication technologies that are being used in the IoT-based network are listed below.

2.6.1 WIRELESS FIDELITY (WI-FI)

This technology is widely being used to exchange information among heterogeneous IoT networks and interconnected devices through wireless signals. In literature [27], it is mentioned that in the year 1991 the NCR Corporation developed the first version of the originator of Wi-Fi. WaveLAN has penetrated the market as the first wireless device that provides a speed of 2 Mbps. However, the quick advancement of wireless technology has facilitated innovative discoveries, and now, millions of public areas such as smart transportation systems, smart homes, and smart offices are equipped via Wireless Local Area Network (WLAN). In addition to this, Wi-Fi is now built into almost all electronic gadgets, such as smartphones, computers, televisions, and other handheld devices [28]. Furthermore, with the aid of wireless access points, entire cities may be turned into Wi-Fi corridors.

1. *Bluetooth:* Bluetooth is another technological miracle that employs short-range radio technology to offer seamless connectivity between everyday items such as portable PCs, notebooks, printers, and cameras across a distance of 100 meters. Bluetooth devices can be connected at a 1 megabit per second (Mbps) rate. Piconet is a popular channel of communication used by various Bluetooth devices. It may link two to eight devices at the same time for information exchange in the form of text, voice, picture, or video [29]. Recently, various companies such as Intel, IBM, Toshiba, Cisco, and HP have been contributing their significant efforts to develop the core Bluetooth Special Interest Group, which is responsible for furthering development of the technology.

2. *ZigBee:* ZigBee is an essential protocol that was created to increase the capabilities of WLANs. The decent price, short communication range, dependability, and flexibility are some major characteristics of this protocol. ZigBee is another miracle of a communication platform that provides plenty of benefits. This protocol is widely used in smart home devices, smart manufacturing systems, and smart power grids [30].

3. *RFID:* One of the most recent communication networks for the IoT is a radio-frequency identification (RFID). These are small reading devices that receive the message. The inbuilt radio device and frequency transponders, known as RF tags, are used in this technology. The RF tag is used to carry programmed data and also allows the RFID to receive the signals. In RFID, there are two types of tags: active reader tags and passive reader tags. The main trait of an active tag is its high frequency over passive tags. The RFID technology is widely employed in many IoT-based applications, such as smart healthcare systems [30], smart agricultural, smart transportation systems, and national surveillance systems.

4. *NFC:* NFC (Near-Field Communication) is a networking technology that brings devices closer to establishing short-range communication to exchange sensitive information. The data communication principle of NFC is similar to that of RFID. After intensive study, it has been found that NFC can be utilized for more in-depth two-way communication. In commercial applications, smartphones, and online digital payment services, NFC is widely used. NFC is known for its quick connectivity and user-friendly functionality. In NFC, a peer-to-peer (P2P) network topology can be employed [6].

2.7 VARIOUS ISSUES OF IOT NETWORKS

In our society, the IoT system is being used in a variety of ways. However, significant hurdles have to be overcome to maintain the growing adoption of IoT devices. The difficulties that are being faced in IoT systems are listed below.

2.7.1 THREATS TO SECURITY

Security risks of IoT devices are being investigated by qualified professionals. The hacking of IoT-enabled devices, sensitive private e-mails, and secret data are the most typical security challenges. The rapid increase in security risks of IoT-enabled devices does not only put sensitive data in danger but also the lifestyles and well-being of its users. Therefore, security is the most challenging obstacle that affects the effective deployment of IoT-enabled devices. With the exponential development of technology, various companies are adopting IoT-based solutions to promote their product into the market. To resolve security issues related to e-business and e-marketing, researchers have identified various cyber threats in IoT and also suggested various solutions [31].

2.7.2 CONNECTIVITY ISSUES

Integrating a huge number of IoT-enabled devices into a common network is another important challenge of the IoT that needs to be focused on carefully [32]. Presently, information from different nodes is authenticated and authorized via a centralized mechanism. However, because the existing centralized system will become a bottleneck, this approach will be unsuitable for connecting billions of IoT devices and their potential users. The future capabilities of IoT systems can be increased by adopting decentralized networking that provides facilities with its unbreakable services to interconnect billions of IoT users at the same time [33].

2.7.3 IoT DURABILITY AND COMPATIBILITY

The IoT system is currently undergoing extensive growth, and several recent technologies are developing from it. Compatibility concerns arise as a result of these changing technologies, which necessitate new hardware devices and software systems. In addition to this, due to the lack of firmware in the IoT-enabled devices, problems of long-term viability have arisen [34]. For a successful IoT-based system, endurance and compatibility are critical concerns.

2.7.4 CONSTRAINTS IN COMPUTING

In an IoT-based network system, even a tiny IoT-enabled device requires an advanced communication system and protocols to be interconnected with other devices [35]. The speed of information processing and other useful functionality of the various IoT-enabled devices can be reduced due to certain constraints. These limitations of IoT networks demand secure operations and connectivity so that less power can be consumed by the equipped IoT devices and secure information can be transferred by them to other devices. The main objective of all the protocols over the IoT network is to strengthen the IoT devices in performing their assigned task at an optimum level. The authenticity and privacy of the data maintained on IoT devices are severely harmed by the network's size and power limits. Digital signatures, which need public key infrastructure, can be used to protect these systems.

However, public key infrastructure encrypts data by utilizing computational and memory capabilities that are not available in recent WSN technology, which is especially important when there is a need for frequent data transfer by the system.

2.7.5   BIG DATA

The IoT is composed of a network of billions of items that generate large amounts of data, referred to as big data. The term "big data" refers to the massive amount of data that cannot be effectively handled by traditional analytical methodologies. The massive volume of data generated by IoT devices poses several issues, particularly in terms of security and privacy. It's difficult to come up with appropriate data analytics strategies that extract useful information. Furthermore, ensuring the integrity of data is also a big problem that researchers must consider while delivering appropriate and concrete solutions [36].

2.8   SECURITY THREATS IN IOT

The IoT is a fast-expanding technology, and it has become the basic requirement in our daily lives. Establishing a secure and safe network system in any country plays a significant role. The principles concerned with the IoT serve as the foundation for the development of a secure IoT system that can resolve various primary security issues. All IoT-enabled devices interact with one another and exchange massive amounts of information via the Internet. Due to the exchange of sensitive information, IoT-based systems are vulnerable to security concerns that make the IoT networks inadaptable technology in the coming days [37]. This section presents a summary of IoT security and discusses potential threats that need to be focused more on every layer in the design of secure IoT systems. In addition, this section explores potential security solutions to counteract such risks. The IoT-based systems comprise billions of IoT-enabled devices. When the IoT technology was not advanced, then IoT-enabled devices were manufactured in a very simple way. The inadequate security features and their simple design make them an easy target for many forms of security attacks. Figure 2.3 shows various security vulnerabilities at each layer of IoT architecture.

2.8.1   SECURITY THREATS TO THE PERCEPTION LAYER

This layer of the IoT system is vulnerable to a multitude of security vulnerabilities. Therefore, to remove the weakness and to make a powerful and secure IoT network the perception layer incorporates sensors and intelligence technologies such as RFIDs. Below are some widely known security threats to the IoT system.

1. *Spoofing:* In spoofing, attackers usually broadcast forged messages to the sensor network. These networks have no mechanism to determine the authenticity of the incoming messages originated from the source [38]. As a result, attackers frequently access sensitive information and exploit it to breach network security in the future.

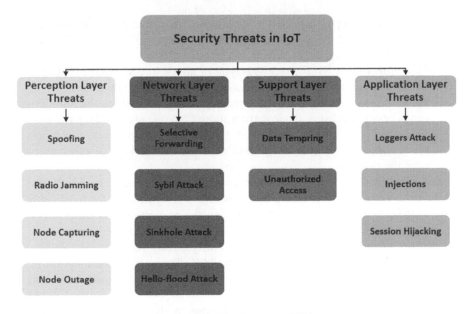

FIGURE 2.3 Various security threats in the Internet of Things.

2. *Radio Jamming:* In this security issue, the attackers utilize Denial of Service (DoS) to prevent the communication channels from sharing sensitive information among the IoT-enabled nodes within the IoT network [39].

3. *Node Capturing:* In this type of attack, a malicious node physically replaces the sensor node. In addition to this, the attacker has complete control of the authentic IoT node. The captured node can be exploited by the attackers to perform harmful activities over the IoT network [40].

4. *Node Outage:* In this type of attack, the network functioning can be interrupted by blocking the IoT nodes. The important sensor nodes over the IoT network can be disrupted either logically or physically by the attackers. As a result, activities such as data collection and data interpretation to obtain and deliver useful information can be entirely hampered [41].

2.8.2 SECURITY THREATS TO THE NETWORK LAYER

In the IoT system, the network layer is vulnerable to fatal security risks. These dangers originate from a variety of places. The security threats that hamper the performance of the network layer are listed below.

1. *Selective Forwarding Attack (SFA):* In this threat, the attackers utilize malicious nodes to stop the transmission of particular packets. The attackers participate in the routing of the message as a normal network node and discard selective messages that are being delivered by neighboring nodes. The malicious nodes do not discard the non-critical data and instead discard the critical message. For example, information originated by the

enemy in an application that is developed to facilitate various military activities is kept. As a result, the entire system is vulnerable to DoS attacks [42].

2. *Sybil Attack:* The Sybil attack is a type of attack in which the IoT device that is recognized as a malicious node tries to make multiple identities or accounts over the network. After creating multiple identities, the intruders can access the network devices from more than one place [43]. After outvoting the non-malicious node from the network, the attackers can block the transmission of information and also initiate blocking of other users over the network.

3. *Sinkhole Attack:* This is another kind of security attack in which the malicious nodes try to affect the network traffic by limiting the bandwidth of the communication channel. Therefore, the congestion over the network significantly increases and hampers the performance of the system. This attack is also used to initiate other security threats such as selective forwarding attacks, spoofing attacks, etc. [44]. The energy consumption of IoT devices can be increased due to the exponential growth of traffic congestion.

4. *Hello-Flood Attack:* This attack is similar to the sinkhole attack as it causes a single communication channel to get clogged with trivial messages due to excessive traffic. As a result, the primary messages become blocked in the clogged channels. A single malicious node generates several meaningless messages and blocks the communication pathways [45].

2.8.3 SECURITY THREATS TO THE SUPPORT LAYER

The main objective of the intruders is to target the storage technologies that are being used on the support layer. These technologies are used to store and manage all kinds of data that are originated from the sensors. The attacks on the support layer are listed below.

1. *Data Tempering:* In a data tempering attack, the authorized person with the right to access the confidential storage technologies alters the sensitive data for their commercial advantage. In this attack, the intruders extract private, sensitive information from the unprotected packets and change the contents as well as the destination address [46]. Data tempering is generally caused for commercial reasons, for example, a competitor company can attack others to obtain sensitive data related to sales, production, and the prototype of a new software system. The day-to-day activities of any company can be hampered after deleting or editing such information from the company's archives.

2. *Unauthorized Access:* In this attack, an unauthorized intruder invades the system and prevents genuine users from accessing it. Aside from that, the intruder destroys the IoT infrastructure and eliminates important information. Hence, these kinds of attacks are devastating to the entire IoT-based network [47].

2.8.4 SECURITY THREATS TO THE APPLICATION LAYER

In the IoT-based network, the application layer provides customizable services to the user based on their choices. The main objective of the intruders is to target customized services that are being offered to the intended users through the application layer. The types of attacks that majorly influence the performance of the application layer are listed below.

1. *Loggers Attack:* In this type of attack, the intruders can send loggers into the IoT-based network to get access to private data such as sensitive documents, messages, and passwords. The most prevalent security vulnerability to the application layer is loggers and sniffers. This strategy is commonly used by hackers to get access to private e-mails and passwords.
2. *Injections:* The intruders in this attack alter the code of the applications through unauthorized access to the servers. The manipulation of code is one of the most commonly exploited flaws in the IoT-based network. Through this attack, sensitive and confidential data and information can be leaked out to the intruders from the security networks [48].
3. *Session Hijacking:* In this type of attack, the intruders utilize the authentication protocols and try to hijack the session management of the network system. As a result, the intruder controls the entire network as a real or authentic user and accesses the personal identities of the intended users [49].

2.9 IOT SECURITY SOLUTIONS

In every IoT-based network system, security is the most prominent area that needs to be focused on more. Researchers and developers have suggested various recent sophisticated security methods. The secure IoT infrastructure is possible, to some extent, by implementing recent security approaches within every aspect of the network. To achieve a secure IoT-based system several security solutions can be utilized by the network administrators. In the subsequent subsections, various security solutions are discussed that are related to each layer of the IoT architecture.

2.9.1 SECURITY SOLUTIONS TO THE PERCEPTION LAYER

RFID readers, gateways, and sensors, which are critical parts of the perception layer, demand extra security procedures to keep them safe from possible security attacks. IoT systems are said to be insecure due to a lack of physical protection. As a result, the most important security endeavor for the IoT system is to ensure that only authorized users can access the private data [50]. To increase the physical security of the system, the IoT system requires strong authentication and authorization procedures. Furthermore, the data collected by sensors require a cryptographic security architecture that guarantees the confidentiality of private data by adopting the procedures of encryption and decryption of the data. Several researchers have shown that cryptographic security protocols and their corresponding algorithms are successful to maintain IoT security. The researchers in their significant research have examined two distinct cryptographic algorithms that are implemented on the sensor nodes. After keen observation, it was found that elliptic curve cryptography is more secure than RSA [51]. The efficiency of cryptographic security mechanisms to secure the IoT system has been demonstrated in a few earlier research studies.

2.9.2 SECURITY SOLUTIONS TO THE NETWORK LAYER

In IoT architecture, the network layer provides security by safeguarding to main sub-layers such as wireless and wired security sub-layers. In the wireless sub-layer, the network can be protected by establishing authentication protocols and key management [52]. In this layer, the Private Pre-Shared Key (PPSK) is used to secure each IoT sensor and other IoT-enabled devices that are interconnected within the system. The wired sub-layer provides a secure communication channel for the transmission of sensitive information in the IoT-based network. In the wired sub-layer, the network can be secure by utilizing firewalls and an Intrusion Prevention System (IPS).

2.9.3 SECURITY SOLUTIONS TO THE SUPPORT LAYER

This layer is a very crucial layer of any IoT network system. It incorporates recent cloud computing technologies to store and manage all the data that are generated by IoT-enabled devices. Moreover, the Cloud Security Alliance (CSA) is a leading organization that provides various guidelines and standards that need to be followed within the security framework to resolve various security issues. This organization promotes best practices and education on the proper utilization of various functionalities related to the cloud computing environment. In the support layer, sensitive data related to intended users and applications are stored and managed; therefore, efficient security processes should be adopted. At this layer, implementation of concrete encryption algorithms is essential, and the definition of antivirus must be regularly updated [53].

2.9.4 SECURITY SOLUTIONS TO THE APPLICATION LAYER

The application layer is the important layer of any IoT network system, which facilitates users to interact with various computer systems integrated over the network. The application layers comprise two sub-layers, the same as the network layer. To prevent unwanted access, all local software systems are required to be protected in one sub-layer by utilizing encryption and authentication processes. In the second sub-layer, the applications that are being used to process the sensitive information of any nation can be secure by adopting authorization, intrusion detection, and access control mechanisms within the IoT network [54].

2.10 INTRODUCTION TO DIGITAL FORENSICS

The number of cybercrimes is exponentially increasing; therefore, the field of digital forensics is grabbing the attention of researchers to contribute their efforts. In this section, firstly digital forensics is introduced. After that, its major steps are discussed that are essential for the development of various digital investigation activities. After the technology revolution in the 1960s, the number of cybercrimes grew exponentially, mainly perpetrated by the heavy use of computer systems. Therefore, digital forensics is currently being utilized to combat any kind of attack or cybercrime that may occur. The National Institute of Standards and Technology (NIST) describes digital forensics as "the science-based process of identifying, gathering, examining, and analyzing data while maintaining data integrity" [55]. The fast growth of network technology has produced issues with data analysis accuracy and efficiency. The study of data obtained from digital devices is known as digital forensics. New devices are introduced into the market with upgraded platforms. Therefore, IT specialists are facing problems with creating new tools to evaluate their retrieved data effectively. The intricacy of digital forensics is the fundamental issue. For example, data from many devices are not easily obtainable using standard techniques; in some cases, the cumulative dataset is stored in several locations. Although the data can be retrieved by conventional digital forensics, their reconstructed form can be unreadable by conventional forensics. Drones, wearables [56], medical equipment, home automation, cars, safety systems, and sensor network technologies are some of the pervasive technologies that provide new problems for digital forensics [57]. When a crime occurs, the forensics team arrives on the site and collects electronic devices to gather forensic evidence. The forensics expert analyzes the electronic tool to gather all relevant evidence about the crime and possible reasons for its occurrence. Both hardware and software digital forensic instruments are employed throughout the digital inquiry. These instruments and incorporated technologies make it easier for the examiner to find and recover the possible evidence. After the completion of the digital inquiry phase, the next phase is the generation of a report that needs to be presented by the investigators in testimony. In this phase, the investigator verifies the validity of digital evidence and provides proof that no data were changed during the inquiry process [58,59]. In the field of digital forensics, blockchain is playing a significant role in cybercrime investigation. The inclusion of blockchain technology is important because it guarantees the correctness of digital evidence as it moves along different levels of hierarchy in the chain of custody during cybercrime investigation [60].

2.10.1 Process Involved in Digital Forensic Investigation

After intensive study and investigation in the field of digital forensics, researchers have concluded that no forensics procedure is best suited to be followed during the investigation process [61]. There are volunteer organizations that define standards that can be applied in every stage of digital forensics. Digital Forensics Research Workshop (DFRW) is a non-profit organization that devotes its efforts to organizing conferences, workshops, and demos that cover various advancements and related issues in the field of digital forensics. To release the useful resources to the digital investigators, three projects – National Software Reference Library (NSRL), Computer Forensic Tool Testing (CFTT), and Computer Forensic Reference Data Sets (CFReDS) – are ongoing at the National Institute of Standards and Technology (NIST). The National Institute of Justice (NIJ) is the research, development, and

FIGURE 2.4 Different phases of the NJR process for digital forensics investigation.

evaluation organization in the United States. This organization is committed to improving awareness and understanding of the challenges that are being faced in crime and justice. Several academicians, practitioners, and researchers have relied on the stages that have been provided by the NIJ [61,62]. In Figure 2.4 different phases involved in the digital investigation process are shown.

1. *Assessment:* Investigators specialized in the field of computer forensics conduct a thorough analysis of all the collected digital evidence according to the depth and sensitivity of the case or crime to decide the course of action.
2. *Acquisition:* Digital evidence is sensitive by nature and can be modified, destroyed, or permanently erased due to improper handling or investigation. Therefore, it is preferable to conduct an investigation using a copy of the original evidence. This unaffected proof should be maintained properly by adopting some concrete investigation methods to protect and preserve its integrity.
3. *Examination*: The goal of the examination is to extract and evaluate digital evidence. Retrieval is essentially the process of recovering data from their storage medium.
4. *Analysis:* In this phase, the data are recovered and interpreted in an organized and meaningful way. A proper data format should be logically selected for data interpretation so that it can be understood easily.
5. *Documenting & Reporting:* In this phase, it is critical to take records on all activities and findings during the forensic analysis of evidence so that they can be preserved for any further investigation. The processes in this phase conclude the findings by preparing a detailed written report on the facts.

2.11   IOT FORENSICS

For those working in the field of digital forensics, the IoT creates a slew of complex issues. According to some predictions, there will be 50 billion interconnected IoT-enabled devices in use by 2022, and these gadgets will be capable of generating massive amounts of data. When massive volumes of IoT data are processed, data centers will face a commensurate increase in workloads; as a result, providers will have to cope with newly emerging issues, such as analytics, privacy, and capacity. Assuring that the aforementioned data are handled efficiently is a critical task, as the application's overall efficiency is heavily reliant on the service features that deal with data management. Figure 2.5 shows three digital forensics schemes – cloud forensics, network forensics, and device forensics – that are widely used in IoT forensics.

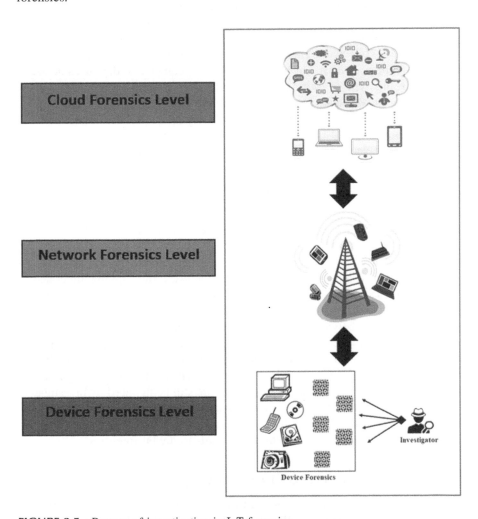

FIGURE 2.5   Process of investigation in IoT forensics.

1. *Cloud Forensics:* In the field of IoT forensics, cloud forensics undoubtedly has a vital contribution. There are several interconnected IoT-enabled devices that have limited storage and processing capabilities. Therefore, all sensitive data and important information generated by IoT devices within the networks are being stored and managed on the cloud. In addition to this, cloud computing services provide various solutions such as high storage capacity, on-demand availability, adaptability, and simplicity [63–65].

2. *Network Forensics:* In IoT-based networks such as local area networks (limited range), metropolitan networks (restricted to metro cities), and Wide Area Networks (across countries), various IoT-based devices are interconnected to transmit and receive messages from one location to another. In the transmission of the data, different types of logs, such as firewall logs and intrusion detection systems, are maintained. To process the criminal cases, these logs are utilized as a piece of probable evidence [66–70].

3. *Device Forensics:* In device forensics, different possible pieces of evidence are collected digitally from the local memory of IoT-enabled devices. These devices can be mobile phones, computers, digital cameras, etc. In this type of forensics, audio and video recording can be obtained from the surveillance system integrated into companies, homes, and other susceptible places. Nowadays, mobile phones are widely used devices that also contain lots of information in the form of images, voice mail, videos, and text. Telephone logs and data may be used by the investigator as a valuable source of proof.

Although a number of models have been created by researchers that uniquely define the significant features of the IoT, there are still various challenges yet to be resolved. The investigator can face difficulties extracting the evidence from the IoT infrastructure.

This particularly happens when the relevant pieces of evidence are found to be concrete and admissible with regard to digital forensics; they are mainly collected from the IoT-enabled devices [71]. The investigators can face complexity in the collection of pieces of evidence due to the existence of multiple challenges, such as no clear relationship between the source of data and their location. The utilization of conventional digital forensic techniques in the process of digital forensics can also be highly responsible to increase the difficulty in finding out better results by the investigators. Although recent technologies have emerged to facilitate the entire process of digital forensics, various challenges are still being faced by investigators that must be overcome. In the next section, various challenges in the field of digital forensics are elaborated. In addition, possible solutions are explained to be considered while developing new schemes in regards to digital forensics.

2.11.1 Related IoT Forensics Frameworks

In earlier days, the framework suggested by researchers was compatible with traditional computing techniques. Based on analysis, traditional techniques are not best suited for recent IoT technologies. In the study, was shown by researchers that recognition of the digital data and the data's proper gathering, protection, and exploration are fundamental activities involved in all the steps of digital forensics. To improve all these activities, some significant processes are needed to develop and further integrate with the IoT. The identified vital challenges that are involved in the development of efficient IoT forensic systems are in the subsequent section. In IoT forensics, various challenges are being faced by investigators that need to be resolved. Researchers are contributing their efforts to propose various types of solutions to improve all the stages of the investigation process. The study carried out by Meffert et al. [72] provides a solution through which Forensic State Acquisition Controller (FSAC) can be adopted to gather the digital data in real time. The adopted approach facilitates monitoring every state of interconnected IoT devices within the network. The study carried out by Hossian et al. [73] provides the solution to ensure that the pieces of evidence that are collected from the public can also be confidential. The concrete evidence can be categorized using proper interfaces, and the incorporation of advanced schemes in the investigation process can guarantee the integrity of the evidence in all the stages of the investigation. Chi et al. [74] proposed a framework that can be used to collect the relevant data from the IoT-enabled devices for further analysis. The centralized collection of data facilities the investigators to formulate new ideas to come up with a specific decision. Chhabra et al. [75] proposed a generalized forensic framework that is capable of disclosing the importance of big data in digital forensics in a well-defined manner. To present the proper utilization of big data in digital forensics, Google's programming model can be used. Al-Masri et al. [76] proposed an efficient framework that is capable of detecting cyberattacks in the early stage. The IoT-based systems that are implemented based on the proposed framework can mitigate the effect of cyberattacks that can hamper the performance of IoT systems. Kebande et al. [77] proposed a framework that is mainly implemented for an IoT ecosystem that is leveraged with the various recent digital forensics technologies. These technologies have the capability of evaluating Potential Digital Evidence (PDE) within the IoT-based ecosystem.

2.11.2 CHALLENGES OF IoT FORENSICS

Current digital forensics is compatible with traditional computing approaches, and in some circumstances, it is not efficient to be interconnected with the recent IoT infrastructure. With the exponential growth of IoT-enabled systems and digital forensics, they must be integrated to secure the admissibility of digital forensics by delivering data swiftly within the IoT system. Taylor et al. [78] have suggested that examination of the real environment is required to allow the interconnection of digital forensics with the IoT. The following are possible issues in the field of IoT forensics:

1. *Development of Investigation Frameworks:* In the conventional digital forensics examination or investigation, a total of six stages are taken into consideration. However, combining digital forensics with the IoT necessitates a new investigation paradigm. IoT devices provide a vast volume

of data that can affect the entire forensic inquiry. As a result, enormous amounts of data gathered at the site might make it difficult for the investigator to determine which digital devices were used to commit a crime. As a result, in the IoT, evidence is gathered to investigate the circumstances surrounding the crime/incident. The process of relevant data collection is the most significant step in any forensics inquiry. The entire investigation process can be thrown off if any mistake is made during the process of data collection. According to studies, the digital forensic equipment that is widely used in the investigation cannot be turned off to accurately record the time in which the data was accessed [79]. Many devices that are not compatible with IoT networks cannot be applicable in digital forensics. Therefore, to make such devices compatible with the IoT, new frameworks need to be designed to collect and preserve forensic data. Researchers in their study have found that the activities that are involved in the collection of evidence are complex due to the availability of various formats of data. Therefore, investigators can face various issues in digital forensics with a variety of protocols and interfaces that are being used in the conventional digital forensics approaches. The extracted data can be temporarily maintained on devices that are interconnected with other IoT devices within IoT networks. As a result, the forensic investigator in their examination and analysis should consider all the interconnected storage devices to extract all the possible evidence.

2. *Multi-jurisdictions:* Investigations in IoT forensics are marred by a lack of defined jurisdictional lines. Data from IoT systems may be sent to other cloud services. As a result, locating data from the servers becomes more complicated for the investigator. In addition, gathering evidence from clouds via IoT forensic equipment is physically inaccessible. As a result, before combining digital forensics with an IoT system, it is necessary to analyze the challenges of numerous jurisdictions. Furthermore, forensic investigators face plenty of legal issues specialized in digital forensics. Problems in the digital forensics process include selecting a law for a particular case that should be prosecuted under device jurisdiction, data storage jurisdiction, or attacker jurisdiction. It will be critical in the future to thoroughly explore legal issues that arise due to multi-jurisdiction in IoT-based systems. The applicability of standard methods would be the crucial requirement to investigate and assess the numerous locations and to deal with various network challenges.

3. *Diverse Range of IoT Devices:* The rapid progress of the IoT is resulting in the creation of new gadgets daily to benefit consumers. To provide excellent services to their clients, service providers also continue contributing their best efforts to explore possible solutions. With regards to technology, IoT-enabled devices run numerous operating systems at the same time. The integration of IoT-enabled devices to exchange information results in a complex IoT network. The intricacy of IoT-enabled devices can have a great influence on forensic investigation methodologies. In the current scenario of digital forensics, only specialized instruments are

employed by forensic investigators. The dedicated tools that are being used in digital forensics are not compatible with the complex IoT-based system. Therefore, IoT is vulnerable to threats [80]. As a result, it's critical to create solutions that can quickly adapt to emerging IoT devices.

4. *Limitations of IoT Devices' Storage:* The IoT-enabled devices that are connected to the network can be equipped with a limited number of computational resources. The data storage capacity of such devices can be very low due to the limited amount of memory. Therefore, the data cannot be stored in these devices for a long time. As a result, there will be a high probability of the forensic evidence being lost or damaged. The investigator can face several challenges while dealing with such devices during the investigation. The investigator can face other challenges due to the utilization of cloud services, particularly for data management and storage. It may be possible that the evidence can be altered or modified by the attackers during their transmission to another network. Therefore, to safeguard the concrete evidence from any kind of tempering, an advanced data transferring approach should be implemented to the IoT-based network.

5. *Poor Evidence Handling:* To prevent manipulation of any evidence in digital forensics, it is critical to treat all evidence with extreme caution. The utilization of traditional cloud computing technique to store and manage data facilitate the attacker to temper the useful facts and evidence explored during the investigation. The management of forensics evidence on clouds is a very complex task in the field of IoT forensics compared to the traditional process. In IoT forensics, the network administrator should maintain and integrate IoT devices that have high storage capacity and computational power into the network. The proper security mechanism should be incorporated within the network to restrict data tampering during transmission.

6. *Lack of Forensics Tools:* It is widely believed that existing forensic tools have several flaws and are unable to adapt to the latest advancements. The existing technologies in the field of digital forensics are incompatible with the IoT environment's infrastructure (which is diverse). The massive volume of potential evidence generated by numerous IoT devices will later give birth to new issues in terms of obtaining evidence from distributed IoT infrastructures [81]. To gather forensic evidence and then evaluate it quickly, a mix of network forensics and computer forensics techniques is required. Traditional forensics technologies can be used to acquire the data (active data) while maintaining their integrity. It is also feasible to collect more data across the network using specialized network forensics tools, such as activity logs.

2.11.3 ADAPTING A REAL-TIME APPROACH FOR IoT FORENSICS

In the field of digital forensics, investigators can be benefited by adopting live forensic investigation that limits the constraints and issues that are mainly faced due to a variety of IoT devices and their handling. Banafa [82] has suggested three major mechanisms that can facilitate the investigators to carry out a real-time forensic investigation. The components that are included in the real-time investigation are listed below.

1. *Time synchronization:* In the IoT network, various devices are interconnected with each other to provide real-time data to the network users. For proper handling of data stored in the IoT-enabled devices, their synchronization is required. In the real-time forensic investigation, all the IoT-enabled devices that contain useful data should be properly synchronized in the detection framework to complete all the stages of real-time forensic investigation.

2. *Enough storage requirements:* All the devices that are storing and managing forensic data must have enough memory space to collect the data. The devices should be capable of providing the data in real time for further analysis by the investigator. It may be possible that the devices interconnected within the network have a small amount of memory to store the useful data. Therefore, the recovered digital data during the real-time forensic investigation are collected and stored in external storage devices.

3. *Communication Requirements:* In digital forensics, the data stored in the devices should not be tempered during communication. Therefore, the proper mechanism is required to extract or safely handle the digital data. A smooth communication process should be implemented within the network to deliver the critical forensic data from one network to another network.

2.12 CONCLUSION AND FUTURE DIRECTIONS

IoT technology has benefited from advancements in network and communication technologies. These technologies integrate billions of communication devices available in the world within the network to exchange sensitive information. Several applications have been developed using these technologies that can facilitate investigators during different phases of digital forensics. Although the IoT provides incalculable benefits, it also poses new concerns, particularly in terms of security. Although various IoT-enabled devices are available with sufficient memory and computing power, by using conventional forensic techniques it is very difficult for investigators to reach a concrete solution, and their efforts can be futile. Therefore, the companies contributing their efforts in the field of digital forensics should come up with an objective in which the development of an IoT-based investigative framework is a top priority. As cybercrimes are exponentially increasing, the field of digital forensics is drawing the attention of researchers to contribute their efforts. There are some major steps in digital forensics that are essential for the development of various digital investigation activities. After intensive study and investigation in the field of digital forensics, researchers have concluded that no forensics procedure is best suited to be followed during the investigation process. There are volunteer organizations that define standards that can be applied in every stage of digital forensics. In the field of digital forensics, several organizations are committed to releasing resources and devoting their efforts toward increasing awareness and understanding of the challenges that are being faced in crime and justice. There are a set of standards established by these organizations that need to be followed by investigators. For those working in the field of digital forensics, the IoT creates a slew of complex issues. In IoT-based systems, massive volumes of data are processed. In this situation, data centers will face a commensurate increase in workloads; as a result, providers will have to cope with newly emerging issues such as analytics, privacy, and capacity. In IoT forensics, several schemes such as network forensics, device forensics, and cloud forensics are widely used to facilitate investigators.

Although several models have been created by researchers that uniquely define the significant features of the IoT, various challenges are yet to be resolved. Investigators can face difficulties extracting evidence from the IoT infrastructure. This particularly happens when the relevant pieces of evidence are found to be concrete and admissible concerning digital forensics; they are mainly collected from IoT-enabled devices. Investigators can face complexity in the collection of pieces of evidence due to challenges such as no clear relationship between the source of data and the location. The utilization of conventional digital forensic techniques in the process of digital forensics can also increase the difficulty of finding better results. Although recent technologies are emerging to facilitate the entire process of digital forensics, various challenges are still being faced by investigators. In earlier days, the frameworks suggested by researchers were compatible with traditional computing techniques. Current digital forensics is compatible with traditional computing approaches, and in some circumstances, it is not efficient to interconnect with the recent IoT infrastructure. With the exponential growth of IoT-enabled systems and digital forensics, they must be integrated to secure the admissibility of digital forensics by delivering data swiftly within the IoT system.

The chapter, in the end, provides future directions to researchers for possible improvement in the field of digital forensics. To improve the entire process of digital forensics, researchers must develop advanced procedures, standards, and concrete guidelines through which recent IoT technologies can easily interact with conventional methods of digital forensics. Investigators can face difficulties while deciding under which law the case should be prosecuted. Therefore, multi-jurisdiction in the IoT-based systems is required. In an IoT-based system, interconnected devices produce a massive amount of data and also share it with other interconnected devices. Sometimes it may be difficult for investigators to deal with an enormous amount of information within the network, and this can influence the investigation. The data analysis procedure during the investigation can also be affected to some extent. Hence, there is a vital requirement to explore new methodologies through which the huge amount of data can be handled effectively. Cyber criminals and attackers can exploit the methodologies and the forensic tools that are being used by the investigator, which is known as anti-forensics. After discovery, the attackers can mislead the investigator during analysis and other tasks. In the current scenario of digital forensics, insufficient data are available. Therefore, government and the private sector should make joint efforts to share their experiences and resources publically.

REFERENCES

[1] Atlam, Hany F., and Gary B. Wills. "IoT security, privacy, safety and ethics." *Digital Twin Technologies and Smart Cities* (2020): 123–149.

[2] Atlam, Hany F., Robert J. Walters, et al. "Fog computing and the Internet of Things: A review." *Big Data and Cognitive Computing* 2, no. 2 (2018): 10.

[3] Statista: Internet of Things (IoT) connected devices installed base worldwide from 2015 to 2025 (in billions). https://www.statista.com/statistics/471264/iot-number-of-connecteddevices-worldwide/. Accessed 05 February 2022.

[4] Jurcut, Anca D., Pasika Ranaweera, et al. "Introduction to IoT security." *IoT security: Advances in Authentication* (2020): 27–64.

[5] Choi, Kyung-Shick, Claire S. Lee, et al. "Historical evolutions of cybercrime: From computer crime to cybercrime." *The Palgrave Handbook of International Cybercrime and Cyberdeviance* (2020): 27–43.

[6] Garg, Ankit, and Anuj Singh. "Applications of Internet of Things (IoT) in green computing." In *Intelligence of Things: AI-IoT Based Critical-Applications and Innovations* (2021): 1–34.

[7] Madakam, Somayya, et al. "Internet of Things (IoT): A literature review." *Journal of Computer and Communications* 3, no. 5 (2015): 164.

[8] Dwivedi Dhar, Ashutosh, Rajani Singh et al. "Blockchain and artificial intelligence for 5G-enabled Internet of Things: Challenges, opportunities, and solutions." *Transactions on Emerging Telecommunications Technologies* (2021): e4329.

[9] Kaushik, Keshav, and Kamalpreet Singh. "Security and trust in IoT communications: Role and impact." In *Intelligent Communication, Control and Devices* (2020): 791–798. Springer, Singapore, 2020.

[10] Adeel, Ahsan, et al. "A survey on the role of wireless sensor networks and IoT in disaster management." *Geological Disaster Monitoring Based On Sensor Networks* (2019): 57–66.

[11] Singh, Anuj Kumar, and B. D. K. Patro. "A novel security protocol for wireless sensor networks based on elliptic curve signcryption." *International Journal of Computer Networks & Communications (IJCNC)* 11, no. 5 (2019): 93–112.

[12] Xiaojiang, Xing, Wang Jianli, and Li Mingdong. "Services and key technologies of the Internet of Things." *Zte Communications* 8.2 (2020): 26–29.

[13] Tewari, Aakanksha, and Brij B. Gupta. "Security, privacy and trust of different layers in Internet-of-Things (IoTs) framework." *Future Generation Computer Systems* 108 (2020): 909–920.

[14] Gokhale, Pradyumna, Omkar Bhat, et al. "Introduction to IOT." *International Advanced Research Journal in Science, Engineering and Technology* 5, no. 1 (2018): 41–44.

[15] Kaur, Karandeep. "A survey on Internet of Things–architecture, applications, and future trends." *2018 First International Conference on Secure Cyber Computing and Communication (ICSCCC)* (2018): 581–583.

[16] Mrabet, Hichem, et al. "A survey of IoT security based on a layered architecture of sensing and data analysis." *Sensors* 20, no. 13 (2020): 3625.

[17] Chandrakanth, S., et al. "Internet of Things." *International Journal of Innovations & Advancement in Computer Science* 3, no. 8 (2014): 16–20.

[18] Syed, Abbas Shah, et al. "IoT in smart cities: A survey of technologies, practices and challenges." *Smart Cities* 4, no. 2 (2021): 429–475.

[19] Rizvi, Syed, et al. "Threat model for securing Internet of Things (IoT) network at device-level." *Internet of Things* 11 (2020): 100240.

[20] Gowda, V. Dankan, et al. "Internet of Things: Internet revolution, impact, technology road map and features." *Advances in Mathematics: Scientific Journal* 9, no. 7 (2020): 4405–4414.

[21] Bures, Miroslav, et al. "Review of specific features and challenges in the current internet of things systems impacting their security and reliability." *World Conference on Information Systems and Technologies* (2021): 546–556.

[22] Fortino, Giancarlo, et al. "Internet of Things as system of systems: A review of methodologies, frameworks, platforms, and tools." *IEEE Transactions on Systems, Man, and Cybernetics: Systems* 51, no. 1 (2020): 223–236.

[23] Garg, Ankit, and Ashish Negi. "A survey on content aware image resizing methods." *KSII Transactions on Internet and Information Systems (TIIS)* 14, no. 7 (2020): 2997–3017.

[24] Garg, Ankit, and Ashish Negi. "Structure preservation in content-aware image retargeting using multi-operator." *IET Image Processing* 14, no. 13 (2020): 2965–2975.

[25] Garg, Ankit, Ashish Negi, and Prakhar Jindal. "Structure preservation of image using an efficient content-aware image retargeting technique." *Signal, Image and Video Processing* 15, no. 1 (2021): 185–193.

[26] Garg, Ankit, Nayyar Anand, and Singh Anuj Kumar. "Improved seam carving for structure preservation using efficient energy function." *Multimedia Tools and Applications* 81, no. 9 (2022): 1283–12924.

[27] Pahlavan, Kaveh, et al. "Handoff in hybrid mobile data networks." *IEEE Personal Communications* 7, no. 2 (2000): 34–47.

[28] Chen, Wenhui, Sangho Jeong, et al. "WiFi-based home IoT communication system." *Journal of Information and Communication Convergence Engineering* 18, no. 1 (2020): 8–15.

[29] Naidu, Gollu Appala, and Jayendra Kumar. "Wireless protocols: Wi-Fi son, bluetooth, Zigbee, z-wave, and Wi-Fi." *Innovations in Electronics and Communication Engineering.* Springer, Singapore (2019): 229–239.

[30] Danbatta, Salim Jibrin, and Asaf Varol. "Comparison of Zigbee, Z-Wave, Wi-Fi, and bluetooth wireless technologies used in home automation." *2019 7th International Symposium on Digital Forensics and Security (ISDFS)* (2019).

[31] Kaushik, Keshav, Dahiya Susheela, and Sharma Rewa. "Internet of Things advancements in healthcare." In *Internet of Things* (2021): 19–32. CRC Press, Boca Rotan, Florida.

[32] Kaushik, Keshav, and Dahiya Susheela. "Security and privacy in IoT based e-business and retail." In *2018 International Conference on System Modeling & Advancement in Research Trends (SMART)* (2018): 78–81.

[33] Singh, Anuj Kumar, and B. D. K. Patro. "Security of low computing power devices: A survey of requirements, challenges & possible solutions." *Cybernetics and Information Technologies* 19.1 (2019): 133–164.

[34] Singh, Anuj Kumar, and B. D. K. Patro. "Elliptic curve signcryption based security protocol for RFID." *KSII Transactions on Internet and Information Systems (TIIS)* 14.1 (2020): 344–365.

[35] Singh, Anuj Kumar, and B. D. K. Patro. "Security attacks on RFID and their countermeasures." *Computer Communication, Networking and IoT.* Springer, Singapore (2021): 509–518.

[36] Balaji, S., Karan Nathani, and R. Santhakumar. "IoT technology, applications and challenges: A contemporary survey." *Wireless personal communications* 108, no. 1 (2019): 363–388.

[37] Solanki, Arun, and Anand Nayyar. "Green Internet of Things (G-IoT): ICT technologies, principles, applications, projects, and challenges." *Handbook of Research on Big Data and the IoT.* IGI Global, Pennsylvania, United States, 379–405, 2019.

[38] Nayyar, Anand, Bao-Le Nguyen, and Nhu Gia Nguyen. "The internet of drone things (IoDT): Future envision of smart drones." *First International Conference on Sustainable Technologies for Computational Intelligence* (2020): 563–580.

[39] Nayyar, Anand, R. U. D. R. A. Rameshwar, and Arun Solanki. "Internet of things (IoT) and the digital business environment: A standpoint inclusive cyber space, cyber crimes, and cybersecurity." *The Evolution of Business in the Cyber Age* 10 (2020): 9780429276484–9780429276486.

[40] Krishnamurthi, Rajalakshmi, et al. "An overview of IoT sensor data processing, fusion, and analysis techniques." *Sensors* 20, no. 21 (2020): 6076.

[41] Patil, Malini M., et al. "Big data analytics using swarm-based long short-term memory for temperature forecasting." *CMC-Computers Materials & Continua* 71, no. 2 (2022): 2347–2361.

[42] Al-Turjman, Fadi, et al. *Intelligence of Things: AI-IoT Based Critical-appllications and Innovations.* Springer Cham, Denmark, 2021.

[43] Khattak, Hasan Ali, et al. "Perception layer security in Internet of Things." *Future Generation Computer Systems* 100 (2019): 144–164.

[44] Aarika, K., et al. "Perception layer security in the Internet of Things." *Procedia Computer Science* 175 (2020): 591–596.

[45] Swamy, Sowmya Nagasimha, Dipti Jadhav, et al. "Security threats in the application layer in IOT applications." *2017 International Conference on i-SMAC (iot in Social, Mobile, Analytics and Cloud) (i-SMAC)* (2017): 477–480.

[46] Siddiqui, Shams Tabrez, et al. "Security threats, attacks, and possible countermeasures in internet of things." *Advances in Data and Information Sciences.* Lecture Notes in Networks and Systems, 94 (2020): 35–46.

[47] Kakkar, Latika, et al. "IoT architectures and its security: A review." *Proceedings of the Second International Conference on Information Management and Machine Intelligence* (2021): 87–94.

[48] Nawir, Mukrimah, et al. "Internet of things (IoT): Taxonomy of security attacks." *2016 3rd International Conference on Electronic Design (ICED)* (2016): 321–326.

[49] Benzarti, Sana, Bayrem Triki, and Ouajdi Korbaa. "A survey on attacks in Internet of Things based networks." *2017 International Conference on Engineering & MIS (ICEMIS)* (2017).

[50] Gurunath, R., et al. "An overview: Security issue in IoT network." *2018 2nd International Conference on I-SMAC (IoT in Social, Mobile, Analytics and Cloud) (I-SMAC) I-SMAC (IoT in Social, Mobile, Analytics and Cloud)(I-SMAC), 2018 2nd International Conference on* (2018): 104–107.

[51] Hassija, Vikas, et al. "A survey on IoT security: Application areas, security threats, and solution architectures." *IEEE Access* 7 (2019): 82721–82743.

[52] Nastase, Lavinia. "Security in the Internet of Things: A survey on application layer protocols." *2017 21st International Conference on Control Systems and Computer Science (CSCS)* (2017): 659–666.

[53] Yang, Guang, et al. "Security threats and measures for the Internet of Things." *Journal of Tsinghua University Science and Technology* 51, no. 10 (2011): 1335–1340.

[54] Jing, Qi, et al. "Security of the Internet of Things: Perspectives and challenges." *Wireless Networks* 20, no. 8 (2014): 2481–2501.

[55] Al Hinai, Siham, and Ajay Vikram Singh. "Internet of Things: Architecture, security challenges and solutions." *2017 International Conference on Infocom Technologies and Unmanned Systems (Trends and Future Directions) (ICTUS)* (2017).

[56] Singh, Anuj Kumar, et al. "Elliptic curve signcryption-based mutual authentication protocol for smart cards." *Applied Sciences* 10, no. 22 (2020): 8291.

[57] Singh, Kamalpreet, Kaushik Keshav, and Shahare Vivek. "Role and impact of wearables in IoT healthcare." In *Proceedings of the Third International Conference on Computational Intelligence and Informatics* (2020): 735–742.

[58] HaddadPajouh, Hamed, et al. "A survey on Internet of Things security: Requirements, challenges, and solutions." *Internet of Things* 14 (2021): 100129.

[59] Ali, Inayat, Sonia Sabir, and Zahid Ullah. "Internet of Things security, device authentication and access control: A review." *arXiv preprint arXiv:1901.07309* (2019).

[60] Kaushik, Keshav, Dahiya Susheela, and Sharma Rewa. "Role of blockchain technology in digital forensics." In *Blockchain Technology* (2022): 235–246.

[61] Pérez, Salvador, et al. "Application layer key establishment for end-to-end security in IoT." *IEEE Internet of Things Journal* 7 no. 3 (2019): 2117–2128.

[62] Kent, Karen, Suzanne Chevalier, and Tim Grance. "Guide to integrating forensic techniques into incident." *Tech. Rep. 800-86* (2006).

[63] Arshad, Humaira, Aman Bin Jantan, et al. "Digital forensics: Review of issues in scientific validation of digital evidence." *Journal of Information Processing Systems* 14, no. 2 (2018): 346–376.

[64] Sharma, Bhoopesh Kumar, et al. "Internet of Things in forensics investigation in comparison to digital forensics." *Handbook of Wireless Sensor Networks: Issues and Challenges in Current Scenario's* (2020): 672–684.

[65] Omeleze, Stacey, and Hein S. Venter. "Digital forensic application requirements specification process." *Australian Journal of Forensic Sciences* 51, no. 4 (2019): 371–394.

[66] Nurhairani, Hijrah, and Imam Riadi. "Analysis mobile forensics on Twitter application using the National Institute of Justice (NIJ) method." *International Journal of Computer Applications* 177, no. 27 (2019): 35–42.

[67] Feucht, Thom. "The National Institute of Justice (NIJ)." *The Encyclopedia of Research Methods in Criminology and Criminal Justice* 2 (2021): 800–803.

[68] Shobana, G. "The state of the art tools and techniques for remote digital forensic investigations." *2021 3rd International Conference on Signal Processing and Communication (ICPSC)* (2021): 464–468.

[69] Stoyanova, Maria, et al. "A survey on the Internet of Things (IoT) forensics: Challenges, approaches, and open issues." *IEEE Communications Surveys & Tutorials* 22, no. 2 (2020): 1191–1221.

[70] Yaqoob, Ibrar, et al. "Internet of Things forensics: Recent advances, taxonomy, requirements, and open challenges." *Future Generation Computer Systems* 92 (2019): 265–275.

[71] Atlam, Hany F., et al. "Security, cybercrime and digital forensics for IoT." *Principles of Internet of Things (IoT) Ecosystem: Insight Paradigm* (2020): 551–577.

[72] Meffert, Christopher, et al. "Forensic state acquisition from internet of things (FSAIoT) A general framework and practical approach for IoT forensics through IoT device state acquisition." *Proceedings of the 12th International Conference on Availability, Reliability and Security* (2017).

[73] Hossain, Mahmud, Yasser Karim, et al. "FIF-IoT: A forensic investigation framework for IoT using a public digital ledger." *2018 IEEE International Congress on Internet of Things (ICIOT)* (2018): 33–40.

[74] Chi, Hongmei, Temilola Aderibigbe, and Bobby C. Granville. "A framework for IoT data acquisition and forensics analysis." *2018 IEEE International Conference on Big Data (Big Data)* (2018): 5142–5146.

[75] Chhabra, Gurpal Singh, Varinder Pal Singh, et al. "Cyber forensics framework for big data analytics in IoT environment using machine learning." *Multimedia Tools and Applications* 79, no. 23 (2020): 15881–15900.

[76] Al-Masri, Eyhab, Yan Bai, et al. "A fog-based digital forensics investigation framework for IoT systems." *2018 IEEE International Conference on Smart Cloud (SmartCloud)* (2018): 196–201.

[77] Kebande, Victor R., et al. "Towards an integrated digital forensic investigation framework for an IoT-based ecosystem." *2018 IEEE International Conference on Smart Internet of Things (SmartIoT)* (2018): 93–98.

[78] Taylor, Mark, et al. "Digital evidence in cloud computing systems." *Computer Law & Security Review* 26, no. 3 (2010): 304–308.

[79] Alabdulsalam, Saad, et al. "Internet of Things forensics–challenges and a case study." *IFIP International Conference on Digital Forensics* (2018): 35–48.

[80] Oriwoh, Edewede, et al. "Internet of Things forensics: Challenges and approaches." *9th IEEE International Conference on Collaborative Computing: Networking, Applications and Worksharing* (2013): 608–615.

[81] Lutta, Pantaleon, et al. "The complexity of Internet of Things forensics: A state-of-the-art review." *Forensic Science International: Digital Investigation* 38 (2021): 301210.

[82] Banafa, Ahmed. (2017). "IoT and blockchain convergence: Benefits and challenges." IEEE Internet of Things 9.

3 Emerging Security Threats and Challenges in IoT

Priyank Parmar and Ravi Sheth
Rashtriya Raksha University, Gujarat, India

CONTENTS

DOI: 10.1201/9781003283003-3

3.1 INTRODUCTION

The incredible growth in the routine use of electronic devices, services, and their applications has led to huge developments in the field of information technology (IT), which triggered the emergence of the new concept of the Internet of Things (IoT). It is expected that by 2024 the number of connected devices will cross 27 million [1]. The IoT is the part of information and communication technology where devices are used as objects or things, and they are responsible for sensing their environment, passing commands to actuators, and exchanging data over the Internet [2,3]. This growth is involved in various areas, such as education, smart homes, elder care, transportation, manufacturing, agriculture, energy management, healthcare, business, and more.

This rapid growth of connected devices in the IoT has led to new challenges to security from various kinds of attacks [4]. The threats to these devices are rising daily, in terms of numbers as well as complexity. These threats make devices vulnerable to potential attackers, who are empowered by various tools, automated scripts, and software. Hence, protection from such vulnerabilities and threats is required.

As these devices are placed in the open, they are vulnerable to physical damage, theft, unauthorized access, and more. CIA (confidentiality, integrity, and availability) needs to be ensured all the time while utilizing these devices. Security requirements for this kind of IoT device are similar to the existing network systems but with some changes. To ensure the availability of data and devices all the time, a strong security mechanism is needed. The key protocols being used by IoT devices are CoAP, MQTT, REST, and AMQP. [5]

If any of the IoT devices are vulnerable, then the enterprise that is utilizing these devices is also vulnerable. Ordinary, classic watches have now changed to smartwatches. These smartwatches keep connected to devices or the Internet almost all the time. This gives an attacker space to compromise the device. For example, people are using smartwatches to remind themselves of medication. If a user is experiencing dementia, he may not remember if he took his medicine earlier. So, by sending frequent and fake reminders, an attacker can overdose the user with the medicine he is supposed to take. [6] This chapter offers a comprehensive overview of various attacks on IoT-based smart devices.

3.2 THE IOT VISION

The contribution of IoT devices has increased the value of information by allowing devices to communicate with each other via the network and converting the processed information to knowledge by edge devices. Eventually, this will benefit society. According to 6-A Connectivity, the IoT will be accessible by anyone for any service from any network, from any place, anytime, and allow the system to connect anytime [7]. Figure 3.1 illustrates this.

FIGURE 3.1 Interconnection of IoT's key elements.

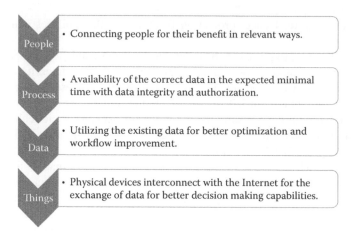

People • Connecting people for their benefit in relevant ways.

Process • Availability of the correct data in the expected minimal time with data integrity and authorization.

Data • Utilizing the existing data for better optimization and workflow improvement.

Things • Physical devices interconnect with the Internet for the exchange of data for better decision making capabilities.

FIGURE 3.2   Internet of everything.

IoT architecture and intelligent middleware enhance the capabilities of the IoT for linking historical and multidimensional aspects to connect it with the physical world. The real physical world is connected with the digital and virtual cyber world, where IoT devices and data integration are established, respectively. The virtual cyber world is semantically integrated with the real physical world to provide better service.

In truth, IoT devices communicate with humans as well as their surroundings for a variety of data. Every object of routine life (e.g. TVs, medical devices, smartphones, food processing units, refrigerators, ACs, vehicles) has unique identification features, which allows them to correspond with other devices. Also, when you consider that those gadgets can sense their surroundings, they may have the ability to confirm identities by talking to each other so that they'll be able to synchronize their data. This may end up a way for information complexity, and the devices may correspond regularly all the time without the intervention of individuals. (Figure 3.2)

IoTs have been given a variety of systems, which work automatically without the intervention of humans. These devices will decentralize and work with their algorithms and eventually with all the other networked things to make collective, intelligent decisions.

3.2.1   IoT Architecture

It's essential to have an open architecture with several layers for maximizing usage and for sharing data across the IoT network (Figure 3.2). Numerous research articles and studies have been done so far on the same topic. Still, there is no single architecture that can fulfill all the requirements. The reason is that for each organization, each user has different requirements. The simple three-layer IoT ecosystem comprises the perception layer, network layer, and Application layer, as shown in Figure 3.3.

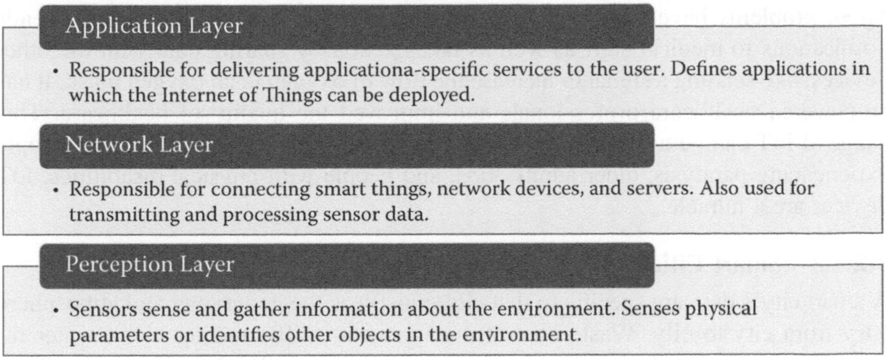

Application Layer
• Responsible for delivering applationa-specific services to the user. Defines applications in which the Internet of Things can be deployed.

Network Layer
• Responsible for connecting smart things, network devices, and servers. Also used for transmitting and processing sensor data.

Perception Layer
• Sensors sense and gather information about the environment. Senses physical parameters or identifies other objects in the environment.

FIGURE 3.3 IoT ecosystem.

This architecture can be expanded to five layers with the addition of the processing layer and transport layer. By considering requirements for individuals, industries, medical sectors, institutes, etc., a layered structure can be designed.

Architecture requirements must include properly described abstract records with replicable standard protocols and interfacing capabilities with proper binding all together to support a wide range of software, smart devices, operating systems, and programming languages [8].

3.2.2 IoT APPLICATION DOMAINS

The IoT covers a wide area and almost every machine. These devices aim for interaction, collaboration, and sharing an exchange experience to reduce human intervention in the machine cycle. The IoT equips a multitude of domains and millions of devices with connectivity every day. The following are some of the important domains.

3.2.2.1 Smart Homes

These days, the IoT has covered a variety of areas and is being used in various devices such as refrigerators, TVs, washing machines, dishwashers, etc. These devices are capable of talking to each other and working accordingly. Apart from these, electricity controls, energy controls, temperature controls, and security systems are IoT devices that have marked their presence. These devices work without human intervention and toward saving the world with various predefined logic. For example, the AC is being controlled at a temperature of 24 degrees Celsius, which is ideal for human beings, and harm to the environment is also under control as there is less heat transfer. The smart refrigerator takes care of food availability within the refrigerator and then makes an order to the pre-registered vendor asking it to deliver dairy products, vegetables, etc.

3.2.2.2 Healthcare

The current problems faced by the healthcare industry are that no real-time data are available, there is a lack of smart care devices, and standard analytics are inaccurate.

These problems have now been addressed by IoT devices. So, the system sends notifications to medical staff as well as takes action by sharing data with the other devices, like sending a signal to increase the flow of oxygen in an oxygen mask. It has empowered healthcare professionals and improved the quality of healthcare. This usage of IoT can be a lifesaver by being a passive health status monitor. For people experiencing paralysis, older adults, kids, and people with physical disabilities, IoT devices are a miracle.

3.2.2.3 Smart Cities

A smart city's data are specific to that city, mostly as the geography and atmosphere vary from city to city. Waste control management, traffic management, water re-source management, housing issues, and pollution – each of these areas collects data that are used to make decisions without human intervention. Along with these data, a huge amount of computations and communications are essential to fulfill the requirements of citizens. Various initiatives have been incorporated by individual governments to help make their city smarter. Smart cities include smart devices, smart homes, smart industries, smart traffic management, etc., and integration amongst these is essential.

3.2.2.4 Agriculture

This is the most neglected sector despite the importance it holds. The IoT can provide solutions like precision farming, smart irrigation, and smart greenhouses, to name a few. This also takes care of soil moisture monitoring and climate difference detection, and it makes decisions accordingly. These smart systems in agriculture can help farmers to select an irrigation technique, maintain the moisture level, make temperature-dependent changes, and feel empowered to get the maximum out of their land and reduce monetary losses.

3.2.2.5 Industrial Automation

This is one of those fields where the IoT can facilitate quick development and quality products by using various sensors and actuators with smart decision-making capabilities. The key areas where the IoT will contribute are optimization, quality control, cost efficiency, and security. One of the applications is an au-tomated guided vehicle can manage the entire warehouse and material handling. IoT devices with long ranges have made work easy for workers in hazardous areas. Boilers, PLC, smart grids, steam devices, turbines, and many more ap-pliances can be controlled and monitored from the central office. This also has the advantage of helping the administrative officer make a smart decision for the next production schedule.

3.2.2.6 Public Safety and Environmental Monitoring

IoT devices nowadays keep their eyes on a specific area and help to monitor ter-ritory along with the environment. There might be an integration of radar, video, and satellite-based surveillance. The installation of emergency/rescue personnel tracking can help in finding personal belongings. Smart cities have started dis-playing air quality, temperature, humidity, and more on public displays.

Apart from these, there are many more domains where IoTs are being used widely with the discussed advantages. Hence, with the increased usage and variety of areas, the possibility of attacks and threats have also increased, which needs attention.

3.2.3 SUPPORTING WIRELESS COMMUNICATION TECHNOLOGIES

As discussed in the introduction, the IoT works as a bridge between any products within the physical world and the virtual world. This setup may require various small modules, each for specific tasks, for example, sensors, actuators, embedded systems, data analytics, mobile applications, cloud computing, and storage; all these become enabling technologies. Further, this can be divided into the following sections.

3.2.3.1 Perception Layer Technologies

It is a bottom layer in the IoT business model, as shown in Figure 3.4. This includes a variety of devices like moisture sensor, camera, OBD-ELM327, PIR sensor, vibration sensor, PH sensor, BME-280, etc. Again, this can be classified as passive, semi-passive, and active.

3.2.3.2 Network Layer Technologies

It is the second layer in the IoT model. Its technology transforms the conventional sensor data into smart and connected nodes. This network layer uses various technologies depending on the requirement [9]. Due to the limitation of power and computing, most IoT nodes are scalable, and efficient routing techniques are required to ensure interoperability among IoT devices. Figure 3.5 illustrates the various wireless communication technologies with their physical ranges.

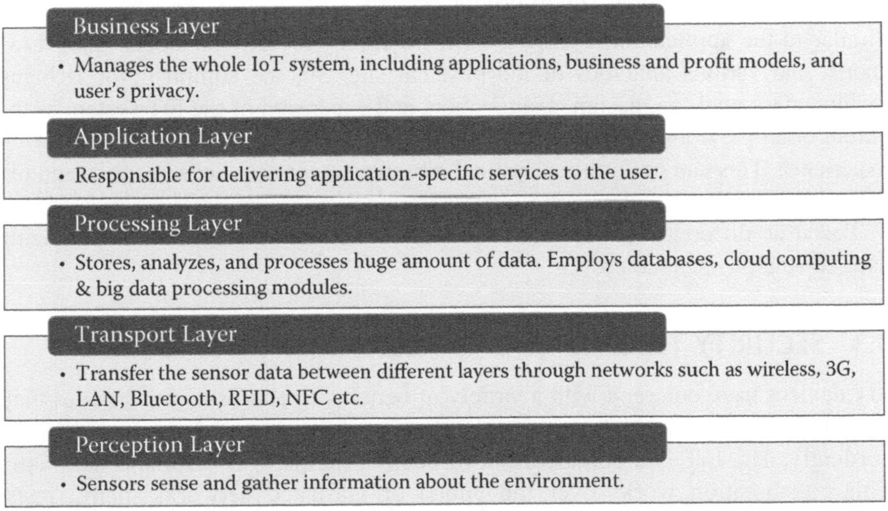

Business Layer
- Manages the whole IoT system, including applications, business and profit models, and user's privacy.

Application Layer
- Responsible for delivering application-specific services to the user.

Processing Layer
- Stores, analyzes, and processes huge amount of data. Employs databases, cloud computing & big data processing modules.

Transport Layer
- Transfer the sensor data between different layers through networks such as wireless, 3G, LAN, Bluetooth, RFID, NFC etc.

Perception Layer
- Sensors sense and gather information about the environment.

FIGURE 3.4 IoT business model.

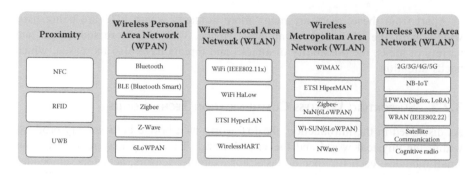

FIGURE 3.5 Wireless communication technologies with their physical ranges.

3.2.3.3   Middleware Technologies

It is the third and essential layer of the IoT environment. Technologies in this layer are frequently supported with the aid of IoT systems. This layer enables offerings to be diagnosed and examined with details, and it empowers the developers to connect with these devices, irrespective of the precise hardware setup [9]. Based on their functionalities, this can be classified as service discovery, data exchange, and computation.

3.2.3.4   Application Layer Technologies

The application layer provides users with requested data, most simply and easily to get the usage of IoT devices. The typical user can use various modes to access information like web portals, mobile applications, etc. This can be further classified into four classes, i.e. collaborative aware services, identity-related services, ubiquitous services, and information aggregation services.

3.2.3.5   Business Layer Technologies

Similar to the application layer, the business layer provides statistical data, flow-charts, and various analytics of the physical site. So, the administrator is being facilitated for analysis, design, examination, and expansion of the IoT system as the output of all previous layers is analyzed and certainly helps in improving the user's experience. This can be further classified into two categories (i.e. semantics and big data analytics).

Based on different scenarios, the combination of various technologies is being used for the physical setup.

3.3   SECURITY THREATS AND CHALLENGES IN THE IOT

IoT devices have emerged with a variety of benefits to end-users but besides that, use of third-party dependency needs to ensure privacy and confidentiality accordingly. The IoT is a collaboration of people, things, software, and hardware. This collaboration works over the public or untrusted networks many times. Security, privacy, and open trust problems need to be addressed [10,11], before moving further with the deployments. In that situation, security can be stated as an organized framework that consists of concepts, beliefs, policies, principles, procedures, measures, and techniques required to secure individual system assets as well as the complete system against any planned threats. All these system interactions must be secured by some means to ensure unrestricted procurement of data and services to all significant entities and limit the number of influential incidents for the entire IoT.

In this section, an overview of existing IoT security challenges and IoT security requirements have been discussed.

3.3.1 INTRUDER MODELS AND THREATS

As the conventional network is vulnerable, the IoT is also vulnerable to various active and passive attacks; these attacks are discussed in the next section of the chapter. These vulnerabilities can nullify the benefits of IoT services. Passive attacks silently keep sniffing the packets moving in the network without affecting the behavior of the IoT device, whereas active attack affects the performance of the IoT device. Consideration of internal threats is crucial as the insider knows the various secret information that might not be known to external attackers, such as API keys, IP addresses, password patterns, etc. Various threats to IoT devices are discussed in the following section.

3.3.1.1 Intruder Model

The Dolev-Yao (DY) intruder shall be used as an example [8,12]. Explicitly, the outsider impacts the network and may intercept packets being transferred between IoT gadgets and hubs.

The DY intruder is extraordinarily successful, but the experts are to some extent unrealistic. Hence, the safety will be much better if IoT devices are robust. But the DY model lacks the functionality of physical damage. Thus, the devices should be tamperproof to prevent such physical damage. This may not seem feasible, but from this point, an attacker can avoid temper detection. Intruders are usually classified as external and internal.

3.3.1.2 Denial of Service Attacks (DoS)

An attempt may be carried out to make the required resources unavailable to users by exhausting the resources allocated to IoT devices. With the limitation of resources and computational power, these devices are vulnerable to resource enervation attacks. DoS attack is realized by flooding the target with traffic or sending it information that triggers a crash [13]. As the IoT devices are resource-constrained, the high computational logic cannot be implemented [14]. The detailed types are discussed in the next section.

3.3.1.3 Physical Attack

As these devices are kept in an open environment and easily accessible by at least internal users, the user may perform various attacks. Moreover, this category also includes assaults that damage the hardware's lifetime or functionality. A few potential problems are described below in the physical attack of the IoT.

3.3.1.3.1 Node Tampering

The attacker may physically replace the complete node or a specific module of the hardware. Using this tempered IoT, the attacker can replace the existing information or may start sending fraudulent requests/data, data stored on it, routing information, stored keys, etc. [15].

3.3.1.3.2 Node Jamming in WSNs

The attacker may use a similar frequency range and interfere with radio frequencies and communicate with other sensors, which will result in jamming signals or DoS attacks. [16]

3.3.1.3.3 Physical Damage

The attacker may physically destruct the node. This attack differs from node tampering in that the attacker is focused on impacting the availability of service by directly damaging the node.

3.3.1.4 Attacks on Privacy

IoT devices collect the information and share it over the network. This information might be captured by internal users also. Such IoT networks increase privacy problems as they make available all information for remote access. Following are the common attacks being done nowadays:

3.3.1.4.1 Eavesdropping and Passive Monitoring

This is the most frequently observed attack on privacy. By sniffing the packets, the adversary may easily find out the conversation contents. When the traffic conveys the managed data approximately the sensor community configuration, which incorporates probably more particular information than accessible through the local server, the eavesdropping can act successfully against privacy protection.

3.3.1.4.2 Traffic Analysis

An attacker may silently monitor all traffic passing through a network. Based on various traffic analyses, attackers can potentially understand the data even if they are encrypted using a strong encryption algorithm.

3.3.1.4.3 Data Mining

Data mining enables the attacker to extract information from the database that is not disclosed directly from the database. It extracts the potential valued data from the comprehensive information for the specific IoT application and makes the decision.

These techniques can provide a variety of ways out of our routine problems. However, this has come up with a new challenge of privacy. Privacy preservation in all these communications is required, and this can be achieved by various techniques, such as key management, encryption, etc.

The following mechanisms are also developed to preserve privacy.

- Anonymity based privacy preservation [17],
- Encryption-based privacy preservation [18],
- Perturbation-based privacy preservation [19].

According to the application, the preferred mechanism should be used by the administrator.

3.3.2 SECURITY AND PRIVACY CHALLENGES IN IoTs

The IoT consists of various sensors and devices that are connected. Based on the scenario, the administrator can apply security, privacy, and trust requirements. For an effective low-cost product, there are a lot of things that need to be incorporated for overcoming such security and privacy challenges [20].

3.3.2.1 User Privacy and Data Protection

Privacy is considered to play a vital role while communicating over the network. The leakage of personal information may result in some crucial attacks. IoT devices are connected and render data over the Internet, which consists of various user data [21–24]. Although there is enough research that has been carried out with concern to user's privacy, this privacy needs to be considered during data collection, data storage, and data sharing over the network.

3.3.2.2 Identity and Access Management

It's a framework consisting of policies and technologies that ensures that authorized users will get appropriate access to services. Identity management ensures access control to the user and keeps track of all activities carried out by the user. It also provides role-based access to the user. This includes a certain task at the administrative level for user privileges, governing user accounts, and policy creations.

3.3.2.3 Trust Management and Policy Integration

As machines/things have started exchanging their information and making a decision, it's essential to have trust amongst each other. It's essential to have trust between all interconnected devices as well as users using this system [25]. In the collaborative environment of IoT devices, an effective mechanism of trust is required. Decentralization in the trust system is essential for the large network where an individual node can trust the other node. As all the data are synchronizing or being sent to the cloud, trust between them is also essential.

Before decision-making a trust, the model is essential for a good policy framework.

3.3.2.4 Authorization and Access Control

After authentication, authorization allows the user to access resources. Access control involves authorization by policies that have been set up by the administration. For establishing a secure network connection, it's essential to have access to a control setup and authorization mechanism. For cases of the IoT, it should be easier to create rules and modify them whenever required.

3.3.2.5 End-to-End Security

Almost all the IoT requires protection from injection, eavesdropping, and modifying packets. Cryptography can be implemented to overcome these issues. The key exchange mechanism needs to be prepared in such a way that the attacker cannot intercept the traffic. With the end-to-end security, various applications can use the IoT devices; otherwise, they would be difficult to use.

3.3.2.6 Resilience to Node Capture

As IoT devices are kept out in the open, they are physically accessible to attackers. Using this exposure, attackers can replace a node with a malicious node that can be controlled by the attacker. A solution with a certain algorithm needs to be designed that can prevent such node capture attacks.

3.4 IOT SECURITY ATTACKS AND THEIR MITIGATION TECHNIQUES BASED ON THEIR LAYERS

This section of the chapter describes the attacks associated with all three layers and provides some mitigation techniques.

3.4.1 PHYSICAL LAYER

The security threats in the physical layer are involved with the node level. As the nodes are comprised of sensors or actuators, the hacker targets such devices to replace the programs with their malicious codes.

3.4.1.1 Node Capture Attacks

With the help of some vulnerability, the attacker gains access to nodes and manipulates existing code with malicious code. This malicious code can capture and share important information like keys, device data, algorithms, data, etc. with the attacker. The attacker can inject malicious nodes within the network, which pretend to be part of the network. Both attacks are very crucial, and for controlling such access, a detailed study of the network is required [26].

3.4.1.2 Malicious Code Injection Attacks

Apart from the node capture attack, the attacker may inject malicious code with the existing source code of the node. This malicious code may create a backdoor connection from where an attacker can gain full access to this node anytime. For prevention, effective code authentication schemes need to be integrated into the IoT [27].

3.4.1.3 False Data Injection Attacks

The compromised node can manipulate the data being communicated with nodes and applications, which may result in the malfunctioning of the device and the ineffectiveness of the IoT applications [28]. For prevention, such false injection data need to be monitored and compared with regex before sending them to the server or receiving them from the server [29,30].

3.4.1.4 Replay Attacks (or Freshness Attacks)

The attacker may use the actual identification information to communicate with the server, to obtain trust from the server. A replay attack is performed to validate the node as authenticated [31]. For prevention, secure two-way authentication and validation should be designed.

3.4.1.5   Cryptanalysis Attacks and Side-Channel Attacks

Here, the attacker retrieves cipher text and plain text to identify the encryption algorithm. However, the impact of this is very low. The attacker may retrieve timing information, power consumption, electromagnetic leaks, and sound to provide an extra source of information. For prevention, secure and efficient encryption algorithms need to be developed in the IoT [32].

3.4.1.6   Eavesdropping and Interference

The majority of IoTs are connected to a wireless network, and these wireless links can be eavesdropped on by an attacker. For prevention, secure and efficient encryption algorithms need to be developed in the IoT. For ensuring the integrity and availability of data, effective noise filtering algorithms are required [16].

3.4.1.7   Sleep Deprivation Attacks

The IoTs operate with very low power. For reducing power consumption, various sleep routines are required. However, the sleep deprivation attack breaks the scheduled sleep routines and keeps the device busy till it consumes all of the available power. For prevention, secured duty cycle mechanisms and other energy sources like solar are required [33].

3.4.2   NETWORK LAYER

As the network layer's primary aim in the IoT is to communicate recorded information, this layer's safety issue concentrates on the effect of network resource accessibility. Moreover, most IoT devices are linked via wireless communication connections to IoT networks. In this layer, therefore, most safety problems are linked to IoT wireless networks.

3.4.2.1   Denial-of-Service (Dos) Attacks

DoS attacks can be achieved by consuming all available resources from the network by large traffic. DoS attack is observed widely, which results in the unavailability of IoT devices [34]. Improper protocol use, a poor encryption algorithm, and vulnerable services may lead the device to be unavailable [35]. Teardrop, SYN flood, tear attack, ping of death, etc. are various types of these attack schemes. For prevention, a detailed working analysis of the attack is needed, followed by a defensive scheme.

3.4.2.2   Spoofing Attacks

The main aim of the attacker is to compromise the IoT device and do some mischievous activity in the network [36]. Spoofing attacks include IP spoofing [37], RFID spoofing, device spoofing, etc. During an IP spoofing attack, the attacker gains access to the network and transmits malicious data with the entire network by spoofed IP address. The attacker with a spoofed valid identity may send malicious data into the network. Specially designed trust management, identification, and authentication systems will help in preventing such attacks. [38].

3.4.2.3   Sinkhole Attacks

High energy is required by a compromised device or node along with good communication capacities, which ultimately allows nearby nodes or devices to select this malicious node for forwarding the information routing process due to the attractive capacities [39]. So, every communication passes through the compromised device or node. This sinkhole attack compromises the confidentiality of data and raises the chance for other attacks. For prevention, multiple secure routing protocols are needed [39].

3.4.2.4   Wormhole Attacks

This attack may be launched by two or more compromised malicious devices or nodes; here these two devices exchange the information of their routing table over the private connection [40]. As the routing table is compromised, the data will travel through malicious nodes, and these nodes can work as a sinkhole attack. For prevention, a routing protocol needs to enhance security in selecting the route or some secure hardware (GPS, directed antenna) can be deployed [40].

3.4.2.5   Man in the Middle Attacks

In this scenario, the attacker remains virtually present between two communicating nodes. By intercepting the identity of these communicating devices, the attacker sniffs the entire communication, and it may be stored or manipulated whenever required. By using this attack, attackers can monitor, tamper, or eavesdrop, and hence the CIA characteristic is compromised. In a malicious node capture attack, the attacker needs to physically tamper with the device, where, in this case, the attack can be launched by only intercepting network traffic. For prevention, secure communication protocols and key management mechanisms are essential to have.

3.4.2.6   Routing Information Attacks

In this attack, the attacker manipulates routing protocols in the IoT network by creating route loops; hence, there is a rise in the end-to-end interval in IoT networks [36]. Implementation of secure routing protocols and trust management techniques should be implemented for mitigation.

3.4.2.7   Sybil Attacks

In this attack, the malicious device claims several valid identities and impersonates them to IoT systems [36]. As the Sybil device has several valid identities, malicious data can be accepted by other neighbor devices. As all the communication is done from the Sybil device, there is a possibility of jamming and DoS. For prevention, secure identification and authentication mechanisms are required [38].

3.4.2.8   Unauthorized Access

There are several IoT devices integrated with RFID, and these RFID tags lack proper authentication mechanisms. The attacker can obtain, modify, or delete the information stored in RFID tags [36]. For prevention, authorization access and authentication mechanisms are required [25].

3.4.3 APPLICATION LAYER

The primary aim of the application layer is to assist user-requested services. Thus, the application layer's difficulties concentrate on software assets. Here, a few potential problems are described below in the application layer of the IoT.

3.4.3.1 Phishing Attack

The attacker can obtain sensitive data (identification and password) of the users, by spoofing the authentication credentials of users via infected email or web pages [36], [33]. For preventing, a secure authorizing access, identification, and authentication system is required. For identifying phishing, intelligent techniques are required. However, the IoT is a machine that might not have such intelligence.

3.4.3.2 Malicious Virus/Worms

These are the other challenges to IoT applications. The attacker can send some self-propagating attacks with the help of a Trojan horse, and then the attacker obtains or tempers sensitive data. For prevention from such attacks, firewalls, anti-virus, or another self-protective algorithm needs to be used [41].

3.4.3.3 Malicious Scripts

These are the scripts added to harm the functioning of IoT devices [36]. These IoT devices are connected to the network and hence to the Internet. Once the attacker compromises the device, data can be manipulated. Malicious scripts can affect the confidentiality, availability, and integrity of the data. For preventing malicious scripts from being executed, detection techniques like honeypot, static, and dynamic code analysis need to be carried out.

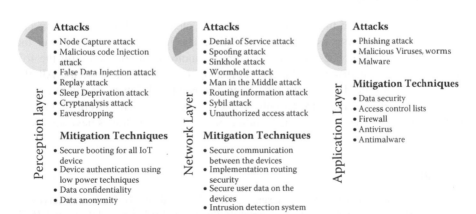

FIGURE 3.6 Graphical representation of attacks on IoT layers and their mitigation techniques.

Figure 3.6 gives a summarization of all the possible attacks on the layers of the IoT along with the possible countermeasures. This extensive list will help researchers to correlate the impact of the various attacks on the IoT.

3.5   FUTURE RESEARCH DIRECTIONS

By now you must understand how these IoT devices are being used in many areas and how day by day the scope is increasing. This may lead to various vulnerabilities; the same has been discussed in this chapter. Here are a few research areas to make the IoT paradigm reality.

- Easy-to-use IoT devices need to be manufactured.
- The end-user needs confidence before becoming dependent on IoT devices, which can be ensured by addressing security and privacy challenges.
- By using various data analysis techniques in real time, better security can be provided.
- The incorporation of blockchain with IoT can be explored for the tamper-proof feature of blockchain.
- Various IDS techniques can be identified for prevention against various intrusions.
- IoT devices have constraints of power, which is advantageous for attackers as these devices don't have the ability to spend their computation power on intrusion detection, so a workaround is required here.
- A privacy-ensuring mechanism is needed to prevent unauthorized identification and tracking.
- The legal liability framework needs to be designed.
- A policy is needed to ensure and verify the CIA characteristics of data sensed and exchanged by IoT devices.

3.6   CONCLUSION

The primary agenda of this chapter is to deliver a clear idea of the various aspects, such as challenges, attacks, and vulnerabilities. The IoT vision will empower the user to utilize IoT devices. The architecture technologies associated with the IoT devices have been discussed to give key insights into all these areas. All the parameters regarding IoT security have been discussed with future directions so that researchers can contribute to the enhancement of security. The future of IoT security threats and challenges in the blending of existing technologies have also been discussed.

REFERENCES

[1] V. Hassija, V. Chamola, V. Saxena, D. Jain, P. Goyal, and B. Sikdar, "A survey on IoT security: Application areas, security threats, and solution architectures," *IEEE Access*, vol. 7, pp. 82721–82743, 2019.
[2] J. Gubbi, R. Buyya, S. Marusic, and M. Palaniswami, "Internet of Things (IoT): A vision, architectural elements, and future directions," *Future Generation Computer Systems* Vol 29, Issue 7, pp. 1645–1660, 2013.

[3] L. Atzori, A. Iera, and G. Morabito, "The Internet of Things: A survey," *Computer Networks*, vol. 54, no. 15, pp. 2787–2805, Oct. 2010. [Online]. 10.1016/j.comnet. 2010.05.010.

[4] M. Shafiq, Z. Tian, Y. Sun, X. Du, and M. Guizani, "Selection of effective machine learning algorithm and Bot-IoT attacks traffic identification for Internet of Things in smart city," *Future Generation Computer Systems*, vol. 107, pp. 433–442, 2020. 10.1016/j.future.2020.02.017

[5] K. S. Raju et al. (eds.), Proceedings of the Third International Conference on Computational Intelligence and Informatics, Advances in Intelligent Systems and Computing 1090, 10.1007/978-981-15-1480-7_67

[6] Sudais Afis "Smartwatch vulnerability allowed hackers to overdose dementia patients". Available from https://www.hackread.com/smartwatch-vulnerability-hackers-overdose-dementia-patients/?web_view=true

[7] O. Vermesan and P. Friess, *Internet of Things: Converging Technologies for Smart Environments and Integrated Ecosystems*. River Publishers ISBN: 978-87-92982-73-5, 2013.

[8] S. Vashi, J. Ram, J. Modi, S. Verma, and C. Prakash, "Internet of Things (IoT): A vision, architectural elements, and security issues," Proceedings of the International Conference on IoT in Social, Mobile, Analytics and Cloud, I-SMAC 2017, 2017, pp. 492–496.

[9] Y. Perwej, M. Ahmed, B. Kerim, and H. Ali, "An extended review on Internet of Things (IoT) and its promising applications," *Communications on Applied Electronics*, vol. 7, no. 26, pp. 8–22, 2019. 10.5120/cae2019652812

[10] J. L. A. Manan, M. F. Mubarak, M. A. M. Isa, and Z. A. Khattak, "Security, trust and privacy – A new direction for pervasive computing," Recent Researches in Computer Science – Proceedings of the 15th WSEAS International Conference on Computers, Part of the 15th WSEAS CSCC Multiconference, pp. 56–60, 2011.

[11] D. Dolev and A. C. Yao, "On the security of public key protocols," *IEEE Transactions on Information Theory*, vol. 29, no. 2, pp. 198–208, 1983.

[12] Korolov, M., NCSC, Information Commissioner's Office, Steve Ranger, Paul Gillin, Venkatesh Sundar, Cisco. (2016). 73% of Companies Using Vulnerable End-of-Life Networking Devices. CSO Online, n/a. 10.1111/j.1751-1097.1994.tb09662.x

[13] S. Alanazi, J. Al-Muhtadi, A. Derhab, and K. Saleem, "On resilience of wireless Mesh routing protocol against DoS attacks in IoT-based ambient assisted living applications," in International Conference on E-Health Networking, Application & Services, 2015.

[14] A. Mehmood, M. Mukherjee, S. H. Ahmed, H. Song, and K. M. Malik, "NBC-MAIDS: Naïve Bayesian classification technique in multi-agent system-enriched IDS for securing IoT against DDoS attacks," *Journal of Supercomputing*, vol. 74, no. 10, pp. 5156–5170, 2018.

[15] A. Perrig, J. Stankovic, and D. Wagner, "Security in wireless sensor networks," *Communications of the ACM*, vol. 47, no. 6, pp. 53–57, 2004.

[16] A. Hamid and C. S. Hong, "Routing security in sensor network: HELLO flood attack and defense," *IEEE ICNEWS*,2, pp. 77–81, 2006.

[17] K. P. N. Puttaswamy et al., "Anonygator: Privacy and integrity preserving data aggregation to cite this version: HAL Id: hal-01055270 anonygator: Privacy and integrity preserving data aggregation," 2014.

[18] J. Girao, D. Westhoff, and M. Schneider, "CDA: Concealed data aggregation for reverse multicast traffic in wireless sensor networks," *IEEE International Conference on Communications*, vol. 5, no. C, pp. 3044–3049, 2005.

[19] W. He, X. Liu, H. Nguyen, K. Nahrstedt, and T. Abdelzaher, "PDA: Privacy-preserving data aggregation in wireless sensor networks," Proc. – IEEE INFOCOM, 2007, pp. 2045–2053.

[20] R. Xu, Q. Zeng, L. Zhu, H. Chi, and X. Du, "Privacy leakage in smart homes and its mitigation: IFTTT as a case study." 2018 IEEE 37th International Performance Computing and Communications Conference, IPCCC 2018, pp. 1–8, 2018.

[21] I. Cervesato, "The Dolev-Yao intruder is the most powerful attacker," in 16th Annual Symposium on Logic in Computer ScienceLICS, vol. 1. Citeseer, 2001.

[22] A. M. Riad, "A survey of Internet of Things," 2013. [Online]. Available: http://www.researchgate.net/publication/257957332 A Survey of Internet of Things.

[23] S. Babar, A. Stango, N. Prasad, J. Sen, and R. Prasad, "Proposed embedded security framework for Internet of Things (iot)," in Wireless Communication, Vehicular Technology, Information Theory and Aerospace & Electronic Systems Technology (Wireless VITAE), 2011 2nd International Conference on. IEEE, 2011, pp. 1–5.

[24] E. Bertino, B. Catania, M. L. Damiani, and P. Perlasca, "Geo-rbac: A spatially aware RBAC," in Proceedings of the tenth ACM Symposium on Access Control Models and Technologies. ACM, 2005, pp. 29–37.

[25] B. Z. Jing et al., "RFID access authorization by face recognition," Proc. 2009 Int. Conf. Mach. Learn. Cybern., vol. 1, no. July, 2009, pp. 302–307.

[26] M. Vivekananda Bharathi, R. C. Tanguturi, C. Jayakumar, and K. Selvamani, "Node capture attack in wireless sensor network: A survey," 2012 IEEE Int. Conf. Comput. Intell. Comput. Res. ICCIC 2012, no. i, 2012.

[27] X. Yang et al., "Towards a low-cost remote memory attestation for the smart grid," *Sensors (Switzerland)*, vol. 15, no. 8, pp. 20799–20824, 2015.

[28] X. Yang, J. Lin, W. Yu, P. M. Moulema, X. Fu, and W. Zhao, "A novel en-route filtering scheme against false data injection attacks in cyber-physical networked systems," *IEEE Transactions on Computers*, vol. 64, no. 1, pp. 4–18, 2015.

[29] J. Lin, W. Yu, and X. Yang, "Towards multistep electricity prices in smart grid electricity markets," *IEEE Transactions on Parallel and Distributed Systems*, vol. 27, no. 1, pp. 286–302, 2016.

[30] Y. Yuan, Z. Li, and K. Ren, "False data injection attacks in smart grid," *Wiley Encyclopedia of Electrical and Electronics Engineering*, pp. 1–2, 2012,10.1002/04 7134608x.w8185.

[31] K. Zhao and L. Ge, "A survey on the Internet of Things security," Proc. – 9th Int. Conf. Comput. Intell. Secur. CIS 2013, 2013, pp. 663–667.

[32] S. Capkun, L. Buttyán, and J. P. Hubaux, "Self-organized public-key management for mobile ad hoc networks," *IEEE Transactions on Mobile Computing*, vol. 2, no. 1, pp. 52–64, 2003.

[33] M. Sarkar and D. B. Roy, "Prevention of sleep deprivation attacks using clustering," ICECT 2011 –l 2011 3rd Int. Conf. Electron. Comput. Technol., vol. 5, 2011, pp. 391–394.

[34] R. Heartfield et al., "A taxonomy of cyber-physical threats and impact in the smart home," *Computers & Security*, vol. 78, pp. 398–428, 2018.

[35] K. Kaushik and S. Dahiya, "Security and Privacy in IoT based E-Business and Retail," 2018 International Conference on System Modeling & Advancement in Research Trends (SMART), 2018, pp. 78–81, 10.1109/SYSMART.2018.8746961.

[36] I. Andrea, C. Chrysostomou, and G. Hadjichristofi, "Internet of Things: Security vulnerabilities and challenges," Proc. – IEEE Symp. Comput. Commun., vol. 2016-Febru, no. August 2017, 2016, pp. 180–187.

[37] A. Mukaddam, I. Elhajj, A. Kayssi, and A. Chehab, "IP spoofing detection using modified hop count," Proc. - Int. Conf. Adv. Inf. Netw. Appl. AINA, 2014, pp. 512–516.

[38] M. C. Chuang and J. F. Lee, "TEAM: Trust-extended authentication mechanism for vehicular ad Hoc networks," *IEEE Systems Journal*, vol. 8, no. 3, pp. 749–758, 2014.

[39] G. Kalnoor and J. Agarkhed, "QoS based multipath routing for intrusion detection of sinkhole attack in wireless sensor networks," Proc. IEEE Int. Conf. Circuit, Power Comput. Technol. ICCPCT 2016, 2016.

[40] P. Lee, A. Clark, L. Bushnell, and R. Poovendran, "A passivity framework for modeling and mitigating wormhole attacks on networked control systems," *IEEE Transactions on Automatic Control*, vol. 59, no. 12, pp. 3224–3237, 2014.

[41] A. K. Sahoo, A. Das, and M. Tiwary, "Firewall engine based on graphics processing unit," Proc. 2014 IEEE Int. Conf. Adv. Commun. Control Comput. Technol. ICACCCT 2014, no. 978, 2015, pp. 758–763.

4 A Review on Security Frameworks and Protocols in the Internet of Things

Meenu Vijarania and Swati Gupta
Associate Professor, Centre of Excellence, Department of
Computer Science, School of Engineering and Technology,
K.R. Mangalam University, Gurugram, Haryana, India

Akshat Agarwal
Assistant Professor, Department of Computer Science,
Amity School of Engineering and Technology, Amity
University Haryana, India

CONTENTS

4.1 IOT INTRODUCTION

The Internet of Things (IoT) is the network that connects different devices, objects, and sensors over the Internet in order to collect and exchange data. With the rapid development of the IoT, these technologies are being used for a variety of purposes, including education, transportation, communication, etc. Individuals and organizations can communicate with each other using the IoT hyperconnectivity concept. Therefore, IoT security is a major concern in order to protect the networks and hardware in the IoT system.

IoT deployment can implement different technologies, architecture, and design methodologies depending on their application usage. For example, for collecting

DOI: 10.1201/9781003283003-4

environmental data in some area, the IoT system can use the capabilities of a wireless sensor network (WSN), and a monitoring application can be run on smartphones to view the data. Middleware can be used to provide easy access to virtual services and resources.

It has been observed that rigorous research and development is being undertaken in the area of IoT privacy and security. Recently, the proposed security techniques have been based on conventional network security methods. But it is very challenging to apply security mechanisms in the IoT system due to device heterogeneity, resource constraints, and trust management.

4.2 IOT SYSTEM COMPONENTS

The IoT has a three-layered architecture that is comprised of the perception layer, network layer, and application layer. Various IoT system components are hardware devices, sensors, localization and tracking, communication protocols, actuators, storage devices, processing, identification, communication, etc. as shown in Figure 4.1.

The IoT consists of a variety of heterogeneous devices connected over the Internet. IoT threats are dissimilar than traditional networks due to different end devices and the availability of resources. The traditional network has powerful servers and resources, whereas IoT devices have very limited computational power and limited memory. Hence, the IoT system cannot afford complex and cross-layer security mechanisms. Bluetooth, Zigbee, 802.15.4, and 802.11a/b/n/g/p are wireless communication media being used by IoT devices. Moreover, the IoT uses different data formats, different operating systems (OS), which makes it very difficult to

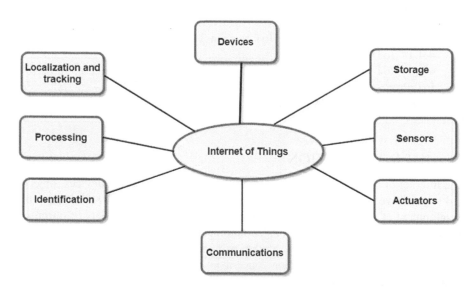

FIGURE 4.1 Components of the IoT system (Based on Deshmukh and Sonavane 2017).

design a standard security protocol (Sadique et al. 2018). All these restrictions and limitations make the IoT prone to various types of attacks, causing security and privacy threats at different layers.

4.3   IOT LAYERED ARCHITECTURES

Multiple IoT architectures exist in the literature. Three-layered, four-layered, and five-layered IoT architectures are shown in Figure 4.2. In five-layered architecture, each layer has a specific functionality in the IoT system. The perception layer, network layer, business layer, middleware layer, and application layer are various IoT layers in the IoT architecture. The perception layer includes hardware like RFID chips, sensors, actuators, barcodes, etc. and further devices connected in the IoT network. The network layer acts as an intermediary layer to pass the information from the perception layer to the processing layer. The processing layer processes the information received from the lower layer and makes decisions based on the ubiquitous computing. The business layer is the topmost layer in the architecture. This layer controls the entire architecture of the IoT system, its services, and its applications.

The business layer helps develop future strategies using the data and statistics received from the lower layer. In addition, the IoT system comprises numerous functional blocks that support several IoT activities, such as control and management, the sensing mechanism, identification, and authentication (Khraisat and Alazab 2021). Figure 4.1 illustrates the IoT components.

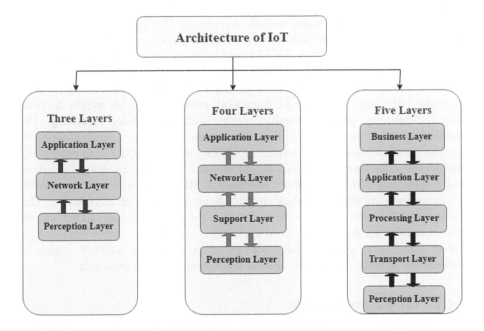

FIGURE 4.2   IoT Architectures (Based on Acharya, V. et al. 2020).

4.4 SECURITY FRAMEWORKS FOR THE IOT SYSTEM

Security frameworks play a crucial role in the implementation of IoT security architectures. The security framework makes the system robust to security attacks. The IoT-based security framework is classified as protocol/functionality specific, application specific, and generic specific.

In Rafique W. et al. 2020, the authors introduced the application-specific, real-time health monitoring system security framework, which ensures authenticity, data integrity, and confidentiality using MTQQ and CoAP protocols. For providing secure end-to-end communication, RESTful, HTTPs, and CoAP are jointly used. Amazon released an IoT-based cloud platform known as Amazon Web Services (AWS) (Aijaz and Aghvami 2015). This framework allows one to connect IoT devices securely with AWS cloud to use various AWS services of Amazon S3 (Meena, S. et al 2015), Amazon machine learning (Acharya and Hegde 2020), Amazon DynamoDB, etc. It uses MTQQ protocol for security.

ARM mbed is an IoT-based platform to develop applications for ARM controllers (Hussain, Tariq). By integrating ARM mbed services and tools, mbed OS, mbed cloud, ARM microcontroller, mbed device controller, and ARM mbed IoT platform aim to provide a scalable, secure, and connected environment for IoT devices. This platform has an advantage over other IoT platforms by using common OS (Bagaa et al. 2020). This provides support for various communication protocols to connect with the cloud and with other devices. Moreover, in order to solve the power consumption problem, it also provides support to automatic power management schemes.

In Horrow and Sardana 2012, the authors proposed a solution that automatically handles the growing need for security aspects associated with the IoT domain using a machine learning (ML) based security framework. To mitigate various threats, this framework used both Software Defined Networking (SDN) and Network Function Virtualization (NFV). An AI-based reaction agent and monitoring agent are combined in this AI framework using ML models. This framework maneuvers neural network, a distributed data mining system, and supervised learning to attain its goals. The functionality-specific framework provides solutions to specific tasks such as enforcing privacy, identity management, and service discovery. The protocol-specific framework provides solutions to the protocol vulnerabilities by designing and eliminating the potential of security attacks. MQTT is an example of publish-subscribe based IoT protocols and services under this category. In Persson and Angelsmark 2015, the authors proposed a MDSIoT (framework for model-driven security enforcement policy) for IoT devices used in an edge server. This framework allows the policies to be executed at the model level and added into the code at runtime for deployment. In Al-Qaseemi et al. 2016, the author proposed the Calvin framework, which includes both cloud programming and IoT models to analyze and develop distributed, diverse, and communication protocols.

4.4.1 IoT Security Domains

Security and privacy include data integrity, data confidentiality, and availability of the network as the primary goals of IoT security. The IoT needs to handle various limitations and restrictions that include devices and components as well as computational resources. In the IoT, data can be anything viz. data sent from a surveillance camera to the server, a user's identity information, or multimedia communication between two individuals. Therefore, IoT security is a critical concern that needs to be addressed while implementing the IoT. Various security domains in the IoT are discussed below.

Confidentiality:

1. The most significant concern in the IoT is confidentiality. Confidentiality makes each device's data private and does not permit the device to share data with neighbors, or it has the capability of hiding the data from a passive invader so that the message that is sent via sensor networks is private. Data may include demographic data, smart meter measurements, personal information, and billing.

2. Integrity: Integrity is the most essential part in the communication network that can be captured by end-to-end security protocols. The data exchange between different devices in the IoT system requires an integrity feature to ensure that the data exchange is correct and accurate between the sender and recipient. During data transmission, no data tampering, loss, or alteration should occur (Sanjana et al. 2021). By utilizing security protocols and services, the information traffic is managed (Hassija, S. et al. 2023).

3. Accessibility: It enables the user to access the information when the different types of smart devices in the network connect with each other Burhan, M. 2018.

4. Authentication: In order to ensure that only the intended users receive the information, it is mandatory to authenticate the source and destination devices. Authentication ensures that only authenticated users have access to this information, and diverse entities are permitted to communicate and exchange correct information (Iwaya et al. 2020)

5. Light-weight Solutions: The power limitations of IoT devices is considered while enabling security procedures and services. The security protocols or procedures are designed to consume less energy. Since the security procedure implanted with certain limited capabilities will be executed on end devices, it has to be compatible with devices with security protocols (Hassan et al. 2021).

6. Heterogeneity in the IoT system is common as different devices can have different underlying hardware and software. IoT devices connected with each other can be from different vendors, can have a different levels of complications, and can have different functionalities. So, in order to deal with these heterogeneous devices efficiently, the security protocol must be designed accordingly. The IoT system needs a heterogeneous network to establish communication between heterogeneous devices. With such heterogeneity, the best security and cryptography protocols must be implemented to guarantee no security breach.

7. Policies: To enable information management in an economical and protected way, a few standards and policies are required. Therefore, tracking

the implementation of these policies and standards is very important, whether the devices are adhering to these policies or not. To deal with such conditions, service-level agreements were presented. The IoT system comprises heterogeneous devices; implications of such procedures and policies form a sense of confidence and trust among users.

8. Key Management Systems: To maintain confidentiality of information between sensors and IoT devices, a key management system is needed. To establish trust among various parties, a lightweight key management system can be used in all frameworks.

4.4.2 IoT Security and Privacy Threats

With the increase in IoT devices and their applications, we must not ignore the security and risk associated with them, as shown in Figure 4.3. IoT safety is the area to focus on to secure connected devices and conserver networks, data, and organization in the IoT.

With the advancements in technology, the usage of Internet devices has increased, which in turn multiplied security problems significantly. Due to the design of IoT system frameworks, traditional security mechanisms cannot be implemented. The problems of heterogeneity and scalability arise due to the large number of devices connected with limited resources available. Hence, it is important that the system is flexible and strong to face predictable and unpredictable risks. As the transmission media is wireless, it is very prone to attacks and security breaches. So, a good framework must be provided with protection measures for exchanged information.

The security mechanism's main (Sadique et al. 2018) intention is to attain availability, integrity, confidentiality, and reliability, which helps to resolve security issues.

Security Issues at the Perception Layer

An IoT node consists of various elements, such as a microcontroller, sensor, memory, transceiver, RFID tags, RFID reader, RFID antennas, etc. The main security threats that come across at this layer are as follows:

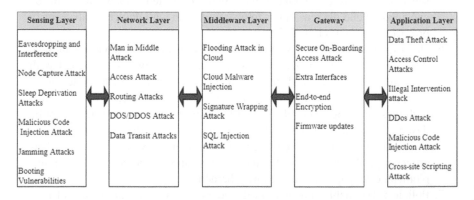

FIGURE 4.3   Attacks associated with different IoT layers (Based on Hassija 2019).

1. Jamming: Jamming is a type of DoS attack where adversaries prevent other nodes from using the channel to communicate by occupying the channel. The node's signal can be interrupted completely or partly with the help of a jammer device. Interfering signals disrupt the wireless communication that allows opponents to easily perform radio interference and cause a denial of service of transmitting or receiving capabilities.

   An adversary without difficulty can accomplish these attacks by detouring the physical layer protocols.

   Various jamming attacks are classified as constant jamming attacks, frequency sweeping jamming attacks, reactive jamming attacks, and deceptive jamming attacks. Reactive jammers, smart hybrid jammers, decoy jammers, and function-specific jammers are varieties of available jammers.

2. Malicious Code Injection Attack: In this attack, the assailant inserts the malicious code in the node's memory and exploits the software. The IoT node's software and firmware are mostly updated using the Wi-Fi network, which provides the gateway for the adversaries to inject malicious code. Using such malicious code, the invaders can access the entire IoT system and may pressurize the device to execute certain unintended functions.

3. Tampering: In this attack, the assailant modifies the compromised node physically, such as a microcontroller, and can acquire sensitive data, like an encryption key. IoT nodes left unattended in the field are more vulnerable to such outbreaks.

4. Eavesdropping and Interference: Nodes in the IoT are of heterogenous types and are placed in open environments. Therefore, IoT applications are vulnerable to eavesdroppers. The attacker can eavesdrop and acquire data during the authentication and transmission phases.

5. Sleep Deprivation Attacks: In this attack, the batteries of IoT devices are drained out by attackers, which leads to denial of service by the IoT nodes. The battery may by drained out by increasing the power consumption of IoT nodes or by running the malicious code infinite times.

6. Booting Attacks: During the boot process, IoT devices are vulnerable to numerous attacks because at that time the security processes are not enabled. The adversaries make use of these vulnerabilities and attack the IoT nodes when they are being restarted.

Network Layer Security Issues

The main activity of the network layer is to transmit the data received from the perception layer to the computation unit for processing. Some more prevalent attacks at this layer are discussed below:

1. Main-in-The-Middle (MiTM) Attack: In the MiTM attack, the attackers intercept and modify data when the sender and receiver are communicating with each other. The attacker can modify the data as per their need and control the entire session. The attacker manipulates and captures real-time

information, which leads to serious threats to online security (Kaushik, K. and Dahiya, S. 2018).

2. Access Attack: In an access attack, the opponent gains unauthorized access to the IoT network. The adversary can be part of the network for a longer duration and have access to important data. As IoT devices endlessly send and receive important data, they are more vulnerable to these attacks (Sha et al. 2018).

3. Routing Attacks: In routing attacks, the routing paths of IoT nodes are diverted to transmit data. There are various types of routing attacks. In a sinkhole attack, the malicious node advertises the shortest path so that data can be transferred through it.

Application Layer Security Issues

The end users directly deal with the application layer and provide services. IoT applications such as smart meters, smart homes, smart grids, and smart cities are part of this layer. Privacy issues and data theft are some specific security issues at this layer. Diverse applications have different security issues. Middleware or the application support layer is the sub-layer in many IoT applications (Sanjay, A. et al. 2020). This sub-layer provides help in optimized resource allocation and computation to support various business services. Various security issues at this layer are discussed as follows:

1. Access Control Attacks: Only authorized users or processes can access data using access control. Therefore, access control attacks are a serious concern in IoT applications. If access to the IoT device is compromised, then the entire IoT system will become vulnerable to attacks. Therefore, in order to thwart these attacks, a robust IoT authentication and access control mechanism is required (Vijarania, M. et al. 2021).

2. Strong IoT access control and authentication technology can help thwart attacks.

3. Data Theft: In IoT applications, a lot of data movement takes place. IoT devices store huge amounts of critical private data. Data during transmission are more at risk than stored data in IoT devices. If IoT applications are vulnerable to these data attacks, then users will be hesitant to register their private information on IoT platforms. A few techniques or protocols can be used to secure the user's data, like data isolation, privacy management, data encryption, etc.

4. Cross-Site Scripting: It is a type of injection attack where the invader injects a side script, like java script, into a trustworthy site. In this way, the attacker can alter the client's content as per their requirements and can make use of the original data in an unlawful way.

4.5   IOT PROTOCOLS AT DIFFERENT LAYERS

This section briefly discusses the routing protocols being used at the network layer for routing. The network layer is divided into two sub-layers, firstly, the routing layer that deals with the routing of information from one place node to another node (Kaushik and Singh 2020). The second layer is the encapsulation layer, which encapsulates the information in the form of packets.

Routing protocol RPL for lossy and low-power networks (RPL)

RPL is a distance vector routing mechanism developed for IoT systems. It is built on destination-oriented directed-acyclic graphs (DODAG) (Makhdoom et al. 2018, Singh, K. et al. 2020). This protocol discovers a distinct path from the terminal node to the root node, which will be used further for packet transmission. Each node sends a DODAG information object in the beginning to advertise itself as a root. The entire DODAG is formed through the propagated DIO from all nodes. The destination sends the DAO (destination advertisement object) when any node wants to communicate to its parent and propagates to the root node. Then, the root node decides the route based on the destination location. By sending the DODAG solicitation message, a new node can join the network and the root node can send the acknowledgment by DAO-ACK message. The entire communication in this protocol goes through the root node (Dhar, D. et al. 2021).

Cognitive RPL (CORPL)

CORPL protocol is the extension of the basic RPL protocol and uses the same method with small modifications (Brandt et al. 2012). This protocol uses opportunistic forwarding in which packets can be forwarded through multiple nodes. Only the best path is chosen to route the packets. Each node maintains the neighbor node list in place of the parent list. DIO messages are sent on any update of neighboring nodes. Each node updates its list of forwarders depending upon the updated information.

MTQQ

Message Queuing Telemetry Transport (MQTT) protocol is commonly used as IoT security protocol. It has been specially designed for unreliable or high-latency and low-bandwidth networks and constraint devices. MQTT protocol provides security at various layers: the transport, network, and application layers. Every layer is responsible for preventing a specific type of attack. MQTT uses a limited security mechanism in order to make it lightweight. A client identifier to authenticate devices on the application level is passed with data packets.

MQTT for Sensor Network

MQTT-SN protocol is used for power-constrained devices of sensor networks. The publisher device is the MTQQ-SN client, which sends a message to the gateway, which transfers the MQTT-SN message to the MQTT message and forwards it to the broker. Hence, the broker delivers the packet to the subscriber on the other gateway (i.e. MQTT-SN client).

Secure MQTT (SMQTT)

MQTT and MQTT-SN both use SSL/TLS for security. Secure MQTT protocol adds security to prevent attacks, such as CRIME and BEAST, to the basic MTQQ protocol (Tawalbeh et al. 2020). It has Spublish message, which is encrypted by attribute-based encryption (ABE) with "0000" message type. So, the subscriber can decrypt the message of whoever satisfies the access policy. ABE supports broadcast encryption, which is a requirement of IoT devices (Saif, A. et al. 2021).

4.6   CONCLUSION AND FUTURE WORK

The IoT is a developing technological field that provides a platform for several opportunities with efficient, cost effective, and convenient services and applications to the end users, though security of IoT systems is a critical concern towards wider deployment of IoT devices. This chapter presented the various security and privacy threats at different layers of IoT architecture and various protocols that deal with security for IoT systems. This chapter has discussed that the existing security frameworks and architectures are not designed to deal with various attacks and threats in a systematic manner. Therefore, a systematic method is required to handle the various IoT security threats in an organized way. A secure IoT architecture needs to be designed that is able to capture the basic IoT security requirements for secure communication.

REFERENCES

Acharya, Vadiraja, and Vinay V. Hegde. "Security frameworks for Internet of Things systems – a comprehensive survey." In 2020 Third International Conference on Smart Systems and Inventive Technology (ICSSIT), pp. 339–345. IEEE, 2020.

Aijaz, Adnan, and A. Hamid Aghvami. "Cognitive machine-to-machine communications for Internet-of-Things: A protocol stack perspective." IEEE Internet of Things Journal 2, no. 2 (2015): 103–112.

Al-Qaseemi, S. A., H. A. Almulhim, M. F. Almulhim, & S. R. Chaudhry, In Future Technologies Conference (FTC) (pp. 731–738). IEEE, 2016.

Bagaa, Miloud, Tarik Taleb, Jorge Bernal Bernabe, and Antonio Skarmeta. "A machine learning security framework for iot systems." IEEE Access 8 (2020): 114066–114077.

Brandt, Aea, J. Hui, R. Kelsey, P. Levis, K. Pister, R. Struik, J. Vasseur, and R. Alexander. "RPL: IPv6 routing protocol for low-power and lossy networks." In RFC 6550. 2012.

Burhan, Muhammad, Rana Asif Rehman, Bilal Khan, and Byung-Seo Kim. "IoT elements, layered architectures and security issues: A comprehensive survey." Sensors 18, no. 9 (2018): 2796.

Dhar Dwivedi, Ashutosh, Rajani Singh, Keshav Kaushik, Raghava Rao Mukkamala, and Waleed S. Alnumay. "Blockchain and artificial intelligence for 5G-enabled Internet of Things: Challenges, opportunities, and solutions." Transactions on Emerging Telecommunications Technologies (2021): e4329.

Deshmukh, S. & Sonavane, S. S. In International Conference on Nextgen Electronic Technologies: Silicon to Software (pp. 71–74). IEEE, 2017.

Hassan, Rondik J., S. R. Zeebaree, Siddeeq Y. Ameen, Shakir Fattah Kak, M. A. Sadeeq, Zainab Salih Ageed, A. Z. Adel, and Azar Abid Salih. "State of art survey for IoT effects on smart city technology: Challenges, opportunities, and solutions." Asian Journal of Research in Computer Science 22 (2021): 32–48.

Hassija, Vikas, Vinay Chamola, Vikas Saxena, Divyansh Jain, Pranav Goyal, and Biplab Sikdar. "A survey on IoT security: Application areas, security threats, and solution architectures." IEEE Access 7 (2019): 82721–82743.

Hassija, S., Y. Arora, K. Tripathi, and M. Vijarania. In Proceedings of the Third International Conference on Information Management and Machine Intelligence, pp. 431–446. Springer, 2023.

Horrow, Susmita, and Anjali Sardana. "Identity management framework for cloud based Internet of Things." In Proceedings of the First International Conference on Security of Internet of Things, pp. 200–203. 2012.

Hussain, Aamir, Tariq Ali, Faisal Althobiani, Umar Draz, Muhammad Irfan, Sana Yasin, Saher Shafiq et al. "Security framework for IoT based real-time health applications." Electronics 10, no. 6 (2021): 719.

Iwaya, Leonardo Horn, Aakash Ahmad, and M. Ali Babar. "Security and privacy for mhealth and uhealth systems: A systematic mapping study." IEEE Access 8 (2020): 150081–150112.

Kaushik, Keshav, and Susheela Dahiya. "Security and privacy in IoT based e-business and retail." In 2018 International Conference on System Modeling & Advancement in Research Trends (SMART), pp. 78–81. IEEE, 2018.

Kaushik, Keshav, and Kamalpreet Singh. "Security and trust in IoT communications: Role and impact." In Intelligent Communication, Control and Devices, pp. 791–798. Springer, Singapore, 2020.

Khraisat, Ansam, and Ammar Alazab. "A critical review of intrusion detection systems in the Internet of Things: Techniques, deployment strategy, validation strategy, attacks, public datasets and challenges." Cybersecurity 4, no. 1 (2021): 1–27.

Makhdoom, Imran, Mehran Abolhasan, Justin Lipman, Ren Ping Liu, and Wei Ni. "Anatomy of threats to the Internet of Things." IEEE Communications Surveys & Tutorials 21, no. 2 (2018): 1636–1675.

Meena, S., M. A., Rajan, V. L. Shivraj, & P. Balamuralidhar. "Secure mqtt for internet of things (IoT)" In Fifth International Conference on Communication Systems and Network Technologies, 2015.

Persson, Per, and Ola Angelsmark. "Calvin–merging cloud and IoT." Procedia Computer Science 52 (2015): 210–217.

Rafique, W., Qi, L., Yaqoob, I., Imran, M., Rasool, R. U., & Dou, W. (2020). Complementing IoT Services Through Software Defined Networking and Edge Computing: A Comprehensive Survey. *IEEE Communications Surveys & Tutorials*, 22, 1761–1804 10.1109/comst.2020.2997475

Sadique, Kazi Masum, Rahim Rahmani, and Paul Johannesson. "Towards security on Internet of Things: Applications and challenges in technology." Procedia Computer Science 141 (2018): 199–206.

Saif, Abdu, Kaharudin Dimyati, Kamarul Ariffin Noordin, G. C. Deepak, Nor Shahida Mohd Shah, Qazwan Abdullah, and Mahathir Mohamad. "An efficient energy harvesting and optimal clustering technique for sustainable postdisaster emergency communication systems." IEEE Access 9 (2021): 78188–78202.

Sanjana, T., B. J. Sowmya, D. Pradeep Kumar, and K. G. Srinivasa. "A framework for a secure e-health care system using IoT-based blockchain technology." In Blockchain Technology for Data Privacy Management, pp. 253–273. CRC Press, 2021.

Sanjay, A., Meenu Vijarania, and Vivek Jaglan. "Security surveillance and home automation system using IoT." EAI Endorsed Transactions on Smart Cities 5, no. 15 (2020): e1.

Sha, Kewei, Wei Wei, T. Andrew Yang, Zhiwei Wang, and Weisong Shi. "On security challenges and open issues in Internet of Things." Future Generation Computer Systems 83 (2018): 326–337.

Singh, Kamalpreet, Keshav Kaushik, and Vivek Shahare. "Role and impact of wearables in
    IoT healthcare." In Proceedings of the Third International Conference on
    Computational Intelligence and Informatics, pp. 735–742. Springer, Singapore, 2020.
Singh, Meena, M. A. Rajan, V. L. Shivraj, and P. Balamuralidhar, "Secure MQTT for
    Internet of Things (IoT)." Published in Fifth International Conference on
    Communication Systems and Network Technologies, 2015.
Tawalbeh, Lo'ai, Fadi Muheidat, Mais Tawalbeh, and Muhannad Quwaider. "IoT Privacy
    and security: Challenges and solutions." Applied Sciences 10, no. 12 (2020): 4102.
Vijarania, Meenu, Neeraj Dahiya, Surjeet Dalal, and Vivek Jaglan. "WSN based efficient
    multi-metric routing for IoT networks." In Green Internet of Things for Smart Cities,
    pp. 249–262. CRC Press, 2021.

5 Application of Artificial Intelligence for DDoS Attack Detection and Prevention on Cyber Physical Systems Using Deep Learning

J. E. T. Akinsola, R. O. Abimbola, M. A. Adeagbo,
A. A. Awoseyi, and F. O. Onipede
First Technical University, Nigeria

A. A. Yusuf
Federal University of Petroleum Resources, Nigeria

CONTENTS

DOI: 10.1201/9781003283003-5

5.1 INTRODUCTION

Cyber physical systems (CPSs) have become sophisticated, multifaceted, independent as well as intelligent. CPSs need a strategy that is different due to its firm interaction among components that are physical as well as cyber, from security of information technology that is traditional. CPSs are also exposed to essential disturbances because of intentional and unintentional events that affect the prediction of their behaviors that was classified as faulty or normal, a task that is very hard to determine. Attention of researchers and scientists is attracted to cybersecurity for CPSs in both academia and industries due to the increase in the number of cyberattacks, such as distributed denial of service (DDoS) attacks and more sophisticated cyber criminals' behavior, which is called zero-day threats. A denial of service (DoS) attack is a type of cyberattack in which the perpetrator attempts to render a machine or network resource unavailable to its intended users by disrupting the services of a host connected to a network for a short or long period of time. A distributed denial of service (DDoS) attack, on the other hand, is a malicious attempt to interrupt the regular traffic of a targeted server, service, or network by flooding the target or its surrounding infrastructure with Internet traffic. The most affected port for DDoS attack is port 22, which is a secure shell (Kuyoro et al., 2017). Mechanisms of conventional cybersecurity, for example, access control as well as the intrusion prevention system/intrusion detection system (IPS/IDS), do not have the ability to block, notice, and avoid this type of cyberattack because of the exhibition of misbehavior that is unidentified from zero-day threats and that is not described in the database signature of the system's security. A new era of artificial intelligence (AI), which is created with mechanisms of cybersecurity, is under development to protect CPSs from zero-day attacks. The technologies of machine learning (ML) are used to manage an enormous amount of data that are heterogeneous and come from different information sources with a purpose of automatic generation of several attack patterns as well as prediction of accurate future attackers' misbehavior. Hence, decision-making issues that are based on cyber defense context have been solved by game-theoretic techniques, that is, detecting if the suspect device is an attacker or not as well as predicting attacks.

Collaboration of several AI systems is required to prevent the occurrence of zero-day attacks, which include game theory, ML, and the involvement of a security expert. Also, there is an improvement in detecting attacks through human involvement in decision making because the purpose of interaction between machine and human is to reduce false positive numbers. It is the best time due to the opportunities brought by AI in deep learning (DL) particularly. DL is used on the contrary rather than traditional ML models due to its use of deeper and more layered artificial neural networks (ANNs). This increases the number of possibilities considered and the overall time the calculative process takes but significantly reduces the gap for the occurrence of false positives. The core function of the DL algorithm would be to formulate scenarios, analyze those scenarios and identify factors of interest, formulate the problem to be solved due to the identified factors, and finally orchestrate an appropriate solution based on the inferences drawn.

CPSs adopt DL models quickly in order to prevent cyberattacks. DL is used to prevent CPSs because it is specially made for handling large sets of data with a huge number of features. A rich class of models that can estimate any function is provided by DL, and these characteristics are desirable by CPSs. This research provides DL solutions to detect cyberattack in the background of CPSs by using DL algorithms on DDoS dataset to generate some ML performance evaluation metrics to validate the best algorithm to use for identifying or detecting attacks in CPSs.

A CPS is a collection of systems comprised of digital devices and intelligent hardware. These systems are a collection of integrated physical and digital devices used in place of traditional physical systems due to their increase in productivity, and they are now commonly used in industrial control systems, water systems, robotics systems, smart grids, smart homes, e-health, and many other aspects of our daily lives, which has made it an essential topic for research. As with other problems, when it is solved, another arises; this study focuses on how to solve cyberattacks on CPSs using AI techniques. The study focuses on building DL models to train the systems and enable them to monitor and potentially flag incoming cyberattacks.

Greater performance is delivered to AI by adopting DL due to its algorithms that are effective as well as its layered setting for useful information extraction from training data. CPSs adopt DL models quickly in order to prevent cyberattacks. Due to the abundance of first-rate datasets, the ease of implementing such models is very high, and the conclusions drawn are extremely accurate, thus reducing the occurrence of the most significant drawback, which would be false positives. An AI-based system was developed to detect cyberattack with a DDoS dataset in the background of CPSs using DL algorithms. Hence, performance evaluation of the algorithms was carried out in order to determine the optimal one for building the DL model when mitigating a DDoS cyberattack on the CPS.

The study evaluated the models and conducted comparative analysis on four algorithms to determine the best DL algorithms that give the best result on the dataset using ML metrics such as accuracy, loss function, precision, recall, and root mean square error (RMSE). Feature extraction was used in classifying a dataset into DDoS attack or normal attack (benign). Based on the DL algorithms used for this study, it was discovered that convolutional neural network (CNN) gives 99.32 accuracy, 0.0353 loss function, 0.9917 precision, 0.994 recall and 0.0805 RMSE; meanwhile, long short-term memory (LSTM) gives 99.92 accuracy, 0.0037 loss function, 0.9997 precision, 0.9992 recall, and 0.026 RMSE. The dense model gives 76.38 accuracy, 0.6132 loss function, 0.7621 precision, 1.0 recall, and 0.4594 RMSE, whereas gated recurrent units (GRU) gives 99.32 accuracy, 0.0353 loss function, 0.9917 precision, 0.994 recall, and 0.0805 RMSE in the training phase on the DDoS dataset. In the testing phase, CNN gives 99.27 accuracy, 0.0401 loss function, 0.991 precision, 0.9995 recall, and 0.0848 RMSE; LSTM gives 99.92 accuracy, 0.0058 loss function, 0.9997 precision, 0.9992 recall, and 0.0278 RMSE; the dense model gives 76.45 accuracy, 0.6131 loss function, 0.763 precision, 1 recall, and 0.4593 RMSE; GRU gives 99.27 accuracy, 0.0401 loss function, 0.991 precision, 0.9995 recall. and 0.0848 RMSE. In conclusion, this research developed a DL model for mitigating CPS attacks using an emerging AI-based method called "deep learning." The results showed that LSTM outperformed other DL algorithms.

5.1.1 CYBER PHYSICAL SYSTEMS

The CPS is a phenomenon that establishes a collection between computational integration and physical processes (Lee & Seshia, 2017). Going by this context, CPSs can be defined as a computational integration with a collection and arrangement of physical objects that together perform a function that the individual object is not capable of, in order to achieve a particular goal. CPSs put together human, physical, and digitized elements in a consolidated process through the integration of logical and physical areas (Mohamed et al., 2020). The sensing, computing, supervision, and networking are integrated into physical elements and infrastructure through CPSs, linking them to one another and the Internet. The most important asset for any individual as well as organizations is holding or keeping data and information intact and safe (Bhardwaj & Kaushik, 2020). In CPSs, monitoring and controlling of the physical process are achieved using networks and embedded computers, commonly with response loops where computations are affected by physical processes and vice versa. Thus, the design of a CPS entails the understanding of collective dynamics of networks, software, and physical processes. A CPS is a multidisciplinary area that requires experts from different domains based on the nature of the problem at hand (Barišić et al., 2022). Based on the foregoing, the CPS has become a prominent domain (Doghri et al., 2021) as its system is a blended engineered system consisting of control systems and different technologies such as communication, electrical, and information (Mohamed et al., 2020). This emerging domain came into being on the occasion of the birth of the CPS, integrating physical and computational capabilities. The Internet of Things (IoT) being among CPSs' important enablers

(Latif et al., 2022), its live data sensor evaluation as well as storage are required widely for further sensor data analysis (Pradeep & Sharma, 2020); the CPS brings forth monitoring and feedback to emergency circumstances, as well as delivery systems. Among the numerous important areas, this concept has revolutionized and brought forth different applications such as healthcare, transportation systems, information systems, and traffic management systems, to mention but a few. Some of other CPS key engineered systems that are facilitating CPS integration are the Internet together with other associated technologies such as cloud computing and software-defined network (SDN), making possible the realization of Industry 4.0, smart security, smart homes, and smart healthcare systems. Also worthy of mentioning is industrial automation, leading to the idea of smart factories, employing the IoT and AI as the CPS key enablers (Latif et al., 2022). The role of cyber threats in the IoT is crucial (Kaushik & Dahiya, 2018). The IoT has transformed the digital world by interconnecting billions of electrical items over the Internet (Dhar Dwivedi et al., 2021), and it is negatively affecting a lot of people (Singh et al., 2020). Some of the areas where the IoT is widely applied are healthcare devices that are wearable, smart homes, smart farming, the smart grid, smart retail, as well as smart supply chain (Hinduja & Pandey, 2020). Security and trust are fundamental threats to the IoT (Kaushik & Singh, 2020). AI in particular as an enabler is a disruptive technology that has revolutionized digital space (Akinsola et al., 2022) and has thus affected every sector of the economy (Hinmikaiye et al., 2021) with specific regard to telecommunications. Some of the examples of CPSs and industrial automation are integration of human to robot, flexibility in the management of supply chain, predictive maintenance, and production quality (Abosaq et al., 2016). A typical example of a CPS is shown in Figure 5.1,

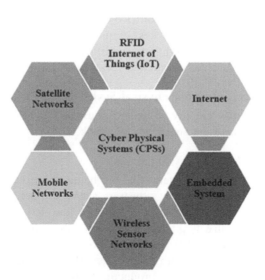

FIGURE 5.1 Different components of the cyber physical system such as embedded systems, wireless sensor networks, the internet, satellite networks, mobile networks, and the Internet of Things.

consisting of different components such as embedded systems, wireless sensor networks, the Internet, satellite networks, mobile networks, and the IoT.

Generally, the CPS is a computational system that relies on computer algorithms that are integrated into real-life applications to monitor and control mechanisms. The CPS, being an emerging domain with potential to revolutionize different areas of life, has attracted a number of researchers working in the different ways to improve on its limitations. The authors (Pivoto et al., 2021) worked on the perception that industries utilize the CPS with a view to provide better, safe, and reliable production. However, there are usually attacks occasioned through SQL injection attacks on intelligent systems and web application (Akinsola et al., 2020). The author (Pivoto et al., 2021) identified possible limitations that AI and IoT can bring forth in Industry 4.0, bringing forth gaps to be enhanced in the CPS model with emphasis on technologies and characteristics. Some of the limitations that AI and IoT can bring about are interoperability, connectivity, resource optimization, smart decisions, and interactivity. In the study by Koren & Krishna, 2021, different approaches CPSs employed for fault tolerance are considered, giving response time great importance, with a view to limiting failure rate in some important applications, such as the power grid, aircraft, automobiles, and so on. In the same vein, Vinogradov et al., 2021 developed a method that utilized four information processing points to bring about logical inference that identifies and constructs a model based on the theory of patterns to ensure robotics' behavior sufficiently guarantees self-actualization of a specific mission. The author's aim is to ensure the CPS effectively transfers experience and also guarantees the cause-and-effect method and compatibility of the theological method. Also, Chechile, 2021, used the CPS that necessitated layered simulation-centric methods that required visualization capabilities of two- and three-dimensions in machine process development, such as space systems for the verification of laws controlled through the creation of synthetic realities, recreating numerical physical decrees in computers and the research laboratory.

5.1.1.1 Applications of Cyber Physical Systems

Some of the systems that employ CPSs are industrial control systems, smart grid systems, medical devices, and smart cars (Ruthvik, 2021).

5.1.1.1.1 Industrial Control Systems

These are regarded as control systems that are being utilized for monitoring, controlling, and production in diverse industries such as water and sewage plants, chemical plants, and nuclear plants, to mention a few. It is generally controlled using a microprocessor that is programmable through a programmable logic controller (PLC) device that involves the connection of sensors and actuators to the physical world. CPSs, together with AI and the IoT, offer industries a system that guarantees reliable, better, and safe production (Pivoto et al., 2021). Typical examples of applications of CPSs are shown in Figure 5.2.

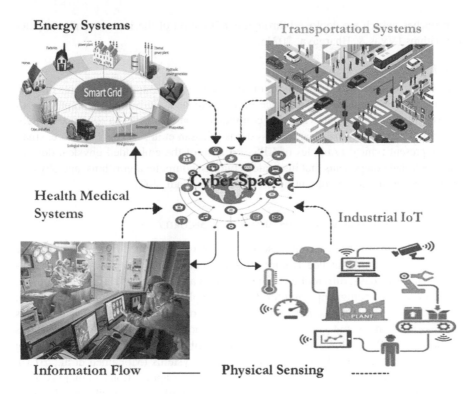

FIGURE 5.2 Typical example of an application of the cyber physical system, comprised of the smart grid, transportation system, healthcare medical center, and Industrial IoT, showing their information flow and physical sensing arrow.

5.1.1.1.2   Smart Grid Systems

The smart grid system efficiently generates, transmits, and distributes electricity because of its ability to globally and automatically maintain voltage load balance based on demand, and it also utilizes windmills' renewable energy generation. CPSs made it possible to control applications, including smart grid systems, because of their real-time and fault-tolerant computational capability, making a response to events possible within a certain time frame (Koren & Krishna, 2021). The introduction of human-computer interaction (HCI), also known as man-machine interaction or interfacing (MMI), has resulted in numerous advances (Alao et al., 2019) and has thus made the devices smart.

5.1.1.1.3   Medical Devices

The need for safety in healthcare applications built on the IoT is important due to different roles on existing wireless systems (Kaushik et al., 2021). Wearable devices that communicate through the use of wireless technology the specific health status of patients to the physician are a typical example of CPSs' application in the medical field. For instance, medical CPSs integrate computational and physical approaches, which are deployed through examination of the Internet and computer algorithms (Vyas & Bhargava, 2021).

5.1.1.1.4 Smart Cars

The smart car is friendly to the environment because of its intelligent features through the use of CPSs and AI that enhance its convenience. Currently, the capability of smart cars to exchange data via many communication channels is a response to high-tech advancement in smart transport systems (Hassan et al., 2018). Therefore, smart cars represent typical examples of CPSs because of the embedded physical devices and electronic components that integrate networks, computer algorithms, and physical approaches to influence computing processes (Alshdadi, 2021).

5.1.2 CYBER PHYSICAL SYSTEMS AND CYBER SECURITY

Recently, there has been an increase in the use of CPSs in different applications because of their intelligence features through computing and physical object integration. Nowadays, different examples of CPSs are emerging in every area of life, and they are also being employed for different applications (Mohamed et al., 2020): cleaning robots at home, smart lighting systems on the street, and other examples such as ventilation and smart heating and air-conditioning (or HVAC) systems (Taha et al., 2020). However, CPSs are susceptible to cyber threats and hacking attempts like other distributed and computerized systems (Mohamed et al., 2020), notwithstanding the growing dependency of numerous applications on them (Gao & Yang, 2022). These susceptibilities have caused numbers of deadly attacks from people of the underworld due to attacks penetrating heterogeneous systems that are highly connected together (Griffioen et al., 2021). Examples of these are thousands of centrifuges being destroyed due to undesirable expedient acceptance of Iran's uranium enhancement capacity by a state enemy (Chen, 2010), numbers of liters of sewage leaked due to undesirable expedient utilization of complete system knowledge to cause havoc on Queensland waste management system by a spiteful insider (Slay & Miller, 2008), and general blackouts in Ukraine due to an undesirable supervisory control and data acquisition system by hackers (Lee et al., 2016). These have drawn the attention of researchers to the different ways attacks can be mitigated, making a secured CPS through safeguarding the heterogeneous items, such as sensors, computation, control, and communication between physical objects. Cybersecurity protects cyber devices such as software applications and hardware from cyberattacks, and businesses and individuals employ this approach to safeguard themselves from undesirable admittance to computerized networks and data centers (Alshdadi, 2021). Some of the defense techniques traditionally employed by cybersecurity are message verification codes, signatures, and authentication encryption, to mention to a few (Mohamed et al., 2020). These techniques use a computational approach to detecting integrity attacks against the highly knowledgeable and resourceful hackers (Griffioen et al., 2021).

5.1.2.1 Defense Techniques in Cyber Physical Systems

CPSs are protected from attacks using different techniques, as discussed below:

5.1.2.1.1 Message Verification Codes

Message verification codes is a method used to protect Internet resources against intruders. Verification codes identify and provide further security when resetting or unlocking user accounts by sending a verification code via the configured medium of communication such as a mobile number or email address. In CPSs, the verification code is one of the key features in building a secured system by ensuring the system meets the configured requirements with high assurance level (Mitra, 2021). Various researchers have applied verification codes to ensure the security of CPSs. For instance, Shen et al., 2013, proposed a cooperative protocol for verification codes that share vehicle verification results with one another in a cooperative way to ensure a significant reduction in the number of verifications of authentication messages by each vehicle. This was done mainly to reduce the complexity of the frequent interplay, such as broadcasting of vehicle geographic information between cyber domains and physical objects.

5.1.2.1.2 Digital Signatures

A digital signature is an electronic signature that routinely employs a mathematical algorithm for the validation of the integrity and authenticity of messages, such as a digital document, online card transaction, email, and so on. It uniquely creates a fingerprint for both the message and the entity or person and subsequently uses the entity's unique fingerprint for the identification of users during online transactions to protect digital messages (CISA, 2020). An example of this application is the enhancement of the security of data in a CPS for a water treatment and supply system (Vegh & Miclea, 2015). Another one is the introduction of a scheme for lightweight signature that protects a CPS from injection of false data to ensure the integrity and authenticity of continuous authentication messages being transmitted (Yang et al., 2020). In fact, injection attack is the most prevalent attack in the last ten years, and it requires taxonomical characterization for its mitigation to be effective (Idowu et al., 2020).

5.1.2.1.3 Authentication Encryption

In encryption, meaningful data transform into unintelligible text (Simplilearn, 2022) using codes that can be employed to reverse the process, called decryption. Also, the authentication process typically needs the codes to unlock and gain entrance to the system. Therefore, further authenticated data are employed in authenticated encryption with a view to providing data integrity and confidentiality as well as assurance of authenticity on data being encrypted.

5.1.3 Emerging Technologies in Mitigating Cyber Physical System Attacks

A number of technologies and methods are emerging to mitigate CPS attacks because of the computational complexity of traditional approaches and their ineffectiveness against physical attacks. Among the emerging technologies employed to mitigate CPS attacks are digital forensics, IoT, AI-empowered CPSs, advanced electronic CPSs, unified approach at run time and design time, moving target defense (MTD) techniques, and so on. They are discussed as follows:

5.1.3.1 Digital Forensics

Digital forensics aims to recover and investigate artifacts established on a digital device such as smartphones, external drives, laptops, memory cards, computers, and so on. Forensic analysis is incorporated in CPSs as a security measure to support the investigation of criminal activities and hacking attempts (Mohamed et al., 2020). Some of the recent trends in the application of digital forensics in cybersecurity include IoT, social media, and cloud forensics. Professionals in cybersecurity use these technologies for digital tracing of data stored electronically and processes involved, to ensure safety of data, while detecting the hackers (Alghamdi, 2021). One of the challenges to digital forensics has been privacy issues. The rise of social media has accelerated the phenomenon of cyberbullying and privacy concerns (Akinsola et al., 2021).

5.1.3.2 Internet of Things (IoT) Security

IoT security is a technological segment used in cybersecurity to protect networks and connected devices of the IoT (Sharon, 2021). Devices of the IoT play an important role in the technology era when devices that are conventional become smarter as well as independent (Dhar Dwivedi et al., 2021). In the study by Alshdadi, 2021, IoT-based advanced electronic features were proposed to safeguard the hijacking of a virtual vehicle in transport networks. CPSs can incorporate advanced electronic features to reduce cyberattacks and improve the security of smart vehicles.

The connection between several devices is leading to various problems related to IoT privacy as well as security. Due to technological advancements, various retail stores and e-businesses use IoT-based techniques for their marketing, promotions, sales, and productivity due to the advantage it brings to their customers as well as the owner of the business (Kaushik & Dahiya, 2018).

5.1.3.3 Artificial Intelligence (AI)

AI is a technology used in cybersecurity to ensure effective and efficient information security. It makes the system secure ahead of a cyber threat. Examples of the technologies in AI are neural networks, ML, DL, and expert systems. AI uses information from blogs, research, and news stories to curate threat intelligence through the use of natural language processing and ML, providing quick analysis of events and identification of vulnerabilities that may lead to an attack. Cybersecurity uses AI at both a social and a technical level of the CPS's automation during the integration of CPSs and the IoT to mitigate possible attacks (Radanliev et al., 2021).

5.1.3.4 Unified Approach at Design and Run-Time

A unified approach that takes the cognizance of security and safety issues related to the integration of the CPS with the IoT at both design and run time is an approach employed to possibly mitigate cyberattacks (Latif et al., 2022). During the design, the strengths and weaknesses of the SDLC models must be keenly considered

(Adeagbo et al., 2021). Meanwhile, ambiguity in the software performance can be eliminated using a formal method of performance evaluation (Akinsola et al., 2020). Run time analysis and design can be effective when integrated with an intelligent user interface (Akinsola et al., 2021). As a result, it is critical to assess whether the software development paradigm is top-down or bottom-up (Akinsola, Ogunbanwo et al., 2020).

5.1.3.5 Moving Target Defense (MTD)

Application of MTD is a technique used to shield the CPS from memory corruption attacks such as code reuse, code injection, and non-control data attacks. The MTD techniques used in shielding systems from attacks include address space randomization (ASR), instruction set randomization (ISR), and data space randomization (DSR) (Griffioen et al., 2021).

5.2 LITERATURE REVIEW

This section considers related works that have been done by several authors to situate important components of this study.

5.2.1 ARTIFICIAL INTELLIGENCE

Information technology is one of the revolutions in the history of humans. The introduction of smart home technology and the Internet has improved the lifestyle of many people. AI has reduced the Herculean task carried out by humans by building machines that can carry out these tasks. The term "artificial intelligence" was proposed in 1956 during a conference at Dartmouth University (Zhang & Lu, 2021). It was at this point that a new area that studies how machines simulate human intelligence was introduced (Xu, 2013). It is currently the most significant area in computing. It is a production factor that has the potential to introduce growth sources and how work is done across several industries. AI is a way of making a computer or application think like or close to a human. It involves recognizing patterns by analyzing the process to produce intelligent software (Bansal, 2022). AI is a field that cannot be stopped from appearing in different areas of our society. Areas like medicine, agriculture, education, and so on have all benefited from the presence of AI. AI-based applications have shown great potential in several areas. AI has penetrated into all parts of society; this is due to the digital revolution and the COVID-19 pandemic (Tognetto et al., 2021). AI is a technique that allows human behavior to be mimicked by computers so as to behave close to humans in making decisions that can solve difficult tasks with little or no supervision. It can be described as the ability of computers or computing-controlled systems to carry out different tasks that are mostly associated with humans or intelligent beings.

AI is a bigger field than ML, which is a statistical subset of AI, and DL, which is a statistical subset of AI (Krukrubo, 2020). Figure 5.3 shows how AI, ML, and DL have evolved over the years. It can be seen that AI dominated the space between 1950 and 1980, whereas ML dominated the space between 1980 and 2010, and DL has been dominating the space since 2010. Currently, most of the intelligent or

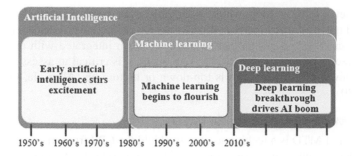

FIGURE 5.3 Artificial intelligence evolution showing the stages from early artificial intelligence to deep learning breakthrough.

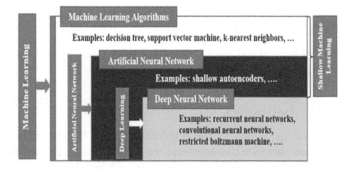

FIGURE 5.4 Foundations of artificial intelligence such as machine learning, artificial neural network, and deep neural network.

smart systems that have AI capabilities rely heavily on DL and ML. ML is used to explain the capability of different systems to learn from training data that are historical in order to predict outcomes of several events based on the training data, thereby solving a problem (Janiesch et al., 2021).

DL is a ML concept that utilizes ANNs. The DL model surpasses ML models in most cases. ML describes how a computer program's performance improves over time in terms of performance metrics and task types.

The foundations of AI as described by Janiesch et al., 2021, include ML algorithms, ANNs, and deep neural networks. The relationships between these items are described in Figure 5.4. ANNs have a flexible structure that can be adjusted for several contexts that cut across the whole ML. The idea was taken from biological systems that consist of representing artificial neurons mathematically as processes. Neurons are arranged in different layers, data input which is received from the input layer and the result received from the output layer. Deep neural networks consist of two or more hidden layers that are arranged in a nested network architecture.

5.2.1.1 Characteristics of Artificial Intelligence

Intelligence is mostly associated with humans describing human beings as intelligent animals. AI is used to describe computers that can reason close to humans.

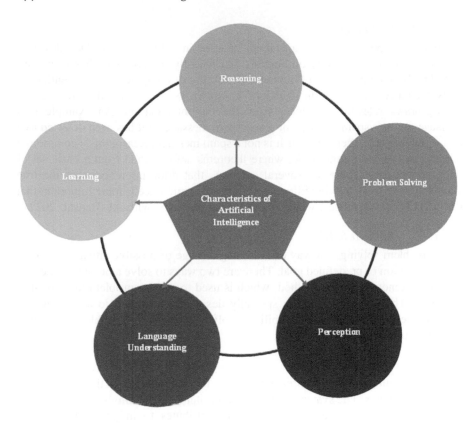

FIGURE 5.5 Characteristics of artificial intelligence which are reasoning, learning, problem solving, language understanding, and perception.

AI contributes and combines its techniques with other disciplines like psychology, philosophy, linguistics, biology, and so on. The characteristics of AI are depicted in Figure 5.5. The authors (Bansal, 2022; Copeland, 2022) describe five major characteristics of AI. They are learning, reasoning, problem solving, perception, and language understanding. They are discussed as follows.

5.2.1.1.1 Learning

Learning can be described as any form of knowledge acquisition through gathering of experience or studying. Computers also learn the way human beings learn. That is, they learn in different ways. AI tries to learn while solving a problem. It continues to find a solution to a problem until it gets the correct result. In this way, the computer keeps track of what it has encountered, takes note of such encounters, and proffers a solution to it if it comes across such an encounter in the future. For example, learning if a message is spam or not, the conditions for categorizing the message are noted for future detection. Trial and error is the simplest form of learning on a computer (Bansal, 2022). The learning component is the most important part of AI because it involves memorizing.

5.2.1.1.2   Reasoning

Reasoning is the act of thinking about an idea in a logical way, Decades ago, reasoning was based wholly on humans, but recently the computer has been subjected to thinking on behalf of humans. The ability of computers to differentiate or draw inferences from certain situations is known as reasoning. Most times, reasoning draws relevant inferences from the current situation. An example is a message can be a spam message or a non-spam message. If it has been detected as a non-spam message, then it means it is not a spam message. Reasoning is common in science, mathematics, and logic, where theorems are designed from a basic set of rules and axioms. There are several solutions that draw inferences, but the true reasoning is beyond drawing inferences. Relevance inference is more important that just identifying inferences, which is one of the problems with AI (Bansal, 2022).

5.2.1.1.3   Problem Solving

In AI, problem solving is a way of searching a range of possible situation so as to attain a solution or predefined goal. There are two ways to solve a problem. The first one is the general purpose method, which is used to solve a problem in a step-by-step way. The second method is specially designed or tailored to a problem. In general, the AI problem-solving ability involves a lot of data. Problem solving is one important component of AI.

5.2.1.1.4   Perception

Perception is an important component of AI as the computer scans the environment to perceive objects. The system analyzes similar items, which might have dissimilar appearance, and uses their relationship and attributes to judge if they can be grouped together. Perception is one of the components used by cars to drive at a moderate speed. The environment is scanned by means of various sensors; an object in an environment can sense the perception of the environment using AI technology (Bansal, 2022).

5.2.1.1.5   Language Understanding

Language is a system of communicating between two entities. Human beings communicate through the language they understand. Computers also communicate with humans via high-level or programming language. It is one of the widely used AI components; understanding a language means the ability to derive meaning from certain terms. One of the important parts of language is object distinction, that is, differentiating between several objects with similar environments. The AI platform makes computers understand and execute programs easily (Bansal, 2022).

5.2.1.2   Applications of Artificial Intelligence in Cyber Physical Systems (CPSs)

CPSs are becoming more sophisticated, very complex, autonomous, and intelligent. Some examples of CPSs include robotic systems, medical systems, intelligent transportation systems, and Industry 4.0 and smart grids that appear in the energy sector (Sedjelmaci et al., 2020). The CPS is an emerging field in cybersecurity that aims to touch every area of someone's life in the future. The Internet and semiconductors transformed and revolutionized our lives, showing how humans interact with information technology growth. The CPS is used to represent a generation of systems that integrate communication capabilities with the flexibility of an engineered and physical system and any other functions (Rho et al., 2016). CPSs are complex systems that are multi-dimensional and that integrate computers, networks, and physical environments. AI in the CPS would involve intelligent edge devices, robotics systems, biomedical monitoring, health systems, and several capabilities that can be used for correcting human errors and natural disasters (Lv et al., 2021).

5.2.1.2.1 Application in Building

Lv et al. (2021) conducted a study that focused on combining AI with CPSs in buildings. The study was based mainly on four modules, which are communication, execution, control, and detection. The lowest unit of control is an agent, and the multi-agent system is used to imitate the connections between human neurons in order to provide flexible and autonomous information access. Multi-agents are utilized to mimic the connections between human neurons. It is possible to construct the physical world link of the physics-based information fusion. The CPS information universe is built using the premise of granular formal concepts and the granular computing paradigm. The back-propagation neural network (BPNN) is used in the environmental information calculation module for pattern recognition and classification. The peak signal-to-noise ratio (PSNR), normalized root mean square error (NRMSE), and mean absolute error (MAE) values of the developed system were determined to be outstanding, indicating that the system's resilience and efficacy were high. The system was put to the test by recognizing scenarios and related temperatures in order to see if the CPS could intelligently meet the requirements for indoor temperature responsiveness.

5.2.1.2.2 Application in Cyber Defense

The authors (Sedjelmaci et al., 2020) described some categories of the CPS: the AI-assisted cyber defense, which uses non-machine learning AI methods to detect attackers targeting CPS, and the ML-based cyber defense for the CPS. A distributed control security architecture for optical networks and fog radio in CPSs is called brain-based distributed control security. Malicious CPS nodes may be discovered with a high degree of precision, whereas blocking likelihood, latency, and packet loss are decreased (Sedjelmaci et al., 2020). Cybercrime is evolving and has infiltrated even the most protected digital businesses and devices (Balogun et al., 2019), including the CPS.

5.2.1.2.3 Application in Resource Optimization

A study by Lv et al., 2021, looked at a method using AI on an edge computing system to optimize the utilization of sensors and secure the CPS from coupling problems; the coupling degree of a system was reduced by two buffer queues in parallel. The result from the study showed that the edge computing-based method reduced the scheduling cost and increased resource utilization while increasing the CPS lifespan.

5.2.1.2.4 Application in Manufacturing Systems

Cisco, GE, and IBM, which are global companies, and some other developed companies in Germany identified the manufacturing CPS as the core infrastructure of the next generation. These companies concentrated on developing CPS utilization platforms and technologies. It is expected that the IoT infrastructure will be converted from a closed system to an open system that can use the centralized cloud and further evolve into an open network that functions in the cloud.

5.2.1.2.5 Application in Medical Systems

Medical cyber physical systems (MCPSs) are a platform in which information about a patient's health can be inferred from IoT sensors, pre-processed locally, and then processed in the cloud using powerful ML algorithms. MCPSs were introduced to improve the quality of life for patients, accelerate the development of new treatments or drugs, and revolutionize remote patient healthcare monitoring.

5.2.1.3 Levels in Cyber Physical Systems

There are five levels in the CPS architecture, as shown in Figure 5.6. These cyber physical levels are mostly referred to the 5Cs architecture (Radanliev et al., 2021). The five levels are:

5.2.1.3.1 Configure

Configure means to allocate supervisory control that might require some actions. This level gives feedback to the physical part through the cyber part. It performs

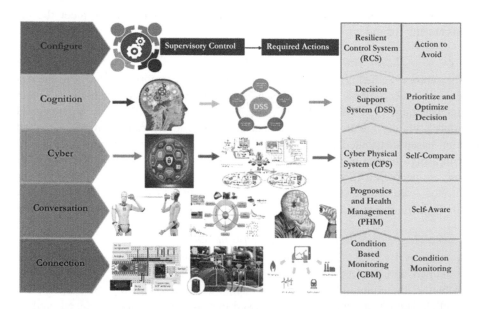

FIGURE 5.6 Five levels of cyber physical system architecture: configure, cognition, cyber, conversation, and connection.

oversight functions so as to make machines self-optimized, self-adjusted, and self-configured. This level applies the controls that correspond to making decisions in the cognition level to monitor the machines.

5.2.1.3.2 Cognition

Cognition describes the condition that could occur in the system. This level provides users with more detailed analytical information so as to make accurate decisions. It makes decision making and collaborative diagnostics possible as the task's priority for maintenance can be easily determined due to the availability of individual machine status and comparative information.

5.2.1.3.3 Cyber

Cyber does a comparative analysis across several machines. This level plays the control information hub role that can gather information across several machine networks. This level allows redundant information about analytics to be extracted for data collection so as to provide a clearer understanding to the machines. This level allows the performance of the machine to be compared with other machines.

5.2.1.3.4 Conversion

Conversion measures the awareness level of machines. Data can be converted into information at the conversion level as several mechanisms can be used to detect the conversion of data to information. An example is converting health information or values to useful information or predictive information about a disease. The machine has the self-awareness property at this level.

5.2.1.3.5 Connection

Connection uses sensors to measure the condition of a machine (Radanliev et al., 2021). The components of machines must be connected as a first step in acquiring reliable and accurate data so as to develop CPSs that can be used in smart factories. Several sensors or devices acquire different data, which could be temperature, current, voltage, oil concentration of machines, and so on.

5.2.1.4 Domains in Artificial Intelligence

AI describes the practice of computer reasoning, action, and recognition, which is all about simulating the behavior of humans, most importantly the ability to be cognitive (Tyagi, 2020). AI is a computer or machine's ability to emulate the intelligence of human beings (i.e. experience acquisition and adapting to the most recent information). Tyagi, 2020, describes six major branches of AI. They include ML, neural network, robotics, expert systems, fuzzy logic, and natural language processing, and they are shown with the aid of the diagram in Figure 5.7. These branches are discussed as follows.

5.2.1.4.1 Machine Learning

The aim of ML is to program computers to have the capability of learning from the input information. Learning literally means to convert a chunk of knowledge or experience into expertise (Shalev-Shwartz & Ben-David, 2014). It is the capacity of

FIGURE 5.7 Six major branches of artificial intelligence such as machine learning, robotics, neural networks, fuzzy logic, expert systems, and natural language processing.

computers to learn with little or no human effort. On the one hand, time required to create a model and precision (accuracy) are factors; while on the other hand, the kappa statistic and mean absolute error (MAE) are factors that must be considered (Osisanwo et al., 2017). Meanwhile, before selecting an effective algorithm for predictive analytics, each performance metric must be analyzed holistically (Akinsola et al., 2019). When a decision is to be made in an objective manner for choosing an algorithm with optimal performance by considering the No Free Lunch Theorem for algorithm performance, then the right approach is multi-criteria decision making (Akinsola et al., 2019).

ML can be categorized into three areas based on the type of data that are available for prediction. They are supervised learning, unsupervised learning, and reinforcement learning. Supervised learning uses a dataset that is categorized by a data expert for training and testing. This type of learning allows the input and output to be categorized before carrying out analysis. Unsupervised learning deals with the unlabeled dataset, that is, the dataset that has not been categorized by data experts. It clusters the data into groups based on their similarities. The idea is to identify a hidden pattern in the dataset. Reinforcement learning teaches a computer to fulfill some defined rules while performing a task. It also categorizes a dataset based on expert knowledge and makes suggestions for the computer if an instance that was not included in the training occurs (Tyagi, 2020).

5.2.1.4.2 Neural Network

A neural network is a collection of algorithms that can be used to search for relationship elements that spans across data by imitating the operational process of the human brain (Tyagi, 2020). It is a collection of neurons that are artificial, also known as perceptrons. A neural network consists of neurons that are mathematical functions that classify and gather information based on a specific structure.

5.2.1.4.3   Robotics

This is an area in AI that focuses mainly on constructing and designing robots. It is a field in science and engineering that incorporates computer science, electrical engineering, mechanical engineering, and many others (Tyagi, 2020). It determines operation, design, production, and usage of robots, that is, dealing with the information transformation and control of computer systems.

5.2.1.4.4   Expert Systems

The first successful model for AI was the Expert System (Shalev-Shwartz & Ben-David, 2014). It came into existence in the 1970s (Tyagi, 2020). An Expert System is a computer system that can imitate the decision-making capability of a human expert. It gets its functionality by extracting knowledge from a knowledge base so as to gain insight and reasoning based on the queries of users. Expert Systems have high execution and are understandable, reliable, and extremely responsive.

5.2.1.4.5   Fuzzy Logic

Fuzzy logic is used to describe the technique that modifies and represents information that is not certain by measuring the level of correctness of its hypothesis. There are conditions where it is difficult to identify if a condition is true or false; such a condition brings about fuzzy logic (Tyagi, 2020). It is also used to create reasoning on uncertain natural concepts. It is used to measure the degree of truth of a particular occurrence, which might fall between 0.0 and 1.0. The occurrence is false if it tends toward 0.0, whereas the occurrence is true if it tends toward 1.0.

5.2.1.4.6   Natural Language Processing

Natural language processing is an area in computing that tries to use AI features to communicate between humans and computers via natural language (Shalev-Shwartz & Ben-David, 2014). It helps to carry out computational processes of natural languages written or spoken by humans. It tries to make the computer imitate human language. Natural language processing deals with deriving, analyzing, searching, and understanding information from textual data.

5.2.2   Applications of Deep Learning in Cyber Physical Systems

One of the evolving technologies is CPSs that contain the cyber system, physical system, as well as systems control integration. Industrial processes such as monitoring, manufacturing, and controlling are automated by the CPS. Due to the complex nature of this system, AI as well as DL provide mechanisms that are effective for determining the performance of such compound systems with focus on optimization as well as design. Mechanisms of AI used in the CPS include scheduling, reorganization, as well as security (Padmajothi & Iqbal, 2022).

DL has attracted a lot of attention in data science due to its enhancement in many areas. DL algorithms contain architectures that are in hierarchical with different layers, where features that are in a higher level are defined based on lower-level features. They are applied in the CPS because they have the ability to extract features as well as abstract from emphasized data (Wickramasinghe et al., 2018). DL acts as an essential tool for identifying attacks as well as inspecting packets due to increases in traffic on the network as well as time consumption and computation for monitoring different attack types (Kamdem & Ziazet, 2019). DL has been effectively useful in CPS security for correlated purposes, which are for detecting malware as well as monitoring of threats, detection of intrusion, detecting anatomy, detecting vulnerability, black-out prevention, destructions, as well as attacks (Wickramasinghe et al., 2018). Finding correlation in data is one of the abilities of DL, so it is used effectively to detect CPS attacks as well as to acquire a high rate of attack identification (Kamdem & Ziazet, 2019). Some DL algorithms that are used in detecting and preventing CPS attacks are CNN, multilayer perceptron (MLP), LSTM, restricted boltzmann machines (RBMs), and deep belief networks (DBNs) (Wickramasinghe et al., 2018).

5.2.2.1   Convolutional Neural Network (CNN)

CNN is the modification of a traditional feedforward neural network. Its inspiration is drawn from the visual cortex of mammals, and it has become the de-facto standard for examining data that are images (Zargar, 2021). CNN is a supervised DL algorithm that makes use of large data for training. It is also useful for object detection, scene classification, LULC classification, and segmentation of semantics (Mohan et al., 2021). Three main types of layers are used in building CNN architectures, which are the convolutional layer, layers that are fully connected, as well as the pooling layer (Karparthy, 2018). CNN is used in the detection of intrusion into the system in the CPS by extracting important features that differentiate one class from the others and by detecting attack-and-train classified data for intrusions on data tested (Kamdem & Ziazet, 2019). CNN is very effective in preventing DoS attacks and detecting cyberattacks in isolation as well as in the CPS. CNN detects as well as puts cyberattacks into isolation, which consists of the elements of the CPS controller and its physical layer, where alerts to detect as well as generates the cyberattack origin location (Paredes et al., 2021).

5.2.2.2   Multilayer Perceptron (MLP)

MLP is a feedforward ANN that contains three minimum layers of nodes, which are layer inputted, layer hidden, as well as layer outputted. A particular output node in a layer is the input linked naturally as all the input in the next layer is fully connected (Khan et al., 2020). It is one of the ANNs that is efficient for classifying data in various areas that are intruding in network detection or network traffic. It is very useful for detecting network traffic by reducing the amount of ANN error (Moghanian et al., 2020).

5.2.2.3   Long-Short-Term Memory (LSTM)

Recurrent neural network (RNN) is a system that is very powerful and useful, which was specifically developed for solving the problem of disappearing as well as gradient explosion, which arises typically during long-term learning dependencies despite the very long minimal lag time (Sood, 2020). This neural network consists of a unit that is special, which is known as blocks of memory in the hidden layer of recurrent. Memory cells, in addition to self-connections that store the state of the network temporarily, is what memory blocks are made of, with multiplicative units that are special, which is known as gates for information flow control (Lee et al., 2017). LSTM is used for detecting anomalies in data that differ from the proper system behavior. It is used as a data-driven model that can learn to predict present as well as future observations of the data. LSTM is very useful in learning sequences in time with changing length of dependencies that are temporal as well as an exciting general-purpose method to behavior learning of randomly compounded CPSs (Eiteneuer & Niggemann, 2018).

5.2.2.4   Restricted Boltzmann Machines (RBMs)

They are models that are graphical and probabilistic in nature, which are understood as stochastic neural networks (SNN) (Fischer & Igel, 2012). RBMs consist of hidden nodes and nodes that are visible where an individual node is linked to every single other node. It assists in understanding anomalies in the system by determining the regular working conditions of a system. A sub-division of Boltzmann machines (BM), which have a boundary or limit on the number of networks between hidden and layers that are visible, is RBMs (Sarker, 2021). RBMs are used to extract features that are new hierarchically from the data that are continuous using a network that is deep of stacked RBMs in development of a cyber physical production system using network timed automaton that is deep (Hranisavljevic et al., 2020). RBMs are used for the development of an intrusion detection framework in smart cities due to unsecured networks, which is DDoS attacks in a smart city. This neural network is used due to its capability to handle as well as learn features of raw data that are high-level in a way that is unsupervised as well as their skill in dealing with data representation that is real (Elsaeidy et al., 2019).

5.2.2.5   Deep Belief Networks (DBNs)

They are types of artificial neural networks derived from stacking many RBMs together. They act as DBN layers as well as networks among the layers introduced but not inside individual layers (Gümüşbaş et al., 2021). This is one of DL algorithms that have the capability and efficient approach to solve neural networks problems with deep layers, for example, the phenomenon of overfitting as well as low velocity in learning. RBMs in conjunction with retuning the whole net with the use of back propagation is that starting point of learning DBN (Algarsamy & Soundar Kathavarayan, 2018). This algorithm is used in the CPS to detect opcode-based malware attack by using data that are unlabeled for a predicting model that is multi-layer generative for solving an overfitting problem during neural network training (Ding et al., 2016). It is also one of the best algorithms for detecting intrusion in the CPS due to fast learning methods by the application of a fashion that is greedy and that is layer by layer in a way that is unsupervised. Due to the DBN capability, it is categorized as one of the best methods for studying and detecting intrusion (Gümüşbaş et al., 2021). DBNs are also used in mitigating attacks and intrusion such as false data injection as well as DoS attacks in the microgrid (Durairaj et al., 2022).

5.3   MATERIALS AND METHODS

The dataset was obtained from https://research.unsw.edu.au/projects/bot-iot-dataset. The study made use of data which consist of 19,771 DDoS attacks and 6,346 normal (benign) attacks. The data were pre-processed after feature selection and normalization were carried out in relation to conversion of categorical values into numerical values for model building after principal components (features) had been determined. The dataset utilized for DDoS attack mitigation consisted of 25 features with 26,117 instances. The approach used in the study to carry out implementation on the DDoS dataset consisted of DL algorithms, which are CNN, LSTM, dense, and GRU. The performances of the DL algorithms were evaluated using hold-out data mining technique with ratio 80 to 20 for training and testing of the DL models using metrics like accuracy, precision, recall, loss function, epoch, RMSE, and confusion matrix.

These materials and methods as implemented in the detection and prevention of DDoS attacks are discussed in ML tools and libraries below.

5.3.1   Tools and Libraries for Deep Learning

DL has been utilized successfully across some knowledgeable parts, such as processing of natural language, computer vision, processing of image, robotics, as well as speech recognition. Its success was achieved due to its ability for data training using multiple artificial neuron layers through the use of some tools and libraries like Anaconda, Jupyter Notebook, scikit-learn, Keras, TensorFlow, and so on (Pandey & Windridge, 2021). DL evolves with a complex ML tools and libraries collection due to its numerous applications in several domains, including CPSs (Acharjee, 2021).

5.3.1.1   Tools for Deep Learning

A wide variety of tools are used for implementing DL. They are open-source tools that are well oriented and can be utilized with little or no experience with self-taught programming (Sánchez-DelaCruz & Lara-Alabazares, 2020). Some of the tools used in this research are discussed below.

5.3.1.1.1   Anaconda

This is Python distribution tool that simplifies the installation process that is required by some packages like Pandas, NumPy, Keras, TensorFlow, matplotlib, scikit-learn, etc. (Ketkar & Moolayil, 2021). It also includes Jupyter Notebooks and Spyder for a development environment for Python and Conda, which is a platform package manager that is independent (Weston & Bjornson, 2016). The tool used in this study is Jupyter development environment to run the Python ML code. This tool is also used to import some libraries such as Pandas, NumPy, TensorFlow, Keras, dense, sequential, and some other ML libraries used in this study.

5.3.1.1.2   Jupyter

It is an interactive web-based development environment (Bloice & Holzinger, 2016). It is a fantastic environment for running DL experiments. Jupyter is often used in data science as well as communities of ML. A file generated by the Jupyter

Notebooks is known as a notebook, and it can be edited on the browser. It is a mixture of executing Python code with text editing that is rich in ability to annotate what is being done on the notebook (Chollet, 2018). This is a development environment used in this study to run or execute Python ML codes, to receive the output of the inputted code, and to display an error or warning if any.

5.3.1.2 Libraries for Deep Learning

DL libraries are used in order to carry out some activities and operations on given data, that is, to determine the training data, testing data, metrics, errors, and some tool use in DL. Some of the tools used in this research are discussed below.

5.3.1.2.1 Keras

It is a ML library written in Python, which operates as TensorFlow and Theano backend. To read and build complete solutions is easier due to the creation of one layer of network by each line of code (Erickson et al., 2017). It is an API for a subset of ML known as neural networks. It provides convolution as well as recurrent network support, and it can run on GPU and CPU (Veena et al., 2020). This toolkit has the selection of state-of-the-art algorithms that are the greatest, which are routines that are normalize, activation of functions, as well as optimizers (Erickson et al., 2017). This library is used in this study to activate, normalize, and optimize the dataset.

5.3.1.2.2 TensorFlow

It is a flexible, fast, as well as open-source ML library that is scalable for invention as well as research (Costa, 2020). This toolkit or library was created by Google, and it has been adopted strongly due to its high performance and provision for multiple GPUs as well as CPU supports (Erickson et al., 2017). This is a tool where dense, sequential, and epoch results are imported, as discussed in this study.

5.3.1.2.3 Scikit Learn

It is the most robust as well as powerful library for Python in ML due to its capability of providing effective tools selected for statistical as well as ML modeling. It is also a library that brings about reduction in dimensionality, classification, clustering, as well as regression through a Python interface that is consistent. It is built upon SciPy, NumPy, Pandas, Matplotlib, and so on.

5.3.1.2.4 PyLearn2

It is Python language that is capable of wrapping other libraries, for example, scikit-learn, to support dataset interface for vector, video, images, etc. It also provides trained models serialization cross-platform (Khan & Zubair, 2018). Classical ML algorithms are introduced by Pylearn2 and algorithms of deep neural networks, which is written in Python. However, this library is not a complete toolkit as others like MXNet and Keras (Erickson et al., 2017).

5.3.1.2.5 Deeplearning4j

It is a DL library that is distributed and also an open-source library that is written for Scala as well as Java. It is an integration of Spark and Hadoop. It is a library designed to be used in business environments on GPUs and CPUs that is distributed (Vinothina, 2017). It provides good performance and multiple supports for GPUs (Erickson et al., 2017).

5.4 DISCUSSION OF RESULTS

The study implemented predictive analytics system on DDoS network traffic da-tasets using four DL algorithms: CNN, LSTM, dense, and GRU. The following results were obtained.

5.4.1 DATA ANALYTIC AND VISUALIZATION

Pandas is used as a data analysis tool is this study. It is a Python-based data ana-lytics framework to analyze the dataset based on DDoS attacks and normal attacks, and the result gives 19,771 DDoS attacks and 6,346 normal attacks in the dataset. The result is comparatively represented in Figure 5.8.

From the data representation shown in Figure 5.8, the DDoS attack covers 76% of the whole dataset used in this study, whereas the normal dataset covers 24%. Furthermore, the dataset is split into the training and testing, or validation, set – 80% of training dataset and 20% of the testing dataset – and this gives 20,893 length of training dataset and 5,224 length of validation or testing dataset, as represented in Figure 5.9.

5.4.2 EVALUATION OF DEEP LEARNING ALGORITHMS

DL algorithms contain architectures that are in the hierarchy with different layers where features that are in a higher level are defined based on lower-level features (Wickramasinghe et al., 2018). DL acts as an essential tool for identifying attacks as well as inspecting packets due to increases in traffic on the network as well as time

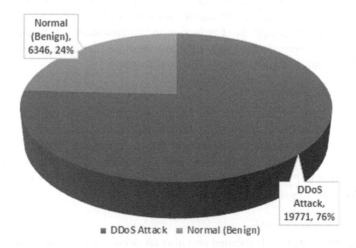

FIGURE 5.8 Dataset representation of a DDoS attack and normal attack using a pie chart.

■ Training Set ■ Testing Set

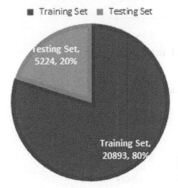

FIGURE 5.9 Training and testing dataset representation using a pie chart.

consumption and severe computation for monitoring different attack types (Kamdem & Ziazet, 2019). There are various types of DL algorithms, but the DL algorithms used are CNN, LSTM, dense, and GRU. They are implemented using the DDoS dataset to evaluate ML metrics such as loss function, accuracy, precision, recall, epoch, RMSE, and confusion matrix.

5.4.2.1 Convolutional Neural Networks (CNN)

CNN is the modification of the traditional feedforward neural network. Three main types of layers are used in building CNN architectures, which are the convolutional layer, layers that are fully connected, as well as the pooling layer (Karparthy, 2018). The ML metrics result generated using the CNN algorithm based on the training set is shown in Table 5.1. Table 5.2 shows the ML metrics result from CNN based on the testing set. Table 5.3 shows the CNN epoch result on the ML metrics based on the training set. The CNN epoch results on the testing set on the ML metrics are shown in Table 5.4.

5.4.2.2 Long Short-Term Memory (LSTM)

LSTM is used in detecting anomalies in the data that differ from the proper system behavior. It is used with data-driven models that can learn to predict present as well as future observations of the data. LSTM is very useful in learning sequences in time with changing length of dependencies that are temporal as well as an exciting

TABLE 5.1

Machine Learning Metrics Result for CNN Based on Training Set

Convolutional Neural Network	
Metrics	Result
Loss Function	0.0353
Accuracy	99.32
Precision	0.9917
Recall	0.994
RMSE	0.0805

TABLE 5.2
Machine Learning Metrics Result for CNN Based on Testing Set

Convolutional Neural Network	
Metrics	Result
Loss Function	0.0401
Accuracy	99.27
Precision	0.9910
Recall	0.9995
RMSE	0.0848

TABLE 5.3
CNN Epoch Result on Training Set Based on Machine Learning Metrics

Epoch Number	Metrics					
	Time	Loss Function	Accuracy	Precision	Recall	RMSE
1	10s	0.66039	70.57	0.7578	0.8982	0.5255
2	8s	0.5892	75.97	0.7591	1	0.4454
3	7s	0.763	76.15	0.7603	1	0.4303
4	6s	0.5498	76.09	0.7602	0.9992	0.4266
5	6s	0.5482	76.17	0.7605	1	0.4259
6	6s	0.5503	76.00	0.7592	1	0.4269
7	6s	0.5491	76.08	0.7599	1	0.4263
8	7s	0.3633	93.85	0.9419	0.9792	0.2318
9	8s	0.047	99.12	0.9903	0.9982	0.0914
10	6s	0.0402	99.33	0.9925	0.9987	0.08

TABLE 5.4
CNN Epoch Result on Testing Set Based on Machine Learning Metrics

Epoch Number	Metrics					
	Time	Loss Function	Accuracy	Precision	Recall	RMSE
1	10s	0.6169	75.81	0.758	1	0.4605
2	8s	0.04	98.39	0.9992	0.9795	0.1
3	7s	0.5488	76.42	0.7627	1	0.4258
4	6s	0.0176	99.56	0.9962	0.998	0.0598
5	6s	0.5501	76.04	0.7598	1	0.4268
6	6s	0.0176	99.6	0.9995	0.9952	0.0593
7	6s	0.5445	76.44	0.7628	1	0.424
8	7s	0.0066	99.88	0.9997	0.9987	0.0315
9	8s	0.0401	99.27	0.991	0.9995	0.0848
10	6s	0.0366	99.23	0.9905	0.9995	0.0831

general-purpose method to behavior learning of randomly compound CPSs (Eiteneuer & Niggemann, 2018). This algorithm is used in this study to generate ML metrics and epoch on the training and testing datasets. Table 5.5 shows the LSTM result of ML metrics on the training dataset, Table 5.6 shows LSTM result on the testing dataset, Table 5.7 shows the LSTM result on the training dataset for epoch, and Table 5.8 shows the LSTM result of epoch for the testing dataset.

TABLE 5.5
LSTM Machine Learning Metrics Result on Training Dataset

Long Short-Term Memory

Metrics	Result
Loss Function	0.0037
Accuracy	99.92
Precision	0.9997
Recall	0.9992
RMSE	0.026

TABLE 5.6
LSTM Machine Learning Metrics Result on Testing Set

Long Short-Term Memory

Metrics	Result
Loss Function	0.0058
Accuracy	99.92
Precision	0.9997
Recall	0.9992
RMSE	0.0278

TABLE 5.7
LSTM Epoch Result on Training Set Based on Machine Learning Metrics

Epoch Number	Metrics					
	Time	Loss Function	Accuracy	Precision	Recall	RMSE
1	73s	0.0621	98.28	0.9839	0.9936	0.1186
2	63s	0.028	99.39	99.59	0.996	0.0735
3	9s	0.5833	76.31	0.7616	1	0.4437
4	26s	0.0226	99.51	0.9965	0.997	0.066
5	7s	0.5469	76.34	0.7619	1	0.4252
6	51s	0.0098	99.78	0.9985	0.9986	0.0449
7	8s	0.5469	76.23	0.7609	1	0.4253
8	26s	0.0073	99.84	0.9987	0.9992	0.0378
9	7s	0.5453	76.36	0.7621	1	0.4245
10	26s	0.011	99.73	0.9982	0.9982	0.0477

TABLE 5.8
LSTM Epoch Result on Testing Set Based on Machine Learning Metrics

Epoch Number	Metrics					
	Time	Loss function	Accuracy	Precision	Recall	RMSE
1	73s	0.04	98.39	0.9992	0.9795	0.1
2	63s	0.6131	76.46	0.763	1	0.459
3	9s	0.0176	99.56	0.9962	0.998	0.0598
4	26s	0.5474	76.46	0.763	1	0.4254
5	7s	0.0176	99.6	0.9995	0.9952	0.0593
6	51s	0.544	76.46	0.763	1	0.4239
7	8s	0.0066	99.88	0.9997	0.9987	0.0315
8	26s	0.544	0.7646	0.763	1	0.4238
9	7s	0.0053	99.83	0.9997	0.998	0.0345
10	26s	0.5439	0.7646	0.763	1	0.4238

5.4.2.3   Dense

A dense network is one in which each node's number of links is near to the maximum number of nodes. Each node is connected to practically every other node. A completely connected network is one in which every node is directly connected to every other node. Higher connection density examples include epidemic spread, the neural network of the brain, and telecommunication networks (Sharma, 2020). Table 5.9 shows the dense result of ML metrics on the training dataset, Table 5.10 shows the dense result on the testing dataset, Table 5.11 shows the dense result on the training dataset for epoch, and Table 5.12 shows the dense result of epoch for the testing dataset.

5.4.2.4   Gated Recurrent Unit (GRU)

GRUs are a gating method in the recurrent neural networks first proposed by Cho et al., 2014 in 2014. The GRU functions similarly to a LSTM with a forget gate, but with fewer parameters because it lacks an output gate. Table 5.13

TABLE 5.9
Dense Machine Learning Metrics Result on Training Dataset

Dense Model	
Metrics	Result
Loss Function	0.6132
Accuracy	76.38
Precision	0.7621
Recall	1
RMSE	0.4594

TABLE 5.10
Dense Machine Learning Metrics
Result on Testing Set

Dense Model	
Metrics	Result
Loss Function	0.6131
Accuracy	76.45
Precision	0.763
Recall	1
RMSE	0.4593

TABLE 5.11
Dense Epoch Result on Training Set for Machine Learning Metrics

Epoch Number	Metrics					
	Time	Loss Function	Accuracy	Precision	Recall	RMSE
1	27s	0.9574	70.88	0.7604	0.8982	0.5318
2	8s	0.5892	75.97	0.7591	1	0.4454
3	8s	0.555	76.25	0.7611	1	0.4291
4	6s	0.5498	76.09	0.7602	0.9992	0.4266
5	7s	0.5458	76.32	0.7617	1	0.4248
6	6s	0.5503	76	0.7592	1	0.4269
7	8s	0.5462	76.28	0.7614	1	0.425
8	7s	0.3633	93.85	0.9419	0.9792	0.2318
9	7s	0.5454	76.34	0.7619	1	0.4246
10	6s	0.0402	99.33	0.9925	0.9987	0.08

TABLE 5.12
Dense Epoch Result on Testing Set for Machine Learning Metrics

Epoch Number	Metrics					
	Time	Loss Function	Accuracy	Precision	Recall	RMSE
1	27s	0.6131	76.46	0.763	1	0.459
2	8s	0.5665	76.44	0.7628	1	0.4346
3	8s	0.5474	76.46	0.763	1	0.4254
4	6s	0.5464	0.7636	0.7622	1	0.4247
5	7s	0.544	76.46	0.763	1	0.4239
6	6s	0.5506	76	0.7595	1	0.427
7	8s	0.544	0.7646	0.763	1	0.4238
8	7s	0.0447	99.02	0.989	0.9982	0.0941
9	7s	0.5439	0.7646	0.763	1	0.4238
10	6s	0.0366	99.23	0.9905	0.9995	0.0831

TABLE 5.13

Machine Learning Metrics Result for GRU Based on Training Set

GRU	
Metrics	Result
Loss Function	0.0353
Accuracy	99.32
Precision	0.9917
Recall	0.994
RMSE	0.0805

TABLE 5.14

Machine Learning Metrics Result for GRU Based on Testing Set

GRU	
Metrics	Result
Loss Function	0.0401
Accuracy	99.27
Precision	0.9910
Recall	0.9995
RMSE	0.0848

TABLE 5.15

Epoch Result of Training Set for GRU on Machine Learning Metrics

Epoch Number	Metrics					
	Time	Loss Function	Accuracy	Precision	Recall	RMSE
1	90s	0.5699	75.89	0.7596	0.9968	0.5518
2	81s	0.552	76.15	0.7604	1	0.4288
3	80s	0.5487	76.38	0.7622	1	0.426
4	65s	0.5481	76.34	0.7618	1	0.4258
5	66s	0.5578	76.06	0.7605	0.9977	0.4285
6	66s	0.5758	75.69	0.7576	0.9985	0.4313
7	67s	0.5569	75.67	0.7567	1	0.4299
8	65s	0.5556	75.73	0.7573	1	0.4293
9	66s	0.5578	75.54	0.7554	1	0.4305
10	66s	0.5553	75.72	0.7572	1	0.4292

shows the GRU result of ML metrics on the training dataset, Table 5.14 shows the GRU result on the testing dataset, Table 5.15 shows the GRU result on the training dataset for epoch, and Table 5.16 shows the GRU result of epoch on the testing dataset.

TABLE 5.16
Epoch Result on Testing Set for GRU on Machine Learning Metrics

Epoch Number	Metrics					
	Time	Loss Function	Accuracy	Precision	Recall	RMSE
1	90s	0.5518	75.79	0.7579	1	0.4275
2	81s	0.5455	76.4	0.7625	1	0.4245
3	80s	0.5452	76.46	0.763	1	0.4244
4	65s	0.544	76.46	0.763	1	0.439
5	66s	0.5589	75.79	0.7579	1	0.4305
6	66s	0.5543	75.79	0.7579	1	0.4287
7	67s	0.5551	75.79	0.7579	1	0.4291
8	65s	0.5546	75.79	0.7579	1	0.4288
9	66s	0.5546	75.79	0.7579	1	0.4289
10	6s	0.5534	75.79	0.7579	1	0.4283

5.4.2.5   Confusion Matrix

This is a classification metric that is made of true positive, false positive, false negative, and true negative. The confusion matrix is a table that describes the classifier or classification model performance on test data for which the values that are true are known. Yes and No are the two possible predicted classes in the confusion matrix. The confusion in this study is labeled as DDoS and normal. Table 5.17 shows the confusion matrix for the four DL algorithms used in this study. The diagrammatic representation of the confusion matrix for the CNN algorithm is shown in Figure 5.10. Figure 5.11 shows the diagrammatic representation of the confusion matrix for the LSTM algorithm. The confusion matrix diagram for the dense model is shown in Figure 5.12. Figure 5.13 shows the confusion matrix for the GRU algorithm.

5.4.3   COMPARATIVE ANALYSIS OF DEEP LEARNING ALGORITHMS

Comparative analysis was done to determine the differences in the performance of DL algorithms used in this study. Training and testing loss function, training and testing accuracy, and the confusion matrix were used for the comparative analysis

TABLE 5.17
Confusion Matrix for Deep Learning Algorithms

Algorithm	Confusion Matrix			
	True Positive	False Positive	False Negative	True Negative
CNN	1265	0	3959	0
LSTM	1265	0	1011	2948
Dense Model	1265	0	3959	0
GRU	1265	0	3959	0

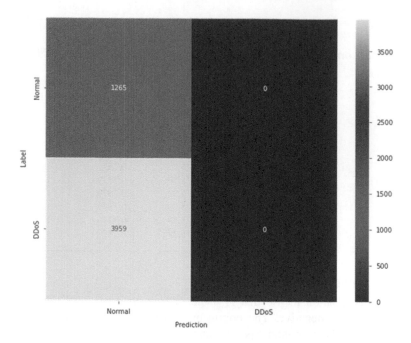

FIGURE 5.10 Confusion matrix for CNN showing true positive, true negative, false positive, and false negative.

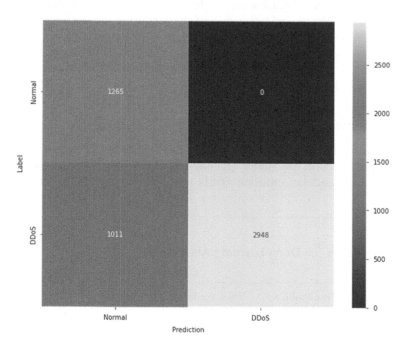

FIGURE 5.11 Confusion matrix for LSTM showing true positive, true negative, false positive, and false negative.

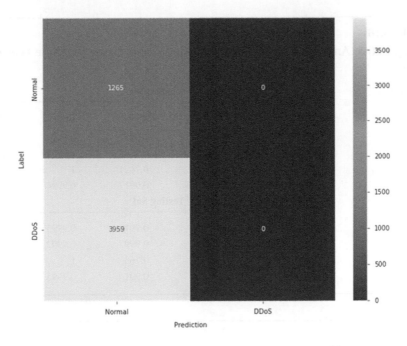

FIGURE 5.12 Confusion matrix for dense model showing true positive, true negative, false positive, and false negative.

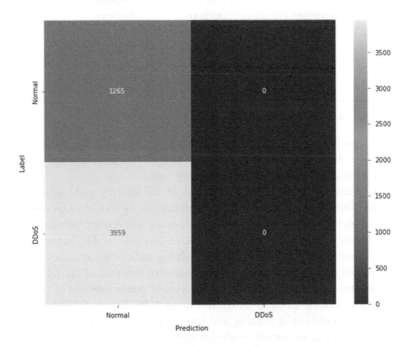

FIGURE 5.13 Confusion matrix for GRU showing true positive, true negative, false positive, and false negative.

TABLE 5.18

Comparative Analysis of Deep Learning Algorithms Using Machine Learning Metrics

Algorithms	Training Set				
	Loss Function	Accuracy	Precision	Recall	RMSE
CNN	0.0353	99.32	0.9917	0.9994	0.0805
LSTM	0.0037	99.92	0.9997	0.9992	0.026
Dense Model	0.6132	76.38	0.7621	1	0.4594
GRU	0.0353	99.32	0.9917	0.9994	0.0805
Algorithms	Testing Set				
CNN	0.0401	99.27	0.991	0.9995	0.0848
LSTM	0.0058	99.92	0.9997	0.9992	0.0278
Dense Model	0.6131	76.45	0.763	1	0.4593
GRU	0.0401	99.27	0.991	0.9995	0.0848

TABLE 5.19

Comparative Analysis Using Training and Testing Loss Function and Accuracy

Algorithm	Training Loss Function	Testing Loss Function	Training Accuracy	Testing Accuracy
CNN	0.0353	0.0401	99.32	99.27
LSTM	0.0037	0.0058	99.92	99.92
Dense Model	0.6132	0.6131	76.38	76.45
GRU	0.0353	0.0401	99.32	99.27

on the four algorithms. Table 5.18 shows the comparative analysis of the algorithms using all the metrics used in this study, such as loss function, accuracy, precision, recall, and RMSE for both training and testing sets.

Table 5.19 shows the comparative analysis of the training and testing results of the DL algorithms. It compares the four algorithms using training loss function and testing loss function in relation to training accuracy and testing accuracy.

Diagrammatic representation of comparative analysis of DL algorithms using training and testing loss function as well as training and testing accuracy is shown in Figure 5.14, and Figure 5.15 shows the comparative analysis of the DL algorithms using the confusion matrix. Comparative analysis of metrics results of both training and testing datasets for CNN is shown in Figure 5.16. Figure 5.17 shows the diagrammatic representation of training and testing results for LSTM. A comparative analysis diagram of dense model results on training and testing datasets is shown in Figure 5.18. Figure 5.19 shows the comparison metrics between training and testing datasets for the GRU DL algorithm.

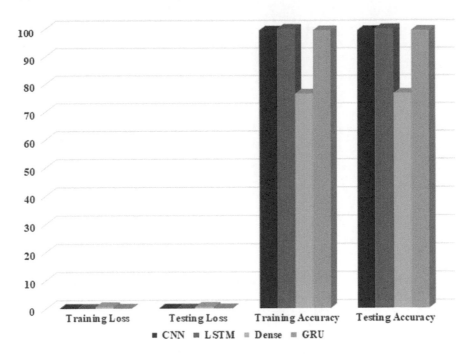

FIGURE 5.14 Comparative analysis of training loss function, testing loss function and accuracy using bar chart.

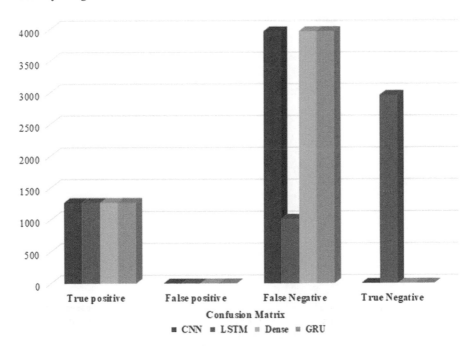

FIGURE 5.15 Comparative analysis of confusion matrix results for deep learning algorithms using bar chart.

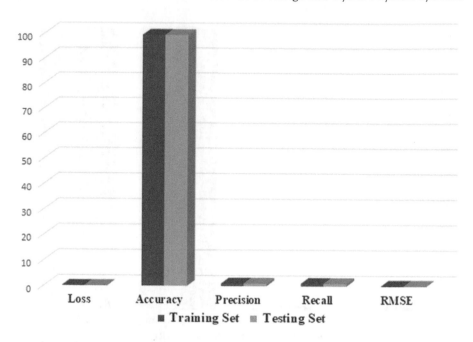

FIGURE 5.16   Comparative analysis of CNN training and testing result using bar chart.

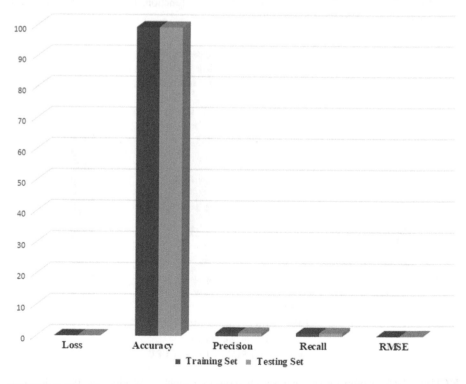

FIGURE 5.17   Comparative analysis of LSTM training and testing result using bar chart.

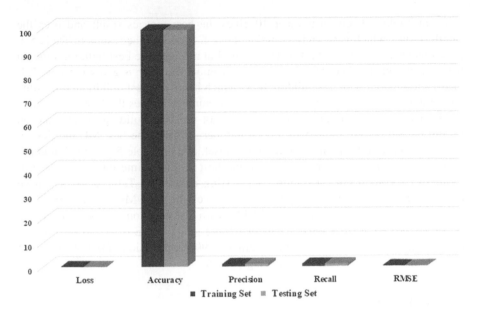

FIGURE 5.18 Comparative analysis of dense training and testing result using bar chart.

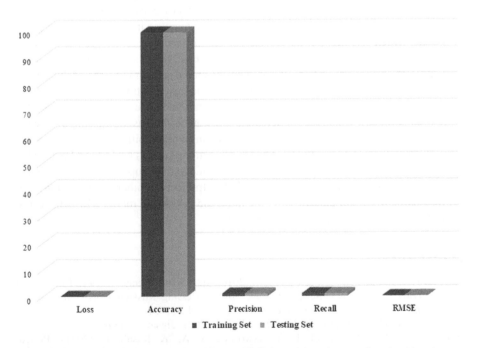

FIGURE 5.19 Comparative analysis of GRU training and testing result using bar chart.

From Table 5.3, epoch number 10 gives the best metrics result and uses the smallest time, which is 6s on the training dataset. Based on the results in Table 5.4, epoch number 8 gives the best metrics result but not with the best building time on the testing dataset. According to Table 5.7, epoch number 8 gives the best ML metrics results but with 21s building time, which is not the best building epoch time on the training dataset. From Table 5.8, epoch number 7 gives the best ML metrics results but with 8s building time, which is not the best building epoch time on testing dataset. From Table 5.11, epoch number 10 gives the best ML metrics results at the best building time on training dataset, and on Table 5.12, epoch number 10 gives the best ML metrics results at the best building time on testing dataset. From the overall result on training and testing dataset on Table 5.18, it can be discovered that the best DL algorithm that gives the best ML metrics result on training and testing dataset used was LSTM, with loss function of 0.0037, accuracy of 99.92, precision of 0.9997, recall of 0.9992, and RMSE of 0.026 on training dataset and loss function of 0.0058, accuracy of 99.92, precision of 0.9997, recall of 0.9992, and RMSE of 0.0278 on testing dataset.

5.5   CONCLUSION

CPSs are a collection of integrated physical and digital devices used in place of traditional physical systems due to their increase in productivity. They are now commonly used in industrial control systems, water systems, robotics systems, smart grids, smart homes, e-health, and many other aspects of our daily lives. Sensing attacks on CPSs became more challenging due to the increase in cyberattacks by cyber criminals, which has made it an essential topic for research. This study considered IoT-based CPSs and cybersecurity as well as the emerging technologies used in the IoT and CPS attack mitigation. It has been observed that among the technologies discussed for mitigating CPS attacks, DL offers the best solution due to its ability to extract features as well as abstract from data. DL has been useful in CPS security for correlated purposes, which are for detecting malware as well as monitoring of threats, detection of intrusion, detecting anatomy, detecting vulnerability, black-out prevention, destruction, as well as attacks. The DL algorithms such as LSTM can be used for detecting and preventing DDoS attacks on CPSs due to their superlative performance. Based on the findings from this study, LSTM outperformed other DL algorithms for the mitigation of DDoS attacks. Consequently, the developed model will help secure cyber space, particularly against DDoS attacks.

REFERENCES

Abosaq, N. H., Alandjani, G., & Pervez, S. (2016). Internet of Things Services Impact as a Driving Force on Future Technologies by Addressing Missing Dots. *International Conference on Applied Computer Science*, 2(April), 31–37.

Acharjee, S. (2021). *7 Best Deep Learning Tools in 2021*. Jigsawacademy.

Adeagbo, M. A., Akinsola, J. E. T., Awoseyi, A. A., & Kasali, F. (2021). Project Implementation Decision Using Software Development Life Cycle Models: A Comparative Approach. *Journal of Computer Science and Its Application*, 28(1). 10.4314/jcsia.v28i1.10

Akinsola, J. E. T., Adeagbo, M. A., & Awoseyi, A. A. (2019). Breast Cancer Predictive Analytics using Supervised Machine Learning Techniques. *International Journal of Advanced Trends in Computer Science and Engineering*, 8(6), 3095-3104. Available at http://www.warse.org/IJATCSE/static/pdf/file/ijatcse70862019.pdf

Akinsola, J. E. T., Adeagbo, M. A., Oladapo, K. A., Akinsehinde, S. A., & Onipede, F. O. (2022). Artificial Intelligence Emergence in Disruptive Technology. *Computational Intelligence and Data Sciences*, 63–90. CRC Press.10.1201/9781003224068-4

Akinsola, J. E. T., Akinseinde, S., Kalesanwo, O., Adeagbo, M., Kayode, O., Awoseyi, A., & Kasali, F. (2021). Application of Artificial Intelligence in User Interfaces Design for Cyber Security Threat Modeling. In R. Heimgärtner (Ed.), *Intelligent User Interfaces* (pp. 1–28). IntechOpen. 10.5772/intechopen.96534

Akinsola, J. E. T., Awodele, O., Adebayo, A. O., Onipede, F. O., & Muhammad, B. A. (2021). Netiquette of Cyberbullying and Privacy Issues. *International Journal of Information Security, Privacy and Digital Forensics*, 5(1), 22–33. https://www.researchgate.net/publication/356128450_Netiquette_of_Cyberbullying_and_Privacy_Issues#fullTextFileContent

Akinsola, J. E. T., Awodele, O., Idowu, S. A., & Kuyoro, S. O. (2020). SQL Injection Attacks Predictive Analytics Using Supervised Machine Learning Techniques. *International Journal of Computer Applications Technology and Research*, 9(4), 139–149. 10.7753/ijcatr0904.1004

Akinsola, J. E. T., Awodele, O., Kuyoro, S. O., & Kasali, F. A. (2019). Performance Evaluation of Supervised Machine Learning Algorithms Using Multi-Criteria Decision Making Techniques. *International Conference on Information Technology in Education and Development (ITED)*, 17–34. https://ir.tech-u.edu.ng/416/1/PerformanceEvaluationofSupervisedMachineLearningAlgorithmsUsingMulti-CriteriaDecisionMaking%28MCDM%29TechniquesITED.pdf

Akinsola, J. E. T., Kuyoro, A., Adeagbo, M. A., & Awoseyi, A. A. (2020). Performance Evaluation of Software using Formal Methods. *Global Journal of Computer Science and Technology: C Software & Data Engineering*, 20(1). https://computerresearch.org/index.php/computer/article/view/1930/1914

Akinsola, J. E. T., Ogunbanwo, A. S., Okesola, O. J., Odun-Ayo, I. J., Ayegbusi, F. D., & Adebiyi, A. A. (2020). Comparative Analysis of Software Development Life Cycle Models (SDLC). *Springer, 1224 AISC*, 310–322. 10.1007/978-3-030-51965-0_27

Alao, O. D., Joshua, J. V., & Akinsola, J. E. T. (2019). Human Computer Interaction (HCI) and Smart Home Applications. *IUP Journal of Information Technology*, 15(3), 7–21. https://search.proquest.com/openview/70e74bf39099ec671c013b7bf9d9258a/1?pq-origsite=gscholar&cbl=2029987

Algarsamy, A., & Soundar Kathavarayan, R. (2018). Classification with MapReduce Based Deep Belief Network (MDBN). *International Journal of Applied Engineering Research*, 13(21), 15255–15260.

Alghamdi, M. I. (2021). Digital Forensics in Cyber Security—Recent Trends, Threats, and Opportunities. In M. Sarfraz (Ed.), *Cybersecurity Threats with New Perspectives* (p. 13). IntechOpen. 10.5772/intechopen.94452

Alshdadi, A. A. (2021). Cyber-physical System with IoT-based Smart Vehicles. *Soft Computing 2021 25:18*, 25(18), 12261–12273. 10.1007/S00500-021-05908-W

Balogun, O., Hinmikaiye, J., Adegbenle, A. A., Oyebode, A. A., Akinsola, J. E. T., Nzenwata U. J., & Adegbenle A. A. (2019). An Analysis of Cybercrime Awareness Amongst First Year Students in Nigerian Private University. *Research Journal of Mathematics and Computer Science*, 3(15), 1–5. https://escipub.com/research-journal-of-mathematics-and-computer-science/

Barišić, A., Ruchkin, I., Mustafa, S., Dušan, A. M., Al-Ali, R. W., Li, L., Mkaouar, H., Eslampanah, R., Challenger, M., Blouin, D., Nikiforova, O., & CicchettiSee, A. (2022).

Multi-paradigm Modeling for Cyber–Physical Systems: A Systematic Mapping Review. *Journal of Systems and Software, 183*, 111081. 10.1016/J.JSS.2021.111081

Bansal, S. (2022). Components Of Artificial Intelligence - How It Works?https://www.analytixlabs.co.in/blog/components-of-artificial-intelligence/

Bhardwaj, A., & Kaushik, K. (2020). Predictive Analytics-Based Cybersecurity Framework for Cloud Infrastructure. *International Journal of Cloud Applications and Computing (IJCAC), 12*(1), 1–20. 10.4018/IJCAC.297106

Bloice, M. D., & Holzinger, A. (2016). A Tutorial on Machine Learning. *Researchgate, 9605*, 435–480. 10.1007/978-3-319-50478-0

Chechile, I. (2021). Simulating Cyber-Physical Systems. *NewSpace Systems Engineering*, 225–261. 10.1007/978-3-030-66898-3_6

Chen, T. (2010). Stuxnet, the Real Start of Cyber Warfare? *IEEE Network, 24*(6), 2–3. 10.1109/MNET.2010.5634434

Cho, K., Merri"enboer, B. van, Bahdanau, D., & Bengio, Y. (2014). On the Properties of Neural Machine Translation: Encoder–Decoder Approaches. *Encyclopedia of Human-Computer Interaction*, 1–16. http://www.interaction-design.org/encyclopedia/cscw_computer_supported_cooperative_work.html

Chollet, F. (2018). *Deep Learning with Python*. MANNING.

CISA. (2020). *Understanding Digital Signatures | CISA*.

Costa, C. D. (2020). *Best Python Libraries for Machine Learning and Deep Learning by Claire D*. Towards Data Science.

CopeLand, B. J.(2022). Definition, Examples, Types, Applications, Companies, & Facts. https://www.britannica.com/technology/artificial-intelligence

Dhar Dwivedi, A., Singh, R., Kaushik, K., Rao Mukkamala, R., & Alnumay, W. S. (2021). Blockchain and Artificial Intelligence for 5G-enabled Internet of Things: Challenges, Opportunities, and Solutions. *Transactions on Emerging Telecommunications Technologies, January*, 1–19. 10.1002/ett.4329

Ding, Y., Chen, S., & Xu, J. (2016). Application of Deep Belief Networks for Opcode Based Malware Detection. *Proceedings of the International Joint Conference on Neural Networks, 7*(29), 3901–3908. 10.1109/IJCNN.2016.7727705

Doghri, W., Saddoud, A., & Chaari Fourati, L. (2021). Cyber-physical Systems for Structural Health Monitoring: Sensing Technologies and Intelligent Computing. *The Journal of Supercomputing, 78*(1), 766–809. 10.1007/S11227-021-03875-5

Durairaj, D., Venkatasamy, T. K., Mehbodniya, A., Umar, S., & Alam, T. (2022). Intrusion Detection and Mitigation of Attacks in Microgrid Using Enhanced Deep Belief Network. *Taylor & Francis*. 10.1080/15567036.2021.2023237

Eiteneuer, B., & Niggemann, O. (2018). LSTM for Model-Based Anomaly Detection in Cyber-Physical Systems. *CEUR Workshop Proceedings, 2289*, 1–8. 10.5281/zenodo.1409642

Elsaeidy, A., Munasinghe, K. S., Sharma, D., & Jamalipour, A. (2019). Intrusion Detection in Smart Cities Using Restricted Boltzmann Machines. *Journal of Network and Computer Applications, 135*, 76–83. 10.1016/j.jnca.2019.02.026

Erickson, B. J., Korfiatis, P., Akkus, Z., Kline, T., & Philbrick, K. (2017). Toolkits and Libraries for Deep Learning. In *Springer*. Journal of Digital Imaging. 10.1007/s10278-017-9965-6

F.Y, O., J.E.T, A., O, A., J. O, H., O, O., & J, A. (2017). Supervised Machine Learning Algorithms: Classification and Comparison. *International Journal of Computer Trends and Technology, 48*(3), 128–138. 10.14445/22312803/ijctt-v48p126

Fischer, A., & Igel, C. (2012). An Introduction to Restricted Boltzmann Machines. *Lecture Notes in Computer Science (Including Subseries Lecture Notes in Artificial Intelligence and Lecture Notes in Bioinformatics), 7441 LNCS*, 14–36. 10.1007/978-3-642-332 75-3_2

Gao, R., & Yang, G. H. (2022). Distributed Multi-Rate Sampled-Data H∞ Consensus Filtering for Cyber-Physical Systems Under Denial-Of-Service Attacks. *Information Sciences*, *587*, 607–625. 10.1016/J.INS.2021.12.046

Griffioen, P., Weerakkody, S., & Sinopoli, B. (2021). A Moving Target Defense for Securing Cyber-Physical Systems. *IEEE Transactions on Automatic Control*, *66*(5), 2016–2031. 10.1109/TAC.2020.3005686

Gümüşbaş, D., Yıldırım, T., Genovese, A., & Scotti, F. (2021). A Comprehensive Survey of Databases and Deep Learning Methods for Cybersecurity and Intrusion Detection Systems. *IEEE Systems Journal*, *15*(2), 1717–1731. 10.1109/JSYST.2020.2992966

Hassan, M. U., Rehmani, M. H., & Chen, J. (2018). Differential Privacy Techniques for Cyber Physical Systems: A Survey. *IEEE Communications Surveys and Tutorials*, *22*(1), 746–789. 10.1109/COMST.2019.2944748

Hinduja, A., & Pandey, M. (2020). Reducing Ping-Pong Effect in Heterogeneous Wireless Networks Using Machine Learning. In *Advances in Intelligent Systems and Computing* (Vol. 989). Springer Nature, Switzerland AG. 10.1007/978-981-13-8618-3_71

Hinmikaiye, J. O., Awodele, O., & Akinsola, J. E. T. (2021). Disruptive Technology and Regulatory Response: The Nigerian Perspective. *Computer Engineering and Intelligent Systems*, *12*(1), 42–47. 10.7176/ceis/12-1-06

Hranisavljevic, N., Maier, A., & Niggemann, O. (2020). Discretization of Hybrid CPPS Data into Timed Automaton Using Restricted Boltzmann Machines. *Engineering Applications of Artificial Intelligence*, *95*, 103826. 10.1016/J.ENGAPPAI.2020.103826

Idowu, S. A., Awodele, O., Kuyoro, S. O., & Akinsola, J. E. T. (2020). Taxonomy and Characterization of Structured Query Language Injection Attacks for Predictive Analytics. *International Journal of Software & Hardware Research in Engineering (IJournals)*, *8*(3), 15–25. https://www.academia.edu/download/65420840/IJSHRE_8306_Taxonomy_and_Characterization_of_SQLIA_Idowu_Sunday_A.1_Awodele_Oludele2_Kuyoro_Shade_O.3.pdf

Janiesch, C., Zschech, P., & Heinrich, K. (2021). Machine learning and deep learning *Electronic Markets*, 31, 685-695. 10.1007/s12525-021-00475-2/Published

Kamdem, G., & Ziazet, J. (2019). Convolutional Neural Network for Intrusion Detection System In Cyber Physical Systems. *Researchgate*, May.

Karparthy. (2018). Convolutional Neural Networks. In *stanford.edu*.

Kaushik, K., & Dahiya, S. (2018). Security and Privacy in iot Based e-business and Retail. *Proceedings of the 2018 International Conference on System Modeling and Advancement in Research Trends, SMART 2018*, 78–81. 10.1109/SYSMART.2018.8746961

Kaushik, K., Dahiya, S., & Sharma, R. (2021). Internet of Things Advancements in Healthcare. In *Internet of Things* (1st Edition, pp. 19–32). Taylor & Francis, CRC Press. 10.1201/9781003140443-2

Kaushik, K., & Singh, K. (2020). Security and Trust in IoT Communications: Role and Impact. In S. Choudhury , R. Mishra , R. G. Mishra , & A. Kumar (Eds.), *Advances in Intelligent Systems and Computing* (Vol. 989). Springer, Singapore. 10.1007/978-981-13-8618-3_81

Ketkar, N., & Moolayil, J. (2021). *Deep Learning with Python: Learn Best Practices of Deep Learning Models with PyTorch*, (2nd Edition).

Khan, A., & Zubair, S. (2018). Machine Learning Tools and Toolkits in the Exploration of Big Data. *International Journal of Computer Sciences and Engineering*, *6*(12), 570–575. 10.26438/ijcse/v6i12.570575

Khan, H. A., Sehatbakhsh, N., Nguyen, L. N., Prvulovic, M., & Zajić, A. (2020). Malware Detection in Embedded Systems Using Neural Network Model for Electromagnetic Side-Channel Signals. *Journal of Hardware and Systems Security*, *3*(4), 1–14. 10.1007/s41635-019-00074-w

Koren, I., & Krishna, C. M. (2021). Cyber-Physical Systems. *Fault-Tolerant Systems*, 237–262. 10.1016/B978-0-12-818105-8.00017-6

Kuyoro, S. O., Akinsola, J. E. T., Fatade, O. B., & Akinjobi, J. (2017). Mitigating Denial of Service (DOS) Attacks In Wireless Networks Using Honeypot. *1st Information Security Conference*, 112–134. 10.1109/ICTC.2014.6983147

Latif, S. A., Wen, F. B. X., Iwendi, C., Wang, L., Li, F., Mohsin, S. M., Han, Z., & Band, S. S. (2022). AI-empowered, Blockchain and SDN Integrated Security Architecture for IoT Network of Cyber Physical Systems. *Computer Communications*, *181*(August 2021), 274–283. 10.1016/j.comcom.2021.09.029

Lee, D., Lim, M., Park, H., Kang, Y., Park, J. S., Jang, G. J., & Kim, J. H. (2017). Long Short-Term Memory Recurrent Neural Network-Based Acoustic Model Using Connectionist Temporal Classification on a Large-Scale Training Corpus. *China Communications*, *14*(9), 23–31. 10.1109/CC.2017.8068761

Lee, E. A., & Seshia, S. A. (2017). Introduction to Embedded Systems. A Cyber-Physical Systems Approach. In *Studies in Systems, Decision and Control: Vol. Version 2*. (2nd Edition). MIT Press.

Lee Robert M., Assante, M. J., & Conway, T. (2016). Analysis of the Cyber Attack on the Ukrainian Power Grid. *Electricity Information Sharing and Analysis Center (E-ISAC)*, *2*, 1–26.

Lv, Z., Chen, D., Lou, R., & Alazab, A. (2021). Artificial Intelligence for Securing Industrial-Based Cyber–Physical Systems. *Future Generation Computer Systems*, *117*, 291–298. 10.1016/j.future.2020.12.001

Mitra, S. (2021). Verifying Cyber-Physical Systems: A Path to Safe Autonomy. In *Cyber Physical Systems Series* (p. 296).

Moghanian, S., Saravi, F. B., Javidi, G., & Sheybani, E. O. (2020). GOAMLP: Network Intrusion Detection With Multilayer Perceptron and Grasshopper Optimization Algorithm. *IEEE Access*, *8*, 215202–215213.

Mohamed, N., Al-Jaroodi, J., & Jawhar, I. (2020). Cyber-Physical Systems Forensics. *Systems Security Symposium, SSS 2020 - Conference Proceedings*. 10.1109/SSS47320.2020.9174199

Mohan, A., Singh, A. K., Kumar, B., & Dwivedi, R. (2021). Review on Remote Sensing Methods for Landslide Detection using Machine and Deep Learning. *Transactions on Emerging Telecommunications Technologies*, *32*(7), 1–23. 10.1002/ett.3998

Osisanwo, F. Y., Akinsola, J.E.T., Awodele, O, Hinmikaiye, J.O., Olakanmi, O., & Akinjobi, J. (2017). Supervised Machine Learning Algorithms: Classification and Comparison. *International Journal of Computer Trends and Technology*, 48, 128–13810.14445/22312803/ijctt-v48p126.

Padmajothi, V., & Iqbal, J. L. M. (2022). Review of Machine Learning and Deep Learning Mechanism in Cyber-Physical System. *IJNAA*, *13*(1), 583–590.

Pandey, H. M., & Windridge, D. (2021). A Comprehensive Classification of Deep Learning Libraries. In *International Congress on Information and Communication Technology*, ISBN 9789811311642. ISSN 2194-5357.

Paredes, C. M., Martínez-castro, D., Ibarra-junquera, V., & González-potes, A. (2021). Detection and Isolation of DoS and Integrity Cyber Attacks in Cyber-Physical Systems with a Neural Network-Based Architecture. *MDPI*, *10*, 1–28.

Pivoto, D. G. S., de Almeida, L. F. F., da Rosa Righi, R., Rodrigues, J. J. P. C., Lugli, A. B., & Alberti, A. M. (2021). Cyber-Physical Systems Architectures for Industrial Internet of Things Applications in Industry 4.0: A Literature Review. *Journal of Manufacturing Systems*, *58*(PA), 176–192. 10.1016/j.jmsy.2020.11.017

Pradeep, S., & Sharma, Y. K. (2020). Study and Analysis of Modified Mean Shift Method and Kalman Filter for Moving Object Detection and Tracking. In K. S. Raju, A. Govardhan, B. P. Rani, R. Sridevi, & M. R. Murty (Eds.), *Advances in Intelligent*

Systems and Computing (Vol. 1090). Springer Nature, Switzerland AG. 10.1007/978-981-15-1480-7_76

Rho, S., Vasilakos, A. V., & Chen, W. (2016). Cyber physical systems technologies and applications. *Future Generation Computer Systems*, 56, 436–437 10.1016/j.future.2015.10.019.

Radanliev, P., De Roure, D., Nicolescu, R., Huth, M., & Santos, O. (2021). Artificial Intelligence and the Internet of Things in Industry 4.0. *CCF Transactions on Pervasive Computing and Interaction*, 3(3), 329–338. 10.1007/s42486-021-00057-3

Ruthvik, R. M. (2021). *What is a Cyber Physical System? – DEV Community.* https://dev.to/ruthvikraja_mv/what-is-a-cyber-physical-system-4e0j

Sánchez-DelaCruz, E., & Lara-Alabazares, D. (2020). Deep Learning: Concepts and Implementation Tools. *CEUR Workshop Proceedings*, 2585, 142–149.

Sarker, I. H. (2021). Deep Learning: A Comprehensive Overview on Techniques, Taxonomy, Applications and Research Directions. *SN Computer Science*, 2(6), 1–20. 10.1007/s42979-021-00815-1

Sedjelmaci, H., Guenab, F., Senouci, S. M., Moustafa, H., Liu, J., & Han, S. (2020). Cyber Security Based on Artificial Intelligence for Cyber-Physical Systems. *IEEE Network*, 34(3), 6–7. 10.1109/MNET.2020.9105926

Shalev-Shwartz, S., & Ben-David, S. (2014). Understanding Machine Learning: From Theory to Algorithms. In *Understanding Machine Learning: From Theory to Algorithms*. Cambridge University Press. 10.1017/CBO9781107298019

Sharma, P. (2020). *Keras Dense Layer Explained for Beginners – MLK – Machine Learning Knowledge.* https://machinelearningknowledge.ai/keras-dense-layer-explained-for-beginners/

Sharon, S. (2021). *What is IoT Security?* Security.(internet of things security). https://www.techtarget.com/iotag

Shen, W., Liu, L., Cao, X., Hao, Y., & Cheng, Y. (2013). Cooperative Message Authentication in Vehicular Cyber-Physical Systems. *IEEE Transactions on Emerging Topics in Computing*, 1(1), 84–97. 10.1109/TETC.2013.2273221

Simplilearn. (2022). *What Is Data Encryption: Algorithms, Methods and Techniques [2022 Edition]| Simplilearn.* Cyber Security.

Singh, K., Kaushik, K., Ahatsham, & Shahare, V. (2020). Role and Impact of Wearables in IoT Healthcare. *Advances in Intelligent Systems and Computing*, 1090, 735–742. 10.1007/978-981-15-1480-7_67

Slay, J., & Miller, M. (2008). Lessons Learned from the Maroochy Water Breach. In E. G. and S. Shenoi (Ed.), *Critical Infrastructure Protection* (Vol. 253, Issue March 2007, pp. 73–82). 10.1007/978-0-387-75462-8_6

Sood, A. (2020). *Long Short-Term Memory.* https://pages.cs.wisc.edu/~shavlik/cs638/lectureNotes/Long%20Short-Term%20Memory%20Networks.pdf

Taha, W., Taha, A.-E. M., & Thunberg, J. (2020). What is a Cyber-Physical System? In *Cyber-Physical Systems: A Model-Based Approach* (pp. 3–18). Springer, Cham. 10.1007/978-3-030-36071-9_1

Tognetto, D., Giglio, R., Vinciguerra, A. L., Milan, S., Rejdak, R., Rejdak, M., Zaluska-Ogryzek, K., Zweifel, S., & Toro, M. D. (2022). Artificial intelligence applications and cataract management: A systematic review. *Survey of Ophthalmology*, 67, 817–829 10.1016/j.survophthal.2021.09.004.

Tyagi, N. (2020). *6 Major Branches of Artificial Intelligence (AI) | Analytics Steps.* Analytics Steps.

Veena, D. S., Shankari, T., Sowmiya, S., & Varsha, M. (2020). A Survey on Tools Used for Machine Learning. *International Journal of Engineering Applied Sciences and Technology*, 4(9), 116–119. 10.33564/ijeast.2020.v04i09.012

Vegh, L., & Miclea, L. (2015). Improving the Security of a Cyber-Physical System using Cryptography, Steganography and Digital Signatures. *International Journal of Computer and Information Technology*, *4*(2), 427–434.

Vinogradov, G., Prokhorov, A., & Shepelev, G. (2021). Patterns in Cyber-Physical Systems. *Studies in Systems, Decision and Control*, *342*, 3–16. 10.1007/978-3-030-66081-9_1

Vinothina, V. (2017). Machine Learning Tools – an Overview. *International Journal of Advanced Research in Science and Engineering*, *6*(2), 169–177.

Vyas, S., & Bhargava, D. (2021). Cyber-physical Systems for Healthcare. *Smart Health Systems*, 71–86. 10.1007/978-981-16-4201-2_7

Weston, S., & Bjornson, R. (2016). *Introduction to Anaconda*. Yale Center for Research Computing.

Wickramasinghe, C. S., Marino, D. L., Amarasinghe, K., & Manic, M. (2018). Generalization of Deep Learning For Cyber-Physical System Security: A Survey. *Proceedings: IECON 2018 - 44th Annual Conference of the IEEE Industrial Electronics Society, October*, 745–751. 10.1109/IECON.2018.8591773

Xu, L. D. (2013). Introduction: Systems Science in Industrial Sectors. *Systems Research and Behavioral Science*, 30, 211–21310.1002/sres.2186.

Yang, Z., Jin, C., Tian, Y., Lai, J., & Zhou, J. (2020). LiS: Lightweight Signature Schemes for Continuous Message Authentication in Cyber-Physical Systems. *Proceedings of the 15th ACM Asia Conference on Computer and Communications Security, ASIA CCS 2020*, 719–731. 10.1145/3320269.3372195

Zhang, C., & Lu, Y. (2021). Study on Artificial Intelligence: The State of the Art and Future Prospects. *Journal of Industrial Information Integration*, 23, 10022410.1016/j.jii.2021.100224.

Zargar, S. A. (2021). Introduction to Convolutional Neural Networks. In *Researchgate*. 10.1007/978-1-4842-5648-0

6 Managing Trust in IoT Using Permissioned Blockchain

Rajesh Kumar and Rewa Sharma
Department of Computer Engineering, J.C Bose University
of Science and Technology, YMCA, Faridabad, Haryana,
India

CONTENTS

DOI: 10.1201/9781003283003-6

6.1 INTRODUCTION

The Internet of Things (IoT) is a system that connects all the things or places in the world to the Internet. These things can be any computing device that can perform some action based on data received from the outside world. Kavin Ashton, the founder and executive director of Auto-ID Center, first coined the term "Internet of Things" in 1999. Because of its features that can directly or indirectly influence human existence in a positive way, IoT grew in popularity quickly. However, managing trust among IoT devices is a very complicated operation due to their functioning mechanisms and features such as their resource-constrained nature, being placed at different and remote locations, the vast scale of the number of devices, and heterogeneous protocols adopted by the devices. It leads to people having concerns about the privacy and integrity of their data, making trust management in IoT systems more important (Frustaci et al. 2018). Trust management identifies malicious nodes based on their reputation, calculated by different techniques, and maintains only trusted nodes or devices in the communication process. Researchers proposed many trust management approaches using conventional methods such as machine learning and mathematical calculations based on the behavior of nodes during the communication process (Ud Din et al. 2019). However, trust-related information propagates through the same network (Internet), which makes it vulnerable to many attacks. These attacks can alter traveling information, and the false reputation of nodes can be provided. Additionally, some other attacks are specially developed for manipulating trust information by misguiding algorithms of trust management.

Furthermore, blockchain technologies such as Bitcoin, Ethereum, Hyperledger, and others have shown their security qualities in a variety of fields outside of cryptocurrencies, attracting a large number of research communities. Moreover, advancements in this technology, such as smart contracts, have widened its application area. Smart contracts add a programmability feature that provides more control over data processing in it. Initially, blockchain was public in nature, which limits its use in some real-world scenarios, where mutual privacy and control over the communication process are more important. Furthermore, the public blockchain has a slow transaction rate, which is incompatible with the need for a quick response system. Lack of adaptability and more energy consumption due to the consensus process are two more major problems of public blockchain. However, the development of private blockchain, which is often referred to as "permissioned" blockchain can address these problems. Unlike public blockchain, where anyone can download the software, form a node, view the ledger, and interact with the blockchain, private blockchain is often run and operated by a trusted intermediary. This type of blockchain system can increase trust among different nodes of the IoT system. Hyperledger Fabric, a popular private blockchain, is primarily targeted for industrial applications and has improved since its initial release (Androulaki et al. 2018).

Maintaining security and trust requires the transformation of safe and original information, which necessitates consideration of some important criteria. It mainly includes authentication, access control, heterogeneity, integrity, and privacy. So, this chapter describes how we can leverage features of private blockchain, such as Hyperledger Fabric, to address these parameters and maintain trust in the IoT environment. The remaining sections of this chapter are as follows: Section 6.2 introduces trust management in the IoT followed by possible security issues and attacks on it. Section 6.3 explains blockchain terminology with its different types and protocols used. This section also highlights some important applications of blockchain. Section 6.4 provides the theoretical background of Hyperledger Fabric, including its architecture and working mechanisms. Section 6.5 provides the main issues and important strategies in integrating blockchain and the IoT. Finally, section 6.6 describes trust management issues and their possible solutions by private blockchain, such as Hyperledger Fabric.

6.2 TRUST MANAGEMENT IN THE IoT: INTRODUCTION AND SECURITY ATTACKS

Unlike other traditional networking environments, the IoT faces new challenges due to its unique characteristics. Apart from privacy and security, trust is the most important of these characteristics. It is difficult for users to accept aggregated information from diverse smart devices if it is harmful and not adequately trustworthy, even if the application and network layers' trust are fully given. The most pressing challenge is how IoT-generated data are transformed into valuable information to enable secure and trusted communication (Ud Din et al. 2019). Consequently, the concept of trust management in the IoT comes to the attention of researchers. The process of removing identified malicious nodes from the communication of the IoT system is called trust management.

Researchers (Manda and Nalini 2019) define three types of trust: The first is "behavior-based trust," defined by nodes' behavior during the communication process. The second type of trust is "computation-based trust," calculated among computational smart devices, and the last and third type of trust is "technology-based trust," calculated and maintained by technology based on evaluating the value of device trust. Additionally, some other researchers (Fortino et al. 2020) divided trust into four parts: The first is "Behaviour Trust," in which the predicted behavior of devices is considered trustworthy, even if it is not constant. The second is "Reputation," where collected information from other nodes of the system is considered as a node's reputation. This collected information is generally based on previous behavior and the present reputation of nodes in a particular environment and period. The third factor is "Honesty," which has a significant role in determining trustworthiness. Decent models do not suggest expecting that nodes will be honest if they are not evaluated. If the information obtained from nodes is similar as predicted in a particular environment and period of time, the recommender is regarded as an honest node. A clever technique is required to find out honest nodes in order to design a good trust management architecture. The last is "Accuracy," wherein a trustworthiness threshold is used as a metric of recommender accuracy. It is considered accurate if the provided and real information fall within a certain range. Information is more dependable over the network if it is accurate. Depending on the requirements, trust management systems with a variety of algorithms and characteristics can be deployed at various points in IoT networks. This heterogeneity of IoT networks makes it difficult to manage trust. Furthermore, because of their limited resources, nodes can or cannot be supportive of this arrangement. As a result, despite many security solutions and standards, trust management systems are vulnerable to a variety of attacks. Some of the important trust-related security attacks are discussed in the next subsection.

6.2.1 TRUST-RELATED SECURITY ATTACKS

Transforma Insights estimates that by 2030, there will be 24.1 billion active IoT devices. The IoT system of these devices has applicability almost everywhere in the world. Despite the numerous solutions available, managing security and trust in applications such as industries and e-businesses is not an easy task (Kaushik and Dahiya 2018). Trust-related attacks should also be examined to better understand trust-related concerns and challenges (Djedjig et al. 2018). Surely, it will help in understanding security and trust-related issues. Some trust-related attacks on the IoT can be seen in Figure 6.1 that are categorized by their biased recommendations, inconsistent behavior, and attacks on the identity of nodes.

6.2.1.1 "Self-Promotion Attacks"

When a malevolent node manipulates its reputation or trust score by making positive suggestions, this is called a "self-promotion attack". It's commonly done with trust management systems that calculate trust via a positive feedback mechanism.

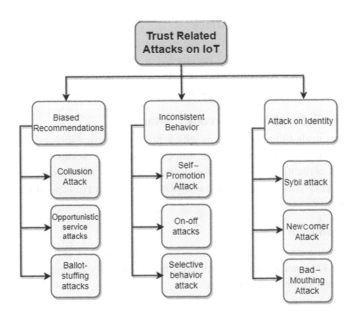

FIGURE 6.1 Security attacks on trust management in the IoT (Modified from (Ahmed et al. 2019)).

Systems with weak or no integrity and authentication mechanisms are more susceptible to this type of attack.

6.2.1.2 "Bad-Mouthing Attacks"

By providing incorrect recommendations for another reputable and trusted node, any malevolent node might influence its reputation. This attack acts opposite of the self-promotion attack.

6.2.1.3 "Ballot-Stuffing Attacks"

Multiple malicious nodes cooperate with each other to trigger this attack. A malicious node provides positive suggestions to another malicious node to make its reputation positive.

6.2.1.4 "Opportunistic Service Attacks"

In this attack, a malicious node provides good services to make its reputation positive and tends to be a trusted node. Later, this node takes advantage of its high reputation for malicious activities.

6.2.1.5 "On-Off Attacks"

Malicious nodes alternate between providing good and bad services in this attack. They want to maintain a good reputation, so they can influence the network by giving good recommendations to malevolent nodes and poor recommendations to trusted nodes. These attacks are not easy to detect.

6.2.1.6 "Selective Behavior Attack"

A malicious node behaves well from the perspective of most of its neighbors, but terribly from the perspective of the remainder of the nodes. As a result, the average recommendation value will stay positive, although some nodes can be harmed. This type of attack is very hard to detect due to its dynamic behavior.

6.2.1.7 "Sybil Attack and Newcomer Attack"

Any malicious node in an IoT system with a poor authentication and access control mechanism can construct, imitate, or impersonate other nodes of the system by changing their reputation values. Using these techniques, these malicious nodes can promote themselves as a trusted node and mask their negative reputation by creating a new identity.

6.2.1.8 "Collusion Attack"

In this scenario, a group of malevolent actors collaborates in order to carry out the illegally biased recommendation. Malicious nodes not only increase their trust value but also decrease others' reputations.

6.3 BLOCKCHAIN TECHNOLOGY AND ITS APPLICATIONS

In 1991, Stuart Haber and W Scott Stornetta introduced the concept of blockchain technology. Later, developer(s) working under the project pseudonym "Satoshi

Nakamoto" successfully implemented the first blockchain network application called Bitcoin. Transactions in this project are made using Bitcoin, which is an electronic currency. To keep track of transactions, a public ledger, subsequently called block-chain, was used. Blockchain keeps every record in continuous blocks, which are chained together using a cryptographic hash. These blocks are interconnected, and all information is dispersed among them. Although blockchain was created to support Bitcoin money transactions, it has many other uses also. In 2014, researchers examined blockchain and discovered that it can protect a variety of other financial applications, including inter-party contracts, IoT applications, banking transactions, etc. Apart from financial uses, blockchain systems like Ethereum and Hyperledger can be used to safeguard crucial information like digital criminal evidence (Kaushik, Dahiya, and Sharma 2022) and educational mark sheets and other documents. Since Bitcoin was the first digital currency, it made a significant contribution to the study of blockchain. In Bitcoin, transactions could be carried out without the involvement of a central authority due to the existence of the distributed ledger. Bitcoin, the largest and original blockchain application, is still operating and processing its transactions successfully. Some other advanced blockchain technology-based projects, such as Ethereum and Ripple, are currently operational and generating revenue.

6.3.1 TYPES OF BLOCKCHAIN

Different researchers have identified that blockchain can be divided into four types based on current requirements and accessibility of information ("What Are The Different Types of Blockchain Technology? l 101 Blockchains" 2021). These types of blockchain are defined below:

6.3.1.1 "Public Blockchain"

This type of blockchain is permissionless and distributed in nature, where anyone is allowed to join, mine, and send transactions to the blockchain. Every entity in the system has equal rights to access blockchain data, functionalities, and features. Bitcoin and Ethereum are two popular examples of public blockchain.

6.3.1.2 "Private Blockchain"

This is the permissioned blockchain that is controlled by some of its entities. The controlling authority determines who can join the blockchain and which service is allowed to which node. Not every node needs to be given equal rights to perform functionalities on the blockchain. Examples of private blockchains include Hyperledger Fabric and Corda. Its applications include supply chain management systems, asset ownership management, etc.

6.3.1.3 "Consortium Blockchain"

This type of blockchain is controlled or administered by a consortium of nodes in the network. Instead of a single administrator like in private blockchain, all forms of blockchain controls are distributed across a group. This form of blockchain is especially useful for firms that require collective work.

6.3.1.4 "Hybrid Blockchain"

This type of blockchain combines the main features of public blockchain and private blockchains, such as access control and transparency. It allows organizations to maintain the information private or public as per their requirements. IBM Food Trust is an example of a hybrid blockchain, which was created to improve efficiency across the whole food supply chain. A popular example is IBM Food Trust, where a complete supply chain is based on hybrid blockchain.

6.3.2 "BLOCKCHAIN BASIC STRUCTURE AND PROTOCOLS"

The basic structure of blockchain consists of a chain of blocks that has mainly two sections. First is the "header" that holds information about the previous block hash and a unique number called "nonce," which is used for the mining process. The second section holds all transactions record. The hash value contained by every block is the combined hash of the previous block and current block.

If an attacker tries to change even a single bit of the hash value of any block, all the hash values of the following blocks will also be changed till the last block. So, for changing hashes of all blocks, attacks have to change and recalculate it, which is nearly impossible as of now. This mechanism makes blockchain completely immutable. Some related protocols and techniques of blockchain are described in detail below (Jesus et al. 2018).

6.3.2.1 Block Identity

The important metadata that identify and locates the block include block height and header hash. Block height indicates the position of blocks in the blockchain by a numeric value, and header hash is defined as the hash value of the block. (Figure 6.2).

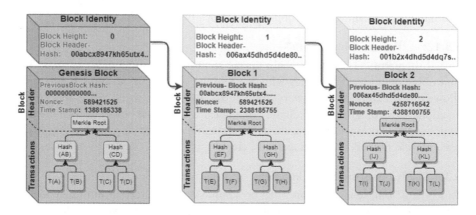

FIGURE 6.2 Structure of blocks in the blockchain (Modified from (Kumar and Sharma 2021)).

6.3.2.2 Block Header

The header of a block in blockchain mainly contains the hash of the immediate last block, nonce, root of Merkle tree, and difficulty. The preceding block's hash linked the current block to the prior one. This technique is found in every block and creates a chain of blocks.

6.3.2.3 Merkle Tree

In 1979, Ralph Merkle patented the name "Merkle tree". This data structure has the same qualities as a binary tree, such as having two children nodes and having the same level of all leaf nodes. The Merkle tree is used to summarize all transactions of blockchain. It composes the hashes of all other nodes. Every parent node in the Merkle tree holds the combined hash of its child node hashes. This process continues until every child node and all transactions of blockchain can be traversed using this data structure. Blockchain systems like Bitcoin and Ethereum use the Merkle tree for their operations.

6.3.2.4 Nonce

It is a variable number used by blockchain miners for meeting difficulty-level restrictions. This number is changed continuously by miners to achieve the desired hash value of the block. For instance, if the difficulty is set to four zeros for the first four digits of the hash, then nonce is changed continuously by miners until the given criterion is satisfied. This process of finding required partial hash collisions is known as the difficulty level of mining.

6.3.2.5 Mining

This process verifies the valid block and adds it to the blockchain. Miners, which are some special nodes developed for the mining process, are responsible and get awarded for this process. This mechanism eliminates the need for a central authority. Miners validate new blocks before adding them to the blockchain using their computation power and special resources. After having some special software and resources, anyone can become a mining node and can communicate with other miners.

6.3.2.6 Consensus

This process maintains a common agreement among nodes of blockchain about the present state of its distributed ledger data (Chen et al. 2011). It ensures any inconsistencies or errors in the data contained by block ledgers. "Proof of Work (PoW)," "Proof of Stake (PoS)," "Practical Byzantine Fault Tolerance (PBFT)," and "Round Robin (RR)" are some important consensus algorithms used by different blockchain networks.

6.3.2.7 Smart Contracts

These are the pieces of software that act as transaction protocols and make blockchain systems programmable. In 2015, Mr. Vitalik Buterin first introduced a programmable blockchain named Ethereum. "Smart Contract" is the main additional feature in Ethereum with basic blockchain features. Some other programmable blockchain examples are Hyperledger, Corda, etc. These technologies use Smart Contracts for the automation of events while maintaining predefined agreements. At first, Smart Contracts were designed in Solidity programming language, but later other popular programming languages such as Go, Python, Java, etc. were also included.

6.3.3 BLOCKCHAIN APPLICATIONS OF IoT

Despite the fact that blockchain technology began with Bitcoin, it already has far-reaching applications outside of the cryptocurrency. Most of the security and trust-related challenges of the IoT can be tackled by blockchain features such as decentralization and encryption of information. Some important IoT-related applications are described below:

6.3.3.1 IoT-based Healthcare Systems

The IoT is widely used in healthcare systems for monitoring sensitive information of patients (Kaushik, Dahiya, and Sharma 2021). Moreover, the use of cutting-edge wearable IoT-based devices can make life easier for those who are afflicted with some serious diseases (Singh et al. 2020). So, the IoT and blockchain can be used to store and share the important medical data of patients securely and in a distributed way. And not only can this information be safely exchanged via blockchain in real time, but it can also be utilized to assure authorized user access (Ramani et al. 2018).

6.3.3.2 Internet of Vehicles (IoV)

Blockchain can assure basic trust and security characteristics such as vehicle identification management, reputation and communication channel integrity, system automation, etc. in connected vehicles over the Internet. Blockchain can also ensure trust management and social relationships in social IoV applications efficiently (Iqbal et al. 2019). With the advancement of blockchain, all vehicle communications can be performed in real time also.

6.3.3.3 IoT-based Supply Chain Management Systems

Using the IoT, we can develop a smart supply chain management system, allowing for efficient control of product and service flow from manufacturer to end-user. However, to create a robust and trusted supply chain management system, the safeguarding of the information that flows through it is a must. Blockchain technology has the potential to be the ultimate solution to this issue (Hasan et al. 2019). It can eliminate the need for centralized authority and provide a secure, fully automated, and robust supply chain management system that can maintain the integrity of data also.

6.3.3.4 Industrial Internet of Things (IIoT)

The integrated architecture of the IoT and industries allows us to monitor its activities with minimal or no human participation. Integrating blockchain with IIoT can solve most of the issues such as access control, authentication, privacy, transparency, etc. (Latif et al. 2021) and can develop a smart and trusted industrial infrastructure.

6.3.3.5   Authentication and Access Control in IoT

Important security and trust parameters such as authentication and access control can be tackled by a combination of blockchain and smart contracts (Yavari et al. 2020). Private blockchain such as Hyperledger Fabric has special mechanisms for access control and authentication in terms of policies in addition to smart contracts.

6.3.3.6   Trusted Firmware Updates

Limited resource availability of IoT devices make it difficult to push out correct firmware updates. Another difficulty is scalability, as updating thousands of end devices manually is not feasible. Furthermore, due to the centralized nature of present architectures in front of such a large number of devices, a single point of failure is a possibility. The distributed nature of blockchain can provide the solution to this problem (Pillai, Sindhu, and Lakshmy 2019). The integrity of firmware data can also be managed using blockchain (Yohan and Lo 2019).

6.4   HYPERLEDGER FABRIC ARCHITECTURE AND WORKING MECHANISMS

The blockchain can revolutionize the way we process business information. The combination of a shared immutable ledger and smart contract can reshape how trust is expressed in business organizations. However, privacy, authentication, processing speed or response time, and scalability are some of the important requirements of conducting business properly. So public blockchain mechanisms are not able to handle all these needs, and private blockchain such as Hyperledger Fabric can be a complete solution due to its specific features. This section describes Hyperledger Fabric Blockchain technology in detail.

Hyperledger Fabric is an openly available, private, and permissioned blockchain framework for generating and maintaining distributed ledgers of records. It is a modular framework where different independent technologies can be plugged in and used. It is managed by the Linux Foundation and intended to provide trust operations with confidentiality, flexibility, and scalability. It can operate with such consensus protocols that are pluggable and can work without any cryptocurrency for the costly mining process and smart contract execution. The practice of avoiding cryptocurrencies in the Hyperledger Fabric system enables its deployment with normal operational cost.

6.4.1   Hyperledger Fabric Architecture

The architecture of Hyperledger Fabric is the combination of multiple pluggable components that are integrated for performing specific tasks. Every component works independently and can be configured according to developers and business needs. High-level architecture (see Figure 6.3) and key components of Hyperledger Fabric are given below:

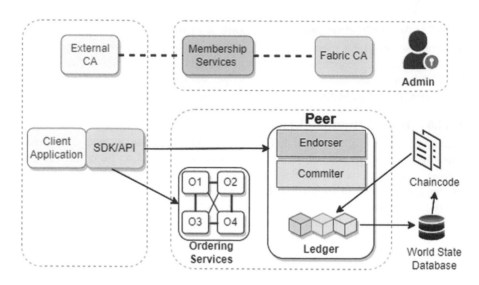

FIGURE 6.3 Architecture of hyperledger fabric network.

6.4.1.1 Peer Nodes

These nodes are the endpoints that reside at organizations and are responsible for all communication processes in Hyperledger Fabric Blockchain. These nodes hold the latest states and copies of distributed ledgers and channels they have joined by receiving orderer state updates in the form of blockchain blocks from the orderers. Based on special tasks performed, peer nodes are of mainly two types: the first is *Commiter Peer,* and the second is *Endorser Peer.* Commiter Peer commits transactions and adds received blocks to its copy of blockchain. This block, which is received from ordering services, contains the list of transactions that are marked either valid or invalid by Committer Peer. Every valid or invalid transaction is committed and added to the blockchain ledger. Endorser Peer performs the additional task of endorsing, which is a process of simulating a client's requests based on the policies defined and smart contract installed. This node generates the result set or reads/writes set after the execution of the transaction and returns it to the client without committing it to the ledger. Additionally, some peer nodes are defined as anchor nodes also that are responsible for all communication processes with other anchor nodes.

6.4.1.2 Ordering Nodes

Ordering is the mechanism that ensures the consistency of distributed ledgers. Consensus algorithms order the transactions and then bundle them into blocks of blockchain. In public blockchains such as Bitcoin and Etherium, any node can participate in the consensus process based on the probabilistic approach. But this approach is very resource-consuming and vulnerable to ledger forks, where different nodes can have a different view of distributed ledgers that is against consistency. But Hyperledger Fabric follows a different approach for ordering services such as Raft ("Raft Consensus Algorithm" 2021). It consists of a special and independent node for ordering services called Orderer. Ordering service can have multiple orders to make it robust against the failure of an orderer node. Orderer services work separately from the chaincode services, which makes them scalable and improves performance. Consensus in Hyperledger Fabric follows a deterministic approach in which final and correct blocks are validated by peers. It simply avoids the ledger fork in Hyperledger Fabric.

6.4.1.3 Membership Service Providers (MSP)

Since Hyperledger Fabric is a permissioned blockchain, every entity in this network must have an identity that needs to be validated before participating in the communication process, and MSP does this job. Certification Authorities provide private and public key pairs to the entities to generate identities where the private key is secretly held by nodes and their corresponding public keys are held by MSP. Nodes have to be digitally signed or endorsed transactions before submitting them, and they are validated by corresponding public keys stored by MSP without revealing nodes' private keys. The MSP implementation process includes the addition of sets of folders to the network configuration and to defining who is the admin within the organization and who has which authority from outside the organization. MSP is defined locally and for channel configurations.

6.4.1.4 Chaincode

Chaincode in Hyperledger Fabric is the group of related smart contracts. Smart contracts are the logic written in some high-level programming language and define some executable logic for the blockchain. They ensure some agreement and define transaction logic among participating organizations before submitting transactions. Smart contracts on Hyperledger Fabric are linked to an endorsement policy that specifies which organization must approve a transaction before it is declared valid or invalid. Chaincode invocation includes a six-step procedure, such as packaging of smart contracts, installing on peers, proving by peer nodes, committing chaincode in the channel, invoking initials, and finally query transactions.

6.4.1.5 Channels

Hyperledger Fabric supports multiple channel capabilities for communication among organizations. This functionality allows enterprises to retain their privacy, and they can join any number of channels also. After the invocation of the chaincode on a channel, all smart contracts of that chaincode become available to participating organizations of that channel. Channels are mainly two types: The "system channel" is the first and only channel. This channel is defined for ordering services and contains all orderer organizations. The second is the "application channel," which can be more than one channel in a Hyperledger Fabric Blockchain network and can provide private communication between participating consortium organizations.

6.4.1.6 Policies

Policies are the set of rules that are defined initially and make Hyperledger Fabric different from other blockchain networks. Policies in the Hyperledger Fabric network are defined at multiple levels such as at the system channel, application channel, and ACL (Access Control Lists). System channel policies define the consensus protocol used by ordering services and govern new block creation. Which member of the consortium is allowed to create a new application channel is also defined by these policies. Application channel policies control adding and removing of member organizations. These policies also govern the system about organizations that are responsible for approving a chaincode before its commitment to the channel. Access control list policies control access to the system's resources, such as functions or block events.

6.4.2 WORKING MECHANISM OF HYPERLEDGER FABRIC

We can divide the working mechanism of Hyperledger Fabric into five steps, which are given below:

First, any member client invokes a request through a client application to initiate a transaction. Client applications broadcast that request to an endorser peer.

Second, after verifying all identities using MSP certificates, the endorser peer executes the chaincodes and sends back a response to the client in terms of approval or rejection of the transaction.

Third, if the transaction is approved by an endorser peer, it is sent to the orderer node or peer to be ordered and included in the block of blockchain.

Fourth, the orderer node orders the transaction according to consensus protocol and adds it to the block. This block is then forwarded to the anchor peers of the remaining participating organizations of the channel.

Finally, these anchor peers broadcast this new block to other peers within their organization. Thus, all peers of all organizations update their local ledgers with this latest block.

6.5 INTEGRATION OF BLOCKCHAIN AND THE IOT: ISSUES AND TRUSTED STRATEGIES

The IoT and blockchain are emerging technologies that are gaining popularity day by day. Features and security mechanisms of blockchain can provide an ultimate solution to many security issues of the IoT. However, the integration of blockchain and the IoT is a very complicated process due to the structure and working nature of both technologies. For instance, the IoT is designed for centralized systems, whereas blockchain is decentralized in nature. In this section, the IoT and blockchain integration issues and some possible solutions are discussed (Kumar and Sharma 2021; Reyna et al. 2018).

6.5.1 Integration Issues

6.5.1.1 Issue of Processing Data Size

The size of data has no limit because some data in terms of transactions and blocks are added to blockchain regularly. According to Statista.com, the size of Bitcoin and Ethereum will be over 380 GB and 1.2 GB, respectively, until May 2022. On the other hand, IoT devices and protocols are designed for processing limited data with limited resource availability. IoT systems are not directly capable of handling such data generated by blockchains. Cloud computing may be an option for storing certain blockchain partial data in the cloud, but cloud computing's centralized nature may conflict with blockchain's decentralization.

6.5.1.2 Issue of Computation Power

The computational power required for blockchain activities is far higher than that required for the IoT. For example, in public blockchains, such as Bitcoin and Ethereum, authentication is done by cryptography, and a complicated problem has to be solved by miners for the consensus process. It requires very high processing machines and energy. However, IoT smart devices are very constrained with different resources, such as processing power and energy, and generally batteries are used for their power sources. So, solving and processing complex tasks and algorithms by IoT devices is not possible directly.

6.5.1.3 Issues of Privacy of Users

The initial architecture of blockchain was intended to be transparent, and privacy was not the main goal. But many applications of the IoT, such as medical systems, business systems, etc., may need a high level of privacy. Some public blockchain systems can have serious privacy issues, which may lead to many severe attacks (Dorri, Kanhere, and Jurdak 2018; Conti et al. 2018). So, integrating blockchain with the IoT can have an issue of privacy of users' data, and private blockchains can have different approaches for handling this issue. For instance, Hyperledger Fabric uses identity management services, access control lists, and the concept of private channels for privacy management (Androulaki et al. 2018).

6.5.1.4 Issues of Processing Speed

The transaction speed of blockchain networks is generally slower than the requirements of modern-day applications. Many blockchain projects such as Bitcoin and Ethereum can process 4–15 transactions per second, which is very slow for many IoT applications and can create a bottleneck for IoT data transmission (Dhar Dwivedi et al. 2021). However, private blockchains like Hyperledger Fabric increased processing speed to 3,000 times per second. This speed makes Hyperledger Fabric eligible for business needs and can be applied for IoT-based applications where a quick response time is required.

6.5.1.5 Issues of Scalability

When the transactions and connected nodes increase in a blockchain system, the main issue that arises is scalability. In most public blockchain networks, every node has to compute and store a complex task to validate a new transaction. It makes it very difficult to scale this network due to the need for very large storage and computation power (Scalability et al. 2021). Along with it, a very high bandwidth network is required for transferring data from one node to another. On the other hand, IoT systems demand a high level of scalability due to their applications such as smart cities, where the home appliances have to increase at any time.

6.5.2 TRUSTED INTEGRATION STRATEGIES

Integration of the IoT and blockchain can cause many issues, as discussed above, but most of them can be tackled with smart strategies. So, a carefully deployed approach based on application requirements must be considered. These strategies are generally based on the communication process between the IoT and blockchain (Reyna et al. 2018). Cloud computing is commonly used by IoT systems for data storage and processing; therefore, we can use it to integrate blockchain with the IoT (Nartey et al. 2021). Possible IoT and blockchain integration strategies are given below:

6.5.2.1 IoT to IoT Model

In this model (see Figure 6.4), different nodes of IoT communicate directly with others, and a network of blockchain is used for holding communication and transaction records. Since there is no direct involvement of blockchain in the communications process among IoT devices, this model responds faster compared to others.

However, the separation of blockchain makes this model more vulnerable to attacks as data injected in blockchain travels through insecure channels. Applications with a low level of latency and security requirements can use this model.

6.5.2.2 IoT-Blockchain-IoT Model

This model (see Figure 6.5) uses most of the security features of blockchain technology. Data from IoT devices is first stored in blockchain and then accessed by other IoT devices or applications. Blockchain ensures the immutability of this data through a ledger of records. But latency of data is the main issue of this model if it uses public blockchain architectures.

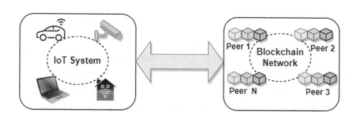

FIGURE 6.4   IoT to IoT model (Modified from (Kumar and Sharma 2021)).

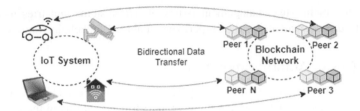

FIGURE 6.5 IoT-blockchain-IoT model of integration (Modified from (Kumar and Sharma 2021)).

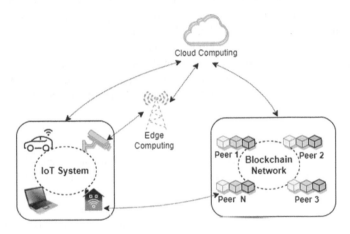

FIGURE 6.6 Cloud-based integration model of IoT and blockchain (Modified from (Kumar and Sharma 2021)).

6.5.2.3 Cloud-based IoT-Blockchain-IoT Model

This model (see Figure 6.6) was designed by taking advantage of both the above models. Cloud computing is a groundbreaking technology that enables us to execute tasks that require a lot of resources in terms of computation power, energy, etc. that are very costly and time-consuming for IoT devices. This model takes advantage of the cloud and fog computing for handling these types of tasks of blockchain, such as hashing and cryptography algorithms.

6.6 IOT TRUST MANAGEMENT ISSUES AND THEIR SOLUTIONS USING HYPERLEDGER FABRIC

IoT systems have many trust-related challenges due to their functioning limitations such as limited resources, lack of proper firmware updation process, the remote location of IoT devices, etc. Private blockchains are more capable of addressing these issues compared to public blockchains because they are designed and developed to overcome the limitations of public blockchain systems. This section describes the main trust management issues of IoT systems and tries to find the solution to those issues using the Hyperledger Fabric Blockchain framework.

6.6.1 TRUSTED AUTHENTICATION ISSUE

Authentication is the process of identifying authentic devices. This process marks authentic devices as trusted so that they can perform operations in the system. For the authentication process, some unique id is provided to the nodes using some cryptographic protocols. These protocols may be based on the symmetric, asymmetric, or hybrid approaches (Ferrag et al. 2017). Due to the availability and diversity of their resources in the connection process, IoT devices can only implement lightweight and multifactor authentication protocols. Many researchers (e.g. Shin and Kwon 2018 and Wang, Wang, and Wang 2020) have proposed a protocol for authentication to authenticate users at both ends of communicating nodes. The bulk of protocols relies on public-key or private-key cryptography, which is difficult for IoT devices with low resources to deal with. Examples of authentication protocols are "X.509 certificates," "Hardware Security Module," "Trusted Platform Module," etc.

6.6.1.1 Possible Solution

Hyperledger Fabric has a separate authentication mechanism called MSP, and this is provided by a separate server named Certificate Authority. From the IoT systems perspective, every node can be first registered and assigned an identity that can be used for authentication of that particular node. Since Certificate Authority resides at a separate location, IoT devices are free of this burden. It not only addressed the computation overhead problem of IoT devices, but any protocol can be plugged into it at any time also (Kurian and Subramanian 2021).

6.6.2 TRUSTED ACCESS CONTROL ISSUE

In IoT systems, access control is used to bind specific services to specific nodes or users. Access control is required to preserve trust among IoT devices, but it is problematic due to the huge number of IoT devices and the variety of protocols they utilize. Furthermore, most of the present access control solutions use local data available in devices for making decisions that cannot be considered secure and trusted mechanisms. Local device information can be easily fabricated, particularly in the case of IoT devices, which are typically located in faraway places. Some other popular techniques, such as OAuth, JASON Web Token, Web Token (CWT), etc. use the authentication server and token-based protocols for access control or authorization. However, these techniques require constant connectivity of IoT devices, which may not be possible for some systems.

6.6.2.1 Possible Solutions

The immutability feature of blockchain can provide an ultimate solution for this problem when we integrate blockchain and authentication protocols such as OAuth 2.0. Some researchers (Siris et al. 2020) combined authentication protocols with public blockchain and successfully addressed most of the access control trust issues. However, as discussed earlier, some limitations of public blockchain are low rates of transactions committed, poor scalability, and privacy management. So, instead of using public blockchain, we can use Hyperledger Fabric, which can address most of the limitations of public blockchain. Hyperledger Fabric has some special mechanisms, such as multiple smart contracts and policies, that can be used for access control (H. Liu, Han, and Li 2020; Iftekhar et al. 2021) in IoT systems.

6.6.3 TRUSTED PRIVACY ISSUE

Privacy is another important parameter that needs to be addressed for trusted IoT scenarios. IoT applications such as healthcare systems, smart homes, industrial IoT, etc. sometimes need more privacy, which is not easily possible in current centralized IoT systems. A single point of failure or compromised central node may breach all private information of the participant nodes. Trust issues become more complicated when users are not aware of how and from where data are coming and are being shared. Some researchers (Luo et al. 2020) have provided cryptography-based privacy solutions, but they may or may not fit in resource-constrained IoT devices.

6.6.3.1 Possible Solution

Private blockchains can address this issue since these are specially designed for privacy preservation, unlike public blockchains, where everyone has access to all the data. Hyperledger Fabric has a great mechanism of separate channels that can be used to communicate privately by different organizations. Since every channel has its separate ledger and other channels cannot access it, users can trust their privacy (Islam, Rehmani, and Chen 2022).

6.6.4 TRUSTED INTEROPERABILITY ISSUE

One of the great features of the IoT is interoperability, which allows IoT systems to work with diverse and heterogeneous environments. But this feature also creates many security and trust issues. IoT systems might include a variety of heterogeneous components, such as smart devices, networks, protocols, and other components that were built by various organizations and adhere to different operating standards. Therefore, interoperability can create compatibility issues in front of third-party systems, and trust cannot be maintained in such scenarios.

6.6.4.1 Possible Solutions

To tackle this problem, blockchain can be used as a service layer that can interact with external different technologies in standardizing a general framework of the IoT. This framework can work in not only an automated way but a trusted decentralized manner (Y. Liu et al. 2020). Hyperledger Fabric supports pluggable standards or protocols that can be a great solution for interoperability in the IoT. Developers can decide the best-suited standards for a particular IoT system and can plug or unplug it as per requirements.

6.6.5 Trusted Integrity Issue

The integrity of data in IoT-like systems is a big concern because data can be transmitted via trusted or untrusted nodes. IoT systems can have a network of thousands of nodes, and it is very hard to monitor them regularly. Reaching these nodes is not difficult for attackers since they don't have trusted security features due to their limited resource availability. Some protocols such as "hash algorithm (SHA)" and "advanced encryption standards (AES)" can maintain data integrity in IoT systems. However, these algorithms use some typical mathematical calculations as their basic techniques, which may or may not be possible to perform for IoT devices. Software-level and hardware-level security systems such as MLS (multilevel security) and TPM (trusted platform module) can be used, but these techniques may not be compatible with IoT system architectures (Musonda 2019).

6.6.5.1 Possible Solutions

Immutability, decentralization, and distributed ledgers are the main features of blockchain that can be used for maintaining IoT data integrity. Hyperledger Fabric is featured with multiple distributed ledgers with respect to channels in the network. These ledgers ensure the integrity of stored information because once a transaction is committed in the ledger, it cannot be updated or removed (Hang and Kim 2019). Hyperledger Fabric can store large-scale IoT data in a special database such as MongoDB, which is cryptographically secured from unwanted access.

REFERENCES

Ahmed, Abdelmuttlib Ibrahim Abdalla, Siti Hafizah Ab Hamid, Abdullah Gani, Suleman Khan, and Muhammad Khurram Khan. 2019. "Trust and Reputation for Internet of Things: Fundamentals, Taxonomy, and Open Research Challenges." *Journal of Network and Computer Applications* 145 (July). 10.1016/j.jnca.2019.102409

Androulaki, Elli, Artem Barger, Vita Bortnikov, Srinivasan Muralidharan, Christian Cachin, Konstantinos Christidis, Angelo De Caro, et al. 2018. "Hyperledger Fabric: A Distributed Operating System for Permissioned Blockchains." *Proceedings of the 13th EuroSys Conference, EuroSys 2018 2018-Janua (April)*. Association for Computing Machinery, Inc. 10.1145/3190508.3190538

Chen, Dong, Guiran Chang, Dawei Sun, Jiajia Li, Jie Jia, and Xingwei Wang. 2011. "TRM-IoT: A Trust Management Model Based on Fuzzy Reputation for Internet of Things." *Computer Science and Information Systems* 8 (4): 1207–1228. 10.2298/csis110303056c

Conti, Mauro, E. Sandeep Kumar, Chhagan Lal, and Sushmita Ruj. 2018. "A Survey on Security and Privacy Issues of Bitcoin." *IEEE Communications Surveys and Tutorials* 20 (4). Institute of Electrical and Electronics Engineers Inc.: 3416–3452. 10.1109/COMST.2018.2842460

Dhar Dwivedi, Ashutosh, Rajani Singh, Keshav Kaushik, Raghava Rao Mukkamala, and Waleed S. Alnumay. 2021. "Blockchain and Artificial Intelligence for 5G-Enabled Internet of Things: Challenges, Opportunities, and Solutions." *Transactions on Emerging Telecommunications Technologies*, no. January: 1–19. 10.1002/ett.4329

Djedjig, Nabil, Djamel Tandjaoui, Imed Romdhani, and Faiza Medjek. 2018. "Trust Management in the Internet of Things." In *Security and Privacy in Smart Sensor Networks*, 122–146. IGI Global. 10.4018/978-1-5225-5736-4.ch007

Dorri, Ali, Salil S. Kanhere, and Raja Jurdak. 2018. "MOF-BC: A Memory Optimized and Flexible BlockChain for Large Scale Networks." *Future Generation Computer Systems* 92 (January). Elsevier B.V.: 357–373. http://arxiv.org/abs/1801.04416.

Ferrag, Mohamed Amine, Leandros A. Maglaras, Helge Janicke, Jianmin Jiang, and Lei Shu. 2017. "Authentication Protocols for Internet of Things: A Comprehensive Survey." *Security and Communication Networks*. Hindawi Limited, London. 10.1155/2017/6562953

Fortino, Giancarlo, Lidia Fotia, Fabrizio Messina, Domenico Rosaci, and Giuseppe M.L. Sarné. 2020. "Trust and Reputation in the Internet of Things: State-of-the-Art and Research Challenges." *IEEE Access* 8: 60117–60125. 10.1109/ACCESS.2020.2982318

Frustaci, Mario, Pasquale Pace, Gianluca Aloi, and Giancarlo Fortino. 2018. "Evaluating Critical Security Issues of the IoT World: Present and Future Challenges." *IEEE Internet of Things Journal* 5 (4): 2483–2495. 10.1109/JIOT.2017.2767291

Hang, Lei, and Do Hyeun Kim. 2019. "Design and Implementation of an Integrated Iot Blockchain Platform for Sensing Data Integrity." *Sensors (Switzerland)* 19 (10). MDPI AG: 2228. 10.3390/s19102228

Hasan, Haya, Esra AlHadhrami, Alia AlDhaheri, Khaled Salah, and Raja Jayaraman. 2019. "Smart Contract-Based Approach for Efficient Shipment Management." *Computers and Industrial Engineering* 136 (July). Elsevier: 149–159. 10.1016/j.cie.2019.07.022

Iftekhar, Adnan, Xiaohui Cui, Qi Tao, and Chengliang Zheng. 2021. "Hyperledger Fabric Access Control System for Internet of Things Layer in Blockchain-Based Applications." *Entropy 2021* 23: 1054 23 (8). Multidisciplinary Digital Publishing Institute: 1054. 10.3390/E23081054

Iqbal, Razi, Talal Ashraf Butt, Muhammad Afzaal, and Khaled Salah. 2019. "Trust Management in Social Internet of Vehicles: Factors, Challenges, Blockchain, and Fog Solutions." *International Journal of Distributed Sensor Networks* 15 (1). 10.1177/1550147719825820

Islam, Muhammad, Mubashir Husain Rehmani, and Jinjun Chen. 2022. "Differential Privacy-Based Permissioned Blockchain for Private Data Sharing in Industrial IoT." *Lecture Notes of the Institute for Computer Sciences, Social-Informatics and Telecommunications Engineering, LNICST* 413 LNICST: 77–91. 10.1007/978-3-030-93479-8_5

Jesus, Emanuel Ferreira, Vanessa R.L. Chicarino, Célio V.N. De Albuquerque, and Antônio A.De A. Rocha. 2018. "A Survey of How to Use Blockchain to Secure Internet of Things and the Stalker Attack." *Security and Communication Networks* 2018. 10.1155/2018/9675050

Kaushik, Keshav, and Susheela Dahiya. 2018. "Security and Privacy in Iot Based E-Business and Retail." *Proceedings of the 2018 International Conference on System Modeling and Advancement in Research Trends, SMART 2018*. IEEE, 78–81. 10.1109/SYSMART.2018.8746961

Kaushik, Keshav, Susheela Dahiya, and Rewa Sharma. 2021. "Internet of Things Advancements in Healthcare." *Internet of Things: Energy, Industry, and Healthcare*, October. CRC Press, 19–32. doi:10.1201/9781003140443-2/INTERNET-THINGS-ADVANCEMENTS-HEALTHCARE-KESHAV-KAUSHIK-SUSHEELA-DAHIYA-REWA-SHARMA

Kaushik, Keshav, Susheela Dahiya, and Rewa Sharma. 2022. "Role of Blockchain Technology in Digital Forensics." *Blockchain Technology*, April. CRC Press, Boca Raton, US, 235–246. 10.1201/9781003138082-14

Kumar, Rajesh, and Rewa Sharma. 2021. "Leveraging Blockchain for Ensuring Trust in IoT: A Survey." *Journal of King Saud University - Computer and Information Sciences*, September. Elsevier. 10.1016/J.JKSUCI.2021.09.004

Kurian, Bibin, and Narayanan Subramanian. 2021. "IoT Device Authentication and Access Control Through Hyperledger Fabric." *Lecture Notes in Electrical Engineering* 735 LNEE. Springer Science and Business Media Deutschland GmbH: 699–713. 10.1007/978-981-33-6977-1_51

Latif, Shahid, Zeba Idrees, Jawad Ahmad, Lirong Zheng, and Zhuo Zou. 2021. "A Blockchain-Based Architecture for Secure and Trustworthy Operations in the Industrial Internet of Things." *Journal of Industrial Information Integration* 21 (September 2020). Elsevier Inc.: 100190. 10.1016/j.jii.2020.100190

Liu, Han, Dezhi Han, and Dun Li. 2020. "Fabric-Iot: A Blockchain-Based Access Control System in IoT." *IEEE Access* 8. Institute of Electrical and Electronics Engineers Inc.: 18207–18218. 10.1109/ACCESS.2020.2968492

Liu, Yinqiu, Kun Wang, Kai Qian, Miao Du, and Song Guo. 2020. "Tornado: Enabling Blockchain in Heterogeneous Internet of Things Through a Space-Structured Approach." *IEEE Internet of Things Journal* 7 (2). IEEE: 1273–1286. 10.1109/JIOT.2019.2954128

Luo, Xi, Lihua Yin, Chao Li, Chonghua Wang, Fuyang Fang, Chunsheng Zhu, and Zhihong Tian. 2020. "A Lightweight Privacy-Preserving Communication Protocol for Heterogeneous IoT Environment." *IEEE Access* 8. IEEE: 67192–67204. 10.1109/ACCESS.2020.2978525

Manda, Sridhar, and Nalini. 2019. "Trust Mechanism in IoT Routing." *Proceedings of the 2nd International Conference on Intelligent Computing and Control Systems, ICICCS 2018*, no. 5: 230–234. 10.1109/ICCONS.2018.8662982

Musonda, Chalwe. 2019. "Security, Privacy and Integrity in Internet Of Things – A Review." *ICTSZ International Conference in ICTs (ICICT2018) Lusak, Zambia (12th -13th December 2018*, no. April: 146–152.

Nartey, Clement, Eric Tutu Tchao, James Dzisi Gadze, Eliel Keelson, Griffith Selorm Klogo, Benjamin Kommey, and Kwasi Diawuo. 2021. "On Blockchain and IoT Integration Platforms: Current Implementation Challenges and Future Perspectives." *Wireless Communications and Mobile Computing*. Hindawi Limited, London. 10.1155/2021/6672482

Pillai, Akshay, M. Sindhu, and K. V. Lakshmy. 2019. "Securing Firmware in Internet of Things Using Blockchain." In *2019 5th International Conference on Advanced Computing and Communication Systems, ICACCS 2019*, 329–334. 10.1109/ICACCS.2019.8728389

"Raft Consensus Algorithm." 2021. Accessed December 23. https://raft.github.io/.

Ramani, Vidhya, Tanesh Kumar, An Bracken, Madhusanka Liyanage, and Mika Ylianttila. 2018. "Secure and Efficient Data Accessibility in Blockchain Based Healthcare Systems." *2018 IEEE Global Communications Conference, GLOBECOM 2018 - Proceedings*. Institute of Electrical and Electronics Engineers Inc. 10.1109/GLOCOM.2018.8647221

Reyna, Ana, Cristian Martín, Jaime Chen, Enrique Soler, and Manuel Díaz. 2018. "On Blockchain and Its Integration with IoT. Challenges and Opportunities." *Future Generation Computer Systems* 88 (2018). Elsevier B.V.: 173–190. 10.1016/j.future.2018.05.046

Scalability, Blockchain, Dodo Khan, Low Tang Jung, and Manzoor Ahmed Hashmani. 2021. "Applied Sciences Systematic Literature Review of Challenges in since. Among the Many Hindrances, Scalability Is Found to Be Has Not Been Well-Defined in the Literature. Issue Task to Validate Every Transaction. The Public Blockchain a High Bandw QoS L."

Shin, Sooyeon, and Taekyoung Kwon. 2018. "Two-Factor Authenticated Key Agreement Supporting Unlinkability in 5G-Integrated Wireless Sensor Networks." *IEEE Access* 6 (January). Institute of Electrical and Electronics Engineers Inc.: 11229–11241. 10.1109/ACCESS.2018.2796539

Singh, Kamalpreet, Keshav Kaushik, Ahatsham, and Vivek Shahare. 2020. "Role and Impact of Wearables in IoT Healthcare." *Advances in Intelligent Systems and Computing* 1090. Springer, Singapore: 735–742. 10.1007/978-981-15-1480-7_67

Siris, Vasilios A., Dimitrios Dimopoulos, Nikos Fotiou, Spyros Voulgaris, and George C. Polyzos. 2020. "Decentralized Authorization in Constrained IoT Environments Exploiting Interledger Mechanisms." *Computer Communications* 152 (September 2019). Elsevier B.V.: 243–251. 10.1016/j.comcom.2020.01.030

Ud Din, Ikram, Mohsen Guizani, Byung Seo Kim, Suhaidi Hassan, and Muhammad Khurram Khan. 2019. "Trust Management Techniques for the Internet of Things: A Survey." *IEEE Access* 7: 29763–29787. 10.1109/ACCESS.2018.2880838

Wang, DIng, Ping Wang, and Chenyu Wang. 2020. "Efficient Multi-Factor User Authentication Protocol with Forward Secrecy for Real-Time Data Access in WSNs." *ACM Transactions on Cyber-Physical Systems* 4 (3). Association for Computing Machinery: 1–26. 10.1145/3325130

"What Are The Different Types of Blockchain Technology? | 101 Blockchains." 2021. Accessed May 21. https://101blockchains.com/types-of-blockchain/.

Yavari, Mostafa, Masoumeh Safkhani, Saru Kumari, Sachin Kumar, and Chien Ming Chen. 2020. "An Improved Blockchain-Based Authentication Protocol for IoT Network Management." *Security and Communication Networks* 2020. 10.1155/2020/8836214

Yohan, Alexander, and Nai Wei Lo. 2019. "An Over-The-Blockchain Firmware Update Framework for IoT Devices." *DSC 2018 – 2018 IEEE Conference on Dependable and Secure Computing.* IEEE, 1–8. 10.1109/DESEC.2018.8625164

7 Cyber Physical System Security

Ankit Kumar Singh
NIT Jamshedpur

CONTENTS

7.1 INTRODUCTION

The term cyber physical system (CPS) emerged for the very first time in 2006 by Helen Gill at NSF (National Science Foundation) in the USA [1]. CPS is a smart and

DOI: 10.1201/9781003283003-7

intelligent computer system whose set of actions and mechanisms are governed through a specific algorithm. It has a deep integration of software components and physical components [2]. In these systems, the computational capabilities are utilized in order to increase the efficiency of the conventional physical systems. CPSs can view things from physical as well as virtual perspectives in order to autonomously evaluate the conditions and then perform the process of decision making based on those sets of conditions without the involvement of any human activity. They have the potential and capability to impact various sectors of the economy. CPSs can bring advancements to the healthcare industry, automobile industry, traffic flow management of the city, smart homes, smart appliances, and anything that can be termed "smart". We can encounter many examples of CPSs surrounding us in our daily lives, such as smart heaters that we have in our homes, which automatically get switched on and adjust the temperature of the room when the room temperature goes below a minimum threshold. Other examples could be an air conditioning system, cleaning robots, and smart ventilation systems. In short and crisp words, CPSs can link the physical world with the virtual world in order to carry out a set of tasks that can impact our daily life tremendously.

7.1.1   3C Concept of Cyber Physical Systems

Just like the transformation of the Internet over the years, the manner or the way in which people have started interacting with information has changed. CPSs have transformed the way in which people interact with intelligent systems. CPSs are integrating computation, communication, sensing, control, and networking into physical objects and then connecting these objects to each other through the Internet. The 3Cs in the concept of CPS stand for computation, communication, and control. The software performs the computation part based on a given or provided code in order to filter out the desired information from the bulk of provided information and then accordingly communicate or interact with the physical system through the networks in order to control the system. The figure shown below depicts the way in which the 3Cs of CPSs work. (Figure 7.1).

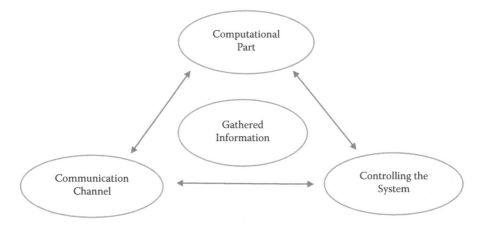

FIGURE 7.1   3C Structure of cyber physical systems.

7.2 FEATURES OF CYBER PHYSICAL SYSTEMS

1. CPSs have the capability to train and adapt themselves under several circumstances under which an ordinary system might not work.
2. The whole principal of CPS is based on the interaction of cyber and physical components that can solve as well as can handle real-time problems that might be a tedious task to solve and overcome.
3. CPSs ensure that the system is reliable and any operation performed must be ensured; for example, we can think about a fire alarm system, which has to be reliable in order to ensure that there is no loss of property or life in an unprecedented situation.
4. CPSs can perform the process of data transmission under wireless networks, which removes the complexities that are associated with the wired connection.
5. Real-time capability is one such feature of the CPS that holds the key to many applications of the CPS as there are certain activities and tasks that require real-time monitoring and viewing (the healthcare sector and automation sectors are perfect examples that require real-time monitoring), and CPSs can be a boon for such sectors of the economy.
6. CPSs have high computational capabilities that can be very useful in solving complex problems that might be a tedious task for a human or any ordinary system.
7. Decentralization refers to the independent decision-making capability of the CPS that must be reliable and should be in alignment with the ultimate goal of the organization.
8. CPSs are also used for efficient, effective, and safe transmission of the energy supply. (Here, smart grids can be a perfect example that uses CPSs.)
9. CPSs are efficient as well as cost effective: energy efficient, where limited amounts of power resources are used, and time efficient, where limited amounts of memory and excessive computational time are avoided. These are a few parameters on which CPSs are efficient. Similarly, because of the features that come with a CPS, its cost in due course of time becomes a good deal for a customer or any user.
10. CPSs have the ability to operate in autonomous as well as semi-autonomous configurations, which gives them an edge over traditional systems.

7.3 CHARACTERISTICS OF CYBER PHYSICAL SYSTEMS

7.3.1 AGRICULTURE

In the next 20 years, it is estimated that the population will grow by double digits; therefore, there is a dire need for incrementing food production, and CPSs can be used for this purpose. CPSs can optimize the quality of food production as well as increase quantity. CPSs can be used to improve agricultural management for the sustainability of agricultural systems, crop production, and maintaining the quality of the environment. CPSs can be used in the agricultural sector in order to perform precise farming. CPSs can monitor climatic changes and the soil on a different set of parameters, like mineral content, moisture, and granularity. Moreover, CPSs can be very useful in scheduling and monitoring irrigation activities, fertilization activities, and harvesting activities. CPSs can help farmers to monitor fields and make resource plans in case there are any unpredictable circumstances and events. Also, CPSs can optimize the schedules of food production by connecting them with the supply chain and can perform activities like harvesting, seeding, and using robots and other intelligent tools.

7.3.2 TRANSPORTATION

When a traditional transportation system is compared to a transportation system that involves the use of CPSs, the later achieves higher reliability, efficiency, and robust performance because of the continuous interaction between the software or the cyber systems and the physical systems involved in transportation. CPSs can effectively reduce road accidents that are caused by human error, and not only that. The CPSs can also effectively manage the flow of the traffic, thereby eliminating the chances of traffic jams and unwanted wastage of time; therefore, all these properties of the CPSs make them very useful in saving time and money and also improving security standards. Many countries are expected to move toward this domain in the near future.

7.3.3 AUTOMATION

CPSs can increase production and also make the process much more flexible by using the self-regulatory system and autonomous production unit. CPSs can automate the industry by using robots, which can result in increases in production as well as quality. Also, the use of CPSs can bring down the cost that the company incurs due to wages given to workers. There would be a cost associated with the purchase and maintenance of the robots, but in due time these costs would come down, thereby providing profit to the organization.

7.3.4 HEALTHCARE

Today most of the components of healthcare systems operate in either limited or complete isolation, which results in a tedious task for the patient as well as the healthcare system to maintain synchronization. However, with the continuous evolution of technology, these devices in the healthcare system may be combined through a network in order to maintain synchronization between the patient and the healthcare system. Also, nowadays CPSs have become important in the healthcare sector. CPSs can limit the cost of healthcare that the patient has to bear by providing real-time monitoring of the patient. CPSs can be extremely helpful in the healthcare industry by providing high-quality treatment and also limiting hospitalization charges, which will ultimately lead to a quality healthcare infrastructure.

7.3.5   OCEAN MONITORING

CPSs can be used for ocean monitoring. Using smart video, unmanned vessels can perform real-time monitoring of the underwater environment. The set of algorithms and information will make sure that the vessel adapts to different challenging conditions that it might have to face underwater. These robots are equipped with high processing powers and sensors to perform navigation operations, process data, and also make sure that they remain charged using natural resources like wind, solar power, etc., to ensure uninterrupted transmission of data.

7.3.6   SMART GRID

Smart grids are essentially a large network of interconnected physical networks that serve as a backbone for the supply of energy. They are basically an electric network that performs the delivery of a reliable energy supply. In recent years, the demand for clean, efficient, reliable, and secure energy generation and transmission has increased tremendously, and deployment of smart technologies has become a must. That's where smart grids could be used that have CPSs already built inside them. These smart grids have advanced monitoring and control technologies. Smart grids are basically a combination of cyber systems and physical networks. These smart grids can adjust to changes if required and can reconfigure themselves in order to avoid blackouts and thereby reduce energy costs.

CPSs are not limited to the applications that we discussed earlier. There are lots more applications that include education, energy management, environment monitoring, smart cities and smart homes, intelligent transportation, and process controls. The figure below shows some of the applications of CPSs. (Figure 7.2).

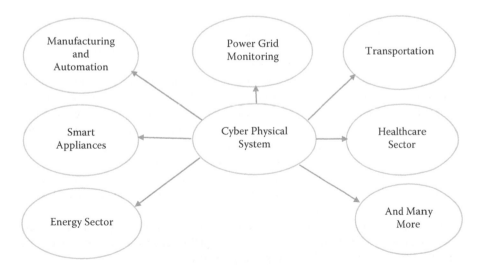

FIGURE 7.2   Applications of cyber physical systems.

7.4 CHALLENGES FACED BY CYBER PHYSICAL SYSTEMS

CPSs involve many interconnected systems that are used for monitoring and processing objects and processes. In today's world, CPSs have evolved our way of life. They are providing services in different sectors, including e-healthcare, smart homes, e-transportation, and many more. Since CPSs deal with several complex components, they are prone to threats and attacks, and there is a need to mitigate such attacks or threats for the security of CPSs and their components.

7.4.1 DATA PRIVACY

Data privacy is the ability of an individual to determine to what extent the personal information of the individual is shared or communicated with a third party. As the use of the Internet has increased drastically over the years, so has the need for data privacy. There are many websites, social media platforms, as well as applications that take the details of the user on the pretext of providing services; however, some of these applications, platforms, and websites use the data in such a way that it compromises the privacy of the user's information. CPSs manage a huge amount of sensitive, confidential, and private data such as phone numbers, addresses, and details; therefore, concerns regarding the privacy of data are always raised in cases of CPSs.

For example, we can think of the healthcare sector where the medical monitoring system contains sensitive information about the patient, such as the patient's medical report, prescriptions, etc. The security of such information must be dealt with high precision so that it does not fall into the hands of someone who could exploit it.

7.4.2 DATA MANAGEMENT

Data management is the practice of collecting, storing, protecting, and organizing data so that proper analysis can be made before making any decision. Data management also provides invaluable insights that can be used by an organization to enrich the user's experience. Data management provides multiple benefits such as visibility, which can help an organization to become more productive and organized by making sure that the right data get accessed by employees quickly and efficiently. Data management also provides reliability for decision making, which is made after analysis of the data, as this will help the organization get synchronized with market changes and customer demands. Similarly, security and scalability are other benefits that data management brings. The data that CPSs receive from various connected modules must be managed and analyzed properly before making any decisions because any decision made without proper study can result in loss of property and even loss of lives.

For example, in a fire alarm detection system, it is necessary that the system analyzes unprecedented situations and makes quality decisions as these decisions hold the key to saving precious lives and properties.

7.4.3 RELIABILITY

Reliability, in simple words, is defined as the probability that the system or software performs the required set of functions for a specified amount of time without failing. Reliability is considered to be one of the most important parameters, along with availability and serviceability, when buying or using a component. Theoretically, reliability means being totally free from any sort of error, but in real life reliability is always specified as a percentage. This percentage value keeps increasing as (and when) the next version of the product comes. Since CPSs are linked to very complex systems configured using several cyber and physical subsystems, the reliability of such systems and subsystems must be ensured. Otherwise, it may lead to a major risk to life and property.

For example, cars have airbag systems that must open up in case of a crash or accident. Therefore, the reliability of such systems must be guaranteed.

7.4.4 REAL-TIME CHALLENGES

Real-time systems are subjected to real time; that is, for such systems, the response should be generated within the specified limit or time constraint. There are two categories of real-time systems. The first is hard real-time systems, which are required to perform the given task within the specified time only. For such systems, if the specified deadline is missed, then it can lead to disastrous consequences. A flight control system can be considered an example of a hard real-time system. The second is soft real-time systems. For such systems, missing the deadline will not lead to a disastrous consequence. These systems can accept the response even if the received response is a little delayed. We can think of telephone switches as example of soft real-time systems. Since the majority of CPSs are required to perform real-time challenges and objectives, the proper configuration and adequate bandwidth should be in place. Otherwise, it may lead to serious consequences in the case of hard real-time CPSs.

For example, in medical monitoring systems present in the healthcare sector, if the system monitors the heart rate of patients, then the system must perform the activity in case of emergency, which could be beeping or informing the doctor and staff.

7.4.5 EAVESDROPPING

Eavesdropping means intercepting the information that is being communicated by the system. These types of attacks are passive attacks, where the attacker does not modify data. Rather, the attacker observes the propagation of data. In today's digital world, eavesdropping has taken the form of sniffing, which is a specialized program created to record the packets flowing over a network and then decrypt them using cryptographic tools to get plain text. For example, in the case of VoIP (i.e. voice over IP), communication can be sniffed and converted to audio data using specialized software. CPSs are prone to this type of attack, where the attacker can perform traffic analysis in order to monitor the transmitting data. Therefore, we need to protect the data flowing through the network in order to protect the data as well as the CPSs.

7.4.6 MAN IN THE MIDDLE ATTACK

The man in the middle attack is a sort of eavesdropping attack where the attacker places itself between legitimate users and then pretends to be a legitimate user to both the actual users. This enables the attacker to catch the data flowing between both the legitimate users and also allows the attacker to send malicious packets to both the users by pretending to be a legitimate user. CPSs are vulnerable and prone to such attacks, where the attacker can send false messages to CPSs through the network in order to make CPSs perform activities that the attacker wants. Such attacks are very dangerous as they may trigger false alarms and create panic among people.

For example, the fire alarm system may get activated and perform activities for which there is no need.

7.4.7 DENIAL OF SERVICE ATTACK

A denial of service (DoS) attack is an attack in which the hacker tries to flood the network with a large amount of malicious packets so that the network becomes so busy that legitimate users are unable to perform activities. DoS attacks generally exploit a vulnerability present in the network or software or even the design of the hardware itself. A DDoS (distributed denial of service) attack is an attack like DoS, but in this case the attackers flood the network through malicious packets coming from different devices that are distributed geographically. Again, the network becomes so busy that legitimate users cannot perform activities. DDoS attacks have more disruptive capabilities compared to DoS attacks because in DoS attacks, the attacker just uses a single system, whereas in DDoS attacks, multiple systems are used. Such types of attacks are possible in CPSs. The attacker can perform flooding of malicious packets on the network and prevent the normal activities of the CPS as well as prevent legitimate users from accessing the CPS.

For example, the attacker makes an ATM or POS server so busy that legitimate users cannot perform their transactions on the ATM or POS machine.

7.4.8 INTEGRITY

The word "integrity" means that the data present in the system have not been modified by an unauthorized user. Integrity involves processes that make data consistent and trustworthy throughout their entire life span. For example, when a message is being sent from entity A to entity B, the message that is being received by entity B should be original. That is, the message should not get tampered with or altered while it reaches entity B. In the context of CPSs, it may happen that the information that a user sends to the system is different from what the system receives; therefore, we can say that an unauthorized entity can make changes to the data or can corrupt the data or programs intentionally if CPSs are not properly controlled and monitored.

7.4.9 ROBUSTNESS

In today's world, CPSs have become an integral part of all major industries and organization. We can view the smart grid as a perfect example of the CPS in which the network of the grid and the communication network are coupled together for operational controls. Here, the communication network controls the grid, and the grid is responsible for providing power to the communication network. Now, such systems in which the components are interdependent upon each other for a particular set of activities tends to make the system fragile. Any failure in one component of the system makes the entire system stop, and this is one of the major problems, where failure of any interconnected component leads to the failure of the entire system.

7.4.10 UNTRAINED EMPLOYEES

CPSs are prone to various threats, and these threats keep on evolving. But one threat that is consistent is the vulnerability of the system due to untrained employees. The people working at an organization are the most frequent cause for the system or data to be compromised. It might happen unintentionally or even with ill intentions in some cases. Users with privileges to access sensitive data are one of the biggest threats to data breach, followed by contractors and regular employees of the organization. There are several reasons why untrained employees are one of the biggest threats to an organization, such as presence of insufficient protection methodologies and solutions, very high volume of devices being given access to sensitive data, everybody associated with the organization accessing the network, and increased usage of cloud storage and other infrastructure.

Therefore, it is necessary to make sure the employees are well trained before they handle real-world activities and tasks.

For example, Snapchat became victim of such an attack in 2016, when an outsider tricked an employee over mail into providing information. This led to the leakage of payroll information of Smapchat employees.

Several other challenges that make CPSs vulnerable, like power management, complexity, connectivity, sensing, data management, and others, are illustrated in Figure 7.3. If these vulnerabilities are not addressed properly, then major risks to life and property are possible.

7.5   REAL-LIFE INSTANCES

- In 2010, an attack named "STUXET" targeted the military and nuclear systems of Iran in order to disrupt services.
- In 2011, the drone system of the US military got hacked. The attacker performed a spoofing attack in order to capture the drone system.
- In 2012, a private gas company in Qatar became the victim of a CPS breach when an attacker tried to disrupt the entire working mechanism of the company using a virus.
- In 2013, the Saudi Arabian defense ministry system was breached through account hijacking in order to extract sensitive information.

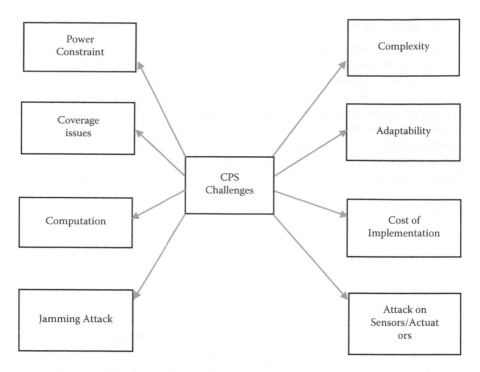

FIGURE 7.3   Challenges to cyber physical systems.

- In 2015, attackers hacked into the Ukraine's power grid, which resulted in power outrages to a population of more than 230,000 for more than 6 hours.
- In 2015, the Istanbul airport online passport system was attacked by hackers who tried to flood the network with malicious packets, preventing legitimate users from accessing the features and facilities.
- In 2015, an energy company in UAE became a victim of a Trojan Horse attack, where hackers tried to extract sensitive information about employees working at the energy company.
- In 2016, Jeep became the victim of a CPS breach when attackers hacked onto the braking and steering system of the car; a similar incident happened with Toyota and Ford in 2009.
- In 2016, the Turkish police database system was hacked in order to extract sensitive information about employees, staff, and prisoners in Turkey.
- In 2017, the power and transmission sector of Turkey became the victim of a CPS breach, where attackers tried to disrupt the transmission of energy across the country.

The graphs provided below indicate the number of CPS breaches that happened per country, as shown in Figure 7.4, and also the number of incidents that happened per year from 2010 to 2017, as shown in Figure 7.5.

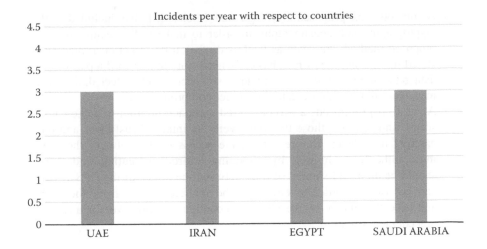

FIGURE 7.4 Incidents with respect to countries.

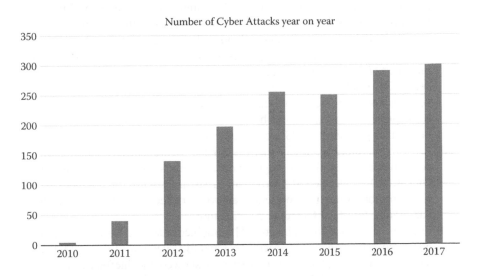

FIGURE 7.5 Number of cyber attacks year by year.

7.6 RISK MITIGATION TECHNIQUES

1. In order to improve the security of the smart grid, a two-step mutual authentication scheme was proposed by Fouda et al. [3]. According to this scheme, "the process of key exchange was done using the Diffie-Hellman exchange algorithm and the message that travels between the smart meters can be authenticated using a key and hash function".

2. Newman [4] provided the "security analysis of the CPSs, which included the CPSs. All these analysis should be done while designing the CPSs in order to make it secure and reliable".

3. A method was proposed by Vegh and Miclea [5] that included both cryptography and steganography in order to make CPSs secure. In this proposed method, "the data as well as the key used to get encrypted and stored in different files which basically made sure that even if a part of the data gets compromised the other data is still secure and protected, that is it made sure that the entire data do not get compromised".

4. Ali et al. [6] proposed "a two tier based approach in order to make CPSs secure and reliable, those two tiers were the internal trust layer and the external trust layer. Before getting the access to the network the user must authenticate himself by providing desired credentials and there should be an establishment of trust between the nodes of the CPS which can be used in order to eliminate the malicious data from the CPS and give the ability to the CPS to reconfigure themselves in any unprecedented situation".

7.7 PREVIOUS SOLUTIONS

1. In terms of confidentiality, securing the communication lines of CPSs is very important. With regard to that, several cryptographic solutions were provided. Using compression technique before performing encryption using this solution, the overhead was reduced, and the problem was also mitigated [7]. Shahzad [8] suggested that if we could install encryption and decryption modules at both ends of a mod bus, then it protects the connection from confidentiality threats. Vegh [9] suggested a hierarchical cryptographic method that can be obtained through the ElGamal algorithm in order to protect the CPS's communication lines.

2. In terms of integrity, where there is a need to prevent any modification done on either incoming or outgoing data, several solutions were provided. Omkar [10] addressed the problems associated with the software reconfiguration through the presented approach called TAIGA (Trustworthy Autonomic Interface Guardian Architecture).

3. In terms of availability, Thiago [11] combined machine learning with an open source PLC in order to secure an OpenPLC version and give it power against numerous attacks. This approach showed the ineffectiveness of attacks like DoS, DDoS, injection, and interception. The Tennessee Eastman Process Control System (TE-PCS) was used to check the DoS attack. Upon testing, it showed how the DoS attacks were ineffective against the sensor networks.

4. In terms of authentication, which is often considered to be a first line of defense, Halperin [12] presented a public key exchange authentication process in order to make sure that no unauthorized entity gains access. This mechanism was based on radio frequency as an energy source. Also, Ibrokhimov [12] presented a user authentication scheme that was based on five-level features, which included security, privacy, and other aspects.

7.8   METHODOLOGY

Certain methodologies can be used in order to provide security to CPSs:

1. Security of sensor networks is very important, and these networks must be prevented from getting hacked by performing several security measures, like user authentication, data confidentiality and integrity check, and detection of intruders in the network using an intrusion detection system.
2. It is also important to protect user data from getting hacked. For example, in the healthcare sector, the medical monitoring system may contain sensitive and confidential data about patients, like patients' medical records, personal information, etc. Therefore, it is important to keep such data private. Several security measures can be taken into consideration, like using security software for such data, access control systems, etc. in order to keep the data safe and secure.
3. CPSs may receive malicious data from attackers. Therefore, it is important for CPSs to analyze collected data before making any decisions. Decisions made without proper analysis can cause catastrophic damage to life or property. Security measures like detection of viruses, verifying the credibility of the sender, and verifying reliability can be used to provide security to CPSs in such situations.
4. Also, the security structure and design of CPSs has to be well structured and maintained in order to avoid security threats like hacking of the internal system, access control of the network resources, etc. Security measures like cross-network authentication and port blocking can be used to provide security to the design and structure of the CPS.
5. In order to counter security threats like data privacy, there is a need to perform security measures like privacy protection mechanisms, updating systems frequently, using access control features, and using standardized security software.
6. In the context of security threats to data confidentiality and the integrity of data, several security measures can be used, like making sure the source of data is reliable, performing encryption of data for its integrity, and using other data mining procedures for maintaining the confidentiality and integrity of data.
7. There are other security threats, like remote accessing. The security of the routing system when the hosts are present in two different networks is also important. Security measures like performing hop-by-hop encryption, doing key management and password negotiation, and performing end-to-end encryption of data are very important for the security of the CPS.

7.9   RESULTS

CPS security has always been important because of the nature of the work and tasks that are performed by CPSs. CPSs' challenges have captured the attention of the industry and researchers around the globe. CPSs involve cybernetics, transdisciplinary approaches, design, and process science, so their complexity is very high. Therefore, security of such systems should be given very high priority in order to avoid any loss of property and life. In this chapter, we looked at the various security aspects of CPSs, reviewed the key issues and challenges of CPSs, discussed mitigation techniques and previously proposed solutions by several researchers that can be helpful in reducing the volume of damage, and dealt with several threats and challenges that were faced by CPSs, which can give the reader a comprehensive overview of security aspects of the CPS.

7.10 CONCLUSION

The security of CPSs is a high priority because CPSs deal with certain applications whose security, if compromised, can cause major risks to life and property. CPSs have become an important component of Industry 4.0. The ultimate aim of CPSs is to enhance quality with reliability intact and to be available whenever required, but there are certain loopholes that make the security of such systems vulnerable. It is necessary to counter those loopholes with high precision. In this chapter, we gave a proper overview of CPSs, their features, different applications, and various threats to which CPSs are vulnerable. Then, we provided various real-life instances where the security of CPSs was compromised, and we looked into methodologies that can protect CPSs from various threats. Several startup companies are now offering security services for CPSs, but they are still few in number. We are at the starting point as far as security of CPSs is concerned, but in the coming years, we may see other threats, challenges, and security measures countering those threats as research moves forward.

REFERENCES

[1] Cyber Physical Systems. Wikipedia a free encyclopedia, en.m.wikipedia.org/wiki/Cyber-physical_system
[2] Fouda M.M., Fadlullah Z.M., Kato N., Lu R., Shen X.S. A lightweight message authentication scheme for smart grid communications. *IEEE Trans. Smart Grid* 2012;2(4):675–685.
[3] Newman C. Challenges in security for cyber physical systems. *DHS ST Work Futur Dir Cyber-Phys Syst Secur* 2009:22–24.
[4] Lu T., Xu, Guo X., Zhao L., Xie F. A new multilevel framework for cyber-physical system security. In First international Workshop on the Swarm at the Edge of the Cloud2013.
[5] Vegh L., Miclea L. Enhancing security in cyber-physical systems through cryptographic and steganographic techniques, Autom. Qual. Testing, Robot. Int. Conf. IEEE, pp. 1–6, 2014.
[6] Zhang M., Raghunathan A., Jha N.K. Trustworthiness of medical devices and body area networks. *Proc. IEEE* 2014;102(8):1174–1188.
[7] Shahzad A., Lee M., Lee Y.-K., Kim S., Xiong N., Choi J.-Y., Cho Y. Real time modbus transmissions and cryptography security designs and enhancements of protocol sensitive information. *Symmetry* 2015;7(3):1176–1210.
[8] Vegh L., Miclea L. *2016* International Conference on Communications (COMM) IEEE; 2016. Secure and efficient communication in cyber-physical systems through cryptography and complex event processing; pp. 273–276.

[9] Harshe O.A., Chiluvuri N.T., Patterson C.D., Baumann W.T. *2015* International Conference on Industrial Instrumentation and Control (ICIC) IEEE; 2015. Design and implementation of a security framework for industrial control systems; pp. 127–132.

[10] Alves T., Das R., Morris T. Embedding encryption and machine learning intrusion prevention systems on programmable logic controllers. *IEEE Embed. Syst. Lett.* 2018;10(3):99–102.

[11] Halperin D., Heydt-Benjamin T.S., Ransford B., Clark S.S., Defend B., Morgan W., Fu K., Kohno T., Maisel W.H. Security and Privacy, 2008. SP 2008. IEEE Symposium on. IEEE; 2008. Pacemakers and implantable cardiac defibrillators: Software radio attacks and zero-power defenses; pp. 129–142.

[12] Ibrokhimov S., Hui K.L., Al-Absi A.A., Sain M. 2019 21st International Conference on Advanced Communication Technology (ICACT) IEEE; 2019. Multi-factor authentication in cyber physical system: A state of art survey; pp. 279–284.

8 Intrusion Detection Systems Apropos of the Internet of Things (IoT)

Abhilasha Chauhan
Department of Computer Science and Engineering,
DIT University, Dehradun, Uttarakhand, India

Sameeka Saini
Indian Institute of Technology, Roorkee, Uttarakhand, India

Luxmi Sapra
School of Computing, Graphic Era Hill University, Dehradun,
Uttarakhand, India

Gesu Thakur
School of Computing, University of Engineering and
technology, Roorkee, Uttarakhand, India

CONTENTS

DOI: 10.1201/9781003283003-8

167

8.1   INTRODUCTION

Tremendous advancements are happening in the technologies implemented in the automotive industry, such as ad-hoc vehicles, electric vehicles, etc. [1]. The Internet of Things (IoT) is one of the major paradigms that is seen in developing smart environments. The key issues that hinder the path of smart environments (Figure 8.1) using the IoT model is privacy and security. Manufacturing can be expanded and public demand fulfilled mainly because of the widespread usage of technology [2]. Because of the important functions they represent, these structures are considered to be critical systems. Use of technology in the role of critical systems, however, permits many attacks to target infrastructures' weaknesses [3]. The research community has focused on determining weaknesses, threats, and attacks on infrastructure systems so that security systems may be constructed to avoid these attacks. The intrusion attack is one of the most well-known and often used forms of attack.

Smart environments have evolved from the usage of the IoT paradigm. To make people's lives more comfortable and productive, smart environments have a major part in resolving issues related to energy consumption, daily life, and various needs of industry. Sensors in smart environments help to carry out processes. The development of smart environments was assisted by wireless sensor nodes, wireless communication techniques, and IPv6. Smart cities and smart buildings, and also smart factories and smart systems, are examples of such environments. If we integrate IoT devices with smart environments, we get more effective results regarding the IoT. IoT applications, however, are prone to a range of security threats, including attacks of denial of service (DoS) and distributed denial of service (DDoS). In an IoT infrastructure, IoT applications and smart applications might be severely harmed as a result of such assaults. As a result, protecting IoT technologies became a top priority [4].

Societies must maintain the resources they use in order to stay productive and preserve their economy from catastrophe [5]. As a consequence, organizations rely on architecture to manage and deliver various resources like electricity, communication, and transportation. Critical infrastructure parameters are water treatments plants, electricity grids, security, the health sector, etc.

Although these structures are centrally managed for the benefit of society's functioning, all vital infrastructures are interrelated and interdependent with one another as well as with the economy's many sectors. Because of the strong link between critical infrastructure, any harm to one industry's services – and worst of all, the elimination of one sector – will undoubtedly affect the other critical structures to the same or larger extent.

The pressing need for countries to meet the aforementioned standards resulted in a flood of technology into vital infrastructures, allowing them to better regulate their operations and optimize their output. Modern computers, meanwhile, have

FIGURE 8.1 IoT-based smart environments.

shortcomings and are unsecure. The increased frequency of cyber threats on key infrastructures, such as the well-known Stuxnet virus, which intended to cause damage to an Iranian nuclear power station [6], highlights the need to develop algorithms, methodologies, and programs to prevent such attacks.

Intrusion detection in infrastructure systems is the topic of this study. More precisely, we're talking about some of the most frequent techniques that an attacker might employ to gain control of a system or destroy it [7]. This study also includes a summary of methodologies and models used in various traditional intrusion detection systems (IDSs). The system where security is applied that works on the network layer of the IoT is an IDS.

Evaluation of data packets should be performed by IDSs in real time. They should not only examine the data packets at various levels of the IoT network but they should also work on various series of protocols and should be adaptable for diverse technology [8].

This chapter describes the most common and well-known attacks that can destroy critical infrastructure and create major issues and losses [9–11].

8.2 IOT PARADIGM

8.2.1 DEFINITIONS

The IoT evolved from the Auto-ID Center at MIT, which was founded in 1999. The EPC (electronic product code), which relies on RFID, was invented by the Auto-ID Center in 2003. This concept is the IoT's most important technology. However, the IoT, being well-established, may be characterized in numerous ways. The IoT is described by [12,13] as a collection of digital and hardware information flow formed on RFID tags. The next sections will go through the various IoT designs and descriptions supplied according to the standards and industries.

8.2.2 ARCHITECTURE

A well-defined project is IEEE P2413, which was developed by IEEE to identify the architectural framework of the IoT. Various fields of the IoT and their applications are briefed in this project [14]. The IoT architecture has three layers: the application layer, network layer, and perception layer.

The IoT's overall design is separated into various layers that cover the three mentioned domains according to [15–17], allowing the IoT to be tailored to meet the demands of various smart settings. Management and usage are included in the application domain. Data transmission is handled by the network domain. The perception domain is in charge of information gathering.

The hardware layer (perception layer) is made up of various sensors and physical things. Identifying, storing, collecting, and processing the information are all provided by these physical parts. This layer's output is forwarded to the next layer (the network layer), where it is processed.

The transmission layer is none other than the network layer that uses a communication system to convey data from a tangible entity or sensors to the processing unit over the protected belt. Determined by the physical entity or sensors, the telecommunication network can be wired or wireless, which can use a variety of technologies. The layer transfers the data on to the middleware layer.

The application layer is responsible for IoT applications worldwide [18]. The information processed at the middleware layer is being used by the application layer. Additionally, the application layer relies on various characteristics of many applications of the IoT that have been developed, such as smart industries, smart buildings, smart cities, and smart applications related to the health sector.

The business layer manages worldwide administration of service of IoT devices. The aim of the business layer is to develop a model based on unified data in the application layer and examine activity output of the processing of the information [19].

8.2.3 CLOUD COMPUTING FOR THE IoT

Various devices and sensors are linked together by the IoT system, which helps them to transfer data and impart a vast number of services. Administration and examination of big data necessitates a number of unique capabilities, including strong computing, huge storage, and high-speed networking [20]. Smart objects can be readily accessible and controlled at any time and location by various systems of cloud computing and smart environments formed on IoT systems, and improved services can be delivered through the IoT paradigm.

The biggest barrier in using a system enabled with cloud computing for the IoT, according to [21], is synchronization across multiple cloud suppliers. A second problem is ensuring that standard cloud service infrastructures and the IoT's needs are compatible. The primary barrier to corporations and government entities adopting cloud computing is security concerns [22]. As a result, the ability to respect the appropriate security limits in a cloud computing platform to meet the objectives of the IoT is a critical necessity.

One approach is to use a reliable and effective security solution like an IDS. Additionally, standardization, improvement, and administration of IoT systems and their connectivity to the cloud needs to be considered.

8.3   SMART ENVIRONMENTS USING THE IOT

8.3.1   DEFINITIONS

"The term smart refers to the ability to independently gain and use information, whereas the term environment refers to the surroundings," [23] write. One sort of smart environment is a smart city.

Smart surroundings can also include smart health, smart industries, smart buildings, and smart residences. The aim of this smart work is delivering services based on data gathered by IoT-enabled sensors that use smart methodologies.

Smart surroundings that use the design of the IoT have unique characteristics, which necessitate specific considerations in their adoption. Smart objects, for example, require remote monitoring and control capabilities in order to gather and analyze data and carry out activities. Furthermore, with such a system, the capacity to make decisions is a critical feature. Using various approaches like data mining to obtain usable information, an object can have the capability of being "smart," or making intelligent judgments without the need for participation of humans [24,25].

Other forms of smart environments include smart health, smart industry, smart buildings, and smart residences. The purpose of various smart surroundings is delivering services that rely on information fetched by the IoT through sensors.

8.3.2   SMART SURROUNDINGS ENABLED IoT

Governments are working over the infrastructure of ICT to tackle challenges in conventional public management activities. Establishing a smart city is one of the most recent and successful options [26]. The smart city notion is a major aspect under the smart environment concept.

The smart city idea has several advantages that are worth transforming conventional user services and measures, including increased public service quality and lower public administration running costs [27,28]. Moreover, the administration and delivery of conventional services in a smart city necessitate the use of a robust network.

However, there are impediments for construction of an IoT-enabled smart city. The most challenging aspect of IoT systems is their novelty, complexity, and technological hurdles. Furthermore, the lack of broadly agreed criteria for a smart city creates governmental and economic impediments that prohibit the smart city idea that is properly implemented.

Various examples of smart cities, like Padova Smart City located in Italy, have successfully surmounted these constraints. The primary purpose behind building this city was to provide information processing systems for administration purposes by utilizing various forms of information and technology [29].

The design of IoT applications for developing smart surroundings, especially smart cities, confronts various technological obstacles. Precision, latency, and available bandwidth are all key factors in many smart contexts, including industrial and healthcare settings. The platforms in IoT systems have the potential to increase the efficiency of data management services and the quality of service of applications in smart environments [30].

8.4   SECURITY AND PRIVACY ISSUES

8.4.1   SECURITY ISSUES IN IoT LAYERS

As growing services and customers enter systems of the IoT, securing systems in the IoT is becoming a real issue. The combination of IoT-enabled systems with smart environments improves the effectiveness of smart items [31].

The major security issues in the IoT make industries that utilize smart environments, like the health sector, at risk. Functions and operations are jeopardized in IoT-enabled smart surroundings that lack adequate security mechanisms.

IoT-based smart houses confront the risk of privacy and security problems that transcend the layers in the IoT infrastructure [32].

Establishment of smart environments faces two significant hinderances: IoT system privacy and the intricacy and affinity of IoT settings. Attacks on IoT networks affect IoT services and, as a result, the services supplied by smart environments.

Scholars investigate the various security concerns of the IoT from all perspectives, among which is the susceptibility of IoT communication protocols [33].

The major inclination is to add IDSs to the design of the IoT, regardless of rules defined; consequently, the research relies on the security concerns confronting IoT systems based on the IEEE definition and the overall IoT architecture.

8.4.2   CHALLENGES

As per the author [34], every IoT system's privacy vulnerabilities can be placed into four categories: authentication & physical dangers, confidentiality hazards, data integrity difficulties, and privacy concerns. Figure 8.2 depicts the relationships between these groupings. The security issues that happen in the various IoT tiers are briefly explored here.

The initial obstacles that an IoT system faces are authentication issues and physical dangers. Many IoT devices, such as sensors, are included in the perception layer and rely on their own security systems, making them vulnerable to physical attacks.

Risks to confidentiality exist in devices enabled with the IoT and gateways on the network layer [35,36].

The integrity of information between applications and services is the subject of the third class of security difficulties. Attacks like spoofing or noise disrupt an IoT system; then, data integrity issues arise. DoS, DDoS, and probe assaults are illegitimate attacks that disrupt IoT approaches and resources [37].

Smart surroundings that incorporate IoT technology are complicated systems since they comprise goods from various firms that rely on various technology that

FIGURE 8.2 Different challenges in security IoT layers.

has no common language. As a result, uniformity is another critical feature of security in IoT systems. Developing a common IoT design to establish a single standard technology for all users will improve the integration of all devices and sensors in an IoT system. The success of this integration will be determined by company participation in developing a uniform standard. Such standardization will make IoT network deployment much easier.

8.5 INTRUSION DETECTION SYSTEMS

8.5.1 OVERVIEW

IDSs' performance is separated into the mentioned parts. The first part is observation, which employs the network. The next part is analysis, which is based on characteristics of algorithms. The detection step that is final level, and it is abnormality based. IDS copies data flow in an information system and then analyzes it to find destructive actions [38]. Over the last 30 years, the notion of IDS as a securing system has evolved significantly. Throughout these years, researchers have presented a variety of ways and tactics for employing IDSs to secure various systems [39].

8.5.2 METHODS AND TECHNIQUES

The deployment of an IDS is dependent on the surroundings. An IDS that is host enabled (HIDS) is intended to defend system against encroachment or incursion assaults that might destroy its operating system or data [40].

Algorithms are used by IDSs to implement the various phases of intrusion detection. There are several algorithms available for IDS kinds and approaches. Out of those algorithms, IDS will be summarily explored in this section [41,42].

Furthermore, several of these IDS methods may be employed for various detection strategies. As a result, this part is inclined toward the IDS algorithm's lightweight anomaly, which depends on the intricacy, implementation time, and detection time requirements, that can be employed in IoT-based contexts. A lightweight method, principal component analysis (PCA), may be utilized for a variety of detection strategies in IDSs. [43,44].

8.6 IDS FOR THE IOT

8.6.1 METHODS AND TECHNIQUES

According to the author [45–51], "principal component analysis (PCA) is a widely used descriptive multivariate approach for dealing with quantitative data and may be expanded to deal with mixed measurement level data." As a result, the algorithm is broadly used in a variety of disciplines. According to [46], the algorithm creates a collection of variables based on the original variables' variance-covariance structure.

8.6.2 INTRUSION DETECTION BASED ON ANOMALIES

Formal data create patterns built on information fetched from regular users. They are compared against current data patterns online to find abnormalities in the intrusion detection approach. Such abnormalities occur as a result of noise or other phenomena that may have been caused by hacking tools.

Anomalies are thus unexpected actions generated by attackers who leave traces in the computer's surroundings. The traces are used to identify assaults, particularly unknown ones.

IDS containing abnormalities finds deflection from normal behavior in the computer surroundings by continually updating a model of fine behavior in the working environment based on input from normal users [47]. Table 8.1 summarizes the benefits and drawbacks of several anomaly-based intrusion detection approaches. These methods will be explained more below.

TABLE 8.1
IDS Survey

Survey	SIDS	Intrusion Detection System						Attacks on IoT	Deployment strategy
		AIDS					Hybrid IDS		
		Supervised	Un-supervised	Semi-supervised	Deep Learning	Ensemble Methods			
[5]	YES	NO	NO	NO	NO	NO	NO	NO	NO
[8]	YES	YES	NO	NO	NO	NO	NO	NO	NO
[10, 11]	YES	YES	YES	NO	NO	NO	YES	NO	NO
[12, 13]	YES	YES	YES	YES	NO	YES	YES	NO	NO
[15–20]	YES	YES	YES	NO	NO	YES	YES	YES	NO
[22–25]	NO	YES	YES	NO	NO	NO	NO	YES	YES
[30]	YES	YES	YES	YES	YES	YES	NO	NO	NO
This Survey	YES	YES	YES	YES	YES	YES	YES	YES	YES

A data mining strategy is a method of obtaining information from enormous amounts information, similar to digging coins from various mountains [48]. The retrieved information is characterized as intriguing data samples.

The technology machine learning contains two parts (i.e., training and testing). The first step is based on calculation-based algorithms or methods that learn the properties of the computer environment by using basic data as a reference input. These traits are then employed for detection and categorization during the detection step. Statistical mathematical operations are used in an analytical procedure.

This method enables a model to develop a set of rules based on the computer's surroundings. The rules are derived from patterns of data transmission. The model-enabled rules for IDS identify any unusual data flow that violates these criteria and classifies it as an attack. For a given application, the payload model method is determined by the packet flow of a certain port or user.

The protocol model technique is based on monitoring protocols at various levels of the computer environment. Based on this method, an IDS Table 8.2 identifies anomalies linked by a certain set of rules or such rules that cannot be included in regular designs.

The methodology based on signal processing technologies is used in traffic analysis.

TABLE 8.2
IDS Techniques With Advantages and Disadvantages

Techniques	Advantages	Disadvantages
Data Mining	1. Models are created automatically	1. Based on historical data
	2. Applicable in different environments	2. Depends on complex algorithm
	3. Suitable for online datasets	
Machine Learning	1. High detection accuracy	1. Requires training data
	2. Suitable for massive data volumes	2. Long training time
Statistical Model	1. Suitable for online dataset	1. Based on historical behavior
	2. System simplicity	2. Detection accuracy depends on statistical and mathematical operations
Rule Model	1. Suitable for online datasets	1. High false positive rate
	2. System simplicity	2. Privacy issues
Payload Model	1. High detection accuracy for known attacks	1. Long processing time
Protocol Model	1. High detection accuracy for a specific type of attack	1. Designed for a specific type of protocol
Signal Processing Model	1. High detection accuracy	1. Depends on complex pattern-recognition methods
	2. Low false positive rate	

8.6.3 Intrusion Detection Based on Specifications

The author [49] presented the notion of a specification-based IDS. They presented an observation and a system to detect the security standards, which defines a typical behavior of the protected system. The security standards are based on the system's functionality and security rules. As a result, operational patterns that are not part of the machine behavior are regarded as privacy breaches . First and foremost, difficulty in establishing a strong requirement-enabled IDS is developing a conformity that encapsulates the system's legitimate operational sequences. As a result, the value of developing the requirement's "trace policy" and complexity of fetching and validating specifications restricts specification-based IDSs' real-world usefulness. A specification-based IDS, like a misuse-enabled IDS, gains the root features of assaults and finds the familiar attacks, but it also has the capacity of anomaly-based IDSs to find unexpected attacks, like working patterns, which cannot be part of the system's regular behavior.

8.6.4 IDSs With IoT Systems

The study explains the aspects of techniques for IDS in the IoT that may be used in smart settings, based on suggestions from previous studies of IoT-enabled IDS . IoT devices need additional security measures with unique properties that typical IDSs do not provide. The primary characteristics of this system are that it functions in real time and performs well in detecting intrusions in an IoT system utilizing an event-processing mechanism.

For anomaly-based and signature-based intrusion detection, the author [50] suggested a NIDS that relies on machine learning. The system framework is intended for CoAP-enabled smart public transportation applications. This system's major characteristics are its adaptability to CoAP applications and its dependence on a lightweight algorithm.

The author presented a NIDS for WSNs that blends the statistical model method with the rule model approach. According to the hierarchical WSN structure, the system is built on a downward-IDS and an upward-IDS. The downward-IDS identifies anomalous activity in member nodes, whereas the upward-IDS detects abnormal behavior in cluster heads. The major characteristics of this system are its adaptability to hierarchical WSNs and its reliance on WSN clustering.

The author [51] suggested a constraint-based specification IDS for 6LoWPAN-based IoT networks. While identifying sinkhole attacks, our system maintains efficiency in terms of QoS metrics. The technology separates malicious nodes and rebuilds the network in their absence. This is a specification-based IDS that relies on behavioral rules and employs the protocol model methodology.

In this paper, the author [52] suggested a hybrid IDS for IoT networks that uses 6LoWPAN to identify multiple RPL attacks. This system is built on specification-based intrusion detection modules in the router nodes that serve as IDS agents, and an anomaly-based intrusion detection module in the root node that serves as the primary IDS. The key advantages of this system are the reduced amount of communication messages as a result of the lack of extra control messages or monitor nodes in the IDS architecture, as well as its adaptability to large-scale networks.

The author [53] suggested a WSN NIDS based on a machine learning technique and a signature model. To increase the detection rate and FPR, they employed a signature-based detection engine and an anomaly-based detection engine. The technology is intended to assist smart city managers in detecting attacks by utilizing an IDS and an attack categorization schema. The system's goal is to identify intrusions in WSNs in various smart city scenarios. The fundamental advantage of this technology is that it can be used with large-scale WSNs.

This work [54] presents the primary aspects of the mentioned structure categorization assaults in three types and the creation of graphical user interface (GUI) tools to graphically depict the abstract activity flows and identify probable intrusions.

This system's major characteristics are its low computational complexity and minimal resource needs. The author suggested a NIDS based on the SFC and PCA designs and algorithms. For the upgradation and enhancement, the competence of intrusion detection in high-dimensional space, mentioned method integrates artificial intelligence and data processing. The PCA technique is used to extract features. The adaptation of this system to provide IoT space for high-dimensional areas is its defining quality. Furthermore, the IDS's efficiency and efficacy are improved by lowering detection time and enhancing accuracy through a frequency self-adjustment algorithm.

The author [55] suggested a simple malicious-pattern-matching IDS. They emphasized that typical IDSs are inapplicable to smart items because of their restricted memory capacity and battery life. As a result of these constraints, a powerful and lightweight IDS is necessary. The key advantages of these algorithms are their small size, low energy consumption, and suitability for use in healthcare settings [56].

8.7 CONCLUSION AND FUTURE DISCUSSIONS

In IoT systems, three critical factors are integrity, confidentiality, and availability. Most IoT-based applications, likely manufacturing and preventive applications, are regarded as critical. Besides, because the mentioned apps might be actual, completeness and latency have a direct impact on their performance. Attacks like DoS, DDoS, and probing, lately, might affect the usefulness of such apps. Consequently, in digital healthcare systems, security concerns might be deemed a life-threatening concern. As a result, strong precautionary systems are essential in networks of the IoT. A protection system of this type must secure the system and its methods while not interfering with system performance or user privacy.

Furthermore, smart surroundings enabled with IoT systems are made up of a diversified machine, objects, and sensors from many suppliers and elicited from various policies and surroundings of the IoT. As a result, interoperability difficulties limit the widespread use of IoT technology [57–59]. When creating IDSs developed to create IoT-based smart environments, interoperability and standards must be taken into account.

IoT networks have poor power efficiency, necessitating the use of a lightweight IDS with a limited amount of computing operations. These challenges should be prioritized in HIDS research for such contexts.

Another major consideration with IoT systems is privacy. Deep packet inspection is seen as a breach of privacy. As a result, such strategies, as well as others with comparable qualities, are undesirable. Furthermore, the blockage of regular data packets has an impact on services and various applications built on the IoT. This impact is extremely damaging, especially in critical and concurring applications such as industrial and medical applications. As a result, implementing a smart system without deep packet inspection necessitates believing that the processes in the IoT system would prevent any illegal access to IoT devices, therefore assisting in the resolution of the user privacy problem.

Several publications were investigated in this chapter. In IoT design, the publications primarily investigated the blueprint and application of IDSs, which may be implemented in smart environments. The characteristics of all IDS approaches reported in these publications have been summarized.

The future studies encourage the development of better outcomes of hybrid IDSs, mostly for IoT-enabled smart settings. Further, the design of IDSs considers the risks related to security of IoT-enabling technologies and sets of rules. Furthermore, it allows adaptability to IoT-based smart settings.

In recent findings, the succeeding research will focus on the enhancement of IDS working performance in the environment, particularly for IoT-based smart settings. Furthermore, the security and privacy risks of the technologies incorporated with the IoT are handled by IDS designs and sets of rules. To allow adaptability to IoT-based smart environments, we apply programmed and reconfigured devices like FP GAs. The design should be adaptable to both distributed and centralized deployment tactics, as well as capable of detecting various forms of threats.

REFERENCES

[1] King J, Awad AI, "A distributed security mechanism for resource-constrained IoT devices", *Informatica (Slovenia)* 40(1) (2016):133–143.

[2] Weber M, Boban M, "Security challenges of the Internet of Things", *In: 2016 39th International Convention on Information and Communication Technology, Electronics and Microelectronics (MIPRO)*, (2016) 638–643

[3] Gendreau AA, Moorman M, "Survey of intrusion detection systems towards an end-to-end secure Internet of Things", In: 2016 IEEE 4th International Conference on Future Internet of Things and Cloud (FiCloud), (2016) 84–90.

[4] Kafle VP, Fukushima YHarai H, "Internet of Things standardization in ITU and prospective networking technologies." *IEEE Commun Mag* 54(9) (2016):43–49

[5] Zanella A, Bui N, Castellani A, Vangelista L, Zorzi M, "Internet of Things for smart cities." *IEEE Internet Things J* 1(1) (2014):22–32.

[6] IoT Bots Cause Massive Internet Outage. https://www.beyondtrust.com/blog/iot-bots-cause-october-21st-2016-massive-internet-outage/. Accessed 22 Oct 2016.

[7] Chauhan Abhilasha, Jain Mukul,"An Enhanced Cluster Feedback System for the Reduction of Jitter ." *Design Engineering* 7:3015–3036.

[8] Ayoub W, Mroue M, Nouvel F, Samhat AE, Prévotet J, "Towards IP over LPWANs technologies: LoRaWAN, DASH7, NB-IoT", In: 2018 Sixth International Conference on Digital Information, Networking, and Wireless Communications (DINWC), IEEE, Beirut. (2018) 43–47.

[9] Aras E, Ramachandran GS, Lawrence P, Hughes D, "Exploring the security vulnerabilities of LoRa", In: 2017 3rd IEEE International Conference on Cybernetics (CYBCONF), (2017) 1–6

[10] Butun I, Pereira N, Gidlund M, "Analysis of LoRaWAN v1.1 security", In: Proceedings of the 4th ACM MobiHoc Workshop on Experiences with the Design and Implementation of Smart Objects, SMARTOBJECTS, (2018) 5–156

[11] Čolaković A, Hadžialić M, "Internet of things (IoT): A review of enabling technologies, challenges, and open research issues." Computer Network 144 (2018):17–39.

[12] The institute, Special Report: The Internet of Things. http://theinstitute.ieee.org/static/special-report-the-internet-of-things. Accessed 8 Jan 2017.

[13] Thiesse F, Michahelles F, "An overview of EPC technology", Sens Rev 26(2) (2006):101–105.

[14] Minerva R, Biru A, Rotondi D, "Towards a definition of the Internet of Things (IoT). Technical report", IEEE, Internet of Things. (2015).https://iot.ieee.org/images/files/pdf/IEEE_IoT_Towards_Definition_Internet_of_Things_Revision1_27MAY15.pdf

[15] SPU The Internet of Things executive summary. Technical report, The ITU Strategy & Policy Unit, (SPU) (2005)

[16] Krčo S, Pokrić B, Carrez F (2014) Designing IoT architecture(s): A european perspective In: 2014 IEEE World Forum on Internet of Things (WF-IoT), 79–84. IEEE, Seoul.

[17] Ray PP, "A survey on Internet of Things architectures", J King Saud Univ Comput Inform Sci 30(3): (2018) 291–319.

[18] Bradley J, Loucks J, Macaulay J, Noronha A, "Internet of everything (IoE) value index", Technical report, Cisco, (2013)

[19] IEEE (2015) Standards, Internet of Things, IEEE P2413. http://standards.ieee.org/develop/project/2413.html. Accessed 8 Jan 2017.

[20] Bandyopadhyay D, Sen J (2011) "Internet of TThings: Applications and challenges in technology and standardization", Wirel Pers Commun 58(1):49–69.

[21] Han C, Jornet JM, Fadel E, Akyildiz IF, "A cross-layer communication module for the Internet of Things", Computer Network 57(3) (2013):622–633.

[22] Khan R, Khan S, Zaheer R, Khan S, "Future Internet: The Internet of Things architecture, possible applications and key challenges", In: 2012 10th International Conference on Frontiers of Information Technology, (2012), 257–260

[23] Rao BBP, Saluia P, Sharma N, Mittal A, Sharma SV, "Cloud computing for Internet of Things & sensing based applications", In: 2012 Sixth International Conference on Sensing Technology (ICST), (2012), 374–380.

[24] Khan Z, Kiani SL, Soomro K, "A framework for cloud-based context-aware information services for citizens in smart cities", J Cloud Computer 3(1) (2014):14.

[25] Al-Fuqaha A, Guizani M, Mohammadi M, Aledhari M, Ayyash M, "Internet of Things: A survey on enabling technologies, protocols, and applications", IEEE Commun Surv Tutor 17(4): (2015):2347–2376.

[26] Charif B, Awad AI, "Business and government organizations' adoption of cloud computing.", In: Corchado E, Lozano JA, Quintián H, Yin H (eds), Intelligent Data Engineering and Automated Learning – IDEAL 2014, 492–501. Lecture Notes in Computer Science. Springer, Cham.

[27] Citron R, Maxwell K, Woods E, "Smart city services market. Technical report, Navigant Research. (2017)

[28] Ahmed E, Yaqoob I, Gani A, Imran M, Guizani M, "Internet-of-Things-based smart environments: State of the art, taxonomy, and open research challenges", IEEE Wirel Commun 23(5) (2016):10–16.

[29] Schaffers H, Komninos N, Pallot M, Trousse B, Nilsson M, Oliveira A, "Smart Cities and the Future Internet: Towards Cooperation Frameworks for Open Innovation", (2011), Springer, Berlin.

[30] Taherkordi A, Eliassen F, "Scalable modeling of cloud-based IoT services for smart cities", IEEE International Conference on Pervasive Computing and Communication Workshops (PerCom Workshops), (2016) 1–6.

[31] Ali B, Awad, "AI Cyber and physical security vulnerability assessment for IoT-based smart homes." *Sensors* 18(3) (2018):1–17.

[32] Granjal J, Monteiro E, SáSilva J, "Security for the Internet of Things: A survey of existing protocols and open research issues", *IEEE Commun Surv Tutor* 17(3) (2015): 1294–1312.

[33] Kumar S, Vealey T, Srivastava H, "Security in Internet of Things: Challenges, solutions and future directions", In: 49th Hawaii International Conference on System Sciences (HICSS), 5772–5781, (2016), Koloa.

[34] Liu X, Zhao M, Li S, Zhang F, Trappe W, "A security framework for the Internet of Things in the future internet architecture", *Future Internet* 9(3), (2017).

[35] Trappe W, Howard R, Moore RS, "Low-energy security: Limits and opportunities in the Internet of Things", *IEEE Security Privacy* 13(1) (2015):14–21

[36] Hassan AM, Awad AI, "Urban transition in the era of the Internet of Things: Social implications and privacy challenges", *IEEE Access* 6 (2018): 36428–36440.

[37] Mohan R, Danda J, Hota C, *"Attack Identification Framework for IoT Devices"*, Springer, New Delhi. (2016)

[38] Jing Q, Vasilakos AV, Wan J, Lu J, Qiu D, "Security of the Internet of Things: perspectives and challenges", *Wireless Network* 20(8) (2014): 2481–2501.

[39] Forsström S, Butun I, Eldefrawy M, Jennehag U, Gidlund M, "Challenges of securing the industrial Internet of Things value chain", *Workshop on Metrology for Industry 4.0 and IoT*, (2018), 218–223. 10.1109/METROI4.2018.8428344

[40] Rubio-Loyola J, Sala D, Ali AI, "Accurate real-time monitoring of bottlenecks and performance of packet trace collection", In: 33rd IEEE Conference on Local Computer Networks (LCN), (2008), 884–891.

[41] Rubio-Loyola J, Sala D, Ali AI, "Maximizing packet loss monitoring accuracy for reliable trace collections", In: 16th IEEE Workshop on Local and Metropolitan Area Networks, (2008) 61–66.

[42] Ghorbani AA, Lu W, Tavallaee M, *"Network Intrusion Detection and Prevention, Advances in Information Security"*, (2010), Springer, US

[43] Anwar S, Mohamad Zain J, Zolkipli MF, Inayat Z, Khan S, Anthony B, Chang V, "From intrusion detection to an intrusion response system: Fundamentals, requirements, and future directions", *Algorithms* 10(2) (2017):1–24.

[44] Denning DE, "An intrusion-detection model", *IEEE Trans Software Engineering* SE-13(2) (1987):222–232.

[45] Stefan A, "Intrusion detection systems: A survey and taxonomy. Technical report", Chalmers University of Technology Göteborg, (2000) Sweden.

[46] Ganapathy S, Kulothungan K, Muthurajkumar S, Vijayalakshmi M, Yogesh P, Kannan A, "Intelligent feature selection and classification techniques for intrusion detection in networks: A survey", *EURASIP J Wirel Commun Netw* 2013(1) (2013):1–16.

[47] Mitchell R, Chen I-R, "A survey of intrusion detection in wireless network applications", *Comput Commun* 42 (2014):1–23.

[48] Butun I, Morgera SD, Sankar R, "A survey of intrusion detection systems in wireless sensor networks", *IEEE Communication Survey Tutor* 16(1) (2014):266–282.

[49] Creech G, Hu J, "A semantic approach to host-based intrusion detection systems using contiguousand discontiguous system call patterns", *IEEE Trans Comput* 63(4) (2014):807–819.

[50] Kumar S, Gautam Om H, "Computational neural network regression model for host based intrusion detection system", *Perspective Science* 8: (2016) 93–95.

[51] Snort, "The Open Source Network Intrusion Detection System", https://www.snort.org. Accessed 1 Nov 2016.

[52] Macia-Perez F, Mora-Gimeno FJ, Marcos-Jorquera D, Gil-Martinez-Abarca JA, Ramos-Morillo H, Lorenzo-Fonseca I, "Network intrusion detection system embedded on a smart sensor", *IEEE Trans Ind Electron* 58(3) (2011):722–732.

[53] Pontarelli S, Bianchi G, Teofili S, "Traffic-aware design of a high-speed FPGA network intrusion detection system", *IEEE Trans Computing* 62(11) (2013):2322–2334.

[54] Mori Y, Kuroda M, Makino N, "Nonlinear principal component analysis and its applications", *JSS Research Series in Statistics*. (2016), Springer, Singapore.

[55] Jolliffe IT, *"Principal Component Analysis, Springer Series in Statistics"*, vol. 2. (2002) Springer, New York.

[56] Kaushik K, Dahiya S. "Security and privacy in IoT based e-business and retail.", In: 2018 International Conference on System Modeling & Advancement in Research Trends (SMART). IEEE, (2018).

[57] Kaushik K, Dahita S, Sharma R. "Internet of Things Advancements in Healthcare." *Intelligent Communication, Control and Devices*. Springer, Singapore, 2020. 791–798.

[58] Singh, K, Kaushik, K, Ahatsham, Shahare, V (2020). Role and Impact of Wearables in IoT Healthcare. In: Raju, K, Govardhan, A, Rani, B, Sridevi, R, Murty, M (eds), *Proceedings of the Third International Conference on Computational Intelligence and Informatics. Advances in Intelligent Systems and Computing*, vol 1090. Springer, Singapore. 10.1007/978-981-15-1480-7_67.

[59] Kaushik K, Dahiya S, Sharma R. "Internet of Things Advancements in Healthcare." *Internet of Things*. Taylor and Francis Group, 2021. 19–32.

9 Intrusion Detection for the Internet of Things

Vikas Kumar, Mukul Gupta, and Shubhika Gaur
Department of Management Studies,
Chaudhary Charan Singh University, India

CONTENTS

DOI: 10.1201/9781003283003-9

9.1 INTRODUCTION

The Internet of Things (IoT) is the most interesting technology in the Information Technology (IT) age. Every day, the Internet allows linked devices to develop tremendously, and it has been predicted that by 2020, more than 50 million gadgets will be connected to the Internet. The goal of IoT technology is to link all devices in such a manner that all computers become programmable, intelligent, and safer to communicate with people. Things can communicate directly with one another because of sensors and networks. Machine-to-machine correspondence (M2M) will be conceivable in the future. Various IoT applications might be utilized in an assortment of enterprises and industries, including savvy/smart city applications (smart houses, smart matrix, smart medical care, and others), where they work on improving an individual's life.

The point of an intrusion detection system (IDS) is to recognize a network assault, and it effectively screens the network by identifying imminent occasions. An IDS is a software or hardware part that identifies and distinguishes destructive movement on PC frameworks or networks, permitting security to be saved. Network intrusion detection systems (NIDSs) focus on a whole network, though host-based intrusion detection systems (HIDSs) focus on a solitary PC framework. NIDSs are network-based equipment or programming parts that analyze and break down traffic created by hosts and gadgets.

The IoT is the newest correspondence worldview in which gadgets with sensors and actuators might work as articles or "things," detecting their environmental factors, speaking or corresponding with each other, and trading information through the web (Elrawy et al., 2018). The IoT needed a stage with which all applications, merchandise, and services might be connected and used to assemble, convey, store, access, and offer/communicate data from this present reality (Muntjir et al., 2017). There are already over 50 billion IoT devices linked to the network, and this number is anticipated to skyrocket in the next few years (Almiani et al., 2020). This massive number of gadgets generates a significant quantity of data. The IoT may be defined as an interconnected system based on authorized protocols that communicate data across Internet-connected objects.

Smartness is being assigned to devices, sensors, homes, streets, and cities as a result of recent breakthroughs in the IoT. The IoT is the most growing, evolving discipline of modern computer and communication technology, with significant contributions in many fields from agriculture to vehicle automation. Because it interacts with each form of linked device in daily life, the IoT is now referred to as the Internet of Everything (IoE) (Statista Research Department, 2020). The number of connected devices is expected to increase to 21.5 billion by 2025 (Statista Research Department, 2020).

As an example, by 2025, there will be 15.3 billion IoT devices for smart and advanced agriculture (Ferrag et al., 2020). For real-time monitoring and environmental control, a huge number of sensors and actuators are needed to give relevant information and make timely choices across a wide range of industrial areas (Ruan et al., 2019). Many obstacles, however, stand in the way of the IoT's widespread acceptance in both academics and industry. These difficulties include but are not limited to, security and trust, dependability, scalability, and mobility, to name a few (Pal et al., 2020).

In recent years, the scientific community has become more interested in the IoT. The IoT is a newly developed technology that will be the web's future, allowing common things to connect without the need for human contact. For present and future study topics, it is one of the most passionately disputed disciplines in both academia as well as industry. The security and privacy of IoT devices have proven to be key goals.

9.1.1 IoT ARCHITECTURE

The IoT is the next generation of the Internet; it comprises various ad-hoc interconnected devices with very limited functionalities. The core of the IoT architecture is made up of three layers, as shown in Figure 9.1.

- Starting with the perception layer, which is the lowest level and inputs data for the IoT, where connections among devices and nodes occur, it is vital to have privacy measures to protect against any compromise. M2M, radio-frequency identification (RFID), and sensor networks are components of the perception layer (Abdul-Ghani and Konstantas, 2019). First, M2M is the key component of the IoT, since it facilitates machine interaction and interoperability through a network (Halak et al., 2016). Second, RFID enables an object to wirelessly send various sorts of data across an IoT environment, allowing data to be monitored. The last sensor network is another characteristic that feeds the signal database and is regarded as vital information in the perception layer.

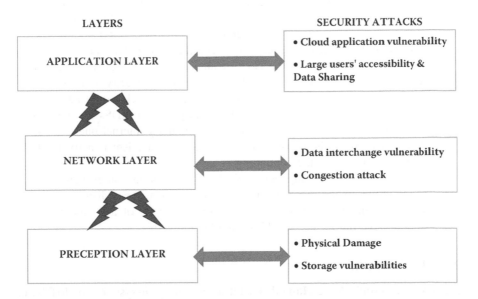

FIGURE 9.1 IoT three-layered architecture.

- The most important is the network layer, which allows IoT devices to connect with application services (Sethi and Sarangi, 2017). Sensor data is processed and sent using network characteristics (Mendez et al., 2017). These sensors are tiny and have limited computational capacity and processing capabilities.
- An IoT structure contains a connection of devices, such as a cloud-based system for data collection and actuators, and an application layer. It's in charge of deciphering the data collected and transmitting them to other IoT layers. The application layer technique filters related data, which are commonly located by transmitting a message from the perception layer via all parts of the network (Zarpelao et al., 2017). Although the application is intended to have high security standards, it does have certain typical security challenges, such as data integrity, dependability, and privacy protection. As a result, IoT security must be addressed.

To reduce security threats, multiple standards and protocols must work together. Besides the IoT industry's various technology, heterogeneity, and scattered nature. The complexity of IoT networks is increased by the nature of IoT applications, which magnify the risks. Because of these flaws, the IoT network is vulnerable to a variety of security threats, concerns, as well as cyberattacks. As a result, having an accurate anomaly-detection IDS model is critical.

In the computer science field, solutions to defend against security attacks or intrusion toward networks comprise three components (Sankar, 2014):

- **Prevention:** This component seeks to prevent threats from happening in the first place. In this instance, any recommended solution must be capable of devising countermeasures to the specific sort of assault(s). Intrusion prevention systems can protect wireless sensor networks (WSNs) and the IoT from external attackers, but they aren't meant to protect internal attackers.
- **Detection:** If an attacker succeeds in advancing the steps taken by the preventive component in the case of an assault, this indicates that the defense against the attack has failed. At the time, security solutions designed for the detection component of the linked attack would take over and focus on detecting the affected nodes in particular. IDSs are the only option to respond to continuing attacks, particularly internal ones (IDSs). When an intrusion is discovered, a mitigation mechanism is activated to reduce the impact of the continuing assault.
- **Mitigation:** The last component seeks to mitigate assaults after they occur. For example, to secure a network, a security step such as "dismissing the afflicted nodes in a network" or "disabling the ports of a computer that were utilized during the attack" should be adopted.

9.2 LITERATURE

Elrawy, M., Awad, A. & Hamed, H. Intrusion detection systems for IoT-based smart environments: a survey. *J Cloud Comp* 7, 21 (2018) This review describes the relationship between IoT architecture, new security vulnerabilities, and architectural layers. Despite earlier research on the design and implementation of IDSs in the IoT paradigm, this study demonstrates that designing efficient, reliable, and resilient IDSs for IoT-based intelligent settings remains a critical job. After this study, important issues for the development of such IDSs are offered as prospects.

Rajni Singh and Keshav Kaushik (2021) This article offers several possibilities and industrial packages of 5G-enabled IoT gadgets together with the supply chain, e-voting, Enterprise 5.0, intelligent home, and so on. Moreover, this study gives the primary stressful conditions integrating blockchain with IoT devices, including storage and throughput scalability, network scalability, and security. In this paper, a designed framework solved network scalability problems by using BDN and the slow throughput problem with the resource of the usage of using Raft consensus.

Keshav Kaushik and Kamal Preet Singh (2020) This paper spotlights a few fundamental threats to protection within the IoT and the current structure. The paper explores numerous commercial possibilities alongside the reason for using the hardware-sponsored protection. With the growing use of IoT programs in numerous businesses, the need to defend those devices against threats has emerged. Various situations for IoT use involve the need for protection, both because of the deployment of IoT devices inside the IoT or their requirement of being flexible. These necessities require a mixed combination of conventional protection enforced alongside device-orientated support. Distribution of this combination of support with constructing-constructing and protection enforcement among IoT devices and the community assists in supplying flexibility and scalability to the ideas of technical tasks.

Kamal Preet Singh, Keshav Kaushik, Ahatsham, and Vivek Shahare (2020) This paper focuses on the position of wearables in IoT healthcare, and the reference structure of today's technology utilized in wearables, as well as the diverse verbal exchange protocols utilized in the IoT. This chapter additionally describes the many wearables utilized in IoT healthcare with their characteristics. These wearable gadgets are synthetic with a few characteristics, which lead them to a suitable part of the human body. New technology like side computing also are supporting wearables to supply the predicted overall performance. Therefore, there may be a want for non-stop improvements in software programs in addition to hardware components to supply the predicted overall performance in close to the future.

Keshav Kaushik and Susheela Dahiya (2018) This study defines the upward push of cybersecurity threats in the IoT, the commercial view of the IoT for Electronic Business & Retail Security, improvements in e-commerce and retail due to the IoT, and risk marketers associated with safety and security worries in e-commerce and retail. The IoT gives quite a few programs in diverse domains. However, while speaking about e-commerce and retail, the IoT will modify this business in the future. This alternative is phenomenal; it gives rise to diverse troubles associated with safety and security, which need to be addressed on precedence with the aid of networks to make e-commerce and retail stable around the IoT. This study has shown the IoT business enterprise structure in e-commerce and retail. In addition, foremost safety and security threats of the IoT in e-commerce and retail with their possible answers are provided.

Allen (2021) Despite investment and promises to become mainstream technology in the future, the IoT still faces challenges that impede its spread. Security challenges are paramount, as the proliferation of IoT devices creates security issues at all three layers of the IoT architecture. Intrusion detection, which has been developed for over 30 years, is said to have the potential to overcome IoT security issues. The information in the article provides an overview of IDSs, IoT security issues, and some research on IoT IDSs.

A. Shaver, Z. Liu, N. Thapa, K. Roy, B. Gokaraju, and X. Yuan, (2020), Inspected the situation of IDSs to provide an alternative to protect IoT devices by using anomaly detection to classify whether network communication represents a potential attack. Integrating various popular machine learning models to improve existing IDSs could be a logical solution to this problem. This study contributes by reviewing various machine learning models and comparing them to intrusion detection. In this comparative analysis, the experimental results of the integrated machine learning model were promising, with 99 achieved accuracy in both binary and multiclass classifiers for intruder detection.

K.V.V.N.L. Sai Kiran, R.N. Kamakshi Devisetty, N. Pavan Kalyan, K. Mukundini, R. Karthi (2020) This paper explains how to create a model; you need to generate regular and attack data from your IoT network. Using the node MCU ESP8266, DHT11 sensor, and WiFi router, the test environment is created to emulate an IoT ecosystem. A laptop system is used to set up the adversary system, which executes sniffing and addiction attacks. Temperature, humidity, and setting data are gathered by the sensors and communicated to the ThinkSpeak platform via the wireless gateway. Sensor values are gathered by the node MCU and communicated to the ThinkSpeak server during the usual period. These servers are saved as regular data and designated as such. The aggressor watchfully intercepts data from the assailant's framework and modifies data communicated between the node and the ThinkSpeak server during the assault stage. During the assault stage, a man-in-the-middle assault utilizing ARP harming/poisoning is performed on the network, and the gathered data are set apart as assault data. Machine learning/artificial intelligence classifiers, for example, NB, SVM, DT, and Adaboost have been formed to arrange data into ordinary, regular, and assault classes.

M. Ge, X. Fu, N. Syed, Z. Baig, G. Teo, and A. Robles-Kelly, This paper focuses on protecting the IoT network against hostile assaults, which may be accomplished by carefully establishing and deploying appropriate security controls, one of which is an IDS. This study offers a new attack detection technique for the IoT that uses deep learning concepts to classify traffic flow. We derive general features from field data at the packet level using a new available IoT dataset. We foster a feedforward neural network model to arrange IoT device assaults into two-fold and multiclass classifications, including disavowal or DoS, dispersed and DDoS, surveillance, and data burglary. The proposed framework has a high arrangement exactness, as per the after-effects of its assessment utilizing the handled dataset.

A. J. Meera, M. V. V. Prasad Kantipudi, Rajanikanth Aluvalu, This paper states that the IoT has recently become important in the creation of smart homes. The IoT connects items to the Internet to make our lives easier, but it also makes IoT environments vulnerable to many types of assaults. Because a significant number of devices with different standards are connected, IoT threats are growing. The IDS is used to defend against a variety of assaults. An IoT system's IDS operates at the network layer. This study analyzes the problems surrounding IoT security. It reviews the literature on IDS for IoT implementation using machine learning and offers a few recommendations. An IDS built for the IoT should be able to withstand extreme environments. To detect important events, more IDS must be developed.

N. Chaabouni, M. Mosbah, A. Zemmari, C. Sauvignac, and P. Faruki, The IoT is rapidly expanding around the globe. The Dyn breach in 2016 uncovered fundamental flaws in smart networks. IoT security has become a major problem. Infested IoT devices pose a threat not just to IoT security, but also to the entire Internet ecosystem, which might be exploited by botnets based on susceptible "things" (smart devices). Mirai malware infiltrated video surveillance systems and used distributed DoS assaults to bring the Internet to a halt. Security assault vectors have advanced both concerning intricacy and variety in recent years. As a result, analyzing approaches in the context of the IoT is critical for identifying, preventing, or detecting novel assaults. The threats and challenges to IoT security are classified in this survey.

E. Hodo et al, This paper explains that the IoT is still in its early stages, but it has piqued interest in a variety of industries, including medicine, logistics, smart cities, and automobiles. It is, nevertheless, vulnerable to a variety of serious infiltration concerns as a paradigm. This study examines IoT security vulnerabilities and employs an ANN to address them. The capacity of a multi-level perception, a kind of administered ANN, to overcome DDoS/DoS assaults is tried by utilizing Internet packet traces. On an IoT network, this examination centers around the order of typical and danger patterns. A simulated IoT network is utilized to test the ANN technique. The findings of the trial show that it is 99.4% accurate and can correctly detect.

Y. Zhang, P. Li, and X. Wang, With the rising use of the IoT, the network layer's security is becoming increasingly important. Previous intrusion detection solutions are less effective with the IoT's complicated Internet. In the case of a deep learning attack detection technique, a neural network algorithm may get an excellent detection result for a similar type of attack but poor detection accuracy for others. As a result, it's critical to create a self-adaptive model that can change the network structure depending on the sort of assault. A detection algorithm is presented in this research paper based on an upgraded Genetic Algorithm (GA) and a Deep Belief Network (DBN). When confronted with various forms of attacks, the ideal number of iterations is the GA.

9.3   IDS CLASSIFICATION (FIGURE 9.2)

9.3.1   SIGNATURE-BASED IDS

These IDSs are used for defending organizations against a variety of known threats where signatures are stored in a database. This search compared a pattern to a list of harmful bytes and recognized patterns. The cause of an intrusion warning is communicated by signature-based IDS (Jacob, 2018). SIDS can quickly detect old assaults, but it fails to detect new assaults when a pattern is unknown or the

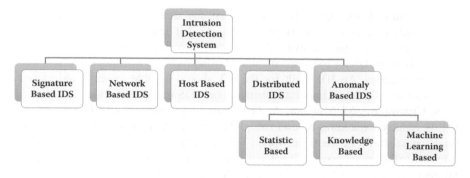

FIGURE 9.2   Intrusion detection classification.

database is not updated. This problem can be solved by updating patterns in the database regularly. Signature-based detection does not perform effectively when the user employs sophisticated technologies to mount attacks, such as No Operation generators and encrypted data channels. Creating a fresh signature for each alteration reduces its efficiency greatly (Rao and Raju, 2019). The system engine's performance also degrades as the number of signatures grows. Working in the field of anomaly detection is necessitated by a failure to identify innovative assaults and to continually update a database for new patterns (Rao and Raju, 2019; Kang and Kang, 2016).

9.3.2   ANOMALY-BASED IDS

By monitoring the system, AIDS can detect both computer and network breaches. Instead of signatures, it employs rules to characterize occurrences as normal or abnormal and seeks to discover aberrant operations after monitoring (Farzaneh et al., 2019; Worku, 2019). Although anomaly detection systems can identify new assaults, creating the ruleset is a time-consuming effort. As shown in Fig. 9.1, AIDS is again divided into three categories: knowledge-based IDS, statistical IDS, and machine learning approaches.

9.3.2.1   Statistical Anomaly IDS

Previously, IDSs were used to identify intrusions in information systems. To see if the observed behavior differed from the predicted behavior, statistical tests were used. Previous signature knowledge and frequent signature changes are not necessary for statistical techniques. They can identify low-level and slow-moving assaults, as well as DoS attacks. Statistical techniques have drawbacks in that they take a long time to learn how to produce accurate and useful findings. The Markov technique, deviation method, multivariate method, and time series method are the most often used approaches in this area.

9.3.2.2   Knowledge-based IDS

This system works by accumulating information regarding threats and system flaws. To identify an assault, it scans through its knowledge base. Knowledge-based

IDSs include techniques such as expert systems, Petri nets, signature analysis, and state transition. The data provided by these approaches have a high accuracy rate and a low rate of false alarm (FAR). Attack data must be updated frequently to maintain knowledge-based IDS effectiveness. Regular data updates take a long time, which is the fundamental drawback of that IDS (Hussain and Khan, 2020).

9.3.2.3 Machine Learning

Machine learning is a broad topic for research that incorporates principles from a variety of related fields, including artificial intelligence. The field focuses on learning or gaining skills or information via experience. This usually entails combining practical notions with historical facts. Most researchers nowadays concentrate on machine learning approaches because of their inherent qualities such as robustness, tolerance to noisy data, and flexibility. Researchers who are interested in learning more about the subject can visit the website.

9.3.3 NETWORK-BASED IDS

A NIDS, sometimes known as a network-based IDS, is security hardware that monitors vital network traffic from a strategic location. Traditional NIDS can scan network traffic and compare it to a database of known assaults.

9.3.4 DISTRIBUTED IDS (DIDS)

For attack detection, incident monitoring, and anomaly detection, DIDSs will have numerous IDSs spread around a system and linked to one another. To monitor and react to outside actions, DIDSs require a central server with high processing and orchestration capabilities.

9.3.5 HOST-BASED IDS (HIDS)

The server is connected to a HIDS, which monitors the system's harmful or malicious behaviors. The HIDS examines network traffic, system calls, ongoing processes, changes in file communication, and application logs, among other things. The disadvantage of this form of IDS is that it can only detect attacks on the system that it is designed to protect.

9.4 TECHNIQUES OF INTRUSION DETECTION SYSTEMS (FIGURE 9.3)

9.4.1 SUPERVISED LEARNING IN AN INTRUSION DETECTION SYSTEM

IDS-based monitoring systems detected attacks using tagged trained data. The supervised approach has two steps: the training method and the assessment method. During the training phase, appropriate structures and categories are identified, and algorithms learn by samples. In a managed read IDS, all data contain a network pair

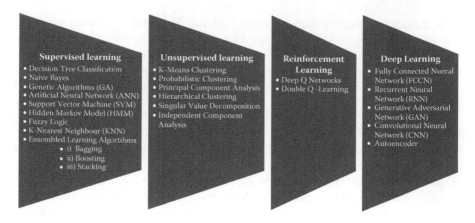

FIGURE 9.3   Techniques applied to IDSs.

of data sources as well as the output (i.e. label), such as login or standard. After that, you may utilize feature selection to delete features that aren't required. Algorithms consist of DT, rule-based systems, SVM, N-Bayes, and KNN, to name a few. Each approach makes use of a getting to know the technique to expand a classification model.

9.4.1.1   Decision Trees

The decision tree is made up of three parts. The decision node is the first component and is used for identifying the test attribute. A second type is a group of the branch, in which every one indicates a potential decision depending on the result of the test attribute. The third element is the last, which contains the model section (Rutkowski et al., 2014). ID3, C4.5, and CART are the few available algorithms of the decision tree (Breiman, 1996).

- **Naïve Bayes**

The Bayes principle is used in conjunction with the strongest independent assumptions among the characteristics in this technique. Using conditional probability equations, Naive Bayes solves queries like "What is the likelihood that a specific type of assault is occurring, given the observed system activities?" Traits that have a different probability of arising in assaults and normal behavior are used by Naive Bayes.

- **Genetic algorithms (GA)**

GA is a heuristic approach of optimism based on a theory of evolution. Every possible solution is represented by a set of bits, and the accuracy of the output increases over time due to the use of optional production operators in favor of better responses. There are usually two chromosome transcription methods in which a genetic algorithm is used to solve an entry phase problem: one is based on merging to create a binary chromosome code, and the other is based on the choice of clustering prototype matrix.

- **Artificial neural network (ANN)**

ANN is the most widely used machine learning method, and it is effective in identifying many types of malware. The backpropagation algorithm is the most widely used learning method for supervised learning. This method assesses the gradient error network concerning its variable weights. The detection accuracy and accuracy of ANN-based IDS still need to be improved, especially in rare attacks. Common attacks have a smaller training database than regular attacks, making it difficult for an ANN to understand the characteristics of various attacks accurately. ANNs have become useful tools for a variety of classification problems, including IDSs, due to the development of many species such as duplicate neural networks and convolution.

- **Fuzzy logic**

There is a common Boolean concept of truth or fiction based on modern PCs. This approach is based on uncertainties. As a result, it provides an easy way to reach data-based input that is confusing, ambiguous, noisy, erroneous, or non-existent. With an obscure background, the subconscious mind allows, for example, that we have multiple classes at once, almost partially. As a result, the unconscious mind is an excellent source of IDS problems, because security is not inherently accurate, and the line between normal and unusual situations is not clearly defined. Additionally, the problem of access detection includes many aspects of quantitative data obtained and the number of mathematical metrics generated. Creating an IDS using numerical data and strict conditions results in a significant number of false notifications. A slight deviation from the model may not be noticeable, or a slight change in normal behavior may trigger false alarms. This slight inconsistency can be modeled in an incomprehensible way to keep false positives low.

- **Support vector machines (SVM)**

The dividing hyperplane defines SVM, which is a discriminatory category. SVMs use the kernel function to transfer training data to a high-density area, allowing linearization of interference. SVMs are best known for their practical capabilities and are very useful when there is a high number of signals and a limited number of data points. By using a kernel, such as linear, polynomial, Gaussian Radial Basis Function (RBF), or hyperbolic tangent, many types of hyperplanes can be created. Many features in IDS data sets are unnecessary or have little effect on separating data items. As a result, feature selection should be considered during SVM training. SVM can also be used to classify data into multiple categories.

- **Hidden Markov model (HMM)**

HMM is a Markov mathematical model that assumes that the simulation system is a Markov process with anonymous data. HMM analysis is already being used to identify certain types of computer malware, according to a previous study (Annachhatre et al., 2015). In this way, the Markov Hidden Model is trained against the known features of a malware program (e.g. performance code sequence) and used to receive incoming traffic when the training step is complete. After that, the result is compared to a predetermined limit, with a higher score than the limit indicating a malware program. Similarly, if a school falls below the limit, traffic is considered normal.

- **K-Nearest Neighbours (KNN) classifier:**

The KNN algorithm is a common non-parametric classifier (Lin et al., 2015). The goal of these methods is to give uncategorized data names based on the class of their K closest neighbors (where k defines the number of neighbors to be considered). Because it delivers high classification performance in most IDSs, KNN may be used as a baseline for all the other classifiers.

- **Ensemble methods**

A few machine learning algorithms can be combined to improve predictive performance over any individual algorithms. Multiple class dividers are trained simultaneously to fetch various attacks, and their results are then compiled to increase the acquisition rate. The strength of the cluster is generally higher than that of individual dividers, as it may develop weaker dividers to produce good output than a single component. Boosting, bagging, and stacking are some of the few integrated methods introduced. Boosting is a term that describes a group of algorithms that can convert weak students into strong students. Training divides the same categories into different subsets of the same database called folding bags. Packing uses a meta-classifier to mix several categories. The authors have proposed a compounding approach that combines a compound that combines the C5 decision tree section with a single-phase vector machine. In the IoT data entry database C5, the mean accuracy of malware detection is 94%, whereas it is 92.5% in the second phase. They reported that the accuracy of the sections was 99.97% in the stacking ensemble.

9.4.2 UNSUPERVISED LEARNING IN AN IDS

It is a machine learning type that extracts useful information from input databases outside of class labels. In most cases, input data act as a group of random variables. The data collection is then assigned to a shared density model. Output labels are provided and used for teaching the system to achieve the desired results of a data point that is not visible in the supervised reading. Unattended reading, on the other hand, does not require labels; instead, data are automatically grouped into several groups throughout the learning process. Unregulated reading refers to the use of labeled data to train the model to detect interference in the context of building IDS network traffic. The IoT is grouped, based on traffic similarities, without the need to define these groups.

- **K-means**

This method is a popular method for combining the need to separate the data of "n" into a "k" cluster, each data object is assigned to a group with a nearby definition. It is a multiplication method that helps to obtain the maximum amount of each multiplication, as shown by the letter K.

As a metaphor, it uses the Euclidean metric. The user selects several collections ahead of time. Generally, many options will be tried before the best option is selected.

- **Probabilistic clustering**

Probabilistic clustering is a process that uses the distribution of opportunities to create clusters. The probability phase is a machine learning phase that can predict the distribution of opportunities over a set of classes given input inputs, rather than the most likely phase of awareness to be related.

- **Key component analysis**

It is a common way to obtain the set of bottom-level features from a large collection of features. PCA is a method for minimizing the size of big data sets by converting a large collection of the variables into a few that store most of the information in a large set.

- **Hierarchical clustering**

It is a merging method that generates a cluster category. The data are collected into a group tree through the merging process of categories. Every data point is considered to be a separate set of consecutive combinations. Thereafter, it repeats the following steps:

- Find out which two groups are most closely related, then combine the two groups most closely related.
- We should repeat these processes until all the collections are put together.

Agglomerative – Bottom-to-bottom combining methods, where clusters have small clusters, with their cluster, and clusters of clusters are joined as move upward in a phase. (Figure 9.4)

Divisive – It is the exact opposite of agglomerative hierarchical clustering. In divisive hierarchical clustering, we treat all data points as one group and remove data points from incomparable clusters for each duplication. Frequently, a group with the largest width in the feature spaces is selected and divided into smaller two groups. (Figure 9.5)

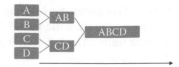

FIGURE 9.4   Agglomerative hierarchical clustering.

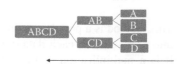

FIGURE 9.5   Divisive hierarchical clustering.

The **singular value decomposition** method of decomposing a matrix in other matrices in the order of line values that reflect the basic meaning of the matrix. The purpose of the price decrease is to find the best collection of earning indicators.

- **Independent component analysis**

This analysis is used to display hidden features behind a set of random features. Through unsupervised learning, much work has been done in the domain of CPCS to detect attacks as well as to reduce aggressive attacks.

9.4.3 REINFORCEMENT LEARNING

Deep reinforcement learning builds IDSs by combining deep as well as reinforcement learning techniques. An agent interacts with surroundings in reinforcement learning. Within the surroundings, the agent is trying to obtain a few types of objectives. The agent's purpose is to discover ways to engage with its environment in a manner that lets it perform its objectives. The use of reinforcement studying to teach deep neural networks is called deep reinforcement learning.

Deep Q-network It's a large-scale combination of reinforcement and deep neural networks. The technique was created by combining deep neural networks with a standard RL algorithm called Q-Learning.

9.4.4 DEEP LEARNING

Deep learning is a kind of machine learning in which a computer generates a hierarchy of data layers as an output based on experience. Deep learning may be both supervised and unsupervised. In supervised deep learning, data can be classified, but in unsupervised deep learning, data patterns may be analyzed. Artificial intelligence, in which robots learn via experience and eventually replace human intelligence, is closely connected to deep learning. Deep learning makes effective use of ANN to analyze massive amounts of data using algorithms devised by humans.

- **Fully connected neural networks (FCNN)**

The FCCN approach that is every neuron inside the preceding layer is attached to each neuron inside the subsequent layer. The term "feedforward" refers back to the truth that neurons in a preceding layer are by no means linked to neurons in a later layer. For characteristic extraction, completely connected neural networks may be employed (Wang et al., 2020).

- **Recurrent neural network (RNN)**

The RRN is a procedure for a succession of information with various input lengths effectively. RNNs utilize the records from their previous state as an entry for their modern-day forecast, and we can also additionally hold this procedure for an arbitrary quantity of steps, permitting the network to propagate information throughout time through its internal state. Giving a neural network a short-term memory is essentially the same thing. This property makes RNNs ideal for dealing with data sequences that occur across time. Using RNNs, a deep learning technique for intrusion detection was designed by the authors. (RNN-IDS).

- **Generative adversarial networks (GAN)**

GAN is a deep learning neural network that mixes two deep learning neural networks: a generator network (GN) and a discriminator network (DN). The GN generates artificial data, while the DN tries to differentiate between real and artificial data. These networks are competitors in the feel that they may be each looking to outperform the other.

- **Convolutional neural network (CNN)**

As in an average multilayer neural network, a CNN is made up of one or more convolutional layers, which are then coupled via a means of one or more related layers (Vasan et al., 2020b). An entry and output layer, in addition to numerous hidden layers, make up a CNN. A succession of convolutional layers involved with a multiplication inside the hidden layers of a CNN is usual.

A CNN takes 2-D input and, using a series of hidden layers, abstracts high-level information. CNNs benefit from spatial features because they improve the design of typical neural networks (Vasan et al., 2020c). In the field of IDS, spatial characteristics are the most commonly used forms of traffic features. Network traffic is formed in traffic images when spatial characteristics are applied; as a result, the image classification approach is utilized to categorize the images, achieving the goal of identifying intrusion traffic. Although this approach is relatively new, multiple recent study findings demonstrate its enormous potential.

- **Autoencoder**

An autoencoder is a machine that can be taught to rearrange its inputs. Online IoT IDS has been developed using autoencoders. An autoencoder that has been trained on

X will be able to regenerate unseen instances from the same data distribution as X. If an instance is not suited for the model learned from X, the restructuring is likely to have a high mistake rate.

9.5 SECURITY THREATS TO THE INTERNET OF THINGS (IOT)

9.5.1 PHYSICAL LAYER

Assaults are predicated on characteristics of devices and resources that are hidden. By messing with hardware, these attackers can seize control of the device. When an assault is conducted against a network or an IoT device, it is called a physical attack. The following are major dangers:

* **Node tampering**

A physical attack, such as connecting wires to the sensor node's circuit board and reading its data, allows an attacker to seize control of the sensor node. Furthermore, opponents can alter the original via tampering, modify the composition of the electrical board's wiring, or utilize the seized slave node's memory and the node's memory in any case. Capturing a node may reveal its important information, and data, particularly cryptography-related keys and information. As a result, the entire WSN might be jeopardized.
   In this scenario, there are two issues:

* The captured node can conduct arbitrary requests on behalf of the user or the attacker (DoS attack against availability).
* A captured node may offer erroneous information to genuine users (attack against integrity).

* **Radiofrequency Interface**

RF is a wireless communication technology utilized by the IoT. This wireless data transmission technique is subject to many assaults that can easily harm IoT devices.

* **Node jamming**

These threats are a kind of DoS intrusion wherein an attacker sends out a long-variety signs to disrupt communication. A rogue node inside the sensor community announces a jamming sign that has the same set of frequencies as the sensor nodes in a jamming attack. By generating noise within, the IoT community and rendering offerings inaccessible, this jamming assault prevents sensor nodes from transmitting or accepting data.

* **Node attack**

The cyber criminal may be able to take complete control of the sensor nodes. Because IoT devices are placed in various locations, tags are vulnerable to physical assaults. A cyber criminal might easily clone these tags and pass them off as legitimate ones to take advantage of an RFID system.

- **Physical damage**

In this attack, attackers are physically present within the attack to alter the information or to steal exclusive information. Physical dangers include physical attacks. An attack denotes the presence of an attacker and his purpose to attack, injure, or cause damage.

- **Social engineering attacks**

The attacker utilizes socially engineered techniques to take advantage of unauthorized get admission to a system and discreetly set up victim software. IoT devices, especially wearables, acquire huge quantities of personally identifiable information (PII) with the purpose of offering clients a personal experience. Customers' personal information is also used by IoT devices to provide user-friendly features, such as buying things online using voice control. Cyber criminals, on the other hand, can utilize PII to get unauthorized access to sensitive statistics, which include consumer passwords, buying histories, and private data.

9.5.2 Software/Application Layer

In the IoT, the software is advanced with the usage of API, and those programs are Internet programs that cannot run without putting in a software program. Software assaults are carried out through the usage of the software programs as well the usage of attacks, viruses, or some other malicious content material, which may also consist of spyware and adware.

- **Buffer overflow**

When an attacker manipulates a code flaw to carry out malicious operations and compromise the compromised system, that is referred to as a buffer overflow attack. The attacker modifies the application's execution route and overwrites sections of its memory, inflicting current documents to be broken or information to be exposed. Buffer overflow attacks regularly entail breaking programming languages and overwriting the boundaries of buffers. The majority of buffer overflows are because of a combination of memory manipulation and wrong facts composition or length assumptions.

- **Data privacy issue**

The attackers may use RFID tags on many items. Tracking IoT devices with the use of RFID tags can steal the privacy of users by monitoring their activities and creating a personal profile (Figure 9.6).

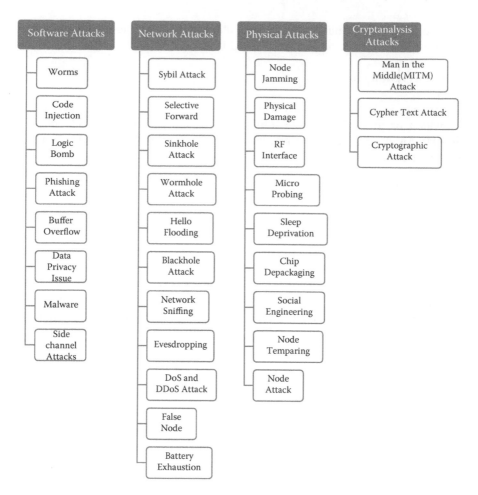

FIGURE 9.6   Attacks on IoT.

- **Malware**

Malware is a malicious software program that is supposed to damage or spoil computer systems and PC systems or harm IoT architecture. The term "malware" is an abbreviation for "malicious software program." A broad variety of malware paperwork exists, together with viruses.

- **Phishing attack**

The attackers make use of an IoT aspect node as a trap. The purpose is to gather records like passwords, usernames, etc. Phishing is a type of cybersecurity risk wherein hostile actors send communications posing as trustworthy persons or organizations. Phishing communications trick users into doing such things as downloading a damaging file, establishing a risky link, or disclosing private data like login credentials. The maximum popular form of social engineering is phishing, that's a big word for trying to misinform or deceive laptop users.

- **Side-Channel attack**

This assault breaks cryptography through records disclosed through cryptography. A side-channel assault makes use of indirect results of the device or its hardware to gather data from or affect the system execution of a machine, instead of immediately attacking this system or its code.

9.5.3   NETWORK LAYER

Data transmission is where security vulnerabilities arise and attacks can occur. Eavesdropping, DoS attacks, storage assaults, exploit attacks, spoofing attacks, and other types of attacks may be used. IoT attacks are a variety of information security threats that can be directed at single components, networks, or data sets. Devices on IoT networks might be targeted, and physical security assaults could be carried out. The bulk of IoT threats are network-based or targeted at individual information attributes. These are frequently premeditated assaults aimed at jeopardizing the IoT application's availability or jeopardizing the data's confidentiality.

- **DoS attack**

A DoS attack prevents a system's services from being available consistently. Legitimate system users are denied access to the system's resources. This attack is known as distributed DoS when it is initiated by a large number of hostile nodes. Instead of losing information owing to service bearers moving from the original provider due to security concerns, a DoS attack costs the victim time and money. There is a massive hazard of an assault on the IoT network for the purpose that devices and gadgets are associated with the Internet for 24 hours and are typically on power-on mode.

- **Distributed denial of service (DDoS)**

In a DDoS assault, an attacker momentarily infects many IoT gadgets right into a botnet, then sends synchronized requests to a server or a group of servers for a sure service, overloading the server and forcing it to reply to valid requests from end-users. It usually happens when all the gadgets are managed and messages are overburdened by IoT devices, and it's far most usually applied to reason traffic congestion within the gadgets.

- **Sybil attack**

This attack is when a group of nodes impersonates different peer identities to corrupt an IoT system. It's used to broadcast erroneous data from a random network. An intruder might utilize phony identities to deliver fraudulent information through these assaults. As a result, either a true emergency is overlooked. A rogue node in a network has numerous identities in this attack. In a peer-to-peer network, a rogue node can impact the routing mechanism and detection method.

- **Sinkhole attack**

It is used to attack data transmission between nodes in the neighborhood. This is mostly accomplished through the use of a routing algorithm. A sinkhole attack is an internal assault in which a rogue node tries to lure network traffic to itself by feigning routing modifications. An attacker launches an attack by inserting bogus nodes into a network (Can & Sahingoz, 2015). The fundamental purpose of that assault is to redirect traffic from a sure region via a hacked node that appears to be specifically attractive to the encircling points (Singh et al., 2015).

- **Wormhole attack**

In this attack, victim nodes provide an illusion to both the sender and recipient devices at all times. A virtual tunnel is created that purports to be the smallest path between the endpoints, which are the malicious nodes, so the base station may send information without it getting lost. The attacker node takes data and sends it to a remote site, where it is then locally sent. The attack can be carried out in either a hidden or participatory mode (Khabbazian et al., 2016).

- **Hello flooding attack**

This type of intrusion, which forces IoT gadgets to emit Hello messages to announce themselves to their neighbors, is one of the most prevalent network layer assaults. The initial message is broadcast as a Hello packet to connect the network node. By sending a Hello message, the cyber criminal can advertise himself as a neighbor node to a large number of nodes. When a node gets a Hello packet, it assumes that it is within the range of the node that delivered it.

- **Blackhole attack**

When a router deletes all messages it is supposed to forward, it is called a blackhole attack. A router may be misconfigured from time to time, resulting in a zero-cost route to every destination on the Internet. As a result, all traffic is routed through this router. The router fails because no device can handle such a load. In that type of attack, a malicious tool incorrectly offers the shortest path to the destination, after which it stealthy drops all packets on its path, creating a blackhole in the network.

- **Man-in-the-middle (MITM)attack**

Wireless sensor networks may be vulnerable to man-in-middle attacks, which might jeopardize the IoT communicant's confidentiality, integrity, and availability (Neshenko et al., 2019). A MITM attack happens when an attacker alters messages between two parties who believe they are secretaries talking with one other without the authenticating user's authorization. It's similar to an eavesdropping attack, in which the attacker may listen in on two people's conversations.

9.6   IOT SECURITY ISSUES AND CHALLENGES

The IoT has a lot of potential, and one of its key goals is to change the way we do things and the quality of life of people in the modern world. Wireless network systems have been vulnerable to security flaws since their beginnings; as a result, it's critical to emphasize the security and privacy challenges of the IoT, which may be described as confidentiality, availability, scalability, and integrity.

- **Confidentiality:** Trust is an important concern for Internet users of devices that share data to help them avoid theft. If the attacker can easily block communication sent by a recipient, the recipient's privacy may be changed and disclosed. As a result, secure messages are required in the IoT context.
- **Availability:** As we depend on IoT security in our daily life, it is necessary to remember the provision of the IoT, the ability to be disrupted due to the failure of communication tools, and powerful attacks including DoS and DDoS, as well as jamming attacks, which are thought to be more of a distraction. That is why the result of the loss of discovery should elevate the loss.
- **Coherence:** Due to the drift of large records generated through a huge quantity of linked devices, making sure the integrity of information in an IoT network is taken into consideration is another difficulty for security. The network needs to assure that messages aren't attacked by an attacker or unwanted person even in transfer over the network to keep the integrity of the IoT. Data integrity can be ensured through efforts. Data integrity in the IoT needs to appeal to several interests in the future.
- **Heterogeneity:** Because IoT-enabled devices have distinctive hardware, including a reminiscence footprint, computation power, protocols, and so on, assaults on confidentiality, availability, and integrity are too complicated to prevent because of IoT safety heterogeneity issues, and the shortage of a not unusual place protection provider is the most important problem.

9.6.1   Challenges

The security as well as privacy of IDSs for the IoT environment are described in this part as it is critical to upkeep and a major concern. Given that the IoT is still a relatively new idea, security goals must be developed. As an output of the dynamic environment of the IoT, many protection concerns remain open at many layers:

- **Attack model:** Considering numerous smart devices are interconnected, cyberattackers can create superior and complex attacks. Therefore, it's important to know the assault models and improve your detection rate and useful resources consumed.

- **Secure alert traffic:** Another continual worry for the IoT system is the safety of IDS communication lines. To protect the connection among IDS nodes, a variety of networks assume control. Weak intrusion detection and protection measures in secure connections between nodes and sensors in the IoT allow hackers to easily monitor and decode network data. IoT security requires a powerful IDS.
- **Trust:** It is based on the assumption nothing will have an impact on the desired individual. As a result, various heterogeneous networks can compromise by linking over the Internet through the IoT program. Because of the link to other systems, security standards are less stringent, which might lead to trust issues. Even though various scholars have suggested assessing only trusted networks, further study is necessary.
- **Malicious code attacks:** Numerous assaults in the IoT that focus on software packages, including DoS and worms, also attack cameras and routers. These styles of assaults can take advantage of the presence of software program vulnerabilities. A commonplace assault mechanism is a new computing gadget that includes IoT protection.
- **Privacy:** The IoT needs to save user's records over the network. Ensuring privacy within the IoT is taken into consideration as a mission for setting up steady verbal exchanges of associated data. Privacy concerns arise because an item inside the IoT collects a mixture of fragments of data.

9.7 IMPORTANCE OF INTRUSION DETECTION SYSTEMS IN CYBERSECURITY

- There is no firewall that anyone can make, and no network that cannot be penetrated. Attackers are constantly developing new exploits and attack methods to evade defenses. Many attacks use other malware or social engineering to obtain user credentials that allow access to networks and data. The benefit of the IDS is that it alerts IT staff in the event of a potential network attack or intrusion.
- NIDS monitors each incoming and outgoing community site visitor, in addition to site visitors among structures inside the community. Network IDS video display units show community site visitors and trigger indicators while suspicious pastimes or regarded threats are detected. This lets IT workers analyze it and take suitable steps to dam or prevent the attack.
- There are no completely secure firewalls and no inadequate networks. Attackers are constantly developing new tricks and techniques to defeat defenses. Most attacks use other social techniques and malware to obtain user credentials that allow access to networks and information.
- Being able to detect and respond to malicious traffic is critical to network security. The agenda of NIDS is to ensure that IT professionals are aware of potential attacks and network intrusions. Incoming and outbound traffic in the network, and traffic between devices in the network, are detected by the NIDS.
- With the proliferation of technology, businesses of all sizes have benefited significantly from the use of resources.

- Virtual security threats are becoming more and more problematic, and the IDS helps protect businesses from external threats and ensure network security.
- IDSs screen community site visitors and alert community directors to uncommon activity, like a house alarm that indicators an interloper has tried to break a window or door. For example, while a hacker tries to get entry to a PC or community, the intrusion detection gadget at once notifies the community administrator of the potential protection breach. Once reported, managers can perceive the precise region of suspicious activity and comply with suitable protection protocols.
- **Wide range of protection**

IDSs can guard your community and your PC from numerous threats. In addition to hackers, IDSs can guard against all sorts of malware and net worms. NIDSs are mainly designed to screen community visitors and monitor for signs of uncommon activity. Whether it is a synthetic virus or a worldwide hacker, community IDSs are the final defense toward all kinds of safety threats. There are three components of an IDS.

Network ID machine includes three specific additives. Sensors are a key aspect that makes it feasible to detect instantaneously protection threats. They typically have a signature database that permits them to identify malicious activity. The backend is the second aspect, chargeable for signals and occasion logging. Alerts may be dispatched in many ways, such as database logs, email, and console displays. Depending on the version, a few backend additives can offer a brief connection lock that forestalls hackers from having access to the unique target. The front end is the remaining aspect that represents the person interface. Through the person interface, the person can view all of the occasions detected through the sensor and set the IDS configuration. Users also can replace the sensor and signature database. All of those additives paintings together offer remaining safety toward hackers and all forms of malicious software programs that threaten community protection.

As you can see, in modern global technology, community protection is important for organizations of all sizes. More state-of-the-art new protection threats are continuously being created. Fortunately, online security is the main enterprise, focusing on online protection. We offer 24/7 tracking offerings and always replace our community assault detection machine. We recognize that the risks of the Internet and protection are our pinnacle priorities.

9.8   FUTURE WORK AND CONCLUSION

Many IoT users, services, and applications are growing, and there is an urgent requirement for a security solution to be used in IoT contexts. Since the IoT is the foundation of intelligent surroundings, any security vulnerabilities in these networks directly impact the intelligent environments in which they are built. DoS, DDoS, and RPL assaults impact services and software available in intelligent IoT-based environments; therefore, the security of the IoT environment is a major concern. A possible solution to this problem is an IDS. In this study, a survey was conducted on IDSs designed for IoT contexts. There were also proposals to develop the strongest and most lightweight IDS.

Several publications were reviewed in this chapter. The design and implementation of IDS for use in the IoT that can be implemented in intelligent systems is the focus of these studies. The properties of all IDS approaches discussed in these publications have been summarized. In addition, this chapter provided several recommendations that need to be considered when creating intrusion detection for the IoT. This chapter has highlighted the need for an integrated IDS that can be used in intelligent IoT-enabled environments. This idea needs to be tested in a centralized IoT database. With this design, the issue of placement strategy needs to be considered.

Based on the recommendations, a future study will explore the creation of a high-performance hybrid intrusion detection specifically designed for intelligent IoT-related environments.

REFERENCES

Abdul-Ghani H. A. and D. Konstantas (2019). "A comprehensive study of security and privacy guidelines, threats, and countermeasures: An IoT perspective," *Journal of Sensor and Actuator Networks*, vol. 8, no. 2, 22.

Abubakar A. and B. Pranggono (2017). "Machine learning-based intrusion detection system for software-defined networks," In Proceedings of 2017 7th International Conference on Emerging Security Technologies (EST), Canterbury, UK, 138–143.

Al-Garadi M. A., A. Mohamed, A. K. Al-Ali, X. Du, I. Ali, and M. Guizani (2020). "A survey of machine and deep learning methods for Internet of Things (IoT) security," *IEEE Communications Surveys Tutorials*, vol. 22, no. 3, 1646–1685.

Almiani M., A. AbuGhazleh, A. Al-Rahayfeh, S. Atiewi, and A. Razaque (2020). "Deep recurrent neural network for IoT intrusion detection system," *Simulation Modelling Practice and Theory*, vol. 101, 102031.

Alsoufi M. A., S. Razak, M. M. Siraj, A. Ali, M. Nasser, and S. Abdo (2021). *Anomaly Intrusion Detection Systems in IoT Using Deep Learning Techniques: A Survey*; Springer International Publishing: Cham, Switzerland.

Atzori L., A. Iera, and G. Morabito (2017). "Understanding the Internet of Things: Definition, potentials, and societal role of a fast-evolving paradigm," *Ad Hoc Networks*, vol. 56, 122–140.

Bouzida Y. and F. Cuppens (2006). "Neural networks vs. decision trees for intrusion detection," In Proceedings of the IEEE/IST Workshop on Monitoring, Attack Detection and Mitigation (MonAM), Tuebingen, Germany, (28), 28–29.

Breiman, L. (1996). Bagging predictors. *Machine learning*, 24(2), 123–140.

Buczak A. L. and E. Guven, (2016). "A survey of data mining and machine learning methods for cyber security intrusion detection," *IEEE Communications Surveys Tutorials*, vol. 18, no. 2, 1153–1176.

Butun I., S. D. Morgera, and R. Sankar (2014). "A survey of intrusion detection systems in wireless sensor networks," *IEEE Communications Surveys & Tutorials*, vol. 16, no. 1, 266–282.

Chaabouni N., M. Mosbah, A. Zemmari, C. Sauvignac, and P. Faruki (2019). "Network intrusion detection for IoT security based on learning techniques," *IEEE Communications Surveys & Tutorials*, vol. 21, no. 3, 2671–2701, third quarter, 10.1109/COMST.2019.2896380

Dubrawsky I. (Ed.) (2007). Chapter 2—General Security Concepts: Attacks. in How to Cheat at Securing Your Network; Syngress: Maryland Heights, MO, USA, 35–64. ISBN 9781597492317.

Dwivedi A. D., R. Singh, K. Kaushik, R. R. Mukkamala, and W. S. Alnumay (2021). "Blockchain and artificial intelligence for 5G-enabled Internet of Things: Challenges, opportunities, and solutions," 10.1002/ett.4329.

Elrawy M. F., A. I. Awad, and H. F. A. Hamed (2018). "Intrusion detection systems for IoT-based smart environments: A survey," *Journal of Cloud Computing*, vol. 7, 21.

Fahim M. and A. Sillitti (2019). "Anomaly detection, analysis and prediction techniques in IoT environment: A systematic literature review," *IEEE Access*, vol. 7, 81664–81681.

Ferrag M. A., L. Shu, X. Yang, A. Derhab, and L. Maglaras (2020). "Security and privacy for green IoT-Based agriculture: Review, blockchain solutions, and challenges," *IEEE Access*, vol. 8, 32031–32053.

Ge M., X. Fu, N. Syed, Z. Baig, G. Teo, and A. Robles-Kelly, (2019). "Deep learning-based intrusion detection for IoT networks," In IEEE 24th Pacific Rim International Symposium on Dependable Computing (PRDC), 2019, 256–25609, 10.1109/PRDC 47002.2019.00056.

Habeeb R. A. A., F. Nasaruddin, A. Gani, I. A. T. Hashem, E. Ahmed, and M. Imran (2019). "Real-time big data processing for anomaly detection: A survey," *International Journal of Information Management*, vol. 45, 289–307.

Halak B., M. Zwolinski, and M. S. Mispan (2016). "Overview of PUF-based hardware security solutions for the Internet of Things," In Proceedings of 2016 IEEE 59th International Midwest Symposium on Circuits and Systems (MWSCAS), Abu Dhabi, United Arab Emirates, 1–4.

Hodo E. et al., (2016). "Threat Analysis of IoT networks using artificial neural network intrusion detection system," In 2016 International Symposium on Networks, Computers, and Communications (ISNCC), 1–6, 10.1109/ISNCC.2016.7746067

Hossain M. M., M. Fotouhi, and R. Hasan (2015). "Towards an analysis of security issues, challenges, and open problems in the Internet of Things," In Proceedings of the 2015 IEEE World Congress on Services, New York, NY, USA, IEEE: Piscataway, NJ, USA, 2015.

Jee K., L. I. Zhichun, G. Jiang, L. Korts-Parn, Z. Wu, Y. Sun, and J. Rhee (2018). "Host level detect mechanism for malicious DNS activities," *U.S. Patent Applications*, vol. 15 644 018.

Kaushik K., and S. Dahiya (2018). "Security and privacy in IoT based e-business and retail," Proceedings of the SMART–2018, IEEE Conference ID: 44078, 78–81.

Kaushik K. and K. Singh (2020). *Security and Trust in IoT Communications: Role and Impact*. Springer Nature Singapore Pte Ltd, 791–798.

Khabbazian M., Kriebel, R., Rohe K., & Ane C. (2016). Fast and accurate detection of evolutionary shifts in Ornstein–Uhlenbeck models. *Methods in Ecology and Evolution*, 7(7), 811–824.

Lin J., W. Yu, N. Zhang, X. Yang, H. Zhang, and W. Zhao (2017). "A survey on Internet of Things: Architecture, enabling technologies, security and privacy, and applications," *IEEE Internet of Things Journal*, vol. 4, 1125–1142.

Meera A. J., M. V. V. Prasad Kantipudi, and R. Aluvalu (2021). Proceedings of the 11th International Conference on Soft Computing and Pattern Recognition (SoCPaR 2019), Volume 1182 ISBN: 978-3-030-49344-8

Mendez D. M., I. Papapanagiotou, and B. Yang (2017). "Internet of Things: Survey on security and privacy," [Online]. Available: https://arxiv.org/abs/1707.01879.

Moustafa N. and J. Slay UNSW-NB15: (2015). "A comprehensive data set for network intrusion detection systems (UNSW-NB15 network data set)," In Proceedings of the 2015 Military Communications and Information Systems Conference (MilCIS), Canberra, ACT, Australia, 10–12.

Moustafa N. and J. Slay (2017). A hybrid feature selection for network intrusion detection systems: Central points. arXiv:1707.05505.

Mukhopadhyay S. C. and N. K. Suryadevara (2014). "Internet of Things: Challenges and opportunities," in *Internet of Things: Challenges and Opportunities*. Cham, Switzerland: Springer International Publishing, 1–17.

Muntjir, M., Rahul, M., & Alhumyani, H. A. (2017). An Analysis of Internet of Things(IoT): Novel Architectures, Modern Applications, Security Aspects and Future Scope with Latest Case Studies. *International Journal of Engineering Research & Technology*, vol. 6no. 6.

Naseer S. and Y. Saleem (2021). "Enhanced network intrusion detection using deep convolutional neural networks," *KSII Transactions on Internet and Information Systems*, vol. 2018, no. 12, 5159–5178.

O. Can and O. K. Sahingoz, "A survey of intrusion detection systems in wireless sensor networks," 2015 6th International Conference on Modeling, Simulation, and Applied Optimization (ICMSAO), 2015, pp. 1–6, doi: 10.1109/ICMSAO.2015.7152200.

Pal S., M. Hitchens, T. Rabehaja, and S. Mukhopadhyay (2020). "Security requirements for the Internet of Things: A systematic approach," *Sensors*, vol. 20, 5897.

S. Rathore, P. K. Sharma, V. Loia, Y. S. Jeong, and J. H. Park, (2017). "Social network security: Issues, challenges, threats, and solutions," *Information Sciences*, vol. 421, 43–69.

Ruan J., Y. Wang, F. T. S. Chan, X. Hu, M. Zhao, F. Zhu, B. Shi, Y. Shi, and F. Lin (2019). "A life-cycle framework of green IoT-Based agriculture and its finance, operation, and management issues," *IEEE Communications Magazine*, vol. 57, 90–96.

Sethi P. and S. R. Sarangi (2017). "Internet of Things: Architectures, protocols, and applications," *Journal of Electrical and Computer Engineering*, article no. 9324035.

T. Sherasiya, H. Upadhyay, and H. B. Patel, (2016). "A survey: Intrusion detection system for Internet of Things," *International Journal of Computer Science and Engineering*, vol. 5, no. 2, pp. 91–98.

Singh K., K. Kaushik, Ahatsham, and V. Shahare (2020). "Role and impact of wearables in IoT healthcare," 978–981, 10.1007/978-981-15-1480-7_67.

Singh, M. Information Security of Intelligent Vehicles Communication.

Soniya S. S. and S. M. C. Vigila (2016). "Intrusion detection system: Classification and techniques," In Proceedings of the 2016 International Conference on Circuit, Power and Computing Technologies (ICCPCT), Nagercoil, India.

Spafford E. and D. Zamboni (2000). Data Collection Mechanisms for Intrusion Detection Systems; CERIAS Technical Report; Center for Education and Research in Information Assurance and Security: West Lafayette, IN, USA, 47907-1315.

Statista Research Department. "IoT: Number of connected devices worldwide 2012–2025," Availableonline:https://www.statista.com/statistics/471264/iot-number-of-connected-devices-worldwide/ (accessed on 20 May 2020).

Tan Z., A. Jamdagni, X. He, P. Nanda, and R. P. Liu (2014). "A system for denial-of-service attack detection based on multivariate correlation analysis," *IEEE Transactions on Parallel and Distributed Systems*, vol. 25, 447456.

The-UNSW-NB15-Dataset. Available online: https://paperswithcode.com/dataset/unsw-nb15.

Wang, W., Lin, H. & Wang, J. CNN based lane detection with instance segmentation in edge-cloud computing. *J Cloud Comp* 9, 27 (2020). https://doi.org/10.1186/s13677-020-00172-z.

Xin Y., L. Kong, Z. Liu, Y. Chen, Y. Li, H. Zhu, M. Gao, H. Hou, and C. Wang (2018). "Machine learning and deep learning methods for cybersecurity," *IEEE Access*, vol. 6, 35365–35381.

Yang Y., K. Zheng, C. Wu, and Y. Yang (2019). "Improving the classification effectiveness of intrusion detection by using improved conditional variational autoencoder and deep neural network," *Sensors*, vol. 19, 2528.

Zarpelao B. B., R. S. Miani, C. T. Kawakani, and S. C. de Alvarenga (2017). "A survey of intrusion detection in Internet of Things," *Journal of Network and Computer Applications*, vol. 84, 25–37.

Zhang Y., P. Li, and X. Wang (2019). "Intrusion detection for IoT based on improved genetic algorithm and deep belief network," *IEEE Access*, vol. 7, 31711–31722, 10.1109/ACCESS.2019.2903723.

10 Cybercrimes and Digital Forensics in Internet of Things

Vinita Sharma
Amity University, Noida, India

CONTENTS

DOI: 10.1201/9781003283003-10

10.1 INTRODUCTION

The Internet of Things (IoT) is technology that does not need human intervention to take many kinds of actions. There are sensors attached to IoT devices to gather, transmit, and analyze data and then act on that data, providing new opportunities for technology, media, and telecommunications companies to produce value.

Consider a car garage door opener that can also deactivate the home alarm system as family members enter. This is a useful function for a homeowner who needs to get into the house quickly. But, if the garage door opener is hacked, the complete alarm system may be disarmed, leaving the house unsafe. In fact, all the devices in the house – TVs, thermostats, door locks, alarms, and garage door openers – create a plethora of opportunities for intruders to get access to the house through the IoT.

IoT technology-based devices are becoming popular worldwide very quickly. The ubiquity, variety, and heterogeneity of this technology is removing all boundaries around the living, non-living, and digital worlds. The presence of IoT technology in the business world cannot be ignored today, hence the attacks and threats on IoT devices, too. Such attacks or crimes are increasing day by day. There is no doubt that IoT technology has shown new paths to organizations for adding value and creating new business models, but at the same time has given opportunities to cyber criminals to hack the systems due to constant connectivity and data sharing.

As every coin has two sides, the risks associated with the IoT cannot be ignored, although the IoT provides many benefits, too. Cyber criminals have become a major threat to the government and business infrastructures all over the globe and are destroying these infrastructures through their criminal behaviors. Cyberattacks over IoT devices and systems are affecting the lives of users, so looking into solutions is mandatory now. Secure IoT is the need of the hour, and understanding of attacks and threats in the IoT structure should be common knowledge.

The IoT invites cyberattacks as it is widely used. The IoT infrastructure can be used as the main platform for cyberattacks, and the IoT infrastructure's security is threatened. IoT forensics supports investigators in gathering clues from smart devices and their network to reconstruct historical incidences. Due to the sophistication of the IoT architecture, digital investigators face lots of obstacles when conducting IoT-related investigations using current investigation methodology, necessitating the creation of a new dedicated forensic framework.

This chapter consists of the below mentioned topics and subtopics to discuss IoT technologies, IoT's main features, security challenges, suggested security solutions, and how the IoT allows cybercrimes to happen. The chapter also explains digital forensics as well as IoT forensics before concluding the chapter.

10.2 INTERNET OF THINGS

The IoT is a group or network of devices, living or non-living things that are able to communicate with each other by exchanging data collected, with the help of Internet connectivity, without any human support. Smart cars and smart homes are few examples that work by using IoT technology.

10.2.1 BASIC CHARACTERISTICS OF THE IoT

Many characteristics in the broader context can be used to define the IoT. There are seven important IoT characteristics: (Figure 10.1)

1. **Connectivity** – Connection of everything in the network is a must. There are multiple levels of connections within IoT devices and other hardware used in the network.
2. **Things** – Any device, hardware, or animal or human that can be labelled or connected in the network is known as a "thing" in the IoT network. Sensors and household equipment are all part of things.
3. **Data** – The content exchanged among the devices and hardware connected through IoT technology is "data." It is the first step toward action and intelligence.
4. **Communication** – Exchanging data among devices is called "communication" among them. There may be short-distance communication or long-distance communication among devices under this technology.
5. **Intelligence** – The sensing capabilities in IoT devices and insight gained from big data analytics is counted as intelligence of IoT devices.
6. **Action** – This is the result of intelligence. Action can be manual or based on debates about phenomena, or automation, which is usually the most essential part of the IoT.

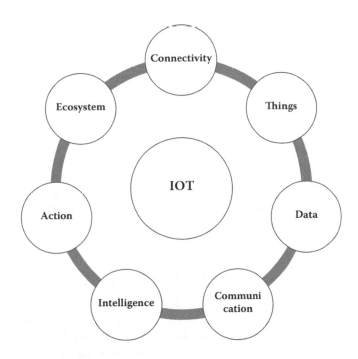

FIGURE 10.1   Characteristics of the Internet of Things.

7. **Ecosystem** – The specific position of the IoT adjusting with other existing technologies, communities, and the overall picture into which the IoT fits automatically is called an "ecosystem."

10.2.2 BUILDING BLOCKS OF THE IoT

There are four basic components of an IoT system. The features of each system are listed below:

1. Sensors

Sensors are the IoT devices' front end. In the IoT, they really mean "things." Their primary responsibility is to collect necessary data from the environment and transmit it on to database or processing systems. Because they are the basic frontend interface in a huge network of other devices, they must be easily searchable via their IP address. Sensors capture data in real time and can either act autonomously or be directed by the user. A gas sensor, a water quality sensor, and a moisture sensor are examples of sensors.

2. Processors

Processors serve as the brain of the IoT system. The main responsibility of processors is to convert raw data gathered by sensors into useful information. Basically, it provides intelligence to the raw data.

Processors are easily controlled by applications. Data security is also one of the major tasks done by processors. It is done through cryptography.

3. Gateways

The IoT system needs communication and network access to work properly. Gateways are used to define the route of the processed data for transmitting it to suitable servers or databases. Gateways include LANs, WANs, PANs, etc.

4. Applications

Another end of an IoT system is applications. Applications utilize collected data. They provide users an interface to interact with the data. Most of the time applications are cloud-based and are used to display collected data. These applications can be controlled by users for various activities. A few major examples of such applications are apps for smart homes, security system control, and industrial control.

10.2.3 TECHNOLOGIES USED FOR IoT COMMUNICATION

Smart IoT-connected gadgets are more vulnerable to cyberattacks. And it's critical to utilize the correct protocols to close these security gaps. IoT communication protocols are forms of communication that offer the highest level of security for data shared between IoT-connected devices. The following are the primary advantages of standardized communication protocols:

1. **High quality and credibility**

Communication technologies that adhere to standards provide good service quality and resistance to interference. Furthermore, they provide dependable and secure transmission of large amounts of IoT sensor data at the edge.

2. **Interoperability and innovation flexibility**

Standard protocols can be programmed on a variety of commodity and off-the-shelf hardware, including gateways and chipsets. As a result, multi-vendor support solutions assist end customers in avoiding vendor lock-in issues.

3. **Global scalability**

Every business organization desires IoT connectivity that can be adopted internationally. Furthermore, established communication protocols provide universal connectivity while reducing installation complexity.

10.2.4 IoT PROTOCOLS

There are various IoT protocols that may be used for IoT-related communication.

1. **IoT Network Protocols**

IoT network protocols are intended to connect low- to high-power devices through a network. They enable data communication within the network's boundaries. Some prominent IoT network protocols are HTTP, LoRaWAN, Bluetooth, and Zigbee.

2. **IoT Data Protocols**

IoT data protocols are intended to link low-power IoT devices. They can provide end-to-end communication with the hardware even without an Internet connection. Some common IoT data protocols are MQTT, CoAP, AMQP, and XMPP.

10.2.5 IoT LAYERS

Though IoT components represent the key fundamentals of a complete Information Technology system, IoT layers are the foundation for the overall network and play a significant role in the overall success of the whole IoT network. Each layer has a distinct objective in addressing the IoT complexity across the network. The following are the layers of an IoT system:

1. **Perception Layer**

The perception layer takes care of managing smart devices throughout the system. The digital and physical worlds are connected through this layer. This layer helps in conversion of analog signals into digital signals and vice versa. This layer includes:

a. Sensors: These are very small objects used to recognize and detect changes in their environment and convert that information into digital form to make it more suitable for the system to understand. Since the sensors are relatively small, they need less power to function. Sensors detect physical characteristics of surroundings, such as humidity or temperature, and exchange this information to the next device in the form of electronic signals.
b. Actuators: The actuators are critical components of IoT networks. These receive the electrical signals from sensors and convert them into physical actions.
c. Machine and Devices: These are all the things and devices under the IoT network that hold actuators and sensors.

Without any geographical location restriction, devices can be scattered throughout the globe while being part of the IoT network.

2. **Transport Layer**

It enables data transmission between the cloud and IoT devices. Also, it holds several features of gateways and networks. This layer is responsible for successful communication between devices and the IoT architecture, which occurs in two ways:

1. By using a TCP or UDP/IP stack;
2. Through the gateways, which helps transmission of data through multiple protocols. Several network technologies are integrated into IoT systems. A few are listed below:
   * WiFi – It is the most widely used and adapted technology in the world these days. This is the basic support of smart devices to function. This technology is extensively used for smart buildings and provides flawless connectivity to users in the networking environment.
   * Ethernet – It is the system that helps connect devices like video cameras, gaming consoles, and security devices in the IoT environment.
   * Bluetooth – It is a good technology to use when the devices are placed very near to each other. This technology is also used extensively between devices. For example, headphones that can operate on low power.
   * NFC (Near Field Communications) – When two or more devices are a maximum of 4 inches apart, this technology enables communication between them.
   * LPWAN (Low Power Wide Area Network) – This technology helps connect long-distant devices. The main advantage of this technology is that even after consuming very low power, it supports the network for a long period of time and may provide exact information. Examples are smart homes.
   * ZigBee – This technology is based on a wireless network and uses low power. The limitation of this technology is that it transmits limited data.

ZigBee was designed with home automation in mind, but it has also demonstrated extraordinary effectiveness with medical, scientific, and industrial protocols.

- Cellular networks – These show greater confidence and reliability in long-distance and short-distance communication worldwide. For cellular networks, IoT layers can be classified as below:
  - **LTE-M** – For providing a very high rate of data transmission, Long Term Evolution for Machines networks are used through the cloud.
  - **NB-IoT** – When a low rate of data transmission is required, Narrowband networks are used.

In addition, messaging protocols are incorporated in the IoT system, allowing for easy data sharing. The majority use protocols in the IoT architectural layers, as listed below:

- Data Distribution Service (DDS) – In IoT systems, it represents a machine-to-machine real-time communications infrastructure.
- Advanced Message Queuing Protocol (AMQP) – This protocol encrypts messages or data, which are transmitted between two or more organizations and applications. It is used in client/server messaging services.
- Constrained Application Protocol (CoAP) – It is one-to-one protocol for transferring state information between client and server. It is used for overly controlled devices that have limited power and memory. A good example for this is wireless sensors.
- Message Queue Telemetry Transport (MQTT) – This protocol for IoT is used for data transmission between remote devices when the network bandwidth is very low.

3. Edge Computing Layer

It collects information at the device's edge or close to it. In the beginning, when IoT networks were becoming bigger, the potential of the network became a significant hurdle. When multiple devices try connecting to each other and to the main center, the whole system gets congested. It delays the procedure of data transmission. Edge computing provides a one-of-a-kind solution that increases the overall expansion of IoT systems where multiple devices may get connected to the main server simultaneously.

Systems have started analyzing data conveniently with the help of edge IoT layers. Edge allows the systems to connect to more devices with lower latency. All IoT network procedures happen at the network's edge, resulting in saved time and resources and increased performance.

4. Processing Layer

IoT systems collect, store, and process data to get insights or useful information for further decision making. There are two major phases in the processing layer, which are listed below:

- Data Accumulation

    It is a very important activity in which data from different sources are collected. Every gadget transmits lots of data through the IoT. Data streams may be in a variety of formats, speeds, and sizes.

    In the processing layer, the useful data are filtered from these massive streams. Unstructured data can be larger and must be processed rapidly in order to acquire intelligence aspects for further decision making. The knowledge of corporate activities helps to understand data requirements for future benefits.

- Data Abstraction

    After collection of the data, specific data are extracted from the datasets and are used in optimizing business procedures. The methods used for data abstraction are as follows:

    - Collection of data from the network (CRM, ERP, and ERM)
    - Use of data virtualization for ensuring availability of the data from all sources.
    - Manage data in several systems.

After the completion of data collection and abstraction, data analysts may easily utilize business insight to extract intelligence components.

5. **Application Layer**

The application layer helps in data analytics, device control, and creation of reports by end-users. For business intelligence, the data are processed and analyzed further in this layer. Here, IoT systems are linked with software to understand data. The application layer contains tasks like:

- Maintaining business decision-making software
- Controlling and monitoring the devices
- Finding analytical solutions by using AI and machine learning and
- Maintaining mobile application for further interactions

Every system is designed with specific objectives to meet business requirements. But the maximum IoT applications are complex and use several technology stacks to execute specialized functions for organizations.

Due to the continuous changes in the IT environment, many firms proposed the addition of three more layers to their infrastructure, which are listed below:

6. **Business Layer**

This layer derives data-driven information and decision-making analysis.

Once obtained, IoT data are only useful if they are applied to corporate planning and strategy. Every organization has specific goals to achieve by using data intelligence process. The data collected previously, as well as currently, help the business stakeholders' future predictions.

Now, data analysis has emerged as a magic tool for firms looking forward to increasing production. The firms collect more data to analyze more useful business decisions. To support the betterment of performance, software like CRM and business intelligence solutions are extensively used in almost all business sectors.

7. Security Layer

Security is one of the most important requirements of IT architecture. The security layer protects all components of the IoT architecture. The key issues with the security layer in integrating IoT systems include data leaks, tracking bad software, and hacking.

- Device Security

The security of devices in the IoT layers are of utmost importance. Most manufacturers adhere to security rules when installing IoT integration firmware and hardware. These are:

- Use a secure boot process for preventing malicious programs.
- Trusted Platform Module chips must be used along with cryptographic keys to save devices.
- Use an extra physical layer to prevent direct device access.
- Update security patches on a regular basis.

- Cloud Security
    For data storage and communication of devices, use of clouds is a new normal now. Hence, security of the cloud is very important, especially for IoT systems. The cloud security includes encryption to prevent data breaches. Authorization of devices is a complex procedure, and strong device identity management is required.
- Connection Security

In an IoT network, encryption of data is a must while being transferred across the network. For protection of sensitive data, DDS, AMQP, and MQTT message protocols are used. TSL cryptographic protocol is a proposed industry standard for data transfer across IoT architecture.

10.3   CYBERCRIMES

Although technology provides many benefits to consumers, it also has a negative side effect that degrades the quality of online activities. Cybercrime is one of those negative side effects, which involves the use of a computer, a network, and the Internet. Cybercrime can take several forms:

a. **Computer integrity crimes** – Integrity of data means that the data are trustworthy and have not been modified. These crimes occur when a breach of security of the computer network happens. Data are modified by the intruder, and incorrect data are received by the receiver. For example, hacking; malware creation, possession, and distribution; denial of service (DoS) attacks; distributed denial of service (DDoS) attacks; and website defacement.

b. **Computer-related crimes** – These crimes directly target a computer or computer system and use the Internet to communicate with victims with the goal of defrauding them of cash, commodities, or services. A few examples of such crimes are hacking, criminal damage, online theft, etc.

c. **Computer content crimes** – These crimes involve the illicit circulation of data on a computer network. Examples of such crimes are the trade and distribution of pornographic items and the dissemination of hate crime materials.

10.3.1 Role of the IoT in Assisting Cybercrimes

The IoT connects practically all physical and virtual things in the environment via the Internet to create new digitized services enhancing life's comfort and ease. Smart buildings, smart agriculture, smart energy, smart healthcare, and smart cars may be considered to be applications of IoT technology. Although such applications provide various benefits to mankind, they bring a number of security concerns.

In order to maintain the successful deployment of IoT applications in society, it is necessary to resolve security issues. IoT device owners must ensure that adequate security mechanisms are built into their equipment. Security threats and cybercrimes have increased over the years. With inadequate security measures installed in IoT devices, the IoT system gives more opportunity to cyber criminals to attack various IoT applications and services, resulting in a direct impact on consumers.

10.4 DIGITAL FORENSICS

Digital forensics is the application of scientifically derived and proven methods to the preservation, collection, validation, identification, analysis, interpretation, documentation, and presentation of digital evidence derived from digital sources for the purpose of facilitating or furthering the reconstruction of criminal events or assisting in the anticipation of unauthorized actions that are disruptive to planned operations.

10.4.1 Digital Forensics Process Model

There is a need for an integrated digital forensics process model to solve the problems of forensic investigators. There may be numerous issues faced by the investigators like:

- Differentiability of types of devices used
- Multiple types of media
- High volume of evidence that is distributed across the wireless network.

- Virtualization
- Live response
- Anti-forensics
- Encryption of static data and data in transit
- Dependency on the cloud for data storage and communication
- Lack of use of standards

So far, various models have been proposed, all of which share the same structure or stages. Hence, each new model strives to improve the fineness and clarity of the inherited technique.

Starting from the old and conventional to the most contemporary models, there are several important and notable digital forensic process models with more clarity of the tasks.

The Forensic Process Model, Abstract Digital Forensics Model, and Integrated Digital Investigation Model are among these process models. Another model is based on the digital forensic framework and data protection of cloud-based data collecting for digital investigations. The integrated digital forensic process model includes the phases as shown in Figure 10.2.

10.4.1.1 Preparation

Since the number of cyberattacks has been increasing, preparation and planning are necessary before conducting any forensic investigation. Lack of preparedness results in a delayed inquiry and the loss of essential artefacts, such as volatile data, that are only available shortly after an incident. The preparation phase includes the selection of appropriate persons, tools, and techniques for the security issue. This step adheres to the system's forensic readiness.

10.4.1.2 Incident

A cyber incident is an occurrence that alters the state of a system in such a way that it threatens the necessary security mechanisms and disturbs normal operations of the system. Cyber incidents are defined as violations of a system's privacy policy that result in the loss or breach of secretive information; interruption of services to authorized users; unauthorized data processing, hardware, or software; and so on. As a result, an event has an impact on the availability of information linked with a system. Early detection of an occurrence is critical in forensic investigations and plays a significant role in deciding the effectiveness of an inquiry. Before initiating an incident response, the proper approach must be determined based on the underlying compromised system. Before responding to an IoT-related issue, a number of aspects must be considered.

10.4.1.3 Incident Response

An incident reaction is the sum of all the measures taken prior to conducting the real digital inquiry. Both digital forensic investigations and incident response work together hand in hand. Incident response immediately controls the problem in order to prevent further possible damage. It also helps in recovering from the damage. Therefore, it reduces the overall impact on the compromised system.

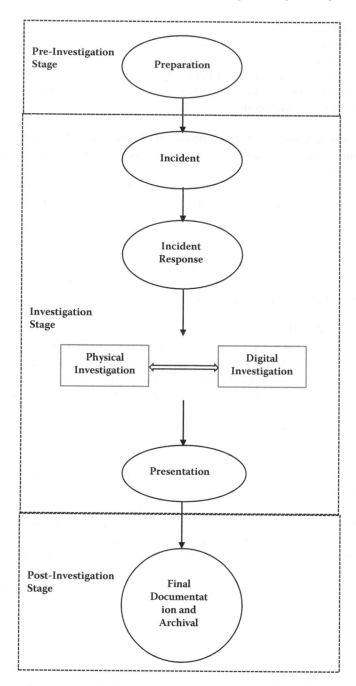

FIGURE 10.2 Digital forensic process model.

An organization needs proper preparation for taking an immediate action in response to an incident. The Computer Security Incident Response Team (CSIRT) or Computer Emergency Response Team (CERT) plan implementation of any incident response. Personnel from the organization, as well as technical and legal support, are part of the team. Occurrence Response entails a team of first responders assessing, analyzing, and reporting on the incident in order to locate and isolate hacked systems and identify artefacts of evidence.

It is always good to respond immediately or as soon as possible to the CSIRT or CERT with an occurrence as it helps to save a significant amount of cost, time, and effort while doing the forensic investigation. The process of digital investigation focuses on its main digital evidence, which has to be presented in front of a court of justice. Originality of the digital evidence is a must before presenting it in front of the court. The digital evidence will be accepted only when the digital investigation is done in the right manner.

Incident Response helps the team collecting all digital evidence, like memory or stored files, configuration of the network, movement of network packets, open and backdoor ports, sockets, and many more. Other than this, information like login session, system time, etc. are also collected, which helps make the plan of investigation.

10.4.1.4 Investigations

Two types of investigations are done throughout the process:

1. Physical
2. Digital

In the case of any cybercrime, both physical and digital evidence may exist, and both must be analyzed and kept in order to obtain a definite solution. The research method for both is distinct, despite the fact that they must be carried out concurrently.

Being the root of the entire Incident Response process, digital investigation plays an important role. It gives a framework of the methodical implementation of several phases to obtain a perfect result. The actual procedure begins with the collection of every small and bigger actions' details or picture of the evidence in response to relevant media proof or direct evidence of acquisition. The confirmation of keeping the original evidence is necessary. Also, it is necessary to check that no changes are made to it for it to be accepted in court. Originality of the evidence makes the task of investigators easier to conduct thorough investigations without danger of unintentional evidence change or deletion. The hash value of both the original and working copy is calculated through a secure hash algorithm just to make the task more authentic and foolproof.

After that, the evidence is checked to see if important data have been erased or if there are any hidden data there or not. Various forensic tools support the completion of such tasks. Investigators look for remains of erased data, such as metadata that can be used to harvest or save the deleted evidence.

Following this phase, certain reduction strategies may be used to further minimize the content base to be studied and inspected, bearing in mind the amount and format diversity of IoT-related data. The evidence may also be reduced by comparing known data and software to the National Software Reference Library. This is a library of calculated hashes of known software with the help of which the hard work and resources required for forensic investigations may be reduced as it eliminates the need to examine the evidence.

The evidence collected from an IoT device is in a highly unstructured form. Hence, extra attention is paid to such evidence as it is converted into structured data through long, technical methods. This whole process helps in the extraction of facts from the acquired data set. The readability of the evidence gets improved in this manner, which helps the organization to reach the final solution.

Based on the comprehension of the available facts, a detailed report of the incident is made. Now, the examination phase is started in which extraction of evidence is done with the help of additional connected procedures to verify the proposed solution. Once established, the chain of events may be reconstructed for security issues. The final decision is conveyed to the appropriate staff for further processing, which includes analyzing and validating the forensic data in relation to the proposed original hypothesis.

10.4.1.5   Presentation

In front of a court of law, the presentation is a short and to-the-point description of inferred investigation results, conclusions, and facts. Since the start of an investigation, a complete record of each and every act has been kept and is presented. It is concerned with facts and the collection of evidence. To add credibility to the final report, supporting papers from the investigations are provided. Records referring to any modifications introduced to the evidence, their relevance, and who they affected, among other things, may be included. In order to uncover the root cause of the incidence, the final report should be accurate and impartial rather than emotional.

The case is decided based on the digital evidence provided.

10.4.1.6   Documentation

Documentation is a crucial component of digital forensic inquiry and begins with an incident involving security. Documentation captures all crucial information about the forensic procedure, which aids investigators and legal personnel in making decisions. The documentation of forensic investigation should be maintained since the beginning of the incident to increase the chances of its approval by a court of law. As the documentation is continuous, it should have all the content that supports a digital witness in court. This may include:

* Duration of the incident
* Evidence procurement
* Digital location of evidence along with details of system software, file system, and computer network
* How many connections were broken
* All kinds of evidence related to as much information as possible.

This documentation aids the final forensic report submitted in court. During the inquiry, any changes made to the evidence or the system are meticulously documented. The sheer volume of digital data complicates the digital investigation process in terms of evidence gathering, storage, processing, and presentation. There is a methodology for dealing with massive amounts of data for fast forensic assessment triage.

The dependence of the IoT on various devices, networks, protocols, services, applications, and technologies raises concerns about hazy network boundaries and ambiguous identification of items of forensic relevance.

10.5 IOT FORENSICS PROCESS

The major infrastructure used for the IoT can be classified as:

- Wireless Sensor Networks
- Near Field Communication
- Radio Frequency Identification

Sensors and actuators in IoT devices help them get information from their surroundings and communicate with people. Software built expressly for interoperability across various, heterogeneous devices does this. The middleware layer supports in developing connections between data, applications, and devices. The IoT software is required to have the quality of accommodating the dynamic, mobile, and massive nature of the information. The IoT architecture is dispersed and highly diverse, involving hardware such as networks, software, processes, and general infrastructure.

However, with the rapid advancement of IoT technology and the penetration of smart devices into almost every sector of the physical world, new avenues for cybercrime are opening up in response to existing weaknesses. As the cybercrimes are increasing day by day, IoT devices are either direct attack targets or are used to carry out a cyberattack. When harmful actions break security barriers, IoT forensics comes into play.

However, due to the vast differences between traditional computing and the IoT, the forensic processes and standards used in IoT-related investigations necessitate a new approach. Standard digital forensic techniques and approaches must be revised to account for the dynamic nature of evidence from the cloud infrastructure. During a digital inquiry, the devices that serve as evidence sources are typically turned off to prevent evidence alteration. The investigators have little or no such provision in IoT-related investigations, which increases the complexity of the investigations.

IoT forensics is a subfield of digital forensics that integrates various subfields of traditional forensics. In the IoT paradigm, they include device forensics, network forensics, cloud forensics, mobile/mobility forensics, live forensics, and so on. Smart forensics and Forensics of Things are other terms for IoT forensics.

Each phase of the forensic model may be subdivided into sub-phases to clarify the entire inquiry. IoT forensics is dependent on modern forensic models.

10.6 THE INTERNET OF THINGS' ROLE IN DIGITAL FORENSICS

The technology of the IoT can be used as a digital witness or a stumbling block in digital investigations. Both the ways are explained below:

10.6.1 ROLE OF THE IoT IN ASSISTING DIGITAL FORENSICS

The IoT is a network of uniquely identified digital devices and digital objects that are networked and interoperable, allowing data to be transferred between them without the need for human interaction. Over time, IoT technology is growing in size as new devices are introduced to the IoT network on a daily basis. These application functions collect an increasing amount of information about their consumers from their daily routines, which can then be used to get access to large amounts of private or confidential data. The information acquired, processed, or transmitted by an object may be crucial to a given investigation case, and when gathered, assessed, and presented correctly, it can operate as a digital witness to assist in the resolution of the case within the time limit. These IoT devices' digital witnesses can either confirm or deny the occurrence of a security incident. As a result, given the IoT's leading role, the data can be used as a gold mine for investigators, assisting in the prompt conclusion of a case by providing the perfect timing of an occurrence or cyber event, as well as other log data essential to break the case.

This information aids detectives in gathering crime-related intelligence and helps them to concentrate on a small number of suspects. This saves forensic resources in terms of money, time, and effort, resulting in a reduction in case backlogs.

10.6.2 ROLE OF THE IoT IN ASSISTING CYBERCRIMES

While the IoT offers countless new opportunities and advantages, the inherent hazards and dangers associated with it should not be overlooked. IoT security vulnerabilities present new opportunities for cyber criminals to commit IoT crime due to its massive diverse and inclusive networks, low standards, and bad design architecture. IoT devices or items can be exploited as a direct target or as a tool or method to commit acts of violence. In either situation, there is a security breach, which leads to the serious problem of compromised information or services. When an IoT device is employed as a target, assaults are carried out directly on the smart device by exploiting its weaknesses. When an IoT device is employed as a tool, it is used to commit the crime, making it more difficult to pinpoint the source of the attack. In the latter situation, often, manufacturer-introduced security flaws or other technical flaws are exploited.

Because IoT security is still in its early stage, the processing power of IoT devices can be used to carry out cyber crimes with disastrous effects that are physically palpable and real in most circumstances. These assaults include remote control of objects, such as cars, light bulbs, or other connected home appliances; eavesdropping on residences; identity theft; DoS or DDoS attacks; and so on. As a result, given the antagonistic function of the IoT, hacked IoT devices can serve as a source of attacks and the most significant barrier for digital forensic investigators.

10.7 CHALLENGES OF IOT FORENSICS

Current digital forensic methods and practices are not specifically designed to meet the requirements of investigations into IoT-related crimes. In dealing with such instances, investigators have significant obstacles, necessitating a shift in forensic approach. Several of these are mentioned below:

10.7.1 DIVERSITY

The IoT has a high level of engagement and dynamicity, which increases its complex nature on all fronts. It also shows that "everything" is rapidly connecting over the network in every domain. As a result, there is diversity in the IoT infrastructure, including gadget type and number, data structures, interfaces, software platforms, and so on. Although this level of heterogeneity is unavoidable in the adoption of IoT ecosystems, it leads to new security threats.

Due to diversity problems, the decline of standard procedures for data storage, processing and maintenance, and forensic investigations is happening. Due to a lack of specific equipment or software support, forensic investigators feel extremely troubled to conduct investigations. The forensic tools must be compatible for investigations to support all types of hardware and software.

Furthermore, investigators struggle to detect and identify devices in a timely manner during the identification process. If it takes a long time to identify devices, they are more likely to be in a passive or off state due to power limits. Aside from the variety of data formats caused by different devices, data generated by an IoT device can be displayed in a different format on the cloud, which further complicates digital investigations.

10.7.2 IoT DEVICES AND DATA LOCATION AND IDENTIFICATION

Multiple connected smart devices disperse throughout cyberspace, making it more difficult for forensics experts to discover or locate the target devices. These devices contain a variety of data that can be beneficial in forensic investigations. More devices collect more data, which leads to a better understanding of whatever happened. Evidence based on the IoT can be found in IoT devices, network devices, cloud infrastructure, and client applications. These data can only be extracted and analyzed if all of the devices are recognized shortly after an occurrence by first responders.

As a result, in the case of an incident, finding and collecting IoT devices is a critical first step in launching a forensic investigation. Because most IoT devices are hidden from view or are located remotely, they might be difficult to uncover or detect and are outside an investigator's control. Devices in IoT environments can be passive or active, posing distinct challenges for investigators. Most IoT-connected devices are mobile, which investigators must take extra time, resources, and skill to identify.

The devices or objects provide raw data collected from their immediate surroundings and may lack any related metadata, whereas the network, cloud, or application maintains complete and processed data as well as any relevant metadata.

However, having quick access to network devices and cloud infrastructure is nearly challenging, if not impossible. Forensic investigators must also deal with a variety of legal and regulatory difficulties that occur as a result of the geographical deployment of IoT ecosystems.

One of the most significant tasks of investigators is to maintain evidence throughout the investigation. The gadgets or nodes have autonomous and real-time interactivity, which makes it difficult to establish specific boundaries to limit the area of investigation.

10.7.3 INADEQUATE STANDARDIZATION

Since properly made standards and uniform agreements are lacking in the IoT system, the current IoT ecosystem is extremely fragmented and badly lacks the ability to collaborate on common ground, which further affects the growth and security of the IoT ecosystem. Due to this lack of uniformity, the open design and architecture of IoT settings is rapidly developing. The immediate consequences of this are a lack of standard or agreed-upon operating systems, programming languages, interfaces, communication protocols, and so on at various layers of IoT systems. Also, the IoT lacks universal standardization, so the diverse IoT ecosystems may never speak the same language.

In forensic investigations, evidence obtained by IoT devices, such as logs, contributes to building a timeline of occurrences. However, because there is no clear structure or standard for representing these evidence logs, the clarity in comprehending and presenting evidence suffers greatly. The connected smart gadgets are further hampered by a lack of wireless protocol standardization, which allows them to operate on different frequencies. Some devices may be forgotten during the forensics device identification process, resulting in insufficient evidence.

As the IoT evolves, gaps of IoT interoperability, portability, and manageability needs will be filled. This will preserve the integrity of evidence in these complicated and distributed systems.

10.7.4 IoT EVIDENCE LIFESPAN

Big data is utilized to derive evidential information from IoT environments during digital forensic investigations. However, it is a must for investigators to gather all necessary artefacts to present those in a court of law.

IoT devices may keep the data for a lesser time as the devices have limited power and storage capabilities. Therefore, the data stored on IoT devices have a short lifespan as they are quickly overwritten. As a result, possible evidence that would have been necessary for investigation may be lost, resulting in gaps in the gathered evidence set.

Furthermore, an IoT device can be either active or passive while working. Active mode may result in quick battery drainage, due to which evidence may be lost. If the device's battery power is depleted, all volatile data may be lost. In contrast, being passive may slow down the process of device tracking and identification.

As a result of the lack of completeness, the trustworthiness of evidence is called into doubt, making it difficult for evidence to be acceptable in court. Therefore, having an incident response team ready to record all possible evidence as soon as feasible is an effective investigation practice. Although the data are stored to the cloud, data volatility will always be a gap.

10.7.5 CURRENTLY AVAILABLE FORENSIC TOOLS

The variety of IoT settings, as well as the massive data created by the IoT setup, pose different problems that render current digital forensics investigation technologies insufficient to meet the actual requirements. As the science of digital forensics is continuously evolving day by day, there are many difficulties dealing with the diversity, heterogeneity, complicated architectures, and huge volume of big data generated by the IoT. As the gadgets based on IoT technology are less secure than traditional digital gadgets, the powerful tools must be used to collect evidence from them. Otherwise, the veracity of the evidence will be called into question.

Furthermore, the IoT requires cloud forensic tools for evidence mining and analysis, but such tools are not successfully developed yet. Due to the lack of suitable tool support, cloud data extraction is difficult. The use of cloud platform implies that forensic tools must deal with virtual environments, which complicates the problems that such tools must encounter. Currently available forensic tools are unsuitable for investigating IoT systems.

The IoT's quick expansion and innovation does not provide enough time to decide and incorporate the required set of protocols for security and privacy concerns, insufficient testing of nodes and communication protocols, and so on. The IoT connects the physical world to the digital world, which reduces the possibility of faults bringing down the entire system or having catastrophic consequences and allowing error propagation to other components. This creates confusion in IoT contexts that must be solved as soon as possible.

If the above-mentioned challenges are not taken into account when investigating an IoT-related case, serious consequences may occur.

10.8 CONCLUSION

As more firms migrate toward these future solutions, the IoT is one of the rising technologies in the worldwide IT market. Advances in network and communication technologies have aided IoT technology in connecting and communicating billions of things over the Internet, allowing it to create a plethora of applications. The IoT can connect practically all physical and virtual items in the globe. Although IoT technology provides innumerable benefits, it also poses unique concerns, particularly in terms of security. Similarly, with the increasing number of cybercrimes, IoT forensics has emerged as one of the hottest subjects attracting the attention of numerous experts and businesses.

Due to the variety of IoT devices, however, using one of the traditional investigative frameworks will be futile. As a result, an IoT-based investigative framework should be one of any organization's top goals. This chapter provided an overview of IoT system security, cybercrime, and digital forensics. It began with a review of the components and building blocks of an IoT device, critical characteristics, architecture levels, communication technologies, and IoT system problems. Then, IoT security was discussed, covering security threats and solutions for IoT architecture levels.

Digital forensics and the major steps of an investigation procedure were also highlighted. Finally, IoT forensics was reviewed by examining similar IoT forensics frameworks, evaluating the need for adopting real-time techniques, and discussing the main issues of IoT forensics.

Given the complexity and rapid growth of IoT systems, security and forensic specialists face a slew of new issues. IoT systems are diverse and highly distributed, with a complicated architecture and limited resources, posing new challenges to researchers. IoT systems generate and consume massive volumes of data, which can be utilized as evidence in forensic investigations.

REFERENCES

Al-Room, K., Iqbal, F., Baker, T., Shah, B., Yankson, B., MacDermott, A., & Hung, P. C. (2021). *Drone Forensics: A Case Study of Digital Forensic Investigations Conducted on Common Drone Models*, 13(1), 1–25. 10.4018/IJDCF.2021010101

Almansoori, A., Ncube, C., & Salloum, S. A. (2021, June). Internet of Things impact on the future of cyber crime in 2050. In *The International Conference on Artificial Intelligence and Computer Vision* (pp. 643–655). Springer, Cham.

Atlam, H. F., & Wills, G. B. (2019). IoT Security, privacy, safety and ethics. In: *Digital Twin Technologies and Smart Cities* (pp. 1–27). Springer, Switzerland, AG

Cristina, G. N., Gheorghita, G. V., and Ioan, U. (2015). Gradual development of an IoT architecture for real-world things. In: 2015 IEEE European Modelling Symposium (EMS) (pp. 344–349). IEEE.

Dhar Dwivedi, A., Singh, R., Kaushik, K., Rao Mukkamala, R., & Alnumay, W. S. (2021). Blockchain and artificial intelligence for 5G-enabled Internet of Things: Challenges, opportunities, and solutions. *Transactions on Emerging Telecommunications Technologies*, e4329.

Kaushik, K., & Dahiya, S. (2018, November). Security and privacy in IoT based e-business and retail. In 2018 International Conference on System Modeling & Advancement in Research Trends (SMART) (pp. 78–81). IEEE.

Kaushik, K., & Singh, K. (2020). Security and trust in IoT communications: Role and impact. In *Intelligent Communication, Control and Devices* (pp. 791–798). Taylor & Francis Group, Singapore.

Kaushik, K., Dahiya, S., & Sharma, R. (2021). Internet of Things advancements in healthcare. In *Internet of Things* (pp. 19–32). CRC Press.

Kebande, V. R., Mudau, P. P., Ikuesan, R. A., Venter, H. S., & Choo, K. K. R. (2020). Holistic digital forensic readiness framework for IoT-enabled organizations. *Forensic Science International: Reports*, 2, 100117.

Kesharwani, S., & Sharma, V. (2018). Cyberbullying in India's capital. *Global Journal of Enterprise Information System*, 10(2), 29–35.

Kirmani, M. S., & Banday, M. T. (2019). Digital forensics in the context of the Internet of Things. In *Cryptographic Security Solutions for the Internet of Things* (pp. 296–324). IGI Global.

Krotov, V. (2017). The Internet of Things and new business opportunities. *Business Horizons*, 60(6), 831–841.

Lee, I. (2020). Internet of Things (IoT) cybersecurity: Literature review and IoT cyber risk management. *Future Internet*, *12*(9), 157.

Madakam, S., Ramaswamy, R., Tripathi, S., Madakam, S., Ramaswamy, R., Tripathi, S. (2015). Internet of Things (IoT): A literature review. *Journal of Computer and Communications*, *03*(05), 164–173

Manocha, T., & Sharma, V. At ease with Industry 4.0 Transition: Readiness of Youth.

Manocha, T., & Sharma, V. (2020). Study on the readiness among youth towards Industry 4.0. ISSN - 2005-4238, Vol. 29 No. 3.

Manocha, T., & Sharma, V. (2021). Essential awareness of social engineering attacks for digital security. *Journal of Applied Management-Jidnyasa*, *13*(1), 25–40.

Nayyar, A., Rameshwar, R. U. D. R. A., & Solanki, A. (2020). Internet of Things (IoT) and the digital business environment: A standpoint inclusive cyber space, cyber crimes, and cybersecurity. *The Evolution of Business in the Cyber Age*, *10*, 9780429276484–9780429276486.

Perumal, S., Md Norwawi, N., Raman, V. (2015). Internet of Things (IoT) digital forensic investigation model: Top-down forensic approach methodology. In: International Conference on Digital Information Processing and Communications (ICDIPC 2015) (pp. 19–23).

Reith, M., Carr, C., & Gunsch, G. (2002). An examination of digital forensic models. *International Journal of Digital Evidence*, *1*(3), 1–12.

Servida, F., & Casey, E. (2019). IoT forensic challenges and opportunities for digital traces. *Digital Investigation*, *28*, S22–S29.

Singh, K., Kaushik, K., & Shahare, V. (2020). Role and impact of wearables in IoT healthcare. In *Proceedings of the Third International Conference on Computational Intelligence and Informatics* (pp. 735–742). Springer, Singapore.

Sharma, V. (2019). Impact of Industry 4.0 over crowdsourcing in Indian Circumstances. *Cybernomics*, *1*(2), 3–10.

Sharma, V. (2020). IoT for crowd sensing and crowd sourcing. In *Internet of Things (IoT)* (pp. 285–300). Springer, Cham.

Sharma, V., & Manocha, T. (2021). Technological influences over factors for sustainability of smart cities. *Global Journal of Enterprise Information System*, *13*(1), 26–41.

Sharma, V., & Manocha, T. (2020). Cyber-crimes-Trends and Awareness: A study on Youth.

Zulkipli, N. H. N., Alenezi, A., & Wills, G. B. (2017, April). IoT forensic: Bridging the challenges in digital forensic and the internet of things. In International Conference on Internet of Things, Big Data and Security (Vol. 2, pp. 315–324). Scitepress.

11 Security and Privacy for IoT-based Smart Cities

Pawan Whig
Vivekananda Institute of Professional Studies,
New Delhi, India

Shama Kouser
Jazan University, Saudi Arabia

Kritika Puruhit
JIET, Jodhpur, Rajasthan, India

Naved Alam
Jamia Hamdard, New Delhi, India

Arun Velu
Equifax, Atlanta, USA

CONTENTS

DOI: 10.1201/9781003283003-11

11.1   INTRODUCTION

The population of urban regions has been quickly expanding in recent decades. According to a survey by the United Nations Populace Account, more than half of the world's population lives in cities [1]. Due more to its possibilities than its practical basis in urbanized environments, the notion of a "smart city" has gained far too much attention from academics and businesses. Some cities have begun to build their smart city initiatives to improve inhabitants' quality of life and deliver healthier facilities [2].

Several nations with growing populations are thinking deeply about smart city initiatives. China, for instance, is working on more than 200 proposals aimed at implementing the smart city model. Smart city-related technology enables urban municipalities to manage their everyday operations to make working class life simpler [3]. The substructure of smart cities consists of various gadgets and interconnected systems that help persons in a range of areas such as smart healthcare, smart transport, smart space, smart traffic systems, smart cultivation, and smart housing, to mention only a few.

Information-centric communication is an interacting architecture that can keep packets delivered even in unstable circumstances. As a result, ICN might be viewed as another IP-based system in smart cities. The addition of multiple affordable smart-sensing strategies and sensors, as well as the quick growth of wireless communication skills allowing small and affordable objects to attach to the Internet, has caused an increase in the implementation of the Internet of Things (IoT) [4], in which things are being replaced by smart devices in everyday life.

Because of its strong, reliable promise and realistic substance in a more built-up sphere, the idea of a "smart city" has shown increasing interest in both industrial and academic disciplines in the last few years [5]. Referring to the most recent United Nations Population Account report, over half of the world's people now live in cities, and it is anticipated that up to 66% of the world's population will live in cities by 2055, subsequent in extreme hardships in the weather, energy, environment, as well as air quality [6].

An increasing number of cities throughout the world have begun to build their smart plans to address these issues and improve inhabitants' well-being, stimulate economic development, and administer contemporary cities sustainably and intelligently [7]. Cisco proclaimed a one billion dollar smart city initiative in 2017. China, being the biosphere's maximum populated country, has more than 200 smart city initiatives in the works. Predictably, a city's infrastructure is interwoven with billions of devices that, via different applications, may be mutually advantageous for people, such as smart transport, etc. [8].

Because of the weaknesses that happen at each layer of a smart design, the growth of these smart applications may pose significant safety and confidentiality concerns [9]. Illegal admission, Sybil, and DoS attacks can all decrease the quality of smart services. For instance, almost 230,000 persons in Ukraine were deprived of power for an extended length of time in 2015 as a result of a Trojan-horse assault on the power network system [10]. Furthermore, over-collection of data by service providers and some third-parties, such as smart cars, smart governance, smart healthcare, smart surroundings, and smart homes, exposes citizens to privacy risks [11].

Several studies on this theme have been done in recent years, the majority of which have focused on the whole IoT ecology. Sicari et al., for example, provided an impression of present concerns and solutions in IoT systems, such as safety, confidentiality, and faith. Recently, Nia et al. explored safety challenges of the IoT. In comparison, the number of review articles on smart city safety and confidentiality remains minimal. Gharaibeh et al. performed a comprehensive study in 2017 that discussed the accomplishments of smart cities and then analyzed existing security challenges from a data-centrical approach. Zhang et al. developed a classification of diverse security answers for dissimilar security concerns, with a focus on security and privacy [12–15].

11.2   OVERVIEW OF A SMART CITY

After studying many designs used in different cities to meet the criteria of a smart city, it is noted that the heavy usage of technology, particularly telecommunications technologies, to enable resource monitoring is valued. It is here that you may discover a method for effective resource management, the need to monitor energy resources, humans, and so on to manage them more efficiently [16].

Then, under the description of smart city, we may use the term "monitoring" to create a system that permits us to be productive and sustainable [17]. To monitor a city, one must first classify the many zones or regions that comprise it, apart from the situation's own set of circumstances [18].

Monitoring the flow of automobiles in the city center is not the same as monitoring the movement of passengers within a railway or bus terminal. Sensors, connection protocols, data analytics, and so forth will all be different [19].

There are two types of architecture in a smart city: one that monitors the city's exteriors, such as its roads and streets, parks and leisure places, and so on, and one that screens the interiors of structures, the movement of persons, and supplies, air conditioning, water, and so on [20].

The architecture used in a city for outside monitoring is based on long-range communication procedures, allowing only a few devices to cover the whole city [21]. Because of interference with walls and electrical or pipe infrastructure, these communication protocols are unable to enter buildings [22].

Building architecture often makes use of the telecommunications infrastructure or, in the absence of one, the wired electrical system; it is easier and less expensive to trust in these resources [23].

The right selection of exterior and interior designs appropriate to the reserves to be covered will allow precise communication with all of the city's devices and equipment, as well as correct and error-free data for resource analysis and optimization [24].

Several designs have been planned to anticipate the growth of smart cities. However, to the best of our knowledge, no universal IoT building exists. Because the focus of this chapter is to outline health and security concerns in smart cities, the building presented here is based on the famous three-layer building and the typically recommended design. The architecture, as seen in Figure 11.1, may be separated into four strata; a quick explanation follows [25].

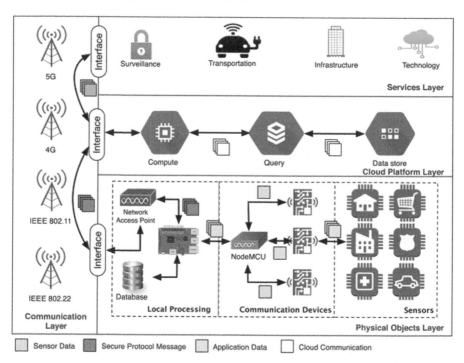

FIGURE 11.1   Architecture of smart cities.

The perception layer, also accompanied by the network layer, support layer, or application layer, is the architecture's lowermost layer. The perception layer is chiefly responsible for gathering data from things in the physical environment and delivering it to the network layer for additional processing [26–28].

The network layer is the substance of the IoT architecture, and it relies on fundamental systems such as the Internet, WSNs, and network services. The support layer, which collaborates closely with the network layer, provides smart computing approaches to satisfy the requirements of diverse requests. The application layer, as the top layer, offers smart and applied facilities or requests to consumers depending on their exact wants. In the next subsection, we offer a full explanation [29].

11.3   ARCHITECTURE ON THE OUTSIDE

To understand what occurs in a city, it is required to install a set of sensors to collect certain characteristics and variables that can be used to make judgments about the procedures that happen in the entire setting [30]. Numerous sensors supply various structures to the city, the most prevalent of which being star architectures or mesh networks.

11.3.1   SENSOR PLACEMENT

Most cities that are pursuing a smart city proposal have chosen to install devices on community lighting. What is the rationale behind this choice? This is in response to numerous factors:

- Because community lighting is an vital city system, it is available in all developed cities.
- Because it is a connected network, electric power is needed to power the sensors; and
- The components may be set at a specific height to minimize vandalism.
- The luminary preparation adjusts to the illumination demands of the road in which they are put, thus there will never be a shortage of locations to install the instruments.
- If the devices screen for people, we will have a system for distant lighting organization, allowing us to save energy.

In certain places, sensors have been placed in various parts of the city, such as trash cans, recycling containers, bus stops, and in specific key areas of the city.

Any element of the city may be placed independently. Every feasible site has more drawbacks than the possibility of being placed in public lights.

11.3.2   INFRASTRUCTURE

The many technologies for smart city sensors create infrastructure in the city; the most frequent mockups are the substructure in star.

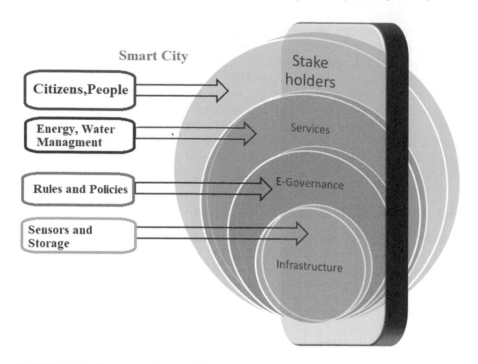

FIGURE 11.2 Structure of smart cities.

Use of a star architecture allows sensors dispersed across a zone to attach straight to an admission point, which transfers the data to a file for collecting and additional analysis.

The mesh net substructure lets the devices communicate with one another, and the information is dumped into the database via the sensors nearest to the access point. The structure of a smart city is shown in Figure 11.2.

11.3.3 INTERNAL STRUCTURE

The method of sensor placement inside a structure is heavily dependent on the following parameters:

- The structure's regular form.
- Whether the structure is designated as a heritage item.
- The usage of the building; sensoring an office building will not be the same as sensing a railway station.
- Private possession or public.
- The existing structure

Another planning milestone in new buildings is the architectural and sensor layout.

However, in the present construction, it is important to analyze the above-mentioned criteria and arrange an appropriate disposition of devices and actuators aimed at the IoT system to work properly [31–33].

11.4 OBJECTIVE OF SMART CITIES

Unique goals of developing smart cities is to help citizens in areas that are carefully connected to their life values, such as health, environment, manufacturing, lifestyle, and facilities. In Figure 11.3, we depict the rising smart requests of smart cities and discuss them in-depth.

11.4.1 SMART GOVERNANCE

A smart city relies heavily on smart government. The goal of smart government is to help residents and groups by linking data, organizations, processes, and bodily substructures through info skill. Furthermore, smart government allows individuals to participate in community choices and city preparation, which can enhance competence while also enhancing info transparency. E-government, for example, enables citizens to access government services online [34–37]. Various objectives of smart cities are shown in Figure 11.3.

11.4.2 TRANSPORTATION

Transportation attempts to enable "smarter" use of transportation designs. Smart transportation networks, in particular, can improve community service by improving safety, speed, and dependability. Consumers may quickly arrange their schedules and identify the most cost-effective and shortest routes by using transportation-related smartphone applications. Driver's passports, credit cards, and

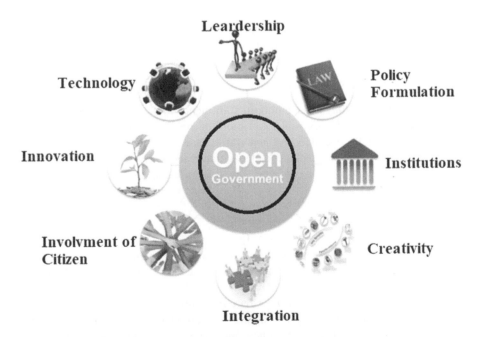

FIGURE 11.3 Various objective of smart cities.

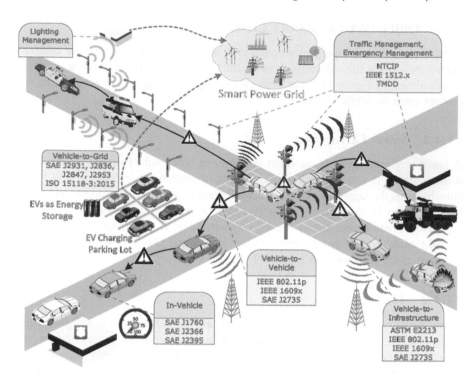

FIGURE 11.4 Transportation mechanism of smart cities.

car parking, traveling, and directions are also typical uses in smart transportation facilities as shown in Figure 11.4 [38].

11.4.3 ENVIRONMENT

A smart environment may make a important influence to the growth of a sustainable society. A smart city, for example, can monitor energy consumption, air quality, building mechanical dependability, and traffic jams, as well as treat pollution or trash effectively, by using technical management tools. In the future, innovative conservational device nets may even be able to foresee and notice usual accidents as shown in Figure 11.5 [39].

11.4.4 UTILITIES

Smart utilities enable smart cities to decrease resource overconsumption, such as water and vapor, while also boosting financial development and contributing to ecological conservation.

Applied smart utility application, smart metering, is frequently used in smart grids to monitor dispersed energy supplies. Smart water meters and smart light devices are also utilized to save money and decrease energy waste as shown in Figure 11.6 [40].

FIGURE 11.5 Smart environment.

FIGURE 11.6 Various utilities in smart cities.

11.4.5 SERVICES

Citizens benefit from smart facilities in a diversity of ways. Smart healthcare apps, for instance, may display common health problems in real time using smart wearables and medical devices. Additionally, certain smart buildings, such as remote switches for home appliances, can help to build pleasant, smart, and energy-saving living quarters. Last but not least, social interacting, entertaining, smart spending, and additional smart facilities must significantly enhance people's daily life as shown in Figure 11.7 [41–44].

11.5 CHARACTERISTICS

It is critical to comprehend the distinctions between the aforesaid smart apps and regular ones.

Furthermore, before building any new security or privacy protection solution, the features of smart cities should be studied and merged as shown in Figure 11.8.

11.5.1 HETEROGENEITY

High heterogeneity is the main distinctive feature of IoT-based systems, which implies the systems are independent, dispersed, and stowed or utilized by diverse operators.

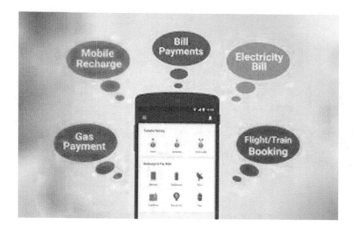

FIGURE 11.7 Various services in smart cities.

FIGURE 11.8 Characteristics of smart cities.

It also mentions to a extensive range of IoT bulges, communication procedures and knowledges, mobility options, hardware performance, platforms, and so on. To the best of our knowledge, there is no universal meaning of a smart city, and an IoT building differs from a smart city. As a result, another important issue is the absence of a unified safety structure and facility [45].

11.5.2 RESOURCES

Many sensor nodes are reserve restricted, which means they have incomplete memory, battery, and processor competences, as well as net borders that are confined owing to low-power radio protocols. In particular, inexpensive, lesser, but energy-inefficient fixed electronics are commonly used in smart cities. With 8-bit or 16-bit embedded systems, these devices often have limited random-access memory and storage capacity. The IEEE 802.15.4 radio in wireless networks results in modest data rates and frame sizes [46].

11.5.3 MOBILITY

Urban mobility has been identified as a critical driver of modern city growth and development. Mobility in smart cities relates not only to movement within a urban and the transportation of commodities from one location to another but also to skill such as citywide wireless connectivity and actual monitoring of air flow, as healthy as adaptable responses to problems [47].

11.5.4 SCALABILITY

Small devices can connect to the smart world thanks to connectivity. It is the greatest essential aspect of a fruitful smart city besides consumers been recognized as critical to bringing smart city designs forward. Simultaneously, scalability is an obvious aspect in smart cities. Smart cities are quickly expanding from small to large scale, subsequent in an short-tempered rise in data and net traffic. As a result, a smart cities cannot function well without scalable systems and procedures.

11.5.5 PARTICIPATION OF USERS

The concept of a smart city includes more than simply leading-edge technology and substructures; human aspects are equally important for the growth of smart cities. Meanwhile, the primary goal of constructing smart cities is to help countries. Besides, community participation can help to recover the excellence of these smart apps. For instance, an early grasp of their security measures and concerns will yield the greatest results in terms of defense solutions (Figure 11.9).

11.6 PRIVACY AND SECURITY

Even though the above-mentioned growths in smart cities have donated significantly to societal developments, almost each smart request is susceptible to hacking via current attacks such as contextual information attacks, conspiracy attacks, Sybil attacks, spying attacks, spam attacks, etc.

In past years, grave concerns have been uncovered in a variety of program settings. Advanced metering technology in microgrids may be used to observe people' private lives, such as their dwelling patterns and working hours. In relation to smart homes or healthcare, device manufacturers and providers may potentially have access to sensitive data. Furthermore, smart mobility applications' massive amounts of trajectory data may be used to deduce a user's location and mobility habits. The following are the most current concerns that have came as a result of the fast growth of smart applications, in additional to these obstacles.

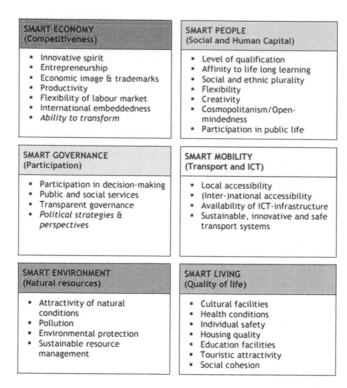

FIGURE 11.9 Various smart objectives.

11.6.1 BOTNET ACTIVITIES IN THE INTERNET OF THINGS (IoT)

Cyberattacks targeting IoT networks have recently emerged as a big threat. For example, the Mirai botnet may attack devices, spread infection to a huge number of disparate IoT devices, and then launch a DDoS attack on target servers. IoT devices, compared to PCs and smartphones, are usually built with insufficient security, if any at all. Sadly, this risk did not become obvious till the second half of 2016. As a result, much more effort will be necessary, and the security community will need to develop new protections. Or else, the IoT-enabled environment will be injured by this new normal of DDoS assaults as shown in Figure 11.10.

11.6.2 DANGERS OF SELF-DRIVING CARS

Robot vehicles have cost billions to develop, and they have helped to minimize car crashes and build a cleaner, more intelligent society.

Nevertheless, because hacking an antivirus puts both life and data secrecy at danger, this rapidly growing application has been labelled a severe security threat.

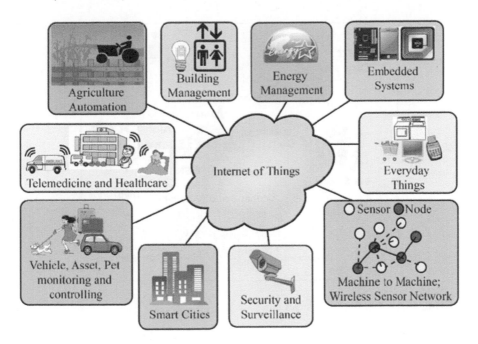

FIGURE 11.10 IoT in smart cities.

11.6.3 VIRTUAL REALITY'S PRIVACY ISSUES

Many governments and items in technology-driven smart cities have used virtual reality technology, such municipality planners, community hospital homemakers, and the industrial industrial sector. Nevertheless, sensitive data traded with third parties, unencrypted VR device interactions, and sensor data all pose privacy concerns.

However, because these new applications were rushed to market, developers and users neglected to adequately manage security.

11.6.4 ARTIFICIAL INTELLIGENCE THREATS IN SMART CITIES

Smart machines are important in a wide range of smart systems, such automatic exchange systems, domestic applications, or pacesetters. The growing use of smart devices, however, presents security issues. Network operators and device makers, for example, might employ data mining to study personal information inappropriately and extract delicate information that goes beyond the primary purpose of linked services. Attackers with AI knowledge are also growing increasingly adept. Hackers could be able to understand how machine learning-based safety systems were built or taught, enabling them to apply specific methods to weaken the learning lessen the systems' reliability as shown in Figure 11.11.

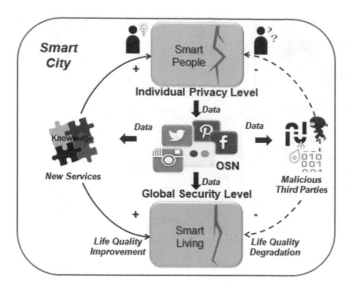

FIGURE 11.11 AI threats in smart cities.

11.7 REQUIREMENTS FOR SECURITY

The remainder of this part focuses mostly on defining the needs associated with safeguarding smart cities, taking into account the features of IoT plans, the multifaceted setting of smart cities, and the security and confidentiality risks outlined previously (Figure 11.12).

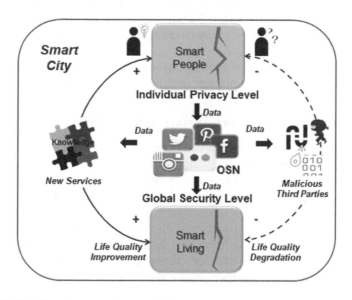

FIGURE 11.12 Requirements for security in smart city.

11.7.1 CONFIDENTIALITY AND AUTHENTICATION

Authentication is a fundamental need for the various levels of a smart design since it is required to prove individualities and guarantee that only authorized customers may access facilities crossways a heterogeneous design. IoT plans in smart cities, for example, can validate the network, other nodes, and organization position communications. Also, because the amount of verification data in smart cities is fast growing, it is dangerous to building superior technology.

11.7.2 INTEGRITY AND AVAILABILITY

In general, availability refers to the capacity of devices and services to function when they are required. About our issue, smart systems or apps should be able to continue to function effectively even when under assault.

Furthermore, because these plans are vulnerable to assaults, a smart design must be able to identify any unusual situations and prevent further system damage.

The capacity of a system to withstand different defects and disappointments produced by assaults and large-scale tragedies is referred to as resilience. To cope with more smart threats, protection methods should have high resilience and the capacity to continue learning adaptively.

11.7.3 DETECTION AND PREDICTION OF LIGHTWEIGHT INTRUSION

Unless a system can monitor its operational circumstances and detect any unexpected events in a timely manner, it cannot be called safe. Classic intrusion detection systems (IDSs) employ three techniques: misuse detection, anomaly-based, and complier detection. In the incredibly diverse smart city context, however, the basic adaptation of a global IDS solution is not adaptive and practicable. Compact IDSs must also be developed so bulky sensors and devices have fewer materials.

11.7.4 PROTECTION OF PRIVACY

Privacy and security are inextricably linked; any of the above requirements might have an impact on privacy protection. This paragraph is necessary because it covers various security requirements that were not enclosed in earlier subsets.

In smart city situations, subtle data leaks, whether deliberate or not, are the major source of confidentiality breaches, adding to other shared damages such as pack capture in message, malware in mobile plans and apps, server riding, and falsifying authorization.

According to a 2017 poll, four types of data may be used to attack privacy, which covers a huge quantity of sensitive information about individuals. Appropriate and effective countermeasures, such as encryption, are required to prevent unwanted usage.

11.7.5 SECURITY AND PRIVACY

This section provides crucial visions into the present and upcoming skills used to address safety and confidentiality issues in the smart city setting.

11.7.6 Cryptography

Cryptographic procedures are the foundation of safety and confidentiality defense for smart application facilities since they prevent unauthorized parties from accessing data along the information lifetime cycle of storage, dispensation, and distribution. In this section, we describe the existing cryptanalytic gears used in smart designs while also highlighting some unique and interesting facts.

11.7.7 Blockchain

Even though the blockchain approach is a skill rather than a punishment, we utilize this part to present it due to the significant increase in interest in recent years. Christidis et al. conducted a comprehensive assessment on this subject in 2016, confirming the feasibility of using blockchain in the IoT area and indicating its substantial request value in developing IoT bionetworks, as shown in Figure 11.13.

11.7.8 Biometrics

Biostatistics are usually used for verification in IoT-based systems. This skill may be used to recognize a person automatically based on their unique behavioral and biological traits. Fingerprints, faces, voices, handwritten signatures, and other

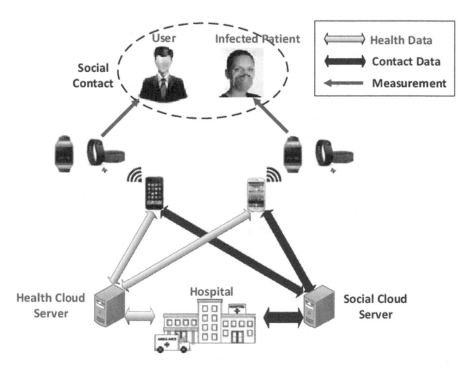

FIGURE 11.13 Application of blockbhain in smart cities.

biometrics are used to extract biometric data. Brainwave-based authentication is one approach worth noting here since it can reach a high level of authentication accuracy while also ensuring efficiency.

11.7.9 DATA MINING

Machine learning skills have been secondhand to increase the performance of interruption discovery designs, which is one used safety substructures to defend networks from assaults, based on current actual conditions. Wireless service networks (WSNs), a critical constituent of the smart world, are gaining popularity. In a detailed review, three benefits of using machine learning technology to protect WSNs were identified, as well as a summary of several machine learning techniques.

11.7.10 ONTOLOGY

Ontology has been highlighted as a viable method for addressing diverse difficulties, particularly for formless data, information, and customizable designs, and is one of the major disciplines of philosophy. Ontology is used to better comprehend, characterize, and reuse certain officially documented information, as well as to hunt for new information and separate discrepancies.

11.7.10.1 Supplements Without a Technical Connection

Protection cannot be achieved just via the use of technical solutions. Existing technological limits can be reduced by strengthening relevant legislation, regulation, governance, and education, among other things. According to [13], effective governance is essential for the development of a dependable smart system. Walravens suggested that governments must carefully assess whether data may be opened and who has access to the data. Likewise, Batty et al. stated that within a smart city architecture, government-enforced policies necessitate secure data and perfect expansion.

11.8 FUTURE PROSPECTS

We looked at existing data security protection measures for smart cities. A flood of innovative responses has been created in a range of fields in recent years. However, based on previous hazards and security requirements, it's reasonable to expect that more efficient security measures will be required to keep up with the growing popularity of smart cities. Based on our analysis, the following things represent future prospects and research paths, as shown in Figure 11.14.

11.8.1 IoT-BASED NETWORK SECURITY

The IoT can be thought of as a network of networks that connects and integrates heterogeneous networks. To deal with the newest issues in this sort of complicated environment, more effective solutions are required.

FIGURE 11.14   Important things for smart cities.

11.8.2   FOG-BASED SYSTEMS

Fog-based structures, as a novel skill for implementing smart cities, provide significant security issues since discrete fog arrangements' operating systems are more susceptable to assaults than central clouds.

11.8.3   PROTECTION METHODS THAT ARE USER-CENTRIC AND PERSONALIZED

Customers must have the ability to remove or change data from one service provider to another at any time in user-centric smart cities. Also, people's preferences for security and privacy must be taken into account, as attitudes and requirements differ from person to person.

11.8.4   COMPLEMENTARY THEORY

Smart applications are being discussed worldwide, and practically every government is working on smart initiatives. However, there is no universally accepted architecture for a smart city. As a consequence, most current security protection mechanisms and network protocols are focused on a specific place, making it difficult to combine or distribute them during the whole urban planning ecosystem. As a result, more theoretical research is needed to reduce the barriers to smart city security.

11.9   CONCLUSION

The rising use of smart applications has resulted in several security and privacy issues. The development of increasingly complicated protection frameworks is vital and in short supply in both business and academic realms. Motivated by these concerns, we investigated current countermeasure initiatives and developments from a variety of perspectives. In order to provide the basis for further studies, we also looked at current problems and unresolved difficulties that have developed in recent years. A range of defensive tactics and procedures have been developed in recent years. Nevertheless, there is also a long gap in terms of addressing the varying security requirements of these rapidly changing smart proposals. It is realistic to expect that in the future, minimizing the issues will be the major focus of the government. The disruption of the IoT and new communication technologies will enable a substantial decrease in global energy usage, and with it, our environmental effect and carbon footprint, in the next few years. It will be a huge step forward for cities in terms of sustainability and resource optimization in the face of the projected super-population challenge in the next 30 years.

We are on the verge of entering a new digital era in which the sensory world will play a more important role in our daily lives.

REFERENCES

[1] L. Xiao, Y. Li, G. Han, G. Liu, and W. Zhuang, "Phy-layer spoofing detection with reinforcement learning in wireless networks," *IEEE Transactions on Vehicular Technology*, vol. 65, no. 12, pp. 10037–10047, 2016.

[2] X. Liu, K. Liu, L. Guo, X. Li, and Y. Fang, "A game-theoretic approach for achieving k-anonymity in location-based services," in INFOCOM, 2013 Proceedings IEEE. IEEE, 2013, pp. 2985–2993.

[3] M. Kearns, M. Pai, A. Roth, and J. Ullman, "Mechanism design in large games: Incentives and privacy," in Proceedings of the 5th conference on Innovations in theoretical computer science. ACM, 2014, pp. 403–410.

[4] L. Xu, C. Jiang, Y. Chen, Y. Ren, and K. R. Liu, "Privacy or utility in data collection? a contract theoretic approach," *IEEE Journal of Selected Topics in Signal Processing*, vol. 9, no. 7, pp. 1256–1269, 2015.

[5] Z. Anwar Razzaq, H. F. Ahmad, K. Latif, and F. Munir, "Ontology for attack detection: An intelligent approach to web application security," *Computers & Security*, vol. 45, pp. 124–146, 2014.

[6] A. Mozzaquatro, R. Jardim-Goncalves, and C. Agostinho, "Towards a reference ontology for security in the internet of things," in Measurements & Networking (M&N), 2015 IEEE International Workshop on. IEEE, 2015, pp. 1–6.

[7] M. Tao, J. Zuo, Z. Liu, A. Castiglione, and F. Palmieri, "Multi-layer cloud architectural model and ontology-based security service framework for IoT-based smart homes," *Future Generation Computer Systems*, vol. 1, pp. 1–10, 2016.

[8] M. Mohsin, Z. Anwar, F. Zaman, and E. Al-Shaer, "Iotchecker: A data-driven framework for security analytics of internet of things configurations," *Computers & Security*, 2017.

[9] S.-H. Kim, I.-Y. Ko, and S.-H. Kim, "Quality of private information (copy) model for effective representation and prediction of privacy controls in mobile computing," *Computers & Security*, vol. 66, pp. 1–19, 2017.

[10] O.-J. Lee, H. L. Nguyen, J. E. Jung, T.-W. Um, and H.-W. Lee, "Towards ontological approach on trust-aware ambient services," *IEEE Access*, vol. 5, pp. 1589–1599, 2017.

[11] R. Kitchin, "Getting smarter about smart cities: Improving data privacy and data security," 2016.

[12] G. Xu, Y. Cao, Y. Ren, X. Li, and Z. Feng, "Network security situation awareness based on semantic ontology and user-defined rules for the internet of things," *IEEE Access*, vol. 5, pp. 21046–21056, 2017.

[13] Meijer and M. P. R. Bolívar, "Governing the smart city: A review of the literature on smart urban governance," *International Review of Administrative Sciences*, vol. 82, no. 2, pp. 392–408, 2016.

[14] N. Walravens, "Mobile business and the smart city: Developing a business model framework to include public design parameters for mobile city services,"

Journal of Theoretical and Applied Electronic Commerce Research, vol. 7, no. 3, pp. 121–135, 2012.

[15] M. Batty, K. W. Axhausen, F. Giannotti, A. Pozdnoukhov, A. Bazzani, M. Wachowicz, G. Ouzounis, and Y. Portugali, "Smart cities of the future," *The European Physical Journal Special Topics*, vol. 214, no. 1, pp. 481– 518, 2012.

[16] S. Misra, M. Maheswaran, and S. Hashmi, *Security Challenges and Approaches in the Internet of Things.* Springer, 2017.

[17] W. Hurst, N. Shone, A. El Rhalibi, A. Happe, B. Kotze, and B. Duncan, "Advancing the micro-ci testbed for IoT cyber-security research and education," *Cloud Computing*, vol. 2017, p. 139, 2017.

[18] N. Aleisa and K. Renaud, "Yes, I know this IoT device might invade my privacy, but I love it anyway! a study of Saudi Arabian perceptions," 2017.

[19] C. Perera, R. Ranjan, L. Wang, S. U. Khan, and A. Y. Zomaya, "Privacy of big data in the internet of things era," *IEEE IT Special Issue Internet of Anything*, vol. 6, pp. 15–27, 2015.

[20] Z. Yan, P. Zhang, and A. V. Vasilakos, "A survey on trust management for internet of things," *Journal of Network and Computer Applications*, vol. 42, pp. 120–134, 2014.

[21] X. Li, R. Lu, X. Liang, X. Shen, J. Chen, and X. Lin, "Smart community: An internet of things application," *IEEE Communications Magazine*, vol. 49, no. 11, 2011.

[22] L. Brandimarte Acquisti, and G. Loewenstein, "Privacy and human behavior in the age of information," *Science*, vol. 347, no. 6221, pp. 509–514, 2015.

[23] C. McCormick Perera, A. K. Bandara, B. A. Price, and B. Nuseibeh, "Privacy-by-design framework for assessing internet of things applications and platforms," in Proceedings of the 6th International Conference on the Internet of Things. ACM, 2016, pp. 83–92.

[24] K. Xu, Y. Qu, and K. Yang, "A tutorial on the internet of things: From a heterogeneous network integration perspective," *IEEE Network*, vol. 30, no. 2, pp. 102–108, 2016.

[25] V. Angelakis, E. Tragos, H. C. Pöhls, A. Kapovits, and A. Bassi, *Designing, Developing, and Facilitating Smart Cities: Urban Design to IoT Solutions.* Springer, 2017.

[26] Z.-K. Zhang, M. C. Y. Cho, and S. Shieh, "Emerging security threats and countermeasures in it," in Proceedings of the 10th ACM Symposium on Information, Computer, and Communications Security. ACM, 2015, pp. 1–6.

[27] A.-S. K. Pathan Abduvaliyev, J. Zhou, R. Roman, and W.-C. Wong, "On the vital areas of intrusion detection systems in wireless sensor networks," *IEEE Communications Surveys & Tutorials*, vol. 15, no. 3, pp. 1223–1237, 2013.

[28] D. Midi, A. Rullo, A. Mudgerikar, and E. Bertino, "Kalis-a system for knowledge-driven adaptable intrusion detection for the internet of things," in 2017 IEEE 37th International Conference onDistributed Computing Systems (ICDCS). IEEE, 2017, pp. 656–666.

[29] K. Xynos, I. Sutherland, and A. Blyth, "Effectiveness of blocking evasions in intrusion prevention system," *University of South Wales*, pp. 1–6, 2013.

[30] J. Wu, K. Ota, M. Dong, J. Li, and H. Wang, "Big data analysis based security situational awareness for smart grid," *IEEE Transactions on Big Data*, vol. 10, pp. 243–253,2016.

[31] C. Dwork, F. McSherry, K. Nissim, and A. Smith, "Calibrating noise to sensitivity in private data analysis," in TCC, vol. 3876. Springer, 2006, pp. 265–284.

[32] L. Xu, C. Jiang, J. Wang, J. Yuan, and Y. Ren, "Information security in big data: privacy and data mining," *IEEE Access*, vol. 2, pp. 1149–1176, 2014.

[33] N. Kumar Dua, A. K. Das, and W. Susilo, "Secure message communication protocol among vehicles in smart city," *IEEE Transactions on Vehicular Technology*, vol. 10, pp. 34–45, 2017.

[34] Abdallah and X. Shen, "A lightweight lattice-based homomorphic privacy-preserving data aggregation scheme for smart grid," *IEEE Transactions on Smart Grid*, vol. 6, pp. 30–37, 2016.

[35] R. Li, T. Song, N. Capurso, J. Yu, J. Couture, and X. Cheng, "IoT applications on secure smart shopping system," *IEEE Internet of Things Journal*, vol. 4, no. 6, pp. 1945–1954, 2017.

[36] M. S. Dousti and R. Jalili, "An efficient statistical zero-knowledge authentication protocol for smart cards," *International Journal of Computer Mathematics*, vol. 93, no. 3, pp. 453–481, 2016.

[37] S. S. Kanhere Dorri, R. Jurdak, and P. Gauravaram, "Blockchain for IoT security and privacy: The case study of a smart home," in *2017 IEEE International Conference on Pervasive Computing and Communications Workshops (PerCom Workshops)*. IEEE, 2017, pp. 618–623.

[38] H. Cruickshank Lei, Y. Cao, P. Asuquo, C. P. A. Ogah, and Z. Sun, "Blockchain-based dynamic key management for heterogeneous intelligent transportation systems," *IEEE Internet of Things Journal*, vol. 21, pp. 21–56, 2017.

[39] H.-S. Choi, B. Lee, and S. Yoon, "Biometric authentication using noisy electro-cardiograms acquired by mobile sensors," *IEEE Access*, vol. 4, pp. 1266–1273, 2016.

[40] Z. Mahmood, H. Ning, and A. Ghafoor, "Lightweight two-level session key management for end-user authentication in the internet of things," in *2016 IEEE International Conference on Internet of Things (iThings) and IEEE Green Computing and Communications (GreenCom) and IEEE Cyber, Physical and Social Computing (CPSCom) and IEEE Smart Data (SmartData)*. IEEE, 2016, pp. 323–327.

[41] N. Li, D. Liu, and S. Nepal, "Lightweight mutual authentication for IoT and its applications," *IEEE Transactions on Sustainable Computing*, vol. 6, pp. 11–21, 2017.

[42] M. S. H. Talpur, M. Z. A. Bhuiyan, and G. Wang, "Shared–node IoT network architecture with ubiquitous homomorphic encryption for healthcare monitoring," *International Journal of Embedded Systems*, vol. 7, no. 1, pp. 43–54, 2014.

[43] Jabbar and S. Najim, "Using fully homomorphic encryption to secure cloud computing," *Internet of Things and Cloud Computing*, vol. 4, no. 2, pp. 13–18, 2016.

[44] S. Goldwasser, S. Micali, and C. Rackoff, "The knowledge complexity of interactive proof systems," *SIAM Journal on Computing*, vol. 18, no. 1, pp. 186–208, 1989.

[45] Christidis and M. Devetsikiotis, "Blockchains and smart contracts for the internet of things," *IEEE Access*, vol. 4, pp. 2292–2303, 2016.

[46] Biswas and V. Muthukkumarasamy, "Securing smart cities using blockchain technology," in *High-Performance Computing and Communications*, 2016, pp. 1392–1393.

[47] P. K. Sharma, M.-Y. Chen, and J. H. Park, "A software-defined fog node based distributed blockchain cloud architecture for IoT," *IEEE Access*, vol. 9, pp. 23–33, 2017.

12 Network Vulnerability Analysis for Internet of Things (IoT)-based Cyber Physical Systems (CPS) Using Digital Forensics

J. E. T. Akinsola, F. O. Onipede, S. O. Osonuga,
S. O. Abdul-Yakeen, R. O. Olopade,
A. O. Eyitayo, and H. A. Badmus
First Technical University, Nigeria

CONTENTS

DOI: 10.1201/9781003283003-12

12.1   CYBER PHYSICAL SYSTEM

Cyber physical system (CPS) refers to the systems developed to perform some actions or work that are performed by humans in order to reduce the stress of carrying out a task and also to perform a task in an accurate and timely manner. These systems have the competency to interrelate with humans with the help of the built-in computational and physical competencies. In other words, a CPS is an advancement in technology that involves creating a human-like system to act on behalf of humans. These systems were created to reduce the effort being done by human beings. These systems have the characteristic of increasing the world of technology with the help of computation (Baheti & Gill, 2011).

CPSs involve the interrelation of software and physical components in order to perform functions on various aspects. Development of CPSs requires different knowledge domains, which include computation, automation, mechatronics, etc. It also involves the use of different algorithms on computer systems to perform human tasks in a very easy and less time-consuming manner (Wikipedia, 2021). CPSs are beneficial in diverse areas such as engineering, medical applications, and airline systems. Health monitoring systems, industrial control systems, and autonomic pilot avionic systems are some of the examples of CPSs. There are

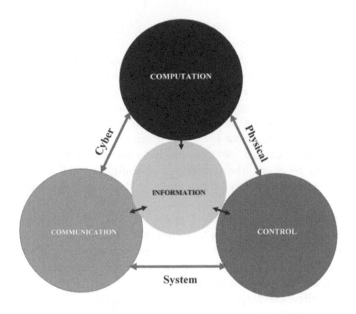

FIGURE 12.1 Components of a cyber physical system: computation, communication, control, and the connection between the components, which is information.

different components that make up a CPS. They are communication, computation, and controls. Figure 12.1 gives the diagrammatic representation of the components of a CPS.

12.1.1 AREAS OF APPLICATION OF CYBER PHYSICAL SYSTEMS IN DIFFERENT DOMAINS

CPSs have been beneficial in many application domains. They perform different works in an efficient and reliable way. The following are areas in which CPSs have been useful (Vanderbilt School of Engineering, 2022):

  i. **Agriculture**: CPSs have been applied in the agricultural domain to make the production of agricultural products more effective. They also involve the innovation of sensors to agricultural machinery to work on the soil. This sensor can detect the type of soil and its characteristics in order to determine the best soil to use for the planting process.
 ii. **Security**: As technology increased, so did fraud. CPSs can be applied to protect technology from easy penetration. An example of a CPS for security purposes is the alarm installed in most organizations that signals if an intruder is trying to break into the organization. With the improvement of innovative technologies, a lot of devices that are computational with networking as well as sensing power are connected to each other with the

communication process, which gives rise to many trust and security concerns (Kaushik & Singh, 2020).

iii. **Medical**: CPSs have caused great advancements in the field of medicine. CPSs can be used to examine patients; for example, a CPS can be used to determine how a cancer patient is responding to medical treatments. This reduces the effort of medical personnel in examining the health condition manually. CPSs will also help in the medical field to get accurate diagnostic results. They have also helped some machines to provide treatments to patients. IoT devices that have the ability to handle a large number of problems like scalability, reliability, as well as security, are pervasive in the system of healthcare and are called smart gateways (Kaushik et al., 2021).

iv. **Industries**: In industries today, many things that were done manually and consumed a lot of effort and time have been automated with the use and knowledge of CPSs. Many industries today use automatic doors. Censors are mounted to the doors, which sense the arrival of a person, and the door automatically opens without any effort.

v. **Automobiles**: Development has been made to the automotive industry using the knowledge and ideas of CPSs. In the United State, censors are used to monitor collisions, lane departures, and the likes. These sensors sense danger and warn the driver in order to reduce the risk of accidents.

12.1.2 DIGITAL FORENSICS

In the modern world, the computer has been used to facilitate and enhance the work of human beings in order to perform some tasks effectively and in a timely manner. The introduction of these modern computers has resulted into a high rate of criminal cases. Many criminals now take advantage of these new technologies to improve the rate of criminal offenses. They indulge in this because they believe it is difficult for them to be caught and punished for their offense. This led to the creation of new ways to track computer-based criminal offenses, known as digital forensics (Reith et al., 2002).

Digital forensics is a method that involves investigation and getting confirmation of digital criminal offences. It involves the use of scientific procedures that are consistent with actions for the purpose of tracing criminal cases. The procedures may involve identification, gathering, and documentation of proof of digital-based criminality (Reith et al., 2002). Digital forensics, in other words, can be defined as a security means for protecting all computer-based devices, such as mobile phones, digital cameras, flash drives, etc. The IoT plays a lot of roles in digital forensics by making it useful in all areas of computer forensics (Kaushik et al., 2022).

Computer forensics is synonymous with digital forensics. Computer forensics can be defined as a way of getting statistical details about an intruder off a computer, whereas digital forensics can be used to get evidence about invaders off all

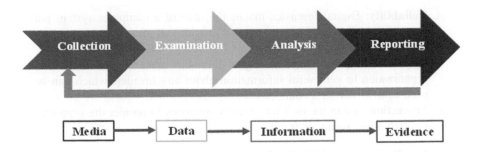

FIGURE 12.2 Phases of digital forensics, which include collection, examination, analysis, and reporting.

digital devices that serve the purpose of data repository (HowStuffWorks, 2000). Smart computing paradigms can be employed for forensic results analysis.

The usage of social networking, microblogging, photo sharing, and video sharing applications has brought about loss of values and disrespect for human dignity (Akinsola, Awodele, et al., 2021). Cybercrimes and other social vices are initiated through these applications, and this has called for serious attention. The pervasiveness of cybercrime in the world portends to destroy the most important component of the essence of human existence – peace (Balogun et al., 2019). There are various phases or procedures to follow when investigating cybercrimes using the knowledge of digital forensics. There are basically four distinct phases of digital forensics, which are acquisition, identification, evaluation, and admission (Patil & Kapse, 2015). Figure 12.2 gives the visual presentation of the four distinct phases of digital forensics.

  i. **Acquisition phase**: This is the first phase of digital forensics. It involves gathering or collecting evidence in a proper way. This evidence must be approved by the authority.
 ii. **Identification phase**: This is the next phase after acquisition. This phase aims at detecting the digital component using evidence from the acquisition phase. This is later converted to human readable form to ease the understating of humans.
iii. **Evaluation phase**: In the evaluation phase, the components that were detected are checked against the evidence in the first phase to assure conformity.
 iv. **Admission phase**: The admission phase involves the exhibition of the gathered proofs in court.

12.1.2.1 Benefits of Digital Forensic
The following are the advantages of digital forensics (Guru99, 2022):

i. **Reliability**: Digital forensics makes the user of a computer system put more trust in the computer system as it provides all means of catching any intruder.
ii. **Apprehending information**: Digital forensics makes it possible for an organization to get useful information about any invader, which can be used as evidence in a court of law.
iii. **Protection**: It can be used for security purposes to protect the organization from any forms of fraud.

12.1.2.2   Drawbacks of Digital Forensics

The following are the drawbacks of digital forensic (Guru99, 2022):

i. **Prosecution of criminal**: Any criminal cases that have been traced with digital forensics might not allow the main invader to be given the deserved punishment.
ii. **Lack of technical knowledge**: Evidence from digital forensics cannot be understood by a jury who has no technical knowledge about the domain.
iii. Any evidence that is derived using tools that are not up to standard can be disregarded in the court of law.

Cyber forensics is the process of analyzing and creating solutions to data or information that have been affected by an attack. Many Information Technology (IT) departments deal with a large amount of data. These data need to be protected from hackers. If there is any attack on the data, cyber forensics is introduced to analyze and create a solution to retrieve the exposed data. It is a way to get rid of a disturbing action that prevents the main functionality (Katz, 2008). Hacking and denial of service has become widespread in society. Cyber forensics can be used to combine information about these problems and analyze the gathered information. This analyzed information is used as evidence in a court of law. Cyber forensics is the intersection between the domain of law, military, and industry (Vidas, 2006). Cyber forensics acquires information about the attacked system. Necessary procedures are carried out such as information gathering, analysis of the information, and documentation (Katz, 2008). This documentation is used in a court of law as evidence for the detected attack. The approved evidence in the court of law will be used in the military department to punish the criminal based on his/her offences. Figure 12.3 below gives the visualization of the three domains in cyber forensics.

12.1.3   AREAS OF APPLICATION OF CYBER FORENSICS

According to the authors (Ademu & Imafidon, 2012), as technology improves, the devices are also exposed to unnecessary attacks such as denial of service (DoS), introduction of viruses, hacking, etc. These vulnerabilities cause great losses to the organization. In order to reduce these defects, the use of cyber forensics is adopted to analyze and track the criminals involved in these cybercrimes. The following are the areas where it can be applied:

FIGURE 12.3 Tripod of digital forensic science showing its three domains that cyber forensics cuts across and their areas of application; law enforcement which is applicable to court, information welfare which is applied in military operation, and critical infrastructure protection which is applied in business and industry.

i. **Embedded system**: Embedded systems such as smart cards, smartphones, and other systems that contain information may be open to threat. Cyber forensics can be used to break down the attacked system, and evidence can be mined from it.

ii. **Communication system**: The systems that are used for easy interaction between people from different places can also be used to generate information about cybercrimes using cyber forensics. Human computer interaction (HCI), also known as man-machine interaction or interfacing (MMI), has resulted in various improvements and has therefore made devices smart (Alao et al., 2019). This, in turn, has created a lead-way for cyber criminals.

iii. **Open source system**: cyber forensic can use the open system which is a combination of hardware, software, and server as source of information. These open systems have the features of increasing repository of information.

12.1.4 NETWORK FORENSICS

One of the most important things for some organizations today is network forensics due to its ability to learn about intruder attack details from similar attacks and prevent future attacks. Network forensics is a network security extension model that emphasizes traditional network attack detection as well as

FIGURE 12.4 OSCAR method of network forensics which is obtaining information, strategizing, collecting evidence, analyzing evidence, and reporting.

prevention (Almulhem, 2010). The various forms of sniffing techniques used in gathering data have brought about legal concerns, privacy concerns, and ethical dilemmas to determine the security vulnerabilities usually exploited by hackers while employing forensic analysis methodology. Nonetheless, the availability of enormous data through sniffing techniques can be efficiently analyzed for mitigating security vulnerabilities using forensic analysis tools such autopsy, FTK imager, and Encase. Intelligent user interface needs to be incorporated into the forensic analysis tool to examine cyber threats effectively (Akinsola, Akinseinde, et al., 2021).

Due to the wide range in the usage of the Internet, network forensics has become a major part of computer forensics. Network forensics captures, analyzes, and records events on the network for evidential information discovery about the security attack source (Meghanathan et al., 2010). Network forensics can also be defined as practices that are proven scientifically for fusing, examining, analyzing, and identifying as well as digital evidence documentation from actively processing multiple as well as digital sources with the aim of exposing related facts for the determined, planned, and successful evaluation of unauthorized activities that are meant to corrupt, compromise, and disrupt components of a system and provision of information to render assistance in response to and recovery from these activities (Pilli et al., 2010). To ensure reproducible and accurate evidence of network forensics, the OSCAR method of network forensics is used. The acronym OSCAR stands for (Qureshi et al., 2021): (Figure 12.4)

  i. O for obtaining information
 ii. S for strategizing
iii. C for collecting evidence
 iv. A for analyzing evidence
  v. R for reporting

12.1.4.1 Network Forensic Tools

These are tools used in carrying out investigations on networks for gathering critical information on the activity of intrusion. Analyzing of traffic on the network is done using network forensics tools for the nature as well of the type

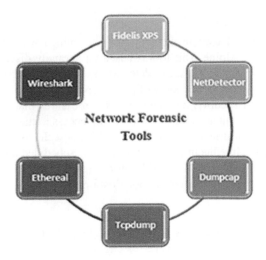

FIGURE 12.5 Network forensic tools such as Fidelis XPS, Wireshark, NetDetector, Ethereal, Dumpcap and TCPDump.

identification of the attack within the network in a duration that is specific. These tools are developed for compatibility with hardware devices of the network, for example, firewalls that make preservation as well as collection of traffic on the network possible (Qureshi et al., 2021). The tools used in network forensics are discussed below. Various types of network analysis discussed in this research is shown in Figure 12.5.

12.1.4.1.1 Fidelis XPS

This type of network forensics tool is used for recording an interesting session of traffic on the network as well as capturing that traffic. Reduction in cost, response that is automatic, alertness that is proactive, bandwidth increment, visualization of real-time results, as well as granular control are provided by this network forensic tool. It brings about information that is sensitive in communication through malicious communication guiding as well as payload collected by systems that are compromised, which is information based (Khan et al., 2016)

12.1.4.1.2 Wireshark

This tool was developed for filtering, analyzing, as well as capturing traffic on the network. It is a graphical user interface (GUI) that is open source that can be used easily as well as help with network forensic analyzing. It has more capabilities of filtering packets, features of protocol decoding, as well as packets detail markup language (PDML). Viewing packets of network is easier and possible as they are captured in real time, and the tool also shows the lost pocket results because of the power of the CPU (Qureshi et al., 2021).

12.1.4.1.3   NetDetector

It is a full-featured tool used in network forensic, which was built on the architecture of NIKSUN's Alpine. This tool is based on anomaly discovery of statistics, which is combined with an intrusion detection system that is based on signature, rebuilding of full application, decoding of packet level, and so on. The user is alerted about the breaches of security, and the tool takes measures that are preventive, for example, blockage of malicious traffic from getting access to the system. Application as well as session reconstruction, analysis of multi-timescale, as well as capturing of traffic on the network, intelligent security for big data, scheduled and ad hoc reporting as well as anomaly identification in addition to signature-based integration are the characteristics of this network forensic tool (Joshi & Pilli, 2016).

12.1.4.1.4   Ethereal

It is a tool that is commonly used for analyzing packets on the network. It is open-source network forensic software for capturing live packets on the network. The information about the packet captured is displayed on the headers of all protocols used in the all-captured packet transmission. Packets are filtered depending on the requirements of the user. This tool allows packet search using some specifications (Meghanathan et al., 2010).

12.1.4.1.5   Dumpcap

This is a network traffic analysis tool (NTST) that was developed for data packets capturing. It is a distribution tool of Wireshark, which arises in command line. Traffic is captured from a network that is live as well as fortified to write the result in a paging file format. It has the merit of fewer resources of the system usage, which makes it possible for capture abilities boosting (Qureshi et al., 2021).

12.1.4.1.6   TCPDump

It is a common command line tool that is available for analyzing as well as capturing traffic on the network. It is based primarily on Unix systems. Capturing of traffic as well as storing of the output in a file that is compatible with TCPDump, such as Wireshark, for analyzing further is possible using this tool. It can be used both for capturing traffic on the network continuously in volumes that are large or on fast packet capture for troubleshooting for carrying out analysis in the future. This tool also has the ability to use filters in addition to its capability to capture a large amount of traffic that is unnecessary avoidance as well as to capture only the interested traffic (Srin, 2021).

12.1.4.2   Network Forensics Challenges

A major network forensics challenge is ensuring whether the network is ready forensically or not. The network must be infrastructurally equipped for a successful investigation of the network to support this investigation fully. The infrastructure should ensure that the needed data exist for a full investigation (Almulhem, 2010).

Some of the major challenges of network forensics are discussed and shown in Figure 12.3.

12.1.4.2.1 Sources of the Data

Unprocessed packets of the network as well as network services and device records are several network data sources. In an ecosystem that consists of a large infrastructure of the network, the option to collect data from all sources is not always feasible. Therefore, selection of sources of data where good coverage of the network is provided is a decision that is important as well as making the process of collection practical (Almulhem, 2010).

12.1.5 IoT AND CPS VULNERABILITIES

There is significant increase in IoT as well as CPS evolvement due to their ability to provide convenience for the industrial production as well as their customers. IoT devices perform an important role in the modern age when devices that are conventional become smart as well as independent (Dhar Dwivedi et al., 2021). Interconnection between different things is leading to many problems in relation to privacy as well as security of the IoT platform. Many electronic businesses as well as retail stores depend on solutions that are IoT based for their everyday marketing, promotions, sales, as well as productivity (Kaushik & Dahiya, 2018). Although the IoT as well as CPSs have some challenges that are new, security is a main concern. The IoT and CPS are suffering from various widespread flaws in security, which is security vulnerabilities, and it ranges the gamut full of faults, from an intruder having the ability to get access to crucial information to having full control of the system. The CPS is even suffering from this fault with greater consequences due to its growth in infrastructure dependence. Vulnerabilities for the IoT and CPSs are vulnerabilities of the booting process, the hash function, encryption, as well as authentication implementations, hardware exploitation, chip-level exploitation, backdoors in remote access channels, and software exploitation (Ly & Jin, 2016).

12.1.5.1 Vulnerabilities of Booting Process

The booting sequence process can be altered by boot process vulnerability injection, and many operations can be interrupted. The initial command in the device is usually interrupted or hackers are tempted to reject the complete process (Prathibanandhi et al., 2020). It is a component that is commonly targeted in attacks because it is the root of trust and the device's operation starting point, and any attacks that successfully gain access to this component have the capability to control anything that happens in a stage of operation that is subsequent (Ly & Jin, 2016).

12.1.5.2 Exploitation of Hardware

Development as well as advancement in devices that are wearable using IoT techniques makes things easier for patients who have some disease issues in healthcare. Some properties are used in manufacturing those devices that make them an approved part of the human's body (Pradeep & Sharma, 2020). This is the critical level, and it's mostly overlooked by designers for whom security at the firmware or software level is their main concern. These attacks depend on the hardware itself, which mostly includes some strategies like looking for debugging ports left exposed by designers, external flash memories modification, address lines glitching, and so on, which thereby causes potential threats to models built on the IoT-CPS (Ly & Jin, 2016). A well-articulated Software Development Life Cycle (SDLC) model (Adeagbo et al., 2021) with dynamic runtime analysis will help forestall the hardware loophole (Akinsola, Ogunbanwo, et al., 2020). Modeling and analytic approaches may be used to evaluate the performance of hardware, systems, and software (Akinsola, Kuyoro, et al., 2020) so that critical parts are not overlooked in the design.

12.1.5.3 Exploitation of Chip-Level

These attacks occur mostly in the IoT-CPS chip. Devices built on IoT-CPS depend on the chip for operation. The complete system is alleviated, and security threats are posed to devices that are connected to the Internet (Prathibanandhi et al., 2020). Exploitation of chip-level includes invasive as well as semi-invasive on the chip itself, and these are serious threats to smart devices that depend on the boot sequence's trust, which relies on the chip assets that are hardware for security (Ly & Jin, 2016).

12.1.5.4 Hash Function, Encryption, and Authentication Implementations

A lot of today's attacks are generated from weak mechanisms of authentication. Strong mechanisms are imposed by system designs such as certificate based. Unless the credentials, such as keys, are stored safely, they can be an attack subject. As IoT devices are visible in public spaces, the attacker's ability to recover credentials becomes an attack that is insignificant, and once the keys are recovered, the identities are compromised, preventing the properties of security afforded by any mechanism of encryption (Ly & Jin, 2016).

12.1.5.5 Backdoors in Remote Access Channels

Smart devices are now equipped with channels that allow for communication that is remote as well as debugging after manufacture for convenience sake. These channels are commonly used for upgrading over-the-air (OTA) firmware. Any insecurities in the protocol used for upgrading OTA firmware would give the attacker control over the device firmware as well as full control over the device consequently. In addition, producers may leave in APLs used during the development that would allow executing commands arbitrarily or it may lead improper communication channel security (Ly & Jin, 2016).

12.1.5.6 Exploitation of Software

General purpose computing software code is mostly reused in software stacks of smart device, which leads to transferring of any vulnerabilities in the existing code to the new code. Therefore, software patches can be used for prevention of these attacks. For example, stack overflow attacks in GNU C Library (glibc) and elsewhere in the code base affect several devices in a smart house (Ly & Jin, 2016).

12.1.6 ATTACKS ON THE IoT AND CPS

The IoT and CPS have been widely used in modern days to interchange data between devices and make connections. The IoT will continue to evolve and be used in a large scale (Butun et al., 2019). These technologies have been opened to different attacks during connection and data exchange due to their wide range of usage. The IoT has the challenge of poor security, which makes it easy for IoT-based devices to be prone to different attacks during communication and data exchange. The rate of risk associated with the IoT increases as it gets vulnerable and open to attack (Kandasamy et al., 2020).

Attacks on the IoT can be grouped into active and passive attacks (Butun et al., 2019). Active attack involves the hacker or attacker trying to intrude data or information that are exchanged between devices. Examples of this attack include masquerade attack, message modification attack, session hijacking attack, DoS, etc. On the other hand, passive attack involves the attacker working on data whereby the intruder is hidden and is hard to detect. In passive attack, the communication link is tapped in order to access useful information. The passive attack categories are node outage, node malfunctioning, eavesdropping, etc.

IoT devices become vulnerable due to some reason (Kandasamy et al., 2020), such as inappropriate security measure, insecure software, composite design, etc.

12.1.6.1 Steps in Preventing Against Attack

Many researches have been learned how to prevent attacks on IoT-based devices. There are three steps to stop IoT-based device attacks. They are avoidance of attack, recognition of attacks ,and mitigation (Butun et al., 2019).

  i. **Avoidance of attack:** This step involves carrying out all activities to prevent devices from all forms of attacks. It is a way to make restrictions to external attacks. Once all prevention activities have been done, the device is said to be safe from external attackers, and all data transmissions are said to be secured. This method contains all activities that are to be done before an attack. These activities are done to repel external attacks and not internal attacks.
 ii. **Recognition of attacks**: This step is carried out to figure out all types of attacks on a device, in order to get solutions to the attack. Sometimes, prevention on a device might fail. Once this happens, this step is done to highlight all attacks on the device. The steps make use of devices known as intrusion detection systems (IDSs) to detect attacks and intrusion on the data on the device. Internal attacks are mostly detected in this step since they cannot be prevented in the above step, that is, avoidance of attacks.
iii. **Mitigation of detected attacks:** This is the last step in preventing attacks and intrusion on IoT-based devices. It is intended to reduce or eradicate the detected attack on any device. When eradicating attacks on any device, the affected part of the device is deactivated.

12.1.6.2 Classes of Attack and Vulnerabilities on CPS

CPSs are said to be vulnerable if they can be exposed to attacks. A CPS is open to attacks due to the various components, such as network technology and the physical system. These combinations are intended to improve the productivity of the devices. Contrarily attacks on the system cause the opposite, that is, reduce the effectiveness of the device (Sui et al., 2021). The device can be attacked through the physical components such as input and output. Vulnerability of a CPS device is a symbol that the device is weak and is open to attack (Singh & Jain, 2018). Vulnerability can occur in hardware or software, or the device can have technical or network vulnerability:

    i. **Hardware Vulnerability:** This vulnerability indicates weakness in the hardware component. It can allow attackers to get into the device through the input and output devices. Finding these vulnerabilities is somewhat tedious.
    ii. **Software vulnerability:** This is the most vulnerable part of CPSs, which is common to most systems. It is the weakness that happens in the software part of the device, such as the control software (e.g. devices driver), operating system, and application software.
    iii. **Network Vulnerability:** This is the integral weakness of CPSs. It is the combination of hardware, arrangement, and monitoring vulnerabilities.
    iv. **Technical Vulnerability:** It is a type of weakness that mostly occurs as a result of human feebleness.

12.1.7 NETWORK VULNERABILITY ON IoT-BASED CPSs

The IoT consists of many types of networks, including the wireless sensing network (WSN) as well as the Internet. The emergence of artificial intelligence has brought about disruptive technology, which has several pros and cons (Akinsola et al., 2022). Therefore, disruptive technology regulatory response must be institutionalized (Hinmikaiye et al., 2021). Different protocols and devices are used by different networks, which makes network attacks diverse. The most popular of all network attacks is DoS, which has the ability of exhausting resources of the network as well as affecting network service. Eavesdropping can be used to obtain patterns of communication as well as network traffic analyzing. A malicious agent can perform an attack after obtaining the pattern of communication, and the attack is known as replay attack. There are some specific attacks on the node of the network in which the attackers can gain access to information transmitted as well as gain network control, for example, man-in-the-middle attack, replay attack, as well as Sybil attack. A network attack has the ability to damage communication of the network through the use of network protocols and node vulnerabilities (Chen et al., 2018). Network vulnerability on IoT-based CPS is shown in Figure 12.7.

A CPS is the combination of different components, that is, computer and physical systems in order to achieve an efficient operating process. IoT-based CPSs are devices that operate using network protocols (Prathibanandhi, 2020) to communicate with each other. IoT-based CPSs mostly work based on communication protocols, such as CoAP for flexible facility, DCCP to control network congestion, AMQP in business

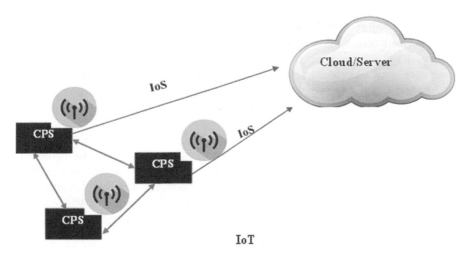

FIGURE 12.6 IoT-based CPS in industries with the connections between CPS and the IoS, which is connected directly to the Cloud/Server.

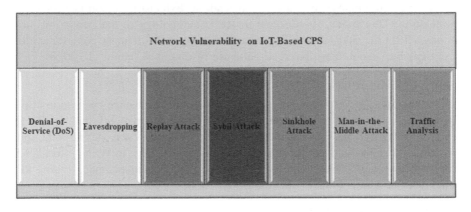

FIGURE 12.7 Network vulnerability on IoT-based CPS which are denial of service, eavesdropping, replay attack, sybil attack, sinkhole attack, man-in-the-middle attack, and traffic analysis.

application for message transfer, MQTT for bandwidth effectiveness, etc. Figure 12.6 gives the graphical representation of IoT-based CPS architecture. In IoT-based CPSs, as they involve communication between devices, data transmission is most essential. The data involved in these devices are stored on the cloud. The security and privacy of these devices are not taken seriously. This makes the devices vulnerable and open to attack. Data in the device can be accessed by external entities (attackers). They either make changes to the data or intrude the privacy of users.

The following are some of the attacks that can be launched against IoT-based CPSs:

12.1.7.1 Denial of Service (DoS)

It is a network attack that denies the mechanism of security to bypass it as well as uncover flaws of the system. It destroys security mechanisms and exploits unresponsive networks (Mourtzis et al., 2019). User information that is unencrypted can be leaked, and it can combine several computers as a platform of attack as well as introduce DDoS attacks to one or more computers (Chen et al., 2018).

12.1.7.2 Eavesdropping

It gains usernames, node identifiers, passwords, as well as other useful data of the system (Millar, 2021). The device can be easily eavesdropped, especially in wireless communications. An attacker can record communication between tags as well as readers that are legitimate through the use of antenna in a RFID system (Mourtzis et al., 2019). In eavesdropping, messages or information are read, saved, and intercepted for future purposes (Millar, 2021).

12.1.7.3 Replay Attack

In this attack, information is gained between the two parties by attackers through the use of eavesdropping. The information received is repeatedly transmitted among the communication pairs, which leads to exhausting resources for communication. This attack often occurs in RFID technology in the communication among RFID tag and reader. This attack can not only exhaust communication resources but also exhaust backend database resources (Chen et al., 2018).

12.1.7.4 Sybil Attack

In this attack, an attacker can be in more than one place at once because multiple identities are presented by one node to other nodes in the network (Millar, 2021), which enables execution of an operation multiple times by the victim node, thus defeating redundancy. Since the attacker has many identities, in WSN, information can be transmitted by the victim node through the compromised node, leading to a route distance that is longer (Chen et al., 2018).

12.1.7.5 Sinkhole Attack

In this attack, all traffic is decoyed from an area through a compromised node, where selective forwarding can follow, with the attacker determining what data to allow through (Millar, 2021). The system is fooled by considering that the data have already reached their destination. The attacker may use a node that is malicious for network traffic attraction in a WSN, and then the sensor data can be arbitrarily operated (Chen et al., 2018).

12.1.7.6 Man-in-the-Middle Attack

This attack occurs between two communication victim nodes where the attacker disguises a malicious node as a node that is genuine and communicates with two victim nodes. The trust of the two nodes is gained by the attacker as well as information about the two victim nodes (Chen et al., 2018). It manipulates routing chain for data packets exfiltration as well as obtaining important information (Mourtzis et al., 2019).

12.1.7.7   Traffic Analysis

Through analyzing number as well as size of the transmitted data packets, the pattern as well as load of communication is detected by attackers. The value of the information available is determined by how large is the number of packets that can be analyzed. Traffic analysis can be applicable to encrypted packets; a communication pattern that can be analyzed. Network activity, physical location of wireless access points, as well as learning the information about the protocol type used in the transmission process by the attackers are the three important things that can be obtained from WSN through analyzing traffic (Chen et al., 2018).

12.2   LITERATURE REVIEW

This section discusses forensic analysis, types of computer forensics, forensics analysis methodology, and related work.

12.2.1   FORENSIC ANALYSIS

Digital forensic analysis is a method used by forensic experts for digital data examination. Forensic analytics, according to Koroniotis et al. (2018), is a forensic technique that utilizes machine learning and big data. In the examination phase, forensic analytics might be employed to identify patterns that would provide answers to the aforementioned queries about the occurrence of a crime. According to Mane & Shibe (2019), the study described Big Data Forensic analytics as a new method for data collection and for analysis of a large bundle of gathered data. Chuprat et al. (2019) created a malware forensic analytic framework that blends big data security solutions with the investigative process to meet the needs of storing malware attack evidence, describing malware trends, visualizing patterns, and predicting future attack patterns. In addition to providing diverse analytics methodologies/algorithms at different phases, the forensic analytics process in big data assists the deep process/methodology in forensic science. Forensic analytics also branches down into network analytics, where analyzing network data is the responsibility of network forensics analytics, such as network packets, emails, and logs in which their data formats are often in packet capture files.

Forensic analysis deals with the examination of data extracted during live or post-mortem forensic investigation. Forensic analysis is a field under computer forensics that deals with preserving data's integrity, availability, and confidentiality. In other words, forensic analysis preserves the security triad of various domains such as network and digital, among others. Bhat and Wani (2018) discussed file system forensics that entailed the forensic analysis investigation of Linux FSs, also known as File Systems, and referred to approaches for retrieving forensic proof or traces by examining various FS data structures and modifications that occur in the directories and files, particularly deletion actions. Wang et al. (2019) studied that forensic analysis details the process users must follow in order to perform well presented digital forensics. The control and analysis of computer network traffic

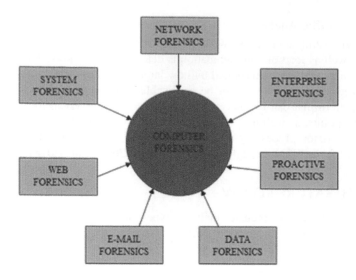

FIGURE 12.8 Types of computer forensics, which includes network forensics, enterprise forensics, system forensics, web forensics, proactive forensics, email forensics, and data forensics.

using both WAN/Internet for the purposes of collecting information, detecting intrusion, and gathering evidence is the primary concern of network forensics. The intercepted data traffic is either archived for later study or filtered in real time (Pansari & Kushwaha, 2019). According to Sridhar et al. (2011), identification, extraction, and reporting on data retrieved from a computer system are all part of forensics analysis.

12.2.1.1 Types of Computer Forensics

Lin (2018) described computer forensics and what it entails. The study discussed retrieval of digital evidence from suspicious systems in a legal-worthy manner, using that evidence to create and confirm hypotheses regarding crimes, and finally providing prosecutors with the proof they need to bring offenders to justice. Computer forensics is a very broad field that can be formed into various types, namely: network forensics, web forensics, system forensics, data forensics, enterprise forensics, proactive forensics, e-mail forensics, and malware forensics (Figure 12.8).

12.2.1.1.1 Network Forensics

Network forensics involves the investigation and analysis of data captured from network traffic. That is, it is the extraction of data from an embodied network, such as a local area network (LAN), personal area network (PAN), metropolitan area network (MAN), wireless local area network (WLAN), wide area network (WAN), etc. It analyzes packets that are being/were transmitted over the network.

12.2.1.1.2   Data Forensics

Data forensics is the detailed observation and investigation of digital evidence or data found in a computer system. It analyzes the data property, such as how the data were created and how they were used. It investigates data from different sources, such as downloaded files, operating system (OS) files, created files and documents, etc.

12.2.1.1.3   System Forensics

System forensics, otherwise known as OS forensics, involves the detailed analysis of important information related to the OS of the mobile phone or PC involved, such as file systems (e.g., FAT, NTFS, Ext3fs) and OSs (e.g. Linux, Windows, Mac OS X, Android).

12.2.1.1.4   Web Forensics

Web forensics, otherwise known as web application forensics, involves the detailed forensic investigation of web applications and their related contents, such as configuration files, logs, www directory, etc. in order to perform identity reversals on the originating attack, to determine the behavior of the attack pattern along with the identification of the device used by the perpetrator.

12.2.1.1.5   Email Forensics

Email forensics involves the detailed investigation and analysis of the component and content of an email source. It analyzes evidence such as the email architecture, the email header, the email data and attachments, and so on.

12.2.1.1.6   Proactive Forensics

Proactive forensics deals with the systematic investigation of digital incidents while the attack is still in place. The organization collaborates with an internal or external investigation team in order to pinpoint the loophole.

12.2.1.1.7   Enterprise Forensics

Enterprise forensics, otherwise known as enterprise computer forensics, involves setting in place security measures that help protect information in an enterprise, ensuring integrity and availability of data. In other words, a security strategy is put in place depending on the amount of data the enterprise wants to protect, and the security strategy helps prevent data loss in the phase of any unexpected incident.

12.2.1.2   Forensics Analysis Methodology

Forensic analysis methodology entails the steps and processes used to carry out a forensic analysis investigation associated with a particular organization. That is, depending on the forensic expert, the methodology of the forensic analysis may vary but will still be in line with the general known methodology. Digital forensic analysis has three (3) process in its methodology, and examiners puts in efforts to be detailed about their methodology process. The digital forensic analysis methodologies are identification, extraction, and analysis.

12.2.1.2.1   Identification

In the digital forensics process, identification is the initial stage. The evidence is assessed in this step according to its nature, location, format, and condition. The process starts by identifying the item's type. Mobile phones, personal computers, servers, networks, and other digital sources can all be used as storage mediums. Identification of potential data sources, acquisition of non-volatile and volatile data, and verification of data integrity to assure chain of custody are among the procedures (Packetlabs, 2021). If an examiner finds something related but outside the scope of the original search warrant, just like in a physical search, it is suggested that the examiner halt immediately and report the case to the appropriate agency in order to get a second warrant to explore the data. But if the examiner finds non-related data during identification, they just mark it as processed and move on as it has no relevance (Carroll et al., 2008)

12.2.1.2.2   Extraction

The examiner analyzes if there is sufficient data to continue the investigation throughout the extraction procedure. The analyst must authenticate each set of hardware and software once it has been brought in and before it is used as part of the digital forensics technique. When the examiner's forensic platform is available, he or she duplicates and verifies the forensic data in the request. This method implies that law enforcement has previously collected the data and developed a forensic copy using the proper legal procedures (Packetlabs, 2021). A forensic copy is a precise replica of the data stored on the initial medium. The important information is gathered then further organized into a list called "extracted data list," which is a separate list. Then, the identification process is repeated by the examiners on the extracted data list items to confirm the integrity of the leads (Carroll et al., 2008).

12.2.1.2.3   Analysis

The analyst tries to figure out the reason why the information is important to the inquiry during the analysis phase. They begin by attempting to envision the sequence of events that occurred during the organization's attack. Examiners connect the dots and give the requester a complete picture. Examiners respond to questions such as who, what, when, where, and how for each item on the relevant data list. They then attempt to investigate any item's creation, alteration, or deletion. Finally, the expert uses digital forensics methodology to try to uncover the attacker's manifesto, which will aid in establishing a theory to law authorities (Carroll et al., 2008).

12.2.2   RELATED WORK

The widespread use of the IoT has also increased the rate of its openness to attack and different threats from cyber criminals. This paper focuses on how to analyze these various attacks and provide security for the devices. Dehghantanha & Franke, 2018, describe in the work the cyberattack issues on the IoT and how to get the IoT more secured. Authentication, privacy, and access control issues were the major security factors that were discussed in their work. Al-sharif et al., 2018, explain in their work a new technique for detecting cyberattacks. This technique is based on getting information about the crime from the executing program. The study was on the use of Java Virtual Machine to capture a cybercrime. It was conducted on three executions of JVM. It was concluded that this will help to detect the software that was used for the attack. In the paper published in April 28, 2021, Rani et al., 2021, carry out a survey on the threat on the IoT and a way to get the corrective measure. The study explains the wide range of use of the IoT and the threat the IoT encountered. The survey was compared with the past work using some features, such as cyberattack and security, cybercrime, security in IoT devices, etc. Vulnerability of CPSs was also discussed in a work published in 2019. Yeboah-Ofori et al. (2019) discussed in their work some vulnerabilities of CPSs and the risk it causes to the systems. They also explained different attacks on CPSs such as ransom ware, malware, DOS, resonance attack, etc. The work also discussed the different weak location CPS that can easily be penetrated by the likes of routers, network, firewalls, HTTP header etc.

　　The IoT is evolving in the modern world. This makes the passing of messages stress-free for people. There is always the need for IoT devices to be linked together to ease communication. The linking of these devices is done through networking. Many intruders and cyber criminals have also sought this advantage to get access to other IoT devices. This has prompted researchers to work on how to secure these devices. Dehghantanha & Franke, 2018, discussed in their work the problem of security encountered by many IoT devices. Some problems were explained, the likes of authorization and access control, privacy and authentication, etc. They also described various ways to capture these attacks with genuine evidence. Jayakrishnan, 2021, carried out a survey on network forensics on IoT devices. He categorized network forensics into two classes. "Catch-it-as-you-can" and "Stop, look and listen". Methods in network forensics were explained in his work. The approaches in network forensics are quite similar to that of digital forensics. It is abbreviated as OSCAR: Obtaining information, Strategizing, Collecting Evidence, Analyzing Evidence, and Report (Qureshi et al., 2021). He also explained that the network forensic process can be automated using some tools to gather information and carry out analysis on them. Examples of the tools are NetDetector, Iris, etc.

12.3　MATERIALS AND METHODS

The study utilized the forensic analysis framework in the examination of vulnerabilities in IoT-based CPSs. Digital forensic analysis was implemented using Autopsy and TCPDump forensic tools.

12.3.1　Forensic Analysis Framework

Forensic Analysis Framework is a method or procedure that guides forensic analysts when performing a forensic examination on any given platform. These frameworks are proposed by experts in the field and adopted overtime. Hikmatyar et al. (2017) proposed a framework model for network forensics called Integrated Digital Forensics Investigation Framework (IDFIF) version 3, branching them all into four processes, namely preparation process, proactive process, reactive process, and presentation process, in which each process has some phases with subphases.

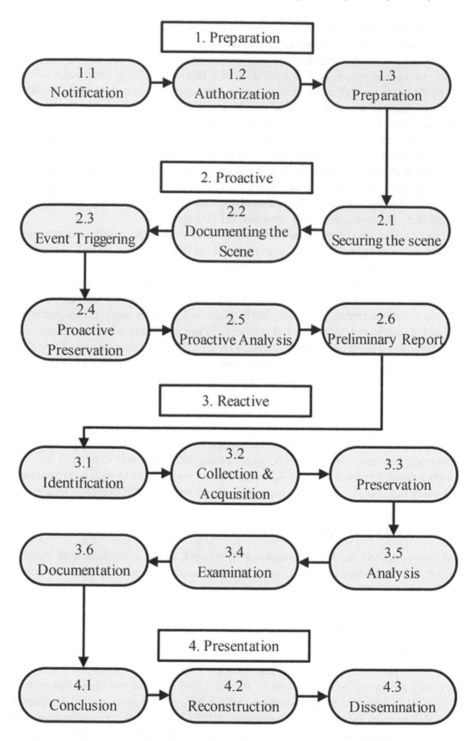

FIGURE 12.9 Framework for forensic analysis.

The study further discussed each process, with the preparation process having the notification, authorization, and preparation phases. Then, the proactive process has securing the scene, documenting the scene, event triggering, proactive preservation, proactive analysis, and preliminary report. The reactive process has identification, collection & acquisition, preservation, examination, analysis, and documentation phases. Finally, the presentation process has the conclusion reconstruction and dissemination phases. Figure 12.9 shows the framework for forensic analysis used for this study. Two digital forensic analysis tools were used to examine the vulnerabilities in IoT-based CPS, which are Wireshark and TCPDump.

12.3.2 WIRESHARK

Wireshark is a digital forensic tool compatible for use with Linux Distribution OS, Windows OS, and OS X, with the graphical interface to the sleuth kit. It is used in the military, in law enforcement, and by corporate examiners to analyze and investigate data stored on a computer. Wireshark has a lot of forensic features, such as multi-user cases, keyword search, timeline analysis, web artifacts, registry analysis, email analysis, LNK file analysis, robust file system analysis, file type detection, Unicode strings extraction, and Android support. It extracts data from call logs, SMS, and contact among many others on Android systems.

12.3.3 TCPDUMP

TCPDump is an effective network packet sniffer tool, which offers an application in the command line of Unix-like OSs, such as Berkeley Software Distribution (BSD), Solaris, OS X, Linux, Android, and HP-UX, among others (Pandit, 2021). It is an open source tool, which is launched as a superuser or as root user in order to make use of promiscuous mode on the network mode. TCPDump has a variety of functions, such as intercepting and outputting data communication occurring between hosts in a network to the user host's terminal. It captures TCP/IP packets only from the network and allows the user to export captured network traffic for further analysis (Goyal & Goyal, 2017). A TCPDump captured packet shows the date in which the packet was captured, followed by the time (including milliseconds), then shows the source IP and port address with destination IP and port address, followed by the TCP flags type (e.g. [S], [F], [.], [P], [R]), still including the sequence number, window number, and length of packet. The TCP flag [S] (Synchronize) is displayed when there is a new synchronization request of a new connection. Flag [F] (Finish) is displayed when there is a closed connection, flag [.] (Acknowledge) is displayed when there is an established connection. Flag [P] (Push) is displayed when there is a push of data from source

FIGURE 12.10 TCPDump TCP packet transmission.

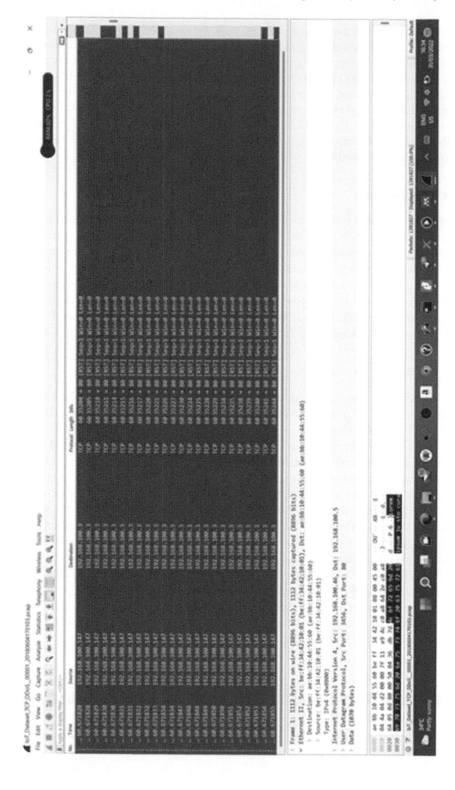

FIGURE 12.11　TCP RST flood attack.

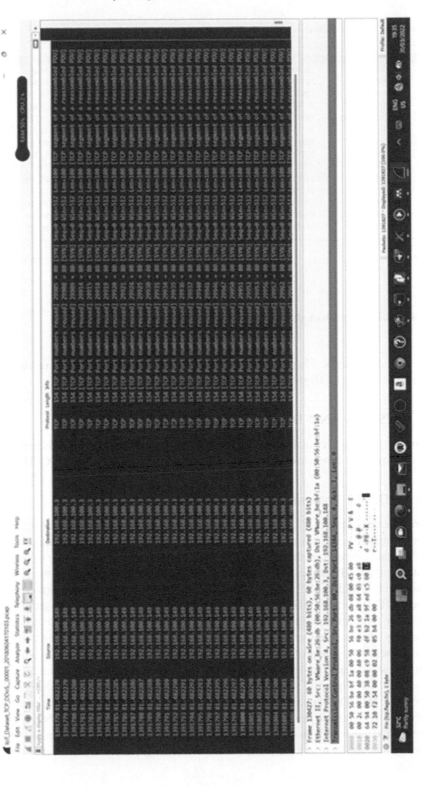

FIGURE 12.12 TCP SYN flood attack.

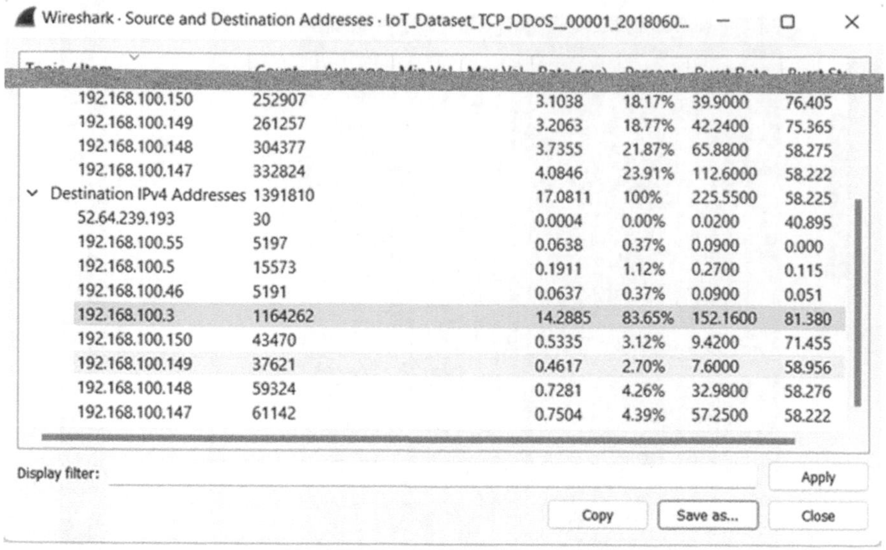

FIGURE 12.13 Wireshark destination packet showing percentage statistics.

to destination address. Flag [R] (Reset) is displayed when either host resets the connection. Figure 12.10 shows a typical TCPDump packet transmission.

12.4 RESULTS AND DISCUSSION OF FINDINGS

The results of forensic analysis of the vulnerabilities on IoT-based CPSs are discussed below. The forensic analysis was carried out using Autopsy and TCPDump.

12.4.1 DIGITAL FORENSIC ANALYSIS USING WIRESHARK

An IoT Packet Capture (PCAP) dataset for network vulnerability assessment on a CPS was analyzed, and it was duly observed that on the captured network, there were a total of four attackers on the network. Figure 12.11 shows that an attacker using the Internet protocol (IP) address 192.168.100.147 directed lots of traffic into the victim machine with IP address 192.168.100.3, overloading the victim's transmission control protocol (TCP) port 80 (HTTP) with a constant length of sixty (60) Reset [RST] packets per millisecond without going through the normal TCP handshake process. One of the attacks discovered on the network was DDoS. A DDOS attack is the process whereby a group of attackers (host) cooperate in the process of flooding a victim's host, causing the device to fail or crash within a short period of time. It was also identified in Figure 12.12 that the attackers with an IP address 192.168.100.149 performed a TCP SYN flooding to the same victim's host 192.168.100.3 with a packet length of 154 per millisecond, causing the network to expectedly go down because in a normal TCP handshake process. After a host sends a SYN packet to another host, the receiving host sends an acknowledge packet to the sender, but in this scenario the

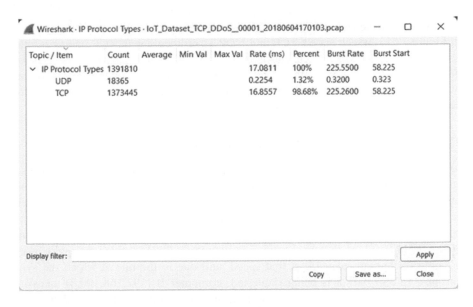

FIGURE 12.14   TCP and UDP network protocol showing percentage statistics.

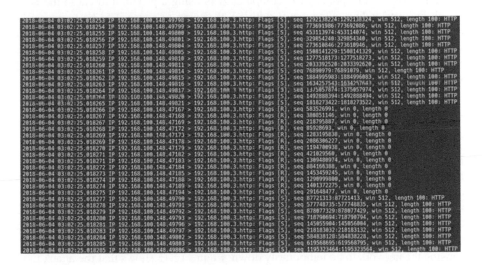

FIGURE 12.15   TCPDump network forensic analysis.

sending host failed to wait to receive an acknowledgment packet and kept transmitting the SYN packet in milliseconds. So, the receiving host got overloaded with SYN packets, causing it to get temporarily down. Then, after a full analysis of the whole packet transmitted over the network, it was discovered in Figure 12.13 that 1,164,262 of 1,391,810 packets that were passed through the network were directed to one destination logical address, being the victim's address 192.162.100.3, at a burst rate of 152.1600 out of 225.5500. That is, 83.65% of packets transmitted on the network were directed to the victim's TCP port 80. The data from the CPS traffic file are shown in Figure 12.14, which shows TCP and UDP as protocols with TCP having a total 1,373,445 of 1,391,810 packets and UDP having a total of 18,365 packets. That is, 98.68% of packets that transmitted on the network were found on the TCP, and that was the only used network protocol in which most of the attack was derived from, being the targeted network protocol.

12.4.2 DIGITAL FORENSIC ANALYSIS USING TCPDUMP

An IoT PCAP dataset for network vulnerability assessment on a CPS was also analyzed using the TCPDump tool, which was implemented through a command line, as shown in Figure 12.15, and the date and time of attack was displayed, which is crucial for detecting time in which an attack took place. In Figure 12.15, it was noticed that computer A (192.168.100.148) was spontaneously sending a synchronize TCP (Flags [S]) packet in a sequence 0.00001s, which normally isn't possible for humans to work at that speed, and due to the rate at which the synchronize (SYN) packet is being requested, computer B (192.168.100.3) takes its time to respond to the packets according to its arrival time, and due to that, computer B wouldn't be able to respond to any other incoming packets until the SYN packets have been responded to. Computer A is using a program to cause the DoS attack by overloading computer B with SYN packet to cause it to be temporarily down, and this is called TCP SYN flood attack. Computer A then floods computer B with the reset TCP (Flags [R]) packet so that it won't be able to acknowledge the connection while computer A keeps flooding computer B with TCP SYN flood attack, causing a full DoS attack.

12.5 COMPARISON OF WIRESHARK AND TCPDUMP FORENSIC ANALYSIS

Digital forensics was carried out on an IoT based CPS network where Wireshark forensic analysis tool was used to capture the traffic going on in the CPS network. The analysis of the traffic was made using Wireshark analyzer, and it was discovered that there was a DDoS attack launched directed to the CPS host, causing downtime on the CPS system. The use of TCPDump was also applied to analyze the traffic that went on in the network, and it was discovered that DDOS attack occurred within 2 minutes, causing the network to go temporarily down. Figure 12.15 shows that the attack took place in the year 2018, 4th of June, and it was duly observed that the attack occurred for 1 minutes and 22 seconds, with a total of 1,373,445 packets transmitted since TCPDump is only capable of capturing traffic that passes through the transmission control protocol. The use of Wireshark analyzer for analyzing the network helps users to get the statistics of the protocol used in the network and also helps users analyze the behavior of the attacker with its interactive graphical interface through a wider scope of protocol analysis, while the use of TCPDump is better for analyzing the data. It helps users track the timestamp of the traffic on the TCP protocol only, but the command line interface is not user friendly as it takes more and dedicated time for analyzing a network traffic using TCPDump.

12.6   CONCLUSIONS AND RECOMMENDATIONS

Wireshark can be used for digital forensics analysis when several network protocols will be examined. The network vulnerability assessment shows that more attacks are targeted at TCP as opposed to UDP. That is, 83.65% of packets transmitted on the network were directed to the victim's TCP port 80. Hence, port 80 should be critically monitored consistently on an IoT-based CPS due to its highly vulnerable exposure components. TCP has a total 1,373,445 of 1,391,810 packets, and UDP has a total of 18,365 packets. Also, this signifies that 98.68% of packets that were transmitted on the network were found on the TCP, and it was the only network protocol used in which most of the attacks were derived from as the network protocol. TCPDump can be used for digital forensics analysis when the date and time of the attack are very crucial. It is effective for detecting the time in which an attack takes place and the period. Through TCPDump network analysis, the attack occurred for 1 minute and 22 seconds, with a total of 1,373,445 packets transmitted since TCPDump is only capable of capturing traffic that passes through the transmission control protocol. The study therefore recommends the usage of other network forensic analysis tools, such as Dumpcap and Ethereal, for live network analysis; NetDetector for instant blockage of malicious traffic; and Fidelis XPS as a type of network forensics tool that is used for recording interested session of traffic that can be used for effective network post mortem analysis.

REFERENCES

Adeagbo, M. A., Akinsola, J. E. T., Awoseyi, A. A., & Kasali, F. (2021). Project Implementation Decision Using Software Development Life Cycle Models: A Comparative Approach. *Journal of Computer Science and Its Application, 28*(1), 121–132. 10.4314/jcsia.v28i1.10

Ademu, I. O., & Imafidon, C. (2012). *The Influence of Security Threats and Vulnerabilities on Digital Forensic Investigation. October 2014.* 10.13140/2.1.2236.8006

Akinsola, J. E. T., Adeagbo, M. A., Oladapo, K. A., Akinsehinde, S. A., & Onipede, F. O. (2022). Artificial Intelligence Emergence in Disruptive Technology. In A. O. Salau, S. Jain, & M. Sood (Eds.), *Computational Intelligence and Data Sciences: Paradigms in Biomedical Engineering*, 63–90. CRC Press, Taylor & Francis Group. 10.1201/9781003224068-4

Akinsola, J. E. T., Akinseinde, S., Kalesanwo, O., Adeagbo, M., Kayode, O., Awoseyi, A., & Kasali, F. (2021). Application of Artificial Intelligence in User Interfaces Design for Cyber Security Threat Modeling. In R. Heimgärtner (Ed.), *Intelligent User Interfaces* (pp. 1–28). IntechOpen. 10.5772/intechopen.96534

Akinsola, J. E. T., Awodele, O., Adebayo, A. O., Onipede, F. O., & Muhammad, B. A. (2021). Netiquette of Cyberbullying and Privacy Issues. *International Journal of Information Security, Privacy and Digital Forensics, 5*(1), 22–33. https://www.researchgate.net/publication/356128450_Netiquette_of_Cyberbullying_and_Privacy_Issues#fullTextFileContent

Akinsola, J. E. T., Kuyoro, A., Adeagbo, M. A., & Awoseyi, A. A. (2020). Performance Evaluation of Software using Formal Methods. *Global Journal of Computer Science and Technology: C Software & Data Engineering, 20*(1), 17-23. https://computerresearch.org/index.php/computer/article/view/1930/1914

Akinsola, J. E. T., Ogunbanwo, A. S., Okesola, O. J., Odun-Ayo, I. J., Ayegbusi, F. D., & Adebiyi, A. A. (2020). Comparative Analysis of Software Development

Life Cycle Models (SDLC). *Springer, 1224 AISC*, 310–322. 10.1007/978-3-030-51 965-0_27

Al-sharif, Z. A., Al-saleh, M. I., Alawneh, L., & Jararweh, Y. (2018). *Live forensics of software attacks on cyber physical systems Live Forensics of Software Attacks on Cyber Physical Systems*. October. 10.1016/j.future.2018.07.028

Alao, O. D., Joshua, J. V., & Akinsola, J. E. T. (2019). Human Computer Interaction (HCI) and Smart Home Applications. *IUP Journal of Information Technology, 15*(3), 7–21. https://search.proquest.com/openview/70e74bf39099ec671c013b7bf9d9258a/1?pq-origsite=gscholar&cbl=2029987

Almulhem, A. (2010). Network forensics: Notions and Challenges. *IEEE International Symposium on Signal Processing and Information Technology, ISSPIT 2009*, 463–466. 10.1109/ISSPIT.2009.5407485

Baheti, R., & Gill, H. (2011). Cyber-physical Systems. In A. M. Annaswamy & T. Samad (Eds.), *The Impact of Control Technology*. IEEE Control Systems Society. http://ieeecss.org/sites/ieeecss/files/2019-07/IoCT-Part3-02CyberphysicalSystems.pdf

Balogun, O., Hinmikaiye, J., Adegbenle, A. A., Oyebode, A. A., Akinsola, J. E. T., Nzenwata U. J., & Adegbenle A. A. (2019). An Analysis of Cybercrime Awareness Amongst First Year Students in Nigerian Private University. *Research Journal of Mathematics and Computer Science, 3*(15), 1–5. https://escipub.com/research-journal-of-mathematics-and-computer-science/

Bhat, W. A., & Wani, M. A. (2018). Forensic Analysis of B-tree File System (Btrfs). *Digital Investigation, 27*, 57–70. 10.1016/j.diin.2018.09.001

Butun, I., Osterberg, P., Song, H., & Member, S. (2019). *Security of the Internet of Things: Vulnerabilities, Attacks and Countermeasures. XX*(X), 1–25.

Carroll, O. L., Brannon, S. K., & Song, T. (2008). Computer Forensics. *The United States Attorneys' Bulletin, 56*(1), 60.

Chen, K., Zhang, S., Li, Z., Zhang, Y., Deng, Q., Ray, S., & Jin, Y. (2018). Internet-of-Things Security and Vulnerabilities: Taxonomy, Challenges, and Practice. *Journal of Hardware and Systems Security, 2*(2), 97–110. 10.1007/s41635-017-0029-7

Chuprat, S., Ariffin, A., Sahibuddin, S., Mahrin, M. N., Senan, F. M., Ahmad, N. A., Narayana, G., Magalingam, P., Anuar, S., & Talib, M. Z. (2019). Malware Forensic Analytics Framework Using Big Data Platform. In *Advances in Intelligent Systems and Computing* (Vol. 881, pp. 261–274). 10.1007/978-3-030-02683-7_19

Dehghantanha, A., & Franke, K. (2018). *Internet of Things Security and Forensics: Challenges and Opportunities*. 2–8.

Dhar Dwivedi, A., Singh, R., Kaushik, K., Rao Mukkamala, R., & Alnumay, W. S. (2021). Blockchain and artificial intelligence for 5G-enabled Internet of Things: Challenges, opportunities, and solutions. *Transactions on Emerging Telecommunications Technologies, January*, 1–19. 10.1002/ett.4329

Goyal, P., & Goyal, A. (2017). Implementasi Keamanan Jaringan Komputer Pada Virtual Private Network (Vpn) Menggungakan. *Implementasi Keamanan Jaringan Komputer Pada Virtual Private Network (Vpn) Menggungakan Ipsec, 2*(1), 65–68. 10.1109/CICN.2017.19

Guru99. (2022). What is Digital Forensics? History, Process, Types, Challenges. In *Guru99* (p. 1).

Hikmatyar, M., Prayudi, Y., & Riadi, I. (2017). Network Forensics Framework Development using Interactive Planning Approach. *International Journal of Computer Applications, 161*(10), 41–48. 10.5120/ijca2017913352

Hinmikaiye, J. O., Awodele, O., & Akinsola, J. E. T. (2021). Disruptive Technology and Regulatory Response: The Nigerian Perspective. *Computer Engineering and Intelligent Systems, 12*(1), 42–47. 10.7176/ceis/12-1-06

HowStuffWorks. (2000). What is the Difference Between Analog and Digital? In *HowStuffWorks.*

Jayakrishnan, A. (2021). *Empirical Survey on Advances of Network Forensics in the Emerging Networks. March.* 10.17781/P002320

Joshi, R. C., & Pilli, E. S. (2016). Network Forensic Tools. In *Computer Communications and Networks* (pp. 71–93). Springer, London. 10.1007/978-1-4471-7299-4_4

Kandasamy, K., Srinivas, S., Achuthan, K., & Rangan, V. P. (2020). IoT Cyber Risk: A Holistic Analysis of Cyber Risk Assessment Frameworks, Risk Vectors, and Risk Ranking Process. *Eurasip Journal on Information Security, 2020*(1). 10.1186/s13635-020-00111-0

Katz, E. (2008). *Cyber Forensics Introduction.*

Kaushik, K., & Dahiya, S. (2018). Security and Privacy in iot Based E-business and Retail. *Proceedings of the 2018 International Conference on System Modeling and Advancement in Research Trends, SMART 2018*, 78–81. 10.1109/SYSMART.2018.8746961

Kaushik, K., Dahiya, S., & Sharma, R. (2021). Internet of Things Advancements in Healthcare. In *Internet of Things* (1st ed., pp. 19–32). Taylor & Francis, CRC Press. 10.1201/9781003140443-2

Kaushik, K., Dahiya, S., & Sharma, R. (2022). Role of Blockchain Technology in Digital Forensics. *Blockchain Technology*, 235–246. 10.1201/9781003138082-14

Kaushik, K., & Singh, K. (2020). Security and Trust in IoT Communications: Role and Impact. In *Advances in Intelligent Systems and Computing* (Vol. 989). Springer, Singapore. 10.1007/978-981-13-8618-3_81

Khan, S., Gani, A., Abdul Wahab, A. W., Shiraz, M., & Ahmad, I. (2016). Network Forensics: Review, Taxonomy, And Open Challenges. *Journal of Network and Computer Applications*, 66, 214–235. 10.1016/j.jnca.2016.03.005

Koroniotis, N., Moustafa, N., Sitnikova, E., & Turnbull, B. (2018). Towards the Development of Realistic Botnet Dataset in the Internet of Things for Network Forensic Analytics: Bot-IoT Dataset. *Future Generation Computer Systems, 100*, 779–796. 10.1016/j.future.2019.05.041

Lin, X. (2018). Introductory Computer Forensics. In *Introductory Computer Forensics.* 10.1007/978-3-030-00581-8

Ly, K., & Jin, Y. (2016). Security Challenges in CPS and IoT: From end-node to the System. *Proceedings of IEEE Computer Society Annual Symposium on VLSI, ISVLSI*, 63–68. 10.1109/ISVLSI.2016.109

Mane, D., & Shibe, K. (2019). Big Data Forensic Analytics. In *Advances in Intelligent Systems and Computing* (Vol. 839, pp. 113–129). Springer, Singapore. 10.1007/978-981-13-1274-8_9

Meghanathan, N., Allam, S. R., & Moore, L. A. (2010). Tools and Techniques for Network Forensics. *International Journal of Network Security & Its Applications (IJNSA), 1*(1), 14–25.

Millar, S. (2021). IoT Security Challenges and Mitigations: An Introduction. *Arxiv, 1*, 1–5.

Mourtzis, D., Angelopoulos, K., & Zogopoulos, V. (2019). Mapping Vulnerabilities in the Industrial Internet of Things Landscape. *Procedia CIRP, 84*, 265–270. 10.1016/j.procir.2019.04.201

Packetlabs. (2021, June). *Here's What You Didn't Know About Digital Forensics Methodology | Packetlabs.*

Pandit, P. D. (2021). *A Study of Packet Sniffer Tools.* 10.13140/RG.2.2.31223.34729

Pansari, N., & Kushwaha, D. (2019). Forensic Analysis and Investigation Using Digital Forensics- An Overview. *International Journal of Advance Research, Ideas and Innovations in Technology, 5*(1), 470–475.

Patil, P. S., & Kapse, A. S. (2015). Survey on Different Phases of Digital Forensics Investigation Models. *International Journal of Innovative Research in Computer and Communication Engineering, 03*(03), 1529–1534. 10.15680/ijircce.2015. 0303018

Pilli, E. S., Joshi, R. C., & Niyogi, R. (2010). A Framework for Network Forensic Analysis. *International Conference on Advances in Information and Communication Technologies,* 142–147.

Pradeep, S., & Sharma, Y. K. (2020). Study and Analysis of Modified Mean Shift Method and Kalman Filter for Moving Object Detection and Tracking. In K. S. Raju, A. Govardhan, B. P. Rani, R. Sridevi, & M. R. Murty (Eds.), *Advances in Intelligent Systems and Computing* (Vol. 1090). Springer Nature, Switzerland AG. 10.1007/978-981-15-1480-7_76

Prathibanandhi, K., Ramesh, S., & Yaashuwanth, C. (2020). Internet of Things (IoT) -Cyber Physical Systems (Cps) An Exploratory Approach on the Security of IoT-CPS Framework Using Blockchain Technologies. *Journal of Xi'an University of Architecture & Technology, XII*(Vii), 1225–1237.

Qureshi, S., Tunio, S., Akhtar, F., Wajahat, A., Nazir, A., & Ullah, F. (2021). Network Forensics: A Comprehensive Review of Tools and Techniques. *International Journal of Advanced Computer Science and Applications, 12*(5), 879–887. 10.14569/IJACSA. 2021.01205103

Rani, S., Kataria, A., Sharma, V., Ghosh, S., Karar, V., Lee, K., & Choi, C. (2021). *Review Article Threats and Corrective Measures for IoT Security with Observance of Cybercrime: A Survey. 2021.*

Reith, M., Carr, C., & Gunsch, G. (2002). *An Examination of Digital Forensic Models, 1*(3), 1–12.

Singh, A., & Jain, A. (2018). Study of Cyber Attacks on Cyber-Physical System. *SSRN Electronic Journal, October.* 10.2139/ssrn.3170288

Sridhar, N., Bhaskari, D. D. L., & Avadhani, D. P. S. (2011). 18: Plethora of Cyber Forensics. *International Journal of Advanced Computer Science and Applications, 2*(11). 10.14569/IJACSA.2011.021118

Srin. (2021). *Network Forensics Tools.* Infosec Resources.

Sui, T., Mo, Y., Marelli, D., Sun, X., & Fu, M. (2021). The Vulnerability of Cyber-Physical System under Stealthy Attacks. *IEEE Transactions on Automatic Control, 66*(2), 637–650. 10.1109/TAC.2020.2987307

Vanderbilt School of Engineering. (2022). *What are the Impacts and Benefits of Cyber-physical Systems?* https://blog.engineering.vanderbilt.edu/what-are-the-impacts-and-benefits-of-cyber-physical-systems

Vidas, T. (2006). Cyber-Forensics: The Basics. In *CERT Conference.*

Wang, N., Tan, Y., & Guo, S. (2019). A Uniformed Evidence Process Model for Big Data Forensic Analysis. In *Lecture Notes in Electrical Engineering* (Vol. 518, pp. 639–645). Springer, Singapore. 10.1007/978-981-13-1328-8_82

Wikipedia. (2021). *Cyber-physical system - Wikipedia.*

Yeboah-Ofori, A., A., J.-D., & K., F. (2019). Cybercrime and Risks for Cyber Physical Systems. *International Journal of Cyber-Security and Digital Forensics, 8*(1), 43–57. 10.17781/p002556

Index

Note: Page numbers in italics indicate tables; page numbers in bold indicate figures